PENGUIN CLASSICS

THE WOMEN'S SUFFRAGE MOVEMENT

SALLY ROESCH WAGNER was awarded one of the first doctorates in the United States for work in women's studies and is a founder of one of the first college-level women's studies programs in the country. She is the founding director of the Matilda Joslyn Gage Foundation in Fayetteville, New York, and currently serves as adjunct faculty in the honors program at Syracuse University. She is a member of the New York State Women's Suffrage Commission and a former consultant to the National Women's History Project. Author of numerous women's history books and articles telling the "untold stories," her recent publications center on the Haudenosaunee influence on the women's rights movement. Wagner appeared in the Ken Burns PBS documentary *Not for Ourselves Alone: The Story of Elizabeth Cady Stanton and Susan B. Anthony*, for which she wrote the accompanying faculty guide for PBS, was a historian in the PBS special *One Woman, One Vote*, and has been interviewed on NPR's *All Things Considered* and *Democracy Now*.

GLORIA STEINEM is a writer, lecturer, editor, and feminist activist. Her books include the bestsellers *My Life on the Road*, *Revolution from Within*, *Outrageous Acts and Everyday Rebellions*, *Moving Beyond Words*, *Marilyn: Norma Jeane*, and *As if Women Matter* (published in India). Steinem has received the National Magazine Award, the Lifetime Achievement in Journalism Award from the Society of Professional Journalists, and the Society of Writers Award from the United Nations. She is a cofounder of *Ms. Magazine*, the Ms. Foundation for Women, the Women's Media Center, Equality Now, and Donor Direct Action. In 2013, she received the Presidential Medal of Freedom from President Barack Obama.

THE
WOMEN'S SUFFRAGE
MOVEMENT

Edited with an Introduction by
SALLY ROESCH WAGNER

Foreword by
GLORIA STEINEM

PENGUIN BOOKS

PENGUIN BOOKS

An imprint of Penguin Random House LLC
penguinrandomhouse.com

First published in Penguin Books 2019
Introduction, notes, afterword, and selection copyright © 2019 by Sally Roesch Wagner
Foreword copyright © 2019 by Gloria Steinem

Ida B. Wells, Crusade for Justice: The Autobiography of Ida B. Wells, edited by Alfreda M. Duster
(University of Chicago Press, 1970) reprinted with permission by University of Chicago Press.

ISBN 9780143132431 (pbk.)
ISBN 9780525504412 (ebook)

Printed in the United States of America
1 3 5 7 9 10 8 6 4 2

Set in Sabon LT Std

To my three grandchildren:
my mentor, Tacoja Michael,
my reality-grounding grandson Tanner,
and Alex, my granddaughter, who moves
the strength of our women-kin forward.
With your clarity and savvy,
you keep me posted on
the change that is coming.
And joyously awaiting it,
since you are in it.

Contents

THE WOMEN'S SUFFRAGE MOVEMENT

IV. THE 1860s: IN FULL STRIDE, THE WAR'S SETBACK, AND REGROUPING AFTER   135

Foreword

With *The Women's Suffrage Movement*, Sally Roesch Wagner has given us a unique gift: the real words and actions, writings and debates, of white and black women who fought for over a century to gain an identity as free human beings and citizens.

For most of those years, black women were legally owned as chattel, forced to work and to suffer the unique punishment of giving birth to children who were also enslaved. White women were not as restricted and endangered as the women or men brought as slaves from Africa. But as the daughters and wives of white men, they were also legal chattel, with no right to leave their homes, disobey orders, profit from their own work, speak in public, have custody of their own children, own property without a guardian, or affect the patriarchal laws that governed their lives.

Even many, or most, white men who fought against slavery supported this subordinate position of their wives and daughters. When Susan B. Anthony, an abolitionist and suffragist, supported not only runaway slaves, but white wives escaping their violent husbands, even male abolitionist allies warned her that she was going too far.

As Frederick Douglass, a freed slave, abolitionist, and suffragist himself, wrote in his autobiography: "When the true history of the antislavery cause shall be written, women will occupy a large space in its pages, for the cause of the slave has been peculiarly women's cause."[1]

And this despite the fact that many white women, especially but not only in the South, aided and abetted black slavery, and also accepted their own subordinate position as natural.

A century later, Gunnar Myrdal would explain in his landmark study of slavery that enslaved African women and men brought to these shores had been given the legal status of wives as the "nearest and most natural analogy" to the status of slaves.[2] As he added, "The parallel between women and Negroes is the deepest truth of American life, for together they form the unpaid or underpaid labor on which America runs."[3]

Wagner takes us into the rooms, writings, and discussions where white and black women and black men, all fighting for legal personhood and full citizenship, were both a miracle of shared purpose, despite all the lethal forces keeping them apart, and later a tragedy of division that echoes in the need for intersectionality and inclusion to this day.

Even the lynchings of black men, crimes designed to maintain the racial order after the Civil War, were most often justified by proximity to white women, however imaginary or freely chosen. This tells us how dangerous and brave was the coalition for universal adult suffrage that you will read about here. It also reveals the betrayal when white men split the coalition apart by offering the vote to black men first, only to then limit their votes with poll taxes, impossible literacy tests, and violence.

Yet despite this tragic division, and despite being labeled as varying degrees of nonhuman, this fractious rebellion and fragile coalition did eventually succeed in gaining citizenship for the majority of people in this country.

Wagner brings us these imperfect and hopeful rebellions of the past as they happened, complete with their courage, divisions, and debates, plus a long organizational disagreement among women suffragists about whether to seek the vote by federal amendment or state by state.

She doesn't attempt to prove a thesis, or to explain mistakes, or to excuse destructive divisions. Other than in the first and last chapters—each one with a very specific purpose—she doesn't insert herself at all. Instead, she allows us to witness the words and acts, dreams and disappointments, victories and defeats, visionary ideas and tactical errors, of people fighting a battle that laid the basis for our continuing movement against hierarchies based on race and gender.

It is this faithfulness to the past that allows us to learn lessons for changes in the present and future.

In thirty or so years, this will no longer be a majority white country. It will better reflect the diversity that has always been its strength and its promise. Indeed, the first generation that is majority babies of color has already been born, and public opinion polls already show that the majority of Americans no longer support divisions by race and gender. Yet there is also a lethal backlash from about a third of the country—including over half of white married women, often also those without a college education and most likely to be dependent on a husband's identity and income—who feel the need to preserve their unearned place in the social and economic hierarchy.

That's why these victories and defeats of the past become the best possible lessons and warnings for our present and future. By taking us into the rooms where history happened, Wagner allows us to see the parallels and differences, empathy and estrangements, connections and isolations, that can hinder or help our shared goals now.

Almost none of the people we meet in these pages will live to celebrate the changes they are working for. This should tell us that social justice movements are not a temporary part of our lives, they *are* our lives. Most of the activists here were not sure that slavery would be abolished, or that universal adult suffrage would ever succeed. This should give us humility about what we can predict, and also arm us with faith and patience.

Few guessed that the legal right to vote would come a half century later for white and black women than for black men, but would be mostly on paper. In the South where most black Americans live, it would take another century plus an entire civil rights movement to overcome procedural and sometimes violent and lethal barriers to voting. This should make us skeptical about changes that come from the top, and that divide us more than they empower us.

And there are other lessons. For instance, decisions can't be made for an unknown future, but we can create an inclusive and democratic way of making decisions. The ends don't justify the means: in real life, the means we choose dictate the ends we get. Most of all, we are still experiencing the scars of divisions based on race and gender; divisions that didn't have to be, and seem not to have existed before Europeans arrived, and conquered or killed most of the advanced cultures already here.

Fortunately, Wagner in her first chapter sends us off with unique encouragement. Unlike almost every other historian, she doesn't treat this country as if it began with Columbus. We are not led to assume that gender and race begin a hierarchy that is decreed by human nature.

On this subcontinent once known as Turtle Island, women's expertise in agriculture and men's expertise in hunting were once equally necessary and equally honored. Many languages had no gendered pronouns, no "he" and "she." Children inherited their clan identity through their mothers. Women knew very well how to have or not have children, and men did not control women's bodies as the means of reproduction. Male leaders were often chosen by female elders, who also decided when to go to war and when to make peace. The paradigm of society was not a hierarchy, but a circle. Human beings were seen as linked, not ranked.

It was the Iroquois Confederacy of six native nations, with layers of talking circles for decision-making, that inspired Benjamin Franklin to invite Iroquois advisors to the Constitutional Convention. Each of the thirteen colonies needed a degree of autonomy, but also a way to make mutual decisions. The Iroquois governance system, the oldest continuing democracy in the world, became a model for our Constitution. Yet the first thing those advisors asked was: *Where are the women?*

Perhaps one day, our schools will teach history that begins when people began. As it is, it is still likely to start when patriarchy, monotheism, and colonialism began. It is rare and important that this book opens by showing us that suffrage leaders were inspired by the example of free and equal Native American women.

Perhaps we may also learn that some African women came from matrilineal cultures, with herbal knowledge of contraceptives and abortifacients that has been well documented. We are discovering from modern public opinion polls and current elections that black women are almost twice as likely to support all the issues of female equality as are white women. Perhaps some of that comes not only from the necessity of their independence, but also from the stories in their memory.

Now, media characterize the suffrage movement, and the modern women's movement, as mostly the activity of white women. But with the growing record of Native American women as the inspiration for white suffragists, and with black women's leadership and activism now better documented—from suffrage to the results of the last presidential election—such fiction cannot survive.

This is why we need to know our history. We walk into rooms of our past, and listen to the conversations. Only after we have had a chance to draw our own lessons and conclusions from events as they happened does Wagner give us her thoughts about what could and should have been—and what could be now.

As Paula Gunn Allen, Native American activist and Laguna Pueblo poet, wrote in *The Sacred Hoop*, "the root of oppression is the loss of memory."

GLORIA STEINEM

Introduction

Writing any history of the woman suffrage movement is an absurdist task. You must be in a million places at once viewing a million things simultaneously from a million different perspectives. It's impossible, but if you take on the job of writing a history anthology you are always aware of the arbitrary nature of what you select.

Given all this, how do you proceed to create an anthology? You may decide to draw out one thread from this thickly woven fabric and follow that single line—like, say, just the vote. But the thread doesn't draw out, it's entangled with too many other threads. You tug and the thread breaks, but you go with that single strand of the thread. It's not complete, it doesn't give you an idea of the vast fabric you've pulled it from or the interrelationships you've torn asunder. That's history. It's a conceit, an impossible task. And, as they say in the biz, you murder a whole lot of little darlings in the process, taking cherished writings out of the manuscript because there just isn't room in the allotted pages.

This is not, then, a definitive collection of primary documents from the movement for the vote. It is rather a sampling of the voices that fought for some of the myriad women's rights issues, those who inspired them, those who opposed them, the documents that defined and reported them, and the writings and speeches they produced embedded in a running narrative.

The book is a journey moving through time, with a tour guide pointing out some high spots along the way, limited by the need to move to the next location before our time together ends; or a train trip through the land of woman's oppression led by a conductor who directs you to various landmarks on the road to freedom land. You know that if you got off at any stop there would many more things to see, but you'd never be able to see them all in one lifetime.

A few things to watch out for along the way. While the suffragists (not suffragettes, that was the British movement) chose the singular, *woman's* rights, you will find used the more contemporary term, *women's* rights. *Suffrage* evokes suffering, as well it should when denied, but it means, of course, the vote. In addition, as our cultural awareness of oppression evolves, we recognize the language fostering racism and sexism in common use in earlier times. For example, our Declaration of Independence refers to the indigenous peoples of this land as "merciless Indian savages," a term continued in usage into the early twentieth century, along with the disrespectful term for female genitalia, squaw, to refer to Native American women. While these words have been kept as they were in the original, you may note our growing cultural awareness as you experience the inappropriateness of each of these words as you read.

Movements don't have a beginning and an end. They are dams historians build in the river of history to capture the flow in a particular moment, and historians regularly move the location of those dams. The standard woman suffrage narrative by historians in the 1950s placed the beginning demarcation of the woman suffrage movement at 1848, marking the local convention for women's rights held that summer in Seneca Falls, New York. That narrative ended the suffrage movement in 1920, when the federal suffrage amendment became part of the Constitution. Scholars studying the pre-Revolution period then recognized propertied women who voted in the colonies, weakening the 1848 dam, while those researching the 1830s Female Anti-Slavery Societies have suggested the beginnings of women organizing are to be found with these abolitionists. You'll see evidence of both in the following chapters.

History is defined less by what happened than by who tells the story. When Elizabeth Cady Stanton sat down with her colleagues Susan B. Anthony and Matilda Joslyn Gage to tell the story of the movement in their three-volume, three-thousand-page *History of Woman Suffrage*, they dammed up the history of their movement from their personal perspective. A planner of the 1848 Seneca Falls convention, Stanton labeled it the first woman's rights meeting held in the country. She may be correct. But it's also possible that a grade school student going through her local newspaper for a History Day project may someday find an account of a woman's rights meeting held before 1848, setting back that beginning marker. The location of the dams keeps shifting as our perspective and knowledge broaden.

Gage pushed back women's rights agitation in the Western world five hundred years in her preface to the first volume of their *History*, excerpted here, but she and Stanton also recognized the earlier existence of gender equality practiced in the nearby Haudenosaunee (Iroquois) nations. This volume, for the first time, places the beginning of women's rights a thousand years ago at the founding of the Iroquois Confederacy on the shores of Onondaga Lake, in present-day Syracuse, New York. Non-native women, on the other hand, were bound by religious dogma instructing them to follow God's edict that they be under the authority of men, with science telling them they were dumber, weaker, and naturally dependent. These women needed a model, a functioning culture where women and men lived in equality. You will read, for the first time, the words of Stanton and Gage, *History* coeditors and the two major theorists of the women's rights movement, documenting the inspiration they received from seeing Native American equality in action. Lucretia Mott, too, as you'll read, brought that energy to the Seneca Falls convention, having just come from a stay in a Seneca community, one of the six Haudenosaunee nations, where her Friends (Quaker) meeting did support work.

Mott is finally redeemed here after years of false intimations of conservative caution on her part for not supporting the call for woman suffrage in the Declaration of Sentiments adopted by the 1848 gathering. It wasn't timidity at all; she was part of two groups that didn't believe in voting, as it supported a government that allowed slavery and war. However, like many pro-choice women today who personally would not have an abortion but support the right of women to make that choice, Mott upheld the right of women to vote.

History is not inevitably progress nor is it linear. Rights gained may be taken away; concerns at one time may remain centuries into the present moment. So it is with Native American women's history. As they were modeling the way for U.S. women to take greater authority over their lives, that authority was at the same time being taken away from them through violence, intimidation, law, and religion, as suffragist-ethnographer Alice Fletcher warned in 1888. Never defeated, these indigenous women rise today, "sovereign women in sovereign nations," inviting us to learn from them as our suffragist foremothers did.

Bringing their voices into the conversation, we come to understand that voting rights for women is not a one-size-fits-all. In her women's rights newspaper, Gage supported the decision of the Haudenosaunee leaders in 1878 to refuse the vote, which was "about to be forced upon them," because with it, as you will read, it failed to recognize them as sovereign nations, with their own governmental structure. Indigenous nations find different means of negotiating physical, cultural, governmental, and spiritual survival against attempts at forced colonization. For some this has meant dual citizenship and accepting the voting rights imposed on them by the federal government with the 1924 Indian Citizenship Act, using the vote and elected representation to ensure their indigenous interests are represented in their complex relationship with the United States. Other native nations, like Onondaga, the center of the Haudenosaunee confederacy, refuse U.S. citizenship and voting rights, maintaining their nation citizenship, with individuals traveling outside their territory on Haudenosaunee passports.

While the United States has forced voting rights on all native women, whether or not they wanted to identify as United States citizens, it has denied them to other groups of women since 1920.

Despite the existing legal assurances, voting rights continue to be eroded in a cat-and-mouse game with the remnants of the country's male founders who continue to sneak in another method of voting suppression each time voting rights are strengthened. This compilation, then, documents not a final victory but one more partial victory as we create democracy in the United States. Each of the markers contains its own truth, which needs to be told in depth. Recognizing that it is a beginning, not an end, this volume ends at 1920, while pointing the way forward for the further story.

Challenged here are the time markers and also the narrative. Women didn't gain legal protection for the ballot in 1920, they regained it. The suffragists knew that women had voted in the colonies. "We are fully awake to the fact that our struggle is not for the attainment of a new right," they said, "but for the restitution of one our fore-mothers possessed and exercised." They echoed Founding Mother Abigail Adams's warning to her future president husband, "We are determined to foment a rebellion, and will not hold ourselves bound by laws in which we have no voice or representation" when they "impeached the government for its treatment of women" on July 4, 1876, declaring they had "greater cause for discontent, rebellion and revolution, than the men of 1776."

Women's rights were old hat by the time the 1848 convention finally rolled around. Individual women, you will learn, had been petitioning for their rights for a decade and had already won victories, such as a Married Woman's Property Act in New York. Nor were they acting alone. Men with voice and authority—attorneys, judges, ministers, journalists—stood against the tide and named the injustices done to women by religion, law, and the family. On the journey, watch for newspaper editor William Ray, who penned a woman suffrage poem in 1821; Judge Hertell, who introduced a married woman's property bill into the New York legislature in 1836; and Unitarian minister Samuel J. May, who preached the first woman's rights sermon in 1845. These individual supporters morphed into organizations of antisexist men who then, as today, prove essential allies in the struggle for justice.

"[A]bove all other causes of the 'Woman Suffrage Movement,'" Gage wrote, "was the Anti-Slavery struggle in this country." It was here, working for an end to slavery, that African American and white women developed skills they would bring into organizing for their own rights the following decade. They learned how to conduct meetings, come to agreement out of disagreement, speak in public, raise funds, and take all forms of action, from petitioning to facing down mobs. Of the five women who organized the Seneca Falls convention, four were seasoned veterans of the Female Anti-Slavery Society activism; only Stanton lacked that background. Many today say, with reason, the women's rights movement started in 1832, when African American women organized the first Female Anti-Slavery Society in Salem, Massachusetts, or when the 139 local societies of black and white women that formed held their first national convention in 1837.

Most remarkably, and seldom recognized because of the delicate language in which they couched it, you will read the words of these anti-slavery activists—women and men—as they publicly exposed the institutionalized rape of enslaved women, an act of tremendous courage at a time when it was considered racy to expose the "leg" of your piano because it might invite men to have inappropriate thoughts. Outraged clergy reminded these women that the Bible clearly instructed them to be under the authority of men, ordering them to go home and behave themselves.

This movement was never about just the vote; nor was it a single movement. Early on, notably in the 1850s, women opened the Pandora's box of their oppression and out popped the Bible, admonishing them to shut their mouths, never wear trousers, obey their husbands, and accept everything about their condition. Some courageous few resisted and attacked the religious dogma, wore pants, and demanded ownership of their property, decent working conditions, and "equal pay for equal work." Pushing open the doors to the higher education that had excluded them, they became doctors, lawyers, professors, business owners, and ministers. They quickly realized, as did feminists in the next century, that the personal is very political, as they raised issues close to home: the right to their

own bodies, to their children, and to leave loveless and dangerous marriages.

For a glorious decade this multi-issue movement gained
ground. With the outbreak of the Civil War, the movement
suspended its women's rights activities and proceeded to make
history, much of which has been lost to us. Surgeon Dr. Mary
Walker was awarded the Congressional Medal of Honor, while
Harriet Tubman was the first woman to lead a military excursion. Anna Ella Carroll developed the Tennessee Plan, which
turned the tide of the war for the North. Dr. Elizabeth Blackwell, the first U.S. woman doctor, started the seven-thousand-
chapter Sanitary Commission to aid sick and wounded soldiers,
which raised more than $92 million, the largest private philan-
thropic effort in the country to that point.

When Abraham Lincoln insisted the war was being fought
to preserve the Union, and had nothing to do with slavery, the
two thousand women, men, and children of the Woman's
Loyal National League collected four hundred thousand signatures, the largest number gathered in the country to that point,
on a petition demanding an end to slavery. The resulting Thirteenth Amendment abolished the ownership of human beings
but made an exception allowing for the virtual enslavement of
prisoners and ushering in the prison-industrial complex.

With slavery legally ended, the pro-slavery Constitution had
to be rewritten. The enslaved people previously counted as
three-fifths of a person for the purposes of representation
would now become citizens—or would they? Internecine warfare broke out among the abolitionists and suffragists, who
had joined together to work for universal suffrage in a merged
organization, the American Equal Rights Association (AERA),
over whether to support the enfranchisement only of black
men or hold out for the vote for everyone. While historians
have often presented this as a simple question of racism, largely
because of the racist statements of Stanton, Anthony, and their
newspaper, funded by a white supremacist, those involved
didn't see it quite that simply. African American men, such as
Charles Remond, said, "In an hour like this I repudiate the
idea of expediency. All I ask for myself I claim for my wife and

sister." Suffragists such as Lucy Stone, on the other hand, declared they were willing to step aside for now because it was the "Negro's hour." When the organization supported the Fifteenth amendment, which enfranchised only African American men, and the Fourteenth amendment introduced the word "male" in describing citizens three times, the progressive suffragists withdrew and formed a new organization to work for women's rights with female-only leadership, the National Woman Suffrage Association (NWSA). The "Negro's hour" women, feeling this group was too radical, formed their own, the American Woman Suffrage Association (AWSA), with a male minister as president.

The women's rights movement, which had addressed a range of issues, now narrowed and focused as the need and momentum for a woman suffrage amendment, first introduced by Representative George W. Julian in 1869, rose to the fore. In the 1850s, they had held women's rights national conventions; now both organizations put the word *suffrage* in their titles.

While both wanted woman suffrage, they worked in seemingly diametrically opposed ways. The NWSA worked for the federal suffrage amendment, while the AWSA put its energy toward securing the right to vote state by state. It is seldom recognized that this strategy, as it supported states' rights, thereby also supported white supremacy. If states could give women the vote, couldn't they also take it away from black men? The federal amendment strategy for woman suffrage, on the other hand, strengthened the national government's authority to enforce equality.

This difference in strategy may help explain why most of the active African American women—Mary Ann Shadd Cary, Sojourner Truth, Harriet Tubman, and Harriet Purvis—went with the NWSA, while Frances Ellen Harper, along with Charlotte Rollin, appear to be the only two who joined the AWSA.

The NWSA campaign of nonviolent civil disobedience is uniquely recognized here, documenting how its members spoke truth to power and broke the law to show the injustice of it. Citing "No taxation without representation," members refused to pay their taxes. They broke the law by voting, and, if not allowed to vote, some sued the registrars who refused to let them register to vote. While history recognizes Susan B. Anthony as the pillar of illegal voting, hundreds —perhaps thousands —of women voted, many up to four years before she did. Far more important than her single act was that of Virginia Minor, who took her case all the way to the Supreme Court, where the nine white male justices ruled unanimously that women did not have the right to vote guaranteed in the United States in 1874. Two years later, Susan B. Anthony and Matilda Joslyn Gage illegally presented a Declaration of Rights of the Women of the United States on July 4, 1876, during the official centennial celebration. They risked arrest, Gage explained, "to place on record for the daughters of 1976, the fact that their mothers of 1876 had . . . impeached the government . . . for its injustice toward woman."

The NWSA continued its direct-action strategy, protesting, in 1886 at the unveiling of the Statue of Liberty, the hypocrisy of the government in representing liberty as a woman in a nation where "not one woman is free." The following year it presented President Cleveland with a protest at the celebration of the centennial of the Constitution, pointing out that the document still failed to recognize half its citizens.

The NWSA had embraced Victoria Woodhull, a brilliant, charismatic newspaper editor and stockbroker, when she presented Congress with a compelling argument to enact woman suffrage by passing simple enabling legislation. The organization then endorsed her self-proclaimed candidacy for president of the United States. Newspaper articles exposing men in high places using their position to sexually violate vulnerable women did not first appear in 2017. Victoria Woodhull and her sister, Tennessee Claflin, published in their newspaper the account of two teenage girls sexually violated by Wall Street operatives. They also exposed the most famous minister in the country for using his position to sexually coerce a parishioner. Woodhull and Claflin were arrested under the newly enacted Comstock law outlawing "obscenity," and the first woman to announce as a candidate for president of the United States spent election night in jail.

Woodhull was also a free lover, proclaiming, "I have an inalienable, constitutional and natural right to love whom I may, to love as long or short a period as I can; to change that love every day if I please." The conservative AWSA, horrified that the suffrage movement now stood aligned in the public's perception with people advocating sexual behavior outside the sanctity of marriage, passed a resolution totally disassociating itself from any connection with free love. The AWSA was on shaky grounds, because the exposed minister, Henry Ward Beecher, was the founding president of the AWSA, and the woman he had sexually coerced, Elizabeth Tilton, was a vice president of the NWSA.

While the major forms of safe, affordable birth control—condoms, spermicide-soaked sponges, diaphragms, and cervical caps—were available by 1870, the Comstock Acts, enacted by states and Congress, made birth control and abortion methods or information about them illegal. Out of the Freethought movement, a body-right movement emerged, supported by Gage, Stanton, and other NWSA members. Included herein is the suicide note of Ida Craddock, who killed herself rather than spend the rest of her life imprisoned under the Comstock laws, perhaps the first martyr of the reproductive justice movement.

The AWSA continued to be critical of the NWSA's actions, increasingly appealing to the conservative groups, including the Woman's Christian Temperance Union (WCTU), which now favored woman suffrage as a tool to both abolish liquor and also create a Christian nation, while the NWSA passed resolutions holding the Christian doctrine that required women to be under the authority of men accountable for their second-class position.

A second NWSA member became a presidential candidate in 1884 when attorney Belva Lockwood announced her candidacy and carried on a campaign, winning the entire electoral vote of Indiana. While the delegates may have cast their vote as a joke, the illegal refusal of the government to accept the results aided the erasure of Lockwood's run from history.

Historians often accept the 1889 merger between the NWSA

and the AWSA as inevitable and expedient, following the description of Anthony and her hand-picked biographer, Ida Husted Harper. It was neither, as you will see documented on these pages. Anthony fervently believed the vote should be the only focus, and the two groups together, working in alignment with the WCTU, could achieve that goal. Unique in the volume is the protest issued by some NWSA leaders to the merger, along with Gage's attempt to stop religious influence on the government.

The merged National American Woman Suffrage Association (NAWSA) increasingly became a top-down, hierarchical organization, focused on achieving the vote state by state and dropping the national amendment. It allowed its state auxiliaries to exclude African American women and to support educated suffrage, a means to the end of maintaining white, native-born sovereignty. You will read the organization's convention proceedings and marketing appealing to white, native-born supremacy as it points out that white, educated, native-born women outnumbered African Americans and immigrants. Immigrants often were not English-fluent upon arrival, and enslaved people had been legally forbidden to learn to read and write, as the organization pointed out with statistics. It justified its xenophobia and racism as "expediency," arguing that women would never achieve suffrage without the support of the South. This volume challenges that argument.

With the influx of orthodox Christian women, the NAWSA became increasingly religiously conservative as well. When Honorary President Elizabeth Cady Stanton released the Woman's Bible she had edited, Carrie Chapman Catt, Reverend Anna Howard Shaw, and the conservative women who increasingly came to control the NAWSA were furious at Stanton for alienating the orthodox Christian women they were courting and ushered through a resolution disavowing any connection with the book. An angry Stanton asked Anthony to resign from the organization, but Anthony chose to continue as president.

History isn't just what happened; it is also what didn't happen. The NAWSA maintained silence as black men were systematically disenfranchised in the South. Lynching became a recognized practice for maintaining white power, and still the NAWSA remained silent. Ida B. Wells, anti-lynching activist and founder of the Alpha, the first suffrage club for black women, pointed out to no avail the contradiction between Anthony's personal commitment to racial justice and her public practice of implicitly condoning racism as an NAWSA tactic. Helen Pitts Douglass, Frederick Douglass's widow, sat outraged through the 1900 NAWSA convention listening to a southern delegate call for white supremacy three times, with no one objecting. Barred from membership and attendance at the NAWSA conventions, their calls for support ignored by the NAWSA leadership, African American women formed their own suffrage organizations, working not just for the vote but also for education, against lynching, and for a host of other issues.

Despite the increased funding that came with increased conservatism, the NAWSA languished, all but dropping the federal amendment, with expensive state suffrage campaigns yielding few victories. Then in 1913 a group of young women, some fresh from training with the militant British suffragettes, brought new tactics and renewed energy to the lagging organization. Unable to work within the NAWSA, Alice Paul and these new suffragists formed the National Woman's Party (NWP). Their direct-action strategies recalled the dynamic NWSA, as they chained themselves to the White House or were arrested and force-fed through feeding tubes down their noses when they went on hunger strikes. They burned a recalcitrant President Wilson's democracy speeches in protest and later, the president's effigy. While working in sometimes opposing ways, the combined efforts of the ladylike NAWSA and the hold-your-feet-to-the-fire NWP—one outside calling out the injustice; one inside, asking politely—created momentum.

When reading about the consequences of the NWSA-AWSA merger, and the energy generated by the dynamic tension of organizations working differently toward the same goal, the reader is invited to question whether there is value in organizations' maintaining their unique integrity and vision, rather than assuming that a merger is always the preferable option.

The congressional hearings slowly progressed in the 1910s as the states' rights strategy paid off. Thousands of women voters in the suffrage states were now watching the actions of their congressional representatives. The amendment wended its way through committees and onto the floor of the Senate and the House until finally, in 1919, it passed both houses and was sent to the states for ratification. The unique account by an on-the-ground activist during the Tennessee campaign takes you inside the final moments as the final state ratifies and the federal suffrage amendment is added to the constitution on August 26, 1920.

These are some of the highlights of the journey, and the reader is invited to step off when one of these stops interests you and travel into the interior. Colleagues have gone deep into all these moments and issues, and continue to with a richness of research too massive to acknowledge in these pages. You are one online search away from a side trip of fascination.

As we move to create a more perfect union in this cultural revolution we are undergoing, we are creating a new history. Not the top-down history that focuses on great white men, their great deeds, and their great wars. We are shaping history to reflect and guide the bottom-up diversity of voices that changed, is changing, and will change the world. Yes, if we don't know our history we are bound to repeat it. But it is also true that if we do know our rich and diverse history of those who worked for social justice, we are empowered to repeat it. Their voices have often been shouted down by those at the top. It's time we gave them a listen.

SALLY ROESCH WAGNER

The
Women's Suffrage
Movement

I.

WOMEN VOTED BEFORE
THE UNITED STATES
WAS FORMED

Women didn't first achieve the vote in 1920; they had political authority on this land before Columbus.

As we celebrate women gaining political voice in the United States, the accurate story begins with a celebration of the women who had political voice on this land a thousand years ago. These women lived in native nations that tenaciously held on, as well as they could, to their system of real equality despite the best efforts of missionaries, boarding schools, and federal and state governments alike to deprive them of it. They still do, and are reclaiming their identity as "sovereign women in sovereign nations."

This story is essential not only because it starts in the right place, but because it helps us understand how any white women, ordered into God-ordained silence and subservience and told by science it was their natural condition, found the courage to challenge all institutionalized society. They had to have seen something that gave them the idea it was even possible. They did. Their native neighbors. They saw, and they were inspired.

Living in an authoritarian culture with no concept of shared power, early suffrage leaders Elizabeth Cady Stanton and Matilda Joslyn Gage saw empowered women, but so locked were they in thinking that required ranking one above the other that they mistakenly thought they saw women with power over men. Although they couldn't recognize gender equality based on balanced responsibilities, they were able to see a model that told them their oppressed condition was neither natural nor spiritually mandated. Another suffragist, ethnographer Alice Fletcher, lived among native people and saw the position of women up close.

Along with Elizabeth Cady Stanton and Susan B. Anthony, Matilda Joslyn Gage (1826–1898) was one of the three major leaders of the National Woman Suffrage Association (NWSA), sharing leadership positions with them, authoring the organization's major documents with Stanton and coediting the first three volumes of *History of Woman Suffrage* with Stanton and Anthony.

Matilda Joslyn Gage saw the Native American model firsthand. She lived in central New York, near the Onondaga nation, which was (and is) the center of the five original nations of the Haudenosaunee (Iroquois, to the French) confederacy: the Mohawk, Oneida, Onondaga, Cayuga, and Seneca—later joined by the Tuscarora. In her newspaper, the *National Citizen and Ballot Box*, Gage recognized the political sovereignty of native nations, writing an editorial in support of the Council of Chiefs in their decision not to accept citizenship in New York State. She demanded that the government honor the treaties it had ratified with these nations.

Perhaps most surprising is that Gage was given an honorary adoption into the Wolf Clan of the Mohawk Nation in 1893, along with a clan name. "I received the name of Ka-ron-ien-ha-wi, or 'Sky Carrier,' or as Mrs. Converse said the Senecas would express it 'She who holds the sky.'" Her Mohawk sister said that "this name would admit me to the Council of Matrons, where a vote would be taken, as to my having a voice in the Chieftainship," Gage wrote. How amazing this must have been to a woman who went to trial the same year for voting in a state school election. Considered for full voting rights in her adopted nation, she was arrested in her own nation for voting.

Gage's publications in a variety of sources reflect her belief that Native American women—specifically the Haudenosaunee (Iroquois)—held a position far superior to that of white women. While serving as president of the National Woman Suffrage Association in 1875, Gage wrote a series of front-page stories for the New York *Evening Post* covering history, ceremony, the role of women, and food practices adopted by European settlers. Excerpts from these articles are included in this chapter.

Gage's major work, *Woman, Church and State* (1893), is now considered a feminist classic. In the book, she designates indigenous, pre-Christian societies her model for a just world, with independence of thought and action, freedom, and perfect equality as the requirements. A portion of this book is included in this chapter, following Gage's *Post* articles.

Gage edited the *National Citizen and Ballot Box*, the official newspaper of the National Woman Suffrage Association, from 1878 to 1881. When the Haudenosaunee Council of Chiefs met to consider a bill to enfranchise Indian men that had been introduced into the New York Legislature, in an editorial titled "Indian Citizenship" Gage supported the chiefs in their decision, while pointing out the hypocrisy of the government. Although she uses the now-racist anthropological language of the time ("barbaric"), Gage demonstrates a sophisticated understanding of the independent sovereignty of native nations and the responsibility of the federal government to live up to its treaties. The article, included in this chapter, also suggests that she either attended the Grand Council or had a Haudenosaunee friend who gave her the details of the meeting.

Witty, brilliant, and iconoclastic, Elizabeth Cady Stanton (1815–1902) was considered one of the country's preeminent and most controversial women. An organizer of the world's first women's rights convention, in 1848, and a widely read author, in 1869 Stanton became a Lyceum lecturer, speaking around the country for twelve years. She saw beyond the vote, espousing social justice issues from reproductive rights to economic justice.

Elizabeth Cady Stanton often stayed with her cousin, Gerrit Smith. Among the many visitors to his palatial mansion would be members of the Oneida Nation, on whose aboriginal territory Smith lived. Gerrit's brother, Peter Skenandoah Smith, was named for an Oneida friend of the family, Chief Skenandoah. In addition, Stanton's nearest Seneca Falls neighbor, Oren Tyler, came from Onondaga, where he "had friendly dealings" with the people there and was given an honorary adoption by a clan. He spoke their language fluently, and parties of Onondagans passing through Seneca Falls to sell their bead work and baskets "sought out their 'brother,' as they called Capt. Tyler, who always befriended them."[1]

It was through reading Karl Pearson's *The Ethic of Free Thought*, Stanton wrote in her autobiography, *Eighty Years and More: Reminiscences 1815–1897*, that she came to believe that the Matriarchate—an egalitarian, female-lineage form of society common to indigenous communities—"[seemed] so natural in the chain of reasoning and the progress of human development."[2]

In *Elizabeth Cady Stanton as Revealed in Her Letters, Diary and Reminiscences*, a book published in 1922 by her children, Theodore Stanton and Harriot Stanton Blatch, Stanton reflects further on the subject in her diary:

> After six months' reading about the matriarchate, I am amazed to find how much more we are indebted to woman than to man for not only the intelligence and the morality of the race but for many of the greatest steps in material progress. Two things are strikingly evident—that woman has not always been the slave of man, nor has she always been his inferior in physical strength. In early savagery he looked out for himself alone, while she looked out for herself and her children. No historian until within thirty years ever noted how long women reigned supreme, and the great physical development and strength they possessed in freedom. Maternity was the source and center of all the first steps in civilization. Because of the variety of things she was forced to do, woman necessarily cultivated many faculties; hence she was better developed physically than the man by her side; and, forced to provide for others, her moral sentiments were roused long before his were.[3]

When Stanton completed her paper, "The Matriarchate, or Mother-Age," she sent it to Susan B. Anthony to read at the 1891 convention of the National Council of Women. She also sent a copy to prominent suffrage lecturer and journalist Clara Colby (1846–1916), for publication in Colby's newspaper, the *Woman's Tribune*. She wrote to Colby fearing "my beloved Susan will not appreciate" the speech, "as the word suffrage does not come in."[4] Anthony by this time had become totally fixated on the vote, and didn't want any other issues of women's equality to stand in its way.

Colby reported in her paper on February 28, three days after the convention, "[T]he reading of Mrs. Stanton's paper was greeted with prolonged applause, both before it began and after it closed." The full paper is included herein, immediately following Gage's works.

Alice Fletcher (1838–1923) was a respected social scientist. President of the Anthropological Society of Washington, vice president of the American Association for the Advancement of Science, and the first woman president of the American Folklore Society, she founded the School of American Archaeology in Santa Fe, New Mexico, while pioneering in the study of Native American music. Fletcher authored forty-six ethnology monographs and developed an intimate personal and professional relationship with members of the influential La Flesche family of the Omaha Nation.

She also was an agent of assimilation. Understanding and respecting indigenous values and institutions, she nonetheless believed that their way of life had become unsustainable and that the key to survival was adopting the European-American culture. To that end, she assisted with the work of the Carlisle Indian School in Pennsylvania, a boarding school where Indian children were taken from their homes and forced, often brutally, to adopt Western ways. At Carlisle, the goal was to "Kill the Indian; Save the Man."

The year before she gave her speech, "The Legal Condition of Indian Women," at the International Council of Women in 1888, Fletcher helped author and lobbied for the Dawes Act of

1887, which tore apart the land of all the indigenous nations. This land had been held collectively since time immemorial, and the Dawes Act forced its division into 160-acre parcels for individual ownership. The land left over after every native nation member had been given a chunk was turned over to whites for settlement. The volume of social, spiritual, economic, and practical destruction caused by the Dawes Act is incalculable.

Revised over the years, land allotment was finally ended under the Franklin D. Roosevelt administration in 1934. Perhaps in an attempt to ameliorate the damage, Fletcher introduced a microloan program through the Women's National Indian Association for native people to buy land and houses.

Fletcher, it must be said, had more knowledge of indigenous people than all but a handful of scholars in her time. Over the course of her lifetime, she lived with or had dealings with the people of the Omaha, Lakota, Ojibwe, Arapaho, Tsêhéstáno (Cheyenne), Winnebago (Ho-Chunk), Pawnee, Oto, Nez Percé, and Ponca nations.

In this talk at the first international gathering of European and American women's rights advocates, Fletcher speaks primarily of her experience with Omaha and Lakota women. While she is acting as an agent of the government's attempted destruction of indigenous culture, in her address she is giving non-native suffragists an idea of what female autonomy and cultural empowerment look like in practice. The full speech is included at the end of this chapter.[5]

The belief runs deep that the history of women in the United States is an undeviating line of steady progress toward greater freedom. In truth, the American woman's story is one of tremendous losses of liberty, regained and extended only through great struggle, and maintained only through continual vigilance. For example, women didn't gain the right to vote in 1920; they regained it. Women voted in the American colonies, a fact the suffragists well knew.

Readers of *The New Era*, a popular feminist journal, in 1885 learned from suffragist Dr. Clemence S. Lozier:[6]

. . . in the colony of New Netherland (later New York), in 1644–5 by the Legislature, a woman, Lady Deborah Moody, was enfranchised by name at the head of the list of voters of Gravesend, and that the men being afterward all disfranchised, she as the sole voter elected the magistrates for years; that through the whole existence of the province the common law . . . recognized woman's right to vote on the same terms with their brothers.[7]

In *History of Woman Suffrage*, Matilda Joslyn Gage documented:

Under the Old Province Charter, women had full suffrage in Massachusetts from 1691 to 1780. With the adoption of the Constitution in 1780, their voting rights were limited, but women still voted for all elective officers except the governor, council and legislature for five years.[8]

Ownership of a certain amount of property was required to vote in many colonies, based on the argument that those without wealth were beholden to the wealthy and therefore highly susceptible to pressure from them to vote a certain way. Women who owned property were logically voters under this system, and when they weren't allowed, a meeting of disgruntled property-holding widows in New York in 1733 protested their disfranchisement in the *New York Journal*, stating they were tax-paying "House Keepers" who paid their taxes, carried on trade—most as "she Merchants"—and as contributors to "the Support of Government," they felt entitled to "some of the Sweets of it."[9]

With women voting in the colonies, the Founding Fathers were forced to consider just how far they would extend the concept of a government of the people. John Adams grappled with the question of woman suffrage in a May 26, 1776, letter to James Sullivan.

It is certain, in theory, that the only moral foundation of government is, the consent of the people. But to what an extent shall we carry this principle? Shall we say that every individual of the community, old and young, male and female, as well as rich and poor, must consent, expressly, to every act of legislation? If not . . . whence arises the right of the men to govern the women, without their consent?[10]

Abigail Adams had challenged her husband in a letter on March 31, which said in part:

That your sex are naturally tyrannical is a truth so thoroughly established as to admit of no dispute; but such of you as wish to be happy willingly give up the harsh title of master for the more tender and endearing one of friend. Why, then, not put it out of the power of the vicious and the lawless to use us with cruelty and indignity and impunity. Men of sense in all ages abhor those customs which treat us only as the vassal of your sex.[11]

In *History of Woman Suffrage*, Matilda Joslyn Gage reminded her readers that Abigail Smith Adams, this Founding Mother and later First Lady, was a feminist and also anti-slavery. And she was not alone. The full writing is included in this chapter.

Abigail Adams was also among those who believed there was a great hypocrisy in opposing English tyranny while practicing slavery, and wrote John in 1774 that "[i]t has always appeared a most iniquitous scheme to me to fight ourselves for what we are daily robbing and plundering from those who have as good a right to freedom as we have."[12]

Woman suffrage ended when Virginia was the first colony to specifically restrict women from voting by statute in 1699. The Election Law of 1704 in South Carolina contained no sex qualification; it was not until the law of 1716 that suffrage was limited to "every [qualified] white man."[13]

The United States Constitutional Convention of 1787 placed voting qualifications in the hands of each state, and the newly formed states specifically denied women suffrage in the constitutions they established. New Jersey and New York voting laws, for example, initially were written in gender neutral language, stating:

> No person shall be entitled to vote in any other township or precinct, or than that in which he or she doth actually reside at the time of the election and Every voter shall openly, and in full view deliver his or her ballot . . . to the said judge.[14]

The new language adopted by states used words like "freemen," "free white men," "male person," and "man" to exclude women and black men from voting.

New York denied women the vote in 1777, followed by Massachusetts in 1780 and New Hampshire in 1784. Maryland inserted the word "male" into the state constitution, thereby excluding women from suffrage, in 1801. Delaware placed the word "male" into its constitution in 1831; Rhode Island followed in the next decade. South and North Carolina, Georgia, Tennessee, and Pennsylvania law didn't deny women suffrage until after the Civil War.[15]

While the Founding Fathers had seen democracy in action among the Iroquois Confederacy and were inspired by the model, they considered, then chose to ignore the critical role of women in government once they established their government.

Free blacks voted, along with women, in many of the colonies and were denied political self-determination by the same legislatures that took away woman suffrage. African American men were denied the vote in the constitutions of New Jersey, Connecticut, New York, and Pennsylvania by 1838, while they still maintained that right in Virginia and North Carolina.[16]

Women and African American men voted in New Jersey from 1790 to 1807. While the law carried a property qualification for voting, there were no race or gender requirements. Once the power of women voters was felt, the appropriateness of their exercising the franchise came into question. Women came close to defeating a candidate when they voted in a bloc in a 1797 election, and the roaring woman suffrage debate that ensued resulted in this poem.

> ... What tho' we read, in days of yore,
> the woman's occupation,
> Was to direct the wheel and loom,
> not to direct the nation:
> This narrow-minded policy
> by us hath met detection;
> While woman's bound, man can't be free,
> or have a fair Election ... [17]

Aware of this early voting history, suffragists a hundred years after the Revolution declared, as stated in *History of Woman Suffrage*:

> ... we are fully awake to the fact that our struggle is not for the attainment of a new right, but for the restitution of one our foremothers possessed and exercised.[18]

A New York State constitutional convention in 1821 removed the property qualification from white men and placed it on black men, who now had to own property valued at $250 in order to vote. Free black men in the state had previously voted without restriction, but few could meet the new requirement. A Negro state convention was later to point out that African American men had helped to elect many of the delegates who now restricted their right to vote.[19]

Therefore, this convention of New York blacks concluded, extending suffrage to white men while limiting it to propertied African American men violated "every principle of justice" and equality "upon which our government is founded."[20]

Woman suffrage came up at this 1821 convention as well and was denied, as it was at another constitutional convention in 1846. Two men were among those who spoke up publicly for women's right to vote in these early years, one a newspaper editor almost thirty years before the first 1848 local women's rights convention, the other a minister who preached the gospel of women's rights two years before. There have always been male allies, their work providing a model and challenge to men today.

William Ray, a newspaper editor and author of *The Horrors*

of Slavery, introduced it in the form of a poem that threatened no less than a Lysistrata-inspired sex boycott if women were refused a political voice:

> A HUMBLE bard who ne'er before,
> Address'd a speaker on the floor
> Of capitol—would mention,
> Without a quibble or a quirk,
> What ladies beg may be one work
> Of your wise state convention.
>
> That ev'ry one must have a vote,
> Who does not wear a petticoat,
> Is generally admitted;
> But why should women be denied,
> And have their tongues completely tied,
> For party broils well fitted.
>
> The question is of great account,
> Which no convention can surmount,
>   Without dissatisfaction
> Amongst the ladies—so I fear,
> And therefore as their friend appear,
>   And counsel in this action.
>
> That women have a right to live,
> Ten thousand reasons I could give,
>   But this was never doubted;
> And he who would their freedom baulk,
> And say they have no right to talk,
>   Would from the world be scouted.
>
> The Turks, I know, who hold no polls,
> Believe that women have no souls;
>   But, when they wear the breeches,
> As oft they do in states like ours,
> Which give them supernatural powers,
>   And hang them up for witches.—

To say that women must be driven
From ev'ry other place but heav'n,
   Is certainly alarming;
And he who would the like maintain,
Ought to be treated with disdain,
   In company so charming.

Man is half-woman, at the least,
Excepting now and then a beast,
   Who forfeits all pretensions
To decency and common sense,
By many a foul and black offence;
   And yet, some state conventions

Have in their wisdom, found it meet
To let such wretches step their feet,
   Polluted with infection,
Into the sacred fane where lies
The ark of all our liberties—
   The birthright of election;

While women, pure as Eden's queen,
Before that world-distressing scene,
   In myst'ry darkly hidden,
Must stand aloof—remaining dumb,
And never to elections come—
   By haughty man forbidden.

But you, immortal statesmen, you,
Keeping the lovely sex in view
   At your august convention,
Will frame the constitution so
That ladies can t' election go,
   Without the least detention;

For, should you otherwise decree,
The direful consequence may be
   Diminish'd population;

> And this I'm authoris'd to say,
> If women's rights are flung away,
> Is their determination [21]

While the "diminished population" did not materialize and children continued to be born in New York State, at the next New York Constitutional Convention in 1846, woman suffrage again came under consideration, with the presence, this time, of petitions from women.[22]

Reverend Samuel J. May, an abolitionist-suffragist Unitarian minister in Syracuse, preached a very political sermon from his pulpit exhorting men to enfranchise the women. At a time when not a single woman was allowed to preach from the pulpit in a Christian church in the United States, this was probably the first women's rights sermon ever delivered. An abridged version is included at the end of this chapter.

1.
"The Remnant of the Five Nations,"
by Matilda Joslyn Gage, the *(New York) Evening Post,*
September 24, 1875

When America first became known to white men as the New World, within the limits of what is now called New York state existed one of the oldest known republics in the world, a confederacy of Five Nations when it was first formed, which added tribes to its numbers as its successor, the American republic, adds states to its Union. So republican was its character that Dr. Peter Wilson, the civilized chief of the Iroquois Indians, in an address before the New York State Historical Society a few years ago, declared that Jefferson borrowed the Declaration of Independence from the Constitution of the Five Nations.[23]

. . . Although it was a confederation of warriors, owing its permanence and its growth to prowess in arms, yet its women exercised controlling power in peace and war, forbidding at will its young braves to enter battle, and often determining its terms of peace. Division of power between the sexes in this Indian republic was nearly equal. Although the principal chief of the confederacy was a man, descent ran through the female line, the sister of the chief possessing the power of nominating his successor. The common interests of the confederacy were arranged in councils, each sex holding one of its own, although the women took initiative in suggestion, orators of their own sex presenting their views to the council of men.[24]

2.
Woman, Church and State,
by Matilda Joslyn Gage, 1893

Woman is told that her present position in society is entirely due to Christianity, that it is superior to that of her sex at any prior age of the world, Church and State both maintaining that she has ever been inferior and dependent, man superior and ruler. These assertions are made the basis of opposition to her demands for exact equality with man in all the relations of life, although they are not true either of the family, the church, or the state. Such assertions are due to non-acquaintance with the existing phase of historical knowledge, whose records the majority of mankind [has] neither time nor opportunity of investigating.

Christianity tended somewhat from its foundation to restrict the liberty woman enjoyed under the old civilizations. Knowing that the position of every human being keeps pace with the religion and civilization of his country—and that in many ancient nations woman possessed a much greater degree of respect and power than she has at the present age—this subject will be presented from a historical standpoint. If in so doing it helps to show man's unwarranted usurpation over woman's religious and civil rights and the very great difference between true religion and theology, this book will not have been written in vain, as it will prove that the most grievous wrong ever inflicted upon woman has been in the Christian teaching that she was not created equal with man, and the consequent denial of her rightful place in Church and State.

The last half century has shown great advance in historical knowledge; libraries and manuscripts long inaccessible have been opened to scholars, and the spirit of investigation has made known many secrets of the past, brought many hidden things to light. Buried cities have been explored and forced to reveal their secrets; lost modes of writing have been deciphered, and olden myths placed upon historic foundations. . . . We are now informed as to the condition of early peoples, their laws, customs, habits, religion, comprising order and rank in the state, the rules of descent, name, property, the circumstances of family life, the position of mother, father, children, their temples and priestly orders; all these have been investigated and a new historic basis has been discovered. Never has research been so thorough or long-lost knowledge so fully given to the world.

These records prove that woman had acquired great liberty under the old civilizations. A form of society existed at an early age known as the Matriarchate, or Mother-rule. Under the Matriarchate, except as son and inferior, man was not recognized in either of these great institutions, family, state or church. A father and husband, as such, had no place either in the social, political or religious scheme; woman was ruler in each. The primal priest on earth, she was also supreme as goddess in heaven. The earliest semblance of the family is traceable to the relationship of mother and child alone. Here the primal idea of the family had birth.[25] The child bore its mother's name, tracing its descent from her; her authority over it was regarded as in accord with nature; the father, having no part in the family, remained a wanderer. Long years elapsed before man, as husband and father, was held in esteem. The son, as child of his mother, ranked the father, the mother taking precedence over both the father and the son.[26] Blood relationship through a common mother preceded that of descent through the father in the development of society.[27] This priority of the mother touched not alone the family, but controlled the state and indicated the form of religion. Thus we see that during the Matriarchate, woman ruled; she was first in the family, the state, religion, the most ancient records showing that man's subjection to woman preceded by long ages that of woman to man. The tribe was united through the mother; social, political and religious life were all in harmony with the idea of woman as the first and highest power. The earliest phase of life being dependent upon her, she was recognized as the primal factor in every relation,[28] man holding no place but that of dependent.

Every part of the world today gives evidence of the system. Reminiscences of the Matriarchate everywhere abound. Livingstone found African tribes swearing by the mother and tracing descent through her. Marco Polo discovered similar customs in his Asiatic voyages, and the same customs are extant among the Indians of our own continent. Bachofen[29] and numerous investigators[30] agree in the statement that in the earliest forms of society, the family, government, and religion were all under woman's control; that in fact society started under woman's absolute authority and power.

The second step in family life took place when the father, dropping his own name, took that of his child. This old and wide-spread custom is still extant in many portions of the globe; the primitive peoples of Java, Australia and Madagascar are among those still continuing its practice.[31] By this step the father allied himself to both mother and child, although still holding an inferior position to both. The matriarchal family was now fully established, descent still running in the female line. Thus, as has been expressed, we find that woman's liberty did not begin to-day nor under modern religions or forms [of] government, but that she was in reality the founder of civilization, and that in the most remote times woman enjoyed superiority of rights in all the institutions of life.[32] And yet so difficult is it to break away from educated thought, so slight a hold have historical facts upon the mind when contrary to preconceived ideas, that we find people still expressing the opinion that man's place has always been first in government. Even under those forms of society where woman was undisputed head of the family, its very existence due to her, descent entirely in the female line, we still hear assertion that his must have been the controlling political power. But at that early period to which we trace the formation of the family, it was also the political unit. And when peoples became aggregated into communities, when tribal relations were ultimately recognized, woman still held superior position, and was the controlling power in government. And never was justice more perfect, never civilization higher than under the Matriarchate. Historians agree as to the high civilization even to-day of those nations or tribes still preserving traces of matriarchal customs. Even under its most degenerate form, the family, governmental and religious rights of women are more fully recognized than under any phase of Christian civilization. . . .

For long years after the decline of the Matriarchate we still discover that among many of the most refined nations, woman still possessed much of the power that belonged exclusively to her during that early period. . . .

The famous Iroquois Indians, or Six Nations, which at the discovery of America held sway from the Great Lakes to the Tombigbee river, from the Hudson to the Ohio, and of whom it has been said that another century would have found them master of all tribes to the Gulf of Mexico on the south, and the Mississippi on the west, showed alike in form of government, and in social life, reminiscences of the Matriarchate. The line of descent, feminine, was especially notable in all tribal relations such as the election of Chiefs, and the Council of Matrons, to which all disputed questions were referred for final adjudication. No sale of lands was valid without consent of the squaws and among the state archives at Albany, New York, treaties are preserved signed by the "Sachems and Principal Women of the Six Nations." The women also possessed the veto power on questions of war. Sir William Johnston mentions an instance of Mohawk squaws forbidding the war-path to young braves. The family relation among the Iroquois demonstrated woman's superiority in power. When an Indian husband brought the products of the chase to the wigwam, his control over it ceased. In the home, the wife was absolute; the sale of the skins was regulated by her; the price was paid to her. If for any cause the Iroquois husband and wife separated, the wife took with her all the property she had brought into the wigwam; the children also accompanied the mother, whose right to them was recognized as supreme. So fully to this day is descent reckoned through the mother, that blue-eyed, fair-haired children of white fathers are numbered in the tribe and receive both from state and nation their portion of the yearly dole paid to Indian tribes. The veriest pagan among the Iroquois, the renowned and important Keeper of the Wampum and present sole interpreter of the Belts which give the most ancient and secret history of this confederation, is Ephraim Webster, descended from a white man, who, a hundred or more years since, became affiliated through marriage with an Indian woman, as a member of the principal nation of the Iroquois, the Onondagas. As of yore, so now, the greater and lesser Council Houses of the Iroquois are upon the "mountain" of the Onondaga reservation a few miles from the city of Syracuse, New York. Not alone the Iroquois but most Indians of North America trace descent in the female line; among some tribes, woman enjoys almost the whole legislative authority and in others, a prominent share. Lafitte and other Jesuit missionary writers are corroborated in this statement by Schoolcraft, Catlin, Clark, Hubert Bancroft of the Pacific Coast, and many students of Indian life and customs. But the most notable fact connected with woman's participation in governmental affairs among the Iroquois is the statement of Hon. George Bancroft that the form of government of the United States was borrowed from that of the Six Nations. Thus to the Matriarchate or Mother-rule is the modern world indebted for its first conception of inherent rights, natural equality of condition, and the establishment of a civilized government upon this basis. Although the reputation of the Iroquois as warriors appears most prominent in history, we nevertheless find their real principles to have been the true matriarchal [ones] of peace and industry. Driven from the northern portion of America by vindictive foes, compelled to take up arms in self-protection, yet the more peaceful occupations of hunting and agriculture were continually followed. Their history was preserved by means of wampum, while under their women the science of government reached the highest form known to the world. Among the Zunis of New Mexico, woman still preserves supreme religious and political authority; the Paramount Council consisting of six priests under control of a supreme priestess who is the most important functionary of the tribe. This form of government is traceable to their earliest civilization at which period their cities were grouped in sevens, six of them constructed upon a uniform plan; the supreme seventh containing six temples clustered about a supreme central seventh temple. While male priests ruled over the six primal cities the central and superior seventh was presided over by a priestess who not alone officiated at the central temple, but to whom the male priests of the six cities and six inferior temples were subservient.[33]

. . . Until the customs of civilization reached the Indians, their wives, according to Catlin, Schoolcraft and others, were not called upon to work with half the severity of the women of to-day, nor had they tradition of children ever born deaf, dumb or blind. Those kinds of labor pointed to as showing the hardships of an Indian woman's life, Schoolcraft dismisses very lightly. The lodge built by her is not made of heavy posts and carpentry, but of thin poles bent over at the top such as a child can lift. When a family changed its residence these poles were not removed; only the thin sheets of birch bark covering, were taken to the new rendezvous. The gathering of the fuel by the women was cutting dry limbs of the forest, not over eighteen inches in length, with a hatchet. The tillage of the fields shared alike by the old men, women and the boys, was very light. No oxen to drive, no plow to hold, no wheat to plant or thresh. The same corn hills were used year after year, forming small mounds that were long a puzzle to the antiquarian. The squash and the pumpkin grew luxuriantly, while the children made holidays of gathering nuts and acorns for winter use.[34]

3.
"Indian Citizenship," by Matilda Joslyn Gage,
National Citizen and Ballot Box,
May 1878

While the United States is trying to force citizenship upon the Indians the latter are everywhere protesting against it. The famous Iroquois, or "Six Nations," held a council at Onondaga the last of March, upon the old, original council grounds, where, before the advent of Columbus, they were wont to meet in settlement of grave questions.

No such important questions ever came up during their old barbaric life as were discussed at the council in March. First among them was the bill recently introduced in the United States Senate by Mr. Kernan of N.Y., to give those tribes the rights of citizenship and allow them to sell their lands in this State.

The Indians decline the gift of citizenship and although Judge Wallace of the Northern District of New York, recently decided in favor of the right of an Oneida Indian who voted at the presidential election of 1876, Chief Skenandoah of the Oneidas, was one of the principal speakers against this innovation.

The Mahommedans have a saying that one hour of justice is worth seventy years of prayer; the Indians seem to think one hour of justice worth a thousand years of citizenship, as the drift of their talk was against any law that should either *allow or compel* them to become citizens, as such a course would open wide the door to the grasping avarice of the white man. They discussed plans to compel the payment due them for lands once deeded them by the United States in treaty, but which were afterwards seized and sold for the benefit of our government.

Over one hundred chiefs and warriors of the different nations took part in this discussion. This council of Indians at Onondaga Castle, in the center of the great Empire State, and the convention of the women of the country at Washington in January, the one protesting against citizenship about to be forced upon them, because with it would come further deprivation of their rights,—the other demanding citizenship denied them, in order to protect their rights, are two forcible commentaries upon our so-called republican form of government. Can woman's political degradation reach much lower depth? She, educated, enlightened, Christian, in vain begs for the crumbs cast contemptuously aside by savages. While some of these red men are educated Christians, others still cling to their pagan rites, yearly celebrating the Green Corn Dance, yearly burning the White Dog.

After close of the council its younger members indulged in a war-dance, and, scalping knife in hand, with painted faces, whirling tomahawk and shrieking war-whoop, recounted their old time prowess.

That the Indians have been oppressed,—are now, is true, but the United States has treaties with them, recognizing them as distinct political communities, and duty towards them demands *not an enforced citizenship* but a faithful living up to its obligations on the part of the Government.

Our Indians are in reality foreign powers, though living among us. With them our country not only has treaty obligations, but pays them, or professes to, annual sums in consideration of such treaties; the U.S. Government paying the Iroquois their annuities in June, the State of New York in September. One great aversion the Iroquois have to citizenship is that they would then be compelled to pay taxes, which they look upon as a species of tribute. From an early day they were accustomed to receiving tribute, sending among the conquered tribes of Long Island for their annual dues of wampum. As poor, as oppressed as they are, surrounded as they now are by the conquering white man, they still preserve their olden spirit of independence, still look upon themselves as distinct nations and in the payment of their annuities, fancy they are receiving, as of old, tribute from their enemies. Compelling them to become citizens would be like the forcible annexation of Cuba, Mexico, or Canada to our government, and as unjust.

A delegation of Indians called at the White House on New Year's day. As a sarcasm of justice, on their "Happy New Year" cards were inscribed extracts from various treaties made with them, and disregarded rights guaranteed them in treaty by the Government.

The women of the nation might take hint from the Indians and on July 4th, send to the legislative, judicial and executive bodies, cards inscribed with such sentiments as "Governments derive their *just* powers from the *consent* of the governed." "Taxation without representation is tyranny," and others of like character.

The black man had the right of suffrage conferred upon him without his asking for it, and now an attempt is made to force it upon the red man in direct opposition to his wishes, while women citizens, already members of the nation, to whom it rightfully belongs, are denied its exercise. Truly, consistency is a jewel so rare its only abode is the toad's head.[35]

4.
"The Matriarchate, or Mother-Age,"
by Elizabeth Cady Stanton,
February 1891

Without going into any of the fine calculations of historians as to the centuries of human growth, I would simply state that some agree on about eighty-five thousand years. They assign sixty thousand to savagery, twenty thousand to barbarism, and five thousand to civilization.

For my present purpose, these facts are only interesting to show for how long a period, in proportion, women reigned supreme; the arbiters of their own destiny, the protectors of their children, the acknowledged builders of all there was of home life, religion, and later, from time to time, of government.

All along from the beginning until the sixteenth century, when Luther eliminated the feminine element wholly from the Protestant religion and brought the full power of the Church to enforce woman's complete subjection, we find traces of the matriarchate. Karl Pearson, in a series of deeply interesting essays, gives us the result of his researches into the works of modern historians, and the startling facts they unearth, from what to most of us is the dead, unknown, eternal past, shadowed in mystery. The publication of Wilkeson's "Ancient Egypt" in 1836, of "Das Mutterecht," by Bachofen in 1861, of Morgan's "Ancient Society" in 1877, with other lesser lights pursuing the same trend of investigation, all show the leading, independent position women held for ages.

What is often said, and repeated from time to time and never contradicted, is accepted as truth. Thus, the assertion that women have always been physically inferior to men, and consequently have always been held in a subject condition, has been universally believed.

This view has furnished the opponents to woman's emancipation their chief arguments for holding her in bondage, and logically so, for if at all periods and in all latitudes and longitudes woman had held the same subordinate position, men would naturally infer that what we choose to call Providence, for wise purposes, had made woman the slave of man. The worst feature of these assumptions is that women themselves believe them, and feel that to strive for their own emancipation is simply an attempt at the impossible. Fortunately, historical research has at last proved the fallacy of these assumptions and all the arguments that grow out of them. Mankind may be traced by a chain of necessary inferences back to a time when, ignorant of fire, without articulate language, without artificial weapons, they depended, like the wild animals, upon the spontaneous fruits of the earth.

Through all this period woman was left to protect herself and forage for her children. Morgan, in his "Ancient Society," gives many remarkable examples of the superior position of women among different tribes in the latter part of the period of barbarism. Among the greater number of the American aborigines the descent of property and children were in the female line. Women sat in the councils of war and peace and their opinions had equal weight on all questions. Among the Winnebagoes that occupied the territory now known as Wisconsin, a woman was at the head of the nation. The same was true among the early tribes or gens in the Eastern Hemisphere. In the councils of the Iroquois gens every adult male or female member had a voice upon all questions brought before it. It elected and deposed its sachem and chief, it elected Keepers of the Faith, it condoned or avenged the murder of a *gentilis,* and it adopted persons into the gens.

At the epoch of European discovery, the American Indian tribes generally were organized into gentes, with descent in the female line. Before paterfamilias was known, the family was nowhere considered a unit around which society centered. Nothing whatever was based on the [nuclear] family in any of its forms, because it was incapable of entering a gens as a whole. The gens was homogenous and to a great extent permanent in duration, and as such the natural basis of a social system. A family of the monogamic type might have individualized and become powerful in society at large, but the gens did not and could not recognize the family as an integer of itself.

This is equally true of the modern family and political society. Although individualized by property rights and privileges, and recognized as a legal entity by statutory enactments, the family is not the unit of the political system. The State recognizes the counties of which it is composed, the county its townships, but the townships take no note of the family. So in the early periods the nation recognized its tribes, the tribes its phratries, and the phratries its gentes, but the gens took no note of the family.

Thus Morgan flatly contradicts modern historians who assert that the social system of the early Greeks "was the home, the hearth, or family." Like our modern opponents, they cling to the idea of "the family unit," because on that is based the absolute power of the father over the property, children, and the civil and political rights of wives. It is worthy of note that our barbarian ancestors seem to have had a higher idea of justice to woman than American men in the nineteenth century, professing to believe, as they do, in our republican principles of government.

During these early periods the property of woman was in her own line and gens, and man's property was in his own line and gens. The following case at the Pueblo of Oraybe shows that the husband acquires no rights over the property of the wife, or over the children of the marriage. A Zunian married an Oraybe woman, and had by her three children. He resided with them at Oraybe until his wife died, when the relatives of the deceased wife took possession of her children and her household property, leaving to him his clothing, horse, and weapons. As was the custom, he returned to his own people at Zuni. A similar case occurred at another of the Moqui Pueblos. A woman died, leaving property, children, and husband. The deceased wife's relatives took the property and children, and all the husband was allowed to take was his own clothing, with the privilege of going whithersoever he desired. From these cases, it appears the children belonged to the mother, not to the father, and that he was not allowed to take them even after the mother's death. Such, also, was the usage among the Iroquois and other Northern tribes, and among the village Indians of Mexico.

The growth of the idea of property, and the rise of monogamy, which in a measure assured the paternity of children, formed motives sufficiently powerful to bring children into the gens of their father and a participation in the inheritance of his estate. But this invasion of the mother's rights was a slow process and for long periods resisted.

Mr. Morgan shows, too, that the early tribes in Greece, like the American aborigines, were essentially democratic in their government. Historians, accustomed to monarchical governments, would naturally interpret words and actions in harmony with their ideas. Thus, Mr. Grote has a memorable dictum of Ulysses in the Iliad to prove that the Greeks had a one-man government: "The rule of many is not a good thing; let us have one ruler only,—one king,—him to whom Zeus hath given the sceptre with the tutelary sanctions." But this saying has no significance as applied to government. Ulysses, from whose address the quotation is taken, was speaking of the command of an army before a besieged city. There was no occasion for Ulysses to discuss or endorse any plan of government; but he had sufficient reason for advocating obedience to a single commander of the army before a besieged city.

As thus we have seen that Grote, in his "History of Greece," writing from his own true inwardness, mistook the spirit of the times of which he wrote, it behooves us women to question all historians, sacred and profane, who teach by examples or precepts any philosophy that lowers the status of the mothers of the race, or favors the one-man power in government.

As far back into the shadowy past as human thought has penetrated, and been able by a process of reason to substantiate the facts of primeval life, we behold woman in all her native dignity, self-poised and self-supporting, her own head and hands her guidance and protection. The instincts of motherhood gave her the first thought of privacy and seclusion, and led her to make a home for herself and children in the caves of the earth, safe from the wild beasts of the forests, and the wily hunter, who lived on uncooked food and slept on the ground, wherever night found him. While his rude activities developed but few of his faculties, the woman, in solitude, was learning the great lessons of life. A new birth! What a mystery for her to ponder! What love and tenderness helpless infancy calls out; what intelligence and activity its necessities compel; what forethought and responsibility in providing for herself and children it involves! Sex relations being transitory and promiscuous, the idea of fatherhood was unknown. As men naturally have no sense of paternal responsibility, no one knew nor cared about the father of a child. To know one's mother was deemed all-sufficient for a legitimate name and an abiding place.

The period of woman's supremacy lasted through many centuries,—undisputed, accepted as natural and proper wherever it existed, and was called the matriarchate, or mother-age. It was plainly traceable among the Aryans, the Germans, the Persians, and indications of it are still seen among uncivilized tribes and nations.

Careful historians now show that the greatest civilizing power all along the pathway of natural development has been found in the wisdom and tender sentiments growing out of motherhood. For the protection of herself and her children woman made the first home in the caves of the earth; then huts with trees in the sunshine. She made the first attempts at agriculture; raised grains, fruits, and herbs which she learned to use in sickness. She was her own physician; all that was known of the medical art was in her hands. She domesticated the cow and the goat, and from the necessities of her children learned the use of milk. The women cultivated the arts of peace, and the sentiments of kinship, and all there was of human love and home-life. The necessities of motherhood were the real source of all the earliest attempts at civilization.

Thus, instead of being a "disability," as unthinking writers are pleased to call it, maternity has been the all-inspiring motive or force that impelled the first steps towards a stable home and family life. Clearly the birth of civilization must be sought in the attempt of woman at self-preservation during the period of pregnancy and lactation.

What man achieved at that period was due to the contest for food with his fellows and the wild beasts. He simply invented and improved weapons of warfare; but the woman, handicapped as she appeared to be by child-bearing, became on this very account the main factor in human progress. The man's contributions at this early period are nothing as compared to woman's. Her varied responsibilities as mother, bread-winner, protector, defender of a group of helpless children, raised her to intellectual and inventive supremacy and made her the teacher and ruler of man.

"Perhaps more interesting for us to-day is the actual existence of the matriarchate in the north of Africa among the Touaregs. 'The matrix dyes the child' is one of their proverbs. The child belongs to the mother and not to the father; it is the blood of the mother, and not that of the father, which confers on the child the rank he is to take. Formerly, when there was a question of territorial distribution, the lands granted to each family were inscribed in the name of the mother. The Berber law gives to women the administration of their property; at Rhat, they alone dispose of houses, gardens,—in a word, of all the landed property in the country. Among the Touaregs, not only is woman held as the equal of man, but she enjoys a preferable condition. She disposes of her hand, and in the conjugal community she administers her own fortune, without being forced to contribute to the expenses of the household. Thus it happens that, as productions accumulate, the greater part of the wealth is in the hands of the women.

"The Targui (which is the adjective for Touareg) woman is monogamous; she has imposed monogamy on her husband, although the Mussulman law permits him several wives. She is independent in regard to her husband, whom she can repudiate on the slightest pretext: she comes and goes freely. These social customs have produced extraordinary developments in the Targui woman. Her intelligence and her initiative spirit are astonishing in the midst of a Mussulman society. She excels in bodily exercises; on the back of a dromedary she travels a hundred kilometers to attend a *soirée*; she competes in races with the boldest cavalier of the desert. She is distinguished by intellectual culture; the ladies of the tribe of Ymanan are celebrated for their beauty and their musical talent; when they give concerts the men come eagerly from the most distant parts, adorned like male ostriches. The women of the Berber tribes sing every evening to the accompaniment of their violin; they improvise; in the open desert they revive the *cours d'amour* of Provence. The Touaregs are the descendants of the Lybians spoken of by Herodotus. This historian tells us that 'in the valley of the Nile the women go to market and traffic, whilst the men, shut up in houses, weave the linen. The male children are not compelled by law to maintain their parents; this charge is incumbent by law upon the daughters.' The imposition of such a duty on the daughters sufficed to establish the rule that the wealth of the family should belong to the women, and wherever the woman possesses this economic position she is not under the guardianship of her husband, but is the head of the family."

The Rev. Samuel Gorman, a missionary among the Taguna Pueblo Indians, remarks, in an address before the Historical Society of New Mexico, that "the right of property belongs to the female part of the family, and descends in that line from mother to daughter. Their land is held in common, as the property of the community, but after a person cultivates a lot he has personal claim to it, which he can sell to one of the community. . . . Their women generally have control of the granary, and they are more provident than their Spanish neighbors about the future. Ordinarily they try to have a year's provision on hand. It is only when two years of scarcity succeed each other that Pueblos, as a community, suffer hunger."

Of the Senecas of North America, the Rev. Arthur Wright wrote in 1873: "As to their family system, when occupying the old long-houses, it is probable that some one clan predominated, the women taking in husbands, however, from other clans. Usually, the females ruled the house. The stores were in common; but woe to the luckless husband or lover who was too shiftless to do his share of the providing. No matter how many children, or whatever goods he might have in the house, he might at any time be ordered to pick up his blanket and budge; and after such an order it would not be healthful for him to attempt to disobey. The house would be too hot for him; and, unless saved by the intercession of some aunt or grandmother, he must retreat to his own clan, or go and start a new matrimonial alliance in some other. The women were the great power among the clan, as everywhere else. They did not hesitate, when occasion required, 'to knock off the horns,' as it was technically called, from the head of a chief and send him back to the ranks of the warriors. The original nomination of the chiefs also always rested with the women."

"The account we find given by the Portuguese navigators of the Nairs, a people inhabiting the coast of Malabar in the fifteenth century, is another proof of the superior condition of women under previous family systems. The Nairs were then in a state of actual civilization; they had a marine and well-organized army; their towns were wealthy and the inhabitants courteous in manners. But the previous notions of the European visitors were strangely upset by what they saw of the social position of the women. There were large families, we are told, consisting of several hundred members bearing the same name. The real estate belonged in common to all members of the gens; the most complete equality reigned among them. The husband, instead of living with his wife and his children, lived with his brothers and sisters in the maternal house; when he left it, he was always accompanied by his favorite sister; at his death his personal property did not go to his children, but was distributed between the children of his sisters. The mother, or, in case of her death, her eldest daughter, was the head of the family; her eldest brother, named the foster-father, managed the estate; the husband was a guest; he only entered the house on fixed days, and did not sit at the table with his wife and children. 'The Nairs,' says Barbosa, 'have an extraordinary respect for their mother; it is from her they receive wealth and honors; they honor equally their eldest sister, who is to succeed the mother and take the management of the family. The children belong to the mother, and she takes their support on herself.' The Nair family system was maintained among the Malabar peoples till the invasion of Hyder Ali in 1766."

Strabo says of the primitive people of Spain, "That they suffered a most foolish governance by women; that the women possessed the property, and it passed from mother to daughter; that the latter gave away their brothers in marriage; that the men took a dowry with them into the houses of their wives; that the women performed all the agricultural work, and were as hardy as men."

The women at a later period were not only the rulers of the home, but they were priestesses; the deities were in a great part goddesses. All there was of learning and tradition was in the hands of the women, and folk custom long recognized their superiority to men.

The woman being the source of traditional religion, the care of the gods was essentially hers. About the hearth arose the first conceptions of the altar and sanctuary and the immortality of the soul. She was essentially the wise, and wrote with her staff in the ashes the will of the gods. Her pots and kettles reappear in every witch trial in the Middle Ages. The safety of mother and child, in the solitudes of the vast primeval forests, was due in no small measure to the superstition that woman was in communion with the gods, who would avenge her wrongs. Her spirit is supposed to linger around the hearth after death, and to-day the solitary student sitting over the fire, or the peasant when his family are out, will tell you they have been alone at the hearth with their mother-soul. As woman forms the religion and tradition of this period, the goddesses, not gods, are the more numerous and most worshipped. The oldest, the wisest, the most mysteriously powerful, of the Teutonic deities are female. Jacob Grimm said of the German goddesses years before modern investigations had brought the mother-age to light:

"In the case of the gods, the previous investigation could reach its goal by considering them separately. It seems advisable, however, to consider the goddesses collectively as well as individually, because a common idea lies at the basis of them all, and will thus be more clearly marked. They are conceived of peculiarly as divine mother (göttermutter) travelling about and visiting mortals. From them mankind has learned the business and the arts of housekeeping, agriculture, cattle-raising, spinning, weaving, sowing, reaping, as well as watching the hearth. These labors bring peace and rest to the land and the memory of them remains firmer in pleasing traditions than war and fighting, which, like women, the majority of the goddesses shun."[36] Karl Pearson says, "A truer although unconscious tribute to the civilizing work of women can hardly be imagined. If we add to the arts mentioned by Grimm the art of healing, the elements of religious faith as a tradition, and the runic art of writing, we have a slight picture of what woman accomplished in the centuries which intervened between the promiscuous period and the complete establishment of the father-age."

With such personal independence and superiority, such authority in the national councils, in religious faith, and at the fireside, with the absolute control of her own home, property, and children, how did it come to pass that the mother was at last dethroned and womanhood degraded in every nation on the globe?

The mother's labors had from an early period been re-enforced by those of her sons whose tastes led them to agriculture and the herding of cattle, to domestic life rather than that of the wandering nomad existence of the wily hunter, but this class was proportionally small. However, in process of time,—as the home with its increasing comforts and attractions, fire, cooked food, and woman's tender care in old age, sickness, and death, the innocent prattle of children, the mother's songs and stories, her religious faith and services, all appealed to the better feelings of the wily hunter also,—men began to think, when weary of the battle and the chase, that they would like a permanent foothold in some family group besides the one into which they were born.

As soon as monogamic marriage appeared with property and descent in the male line, and men found themselves comfortably ensconced in a home of their own, they began little by little to make their aggressions, and in time completely dominated woman, leaving her no remnant of authority anywhere, neither in the home, nor at the altar, nor in the councils of the nation.

Having no paternal instinct, no natural love for children, the devices of men to establish the rights of paternity were as varied as ridiculous. It was the custom at one time when the mother gave birth to a child for the acknowledged father to take to his bed to pretend that he had shared in the perils of labor, and thus prove his identity, while the wife waited on him; for the women, accustomed to agricultural work, were so hardened by it that they did not suffer in childbirth.

On this point Karl Pearson tells us the transition from the mother to the father-age was marked by the appearance of women of gigantic stature. The old legends of contests between men and women for supremacy are not such idle fancies as some would have us believe. Very dark shadows indeed do such figures as those of Ildico, Fredegunde, and Brunhilde cast across the pages of history. Such women were only paralleled by the Clytemnestra and Medea of a like phase in Greek development. Among the Germans, too, the poets represent the contest between men and women for the mastery. Wuodan replaces Hellja; Siegfried conquers Brunhilde; Beovulf, the offspring of Grindel and Thor, fights with Gialp and Griep, the daughters of Geirrod. One great element of physical and mental vigor is freedom, which women have never enjoyed except under the Matriarchate.

The Amazons, the present body-guard of the King of Dahomey, the astounding powers of endurance exhibited by domestic servants and the peasant girls of southern Germany and Italy, the fish-women at Boulogne, all point to the great strength when once the physique has been developed.

The victory of man over woman was not easily accomplished. It took long centuries to fully confirm it, and traces of the mother-age remain throughout the Medieval times. The permanency of sex relations among the agriculturists and the necessity for organization in matters of defense, which must be entrusted mainly to men, were the beginnings of the father-age.

For though women had been compelled to fight for their own protection, and were abundantly able to maintain the contest, yet wars for territory and conquests over other tribes and nations were opposed by all the tenderest sentiments of their nature. Hence they naturally of their own accord would withdraw from the councils of war and the battle-field, but as angels of mercy to minister to the wounded and the dying. Thus man became ruler, tribal organizer, tribal father, before his position of sexual father was recognized. While the mother still ruled the house, "the Alvater" ruled the fight, though ofttimes guided by the woman.

Driven from the commanding position of home mother, and deprived of her rights to property and children, the last fortress of the Teutonic woman was her sacerdotal privileges. She remained holy as priestess. She had charge of the tribal sacrifice and the tribal religion.

From this last refuge she was driven by the introduction of the Christian religion, with its narrow Pauline doctrine, which made woman mentally and physically the inferior of man, and lawfully in subjection to him.

The spirit of the church in its contempt for women, as shown in the Scriptures, in Paul's epistles and the Pentateuch, the hatred of the fathers, manifested in their ecclesiastical canons, and in the doctrines of asceticism, celibacy, and witchcraft, destroyed man's respect for woman and legalized the burning, drowning, and torturing of women by the thousand.[37]

Women and their duties became objects of hatred to the Christian missionaries and of alternate scorn and fear to pious ascetics and monks. The priestess mother became something impure, associated with the devil, and her lore an infernal incantation, her very cooking a brewing of poison, nay, her very existence a source of sin to man. Thus woman, as mother and priestess, became woman as witch. The witch trials of the Middle Ages, wherein thousands of women were condemned to the stake, were the very real traces of the contest between man and woman. Christianity putting the religious weapon into man's hand made his conquest complete. But woman did not yield without prolonged resistance and a courageous final struggle. Driven from the home, an outlaw and wanderer everywhere, ostracized by the State, condemned by the courts, crucified by the Church, the supreme power of the mother of the race was conquered only by the angel of death, and the Dark Ages tolled her funeral knell.

It was this wholesale, violent suppression of the feminine element, in the effort to establish the Patriarchate, that, more than any other one cause, produced the Dark Ages.[38]

Morgan, in his "Ancient Society," attributes the premature destruction of ethnic life, in the societies of Greece and Rome, to their failure to develop and utilize the mental and moral conservative forces of the female intellect, which were not less essential than those of men to their progress.

In closing, I would say that every woman present must have a new sense of dignity and self-respect, feeling that our mothers, during some periods in the long past, have been the ruling power, and that they used that power for the best interests of humanity. As history is said to repeat itself, we have every reason to believe that our turn will come again, it may not be for woman's supremacy, but for the as yet untried experiment of complete equality, when the united thought of man and woman will inaugurate a just government, a pure religion, a happy home, a civilization at last in which ignorance, poverty, and crime will exist no more. Those who watch already behold the dawn of the new day.

> "Night wanes—the vapor round the mountains curled
> Melts into morn, and light awakes the world.
> Mighty Nature bounds as from her birth:
> The sun is in the heavens, and life on earth;
> Flowers in the valley, splendor in the beam,
> Health on the gale, and freshness in the stream."[39]

5.
"The Legal Condition of Indian Women," Alice Fletcher's speech at the 1888 International Council of Women

MISS FLETCHER. The popular impression concerning Indian women is, that they are slaves, possessing neither place, property, nor respect in the tribe. This impression is confirmed by observing that women are the workers and the burden-carriers; that upon them falls all the drudgery of life. They are also said to be bought and sold as wives, and their life is without honor or happiness. In the face of this generally accepted picture of the Indian woman, I can hardly hope to greatly modify this opinion by the statement of facts. I must, therefore, ask you to receive what I say as from one who, having lived among the people, sharing their poverty in summer and in winter, has thus learned their social and religious customs.

The Indian tribe is not a mere collection of men and women; it is a completely organized body, girt about by laws, unwritten, it is true, but rooted in the religion and time-honored customs of the people. The tribe is divided into clans or gens, each division having its location in the camp, and duties in the tribe. These clans are organized and subdivided, having appropriate officers to fulfill their rites and customs. These clans are based upon kinship, and are the fundamental units of the tribe. A man is born into his clan, into this family of kindred. In a large

proportion of our Indian tribes the mother carries the clan—
that is, the man belongs to the clan or kindred of his mother, not
to that of his father. It is a general law among a large portion of
the tribes that a man may not marry in his own clan. The family, as we understand it, can not exist in the tribe, as the husband
and wife represent two distinct political bodies, so to speak,
which can never coalesce, for neither the man nor the woman by
marrying lose or change any of their rights in their respective
clans. There are no family names in an Indian tribe. Of course,
I do not refer to the customs which have been introduced by our
race in many of the tribes, but to the native conditions unmodi-
fied by the white man, which conditions are to-day more or less
potent in every Indian community.

. . . Her children, if the clan follows the mother, are given
names proper to her clan, and are identified with her kindred
and not with that of their father. The child is never the heir of
both his parents, since the claim of the clan into which he is born
is primal, and that of the family, as we know it, secondary. For
the same reason the wife never becomes entirely under the control of her husband. Her kindred have a prior right, and can use
that right to separate her from him or to protect her from him,
should he maltreat her. The brother who would not rally to the
help of his sister would become a by-word among his clan. Not
only will he protect her at the risk of his life from insult and injury, but he will seek help for her when she is sick and suffering. . . .
The woman never, from her birth to her death, is without the
strong protecting arm of her kindred, to whom she can appeal
in the case of injury.

. . . Should the husband prove tyrannical or lazy in providing for his family, the wife tells him to go back to his kindred,
or if the pair are living in a lodge apart from her family she
takes down the lodge and departs, leaving her husband to
watch the dying embers of the fire. Her kindred will not send
her back, nor would her husband be allowed to coerce her to
live with him.

It is true that Indian women are the laborers and burden-
bearers. That is not because they are slaves, but because they
belong to the non-combatant portion of society.

. . . In olden times the women claimed the land. In the early treaties and negotiations for the sale of land, the women had their voice, and the famous Chief Cornplanter was obliged to retract one of his bargains because the women forbade, they being the land-holders, and not the men. With the century, our custom of ignoring women in public transactions has had its reflex influence upon Indian custom. At the present time all property is personal; the man owns his own ponies and other belongings which he has personally acquired; the woman owns her horses, dogs, and all the lodge equipments; children own their own articles, and parents do not control the possessions of their children. There is really no family property, as we use the term. A wife is as independent in the use of her possessions as is the most independent man in our midst. If she chooses to give away or sell all of her property; there is no one to gainsay her.

When I was living with the Indians, my hostess, a fine look- ing woman, who wore numberless bracelets, and rings in her ears and on her fingers, and painted her face like a brilliant sunset, one day gave away a very fine horse. I was surprised, for I knew there had been no family talk on the subject, so I asked: "Will your husband like to have you give the horse away?" Her eyes danced, and, breaking into a peal of laughter, she hastened to tell the story to the other women gathered in the tent, and I became the target of many merry eyes. I tried to explain how a white woman would act, but laughter and con- tempt met my explanation of the white man's hold upon his wife's property.

It has been my task to explain to the Indian woman her legal conditions under the law.

. . . As I have tried to explain our statutes to Indian women, I have met with but one response. They have said: "As an In- dian woman I was free. I owned my home; my person, the work of my own hands, and my children could never forget me. I was better as an Indian woman than under white law." Men have said: "Your laws show how little your men care for their women. The wife is nothing of herself. She is worth little but to help a man to have one hundred and sixty acres." One day, sitting in the tent of an old chief, famous in war, he said to me: "My young men are to lay aside their weapons; they are to take up the work of the women; they will plow the field and raise the crops; for them I see a future, but my women, they to whom we owe everything, what is there for them to do? I see nothing! You are a woman; have pity on my women when everything is taken from them." Not only does the woman under our laws lose her independent hold on her property and herself, but there are offenses and injuries which can befall a woman which would be avenged and punished by the relatives under tribal law, but which have no penalty or recognition under our laws. If the Indian brother should, as of old, defend his sister, he would himself become liable to the law and suffer for his championship.

. . . I crave for my Indian sisters, your help, your patience, and your unfailing labors, to hasten the day when the laws of all the land shall know neither male nor female, but grant to all equal rights and equal justice.[40]

6.
"The Rights and Condition of Women,"
sermon by Samuel J. May, November 1845

. . . During the past summer, a large Convention of delegates, elected by the people of this State, have been in session at the Capitol, framing a new Constitution, which is to affect as vitally the lives, liberties, properties, happiness of women as of men: and yet not a female was there to represent the interests of her sex; nor would one hardly suspect, from the document they have spread before their fellow citizens, that there were any women in the body politic. Nor is this all; but last Tuesday, when the constituents of that Convention were called upon to signify whether they would ratify the new Constitution, the women of New York were not expected, nor would they have been permitted to say, by their votes, whether or not they were willing to live under such a frame of government.

Now this is all unequal, all unrighteous—this utter annihilation, politically considered, of more than one half of the whole community. It is a piece of assumption just as egregious as it would be for the females to call a Convention, frame a state government, and go on to administer it by officers of their own choosing, without any recognition of the rights, and hardly any of the existence even of our sex.

This entire disfranchisement of females is as unjust as the disfranchisement of the males would be; for there is nothing in their moral, mental or physical nature, that disqualifies them to understand correctly the true interests of the community, or to act wisely in reference to them.

. . . To prove, however, that woman was not intended to be the equal of man, the argument most frequently alleged is, that she is the weaker vessel—inferior in stature, and has much less physical strength. This physiological fact of course cannot be denied; although the disparity in these respects is very much increased by neglect or mismanagement. But allowing women generally to have less bodily power, why should this consign them to mental, moral or social dependence? Physical force is of special value only in a savage or barbarous community.

. . . But some would eagerly ask, should women be allowed to take part in the constructing and administering of our civil institutions? Allowed, do you say? The very form of the question is an assumption of the right to do them the wrong that has been done them. Allowed! why, pray tell me, is it from us their rights have been received? Have we the authority to accord to them just such prerogatives as we see fit, and withhold the rest? No; woman is not the creature, the dependant of man, but of God. We may, with no more propriety assume to govern women, than they might assume to govern us. And never will the nations of the earth be well governed, until both sexes, as well as all parties, are fairly represented, and have an influence, a voice, and, if they wish, a hand in the enactment and administration of the laws. One would think, the sad mismanagement of the affairs of our own country should, in all modesty, lead us men to doubt our own capacity for the task of governing a nation, or even a state, alone; and to apprehend that we need other qualities in our public councils—qualities that may be found in the female portion of our race.

. . . Undoubtedly some of you are ready to say to me, "pray would you have women public instructors, lecturing upon moral and political science, and haranguing the people upon their special duties as citizens?" Hear my reply. It is not for me, nor for us men, to prescribe the mode in which the women shall operate. Let us leave this to their own good sense, and taste. . . . To me, it is as grateful to hear words of wisdom and eloquence from a woman as a man; and quite as uninstructive and wearisome to listen to a vapid, inane discourse from the one as from the other. . . . I have heard some women speak in a manner far more convincing and impressive than most men, that I have known, were able to; and so as amply to vindicate their right to stand up in the pulpit or the forum, as teachers of men.

"Ah" say some, "would you then have women engage in the acrimonious contests of the political parties, attend the angry meetings, witness the passion, hear the ribaldry and abuse, that are poured upon each other by the excited opponents; and be tempted perhaps to commit the same offences themselves?" No. Surely not. Neither would I have *men* guilty of such indecorum, folly and wickedness. If political meetings must needs be disgraced by such scenes, they ought not to be held; and those men who would attend them, show that they are careless of their own moral health. It were no more unseemly, no worse any way, for women to be thus defiled than for us men. We are called to be upright, pure and holy beings as well as they. Propriety of conduct, courtesy of manners, purity of speech, delicacy, refinement, gentleness, are just as becoming in one sex as the other. For one, I do not allow it to be a matter of course, that we men should be rough, violent, passionate, abusive, profane, obscene. It is unworthy of any man to be so. He is as much bound as a woman can be, "to keep himself unspotted from the world," and to keep himself away from places where, and from persons by whom, he may be tempted to become thus vile. Is it not indeed a mortifying confession—one that we men ought to be ashamed to make, that political meetings are occasions, from which the delicate and pure would shrink, and yet that we attend them? Nay more, friends, if it be true that they are such,—if our primary political gatherings, at which the people are called to consider their true interests and duties, and to exercise their high prerogatives as a self-governing community,—if these primary meetings are indeed such scenes, that our mothers, wives, sisters and daughters would be disgusted if not corrupted at them, may we not seriously apprehend, that our civil institutions are unsound, rotten at the very core? and anxiously look about us, for healing and purifying influences, from any quarter, to save us from the impending ruin?

. . . Why should man always be spoken of as the moral patient, and woman as the nurse? Surely this is very inappropriate, if man be, as he claims to be, the stronger vessel. Either may have occasion to soothe, comfort, uphold the other; therefore both man and woman should strive to acquire the same dispositions and graces, which adapt us to fulfil the various ministries of love. I can think of no excellence, that would be becoming and beautiful in a true woman, that would not be equally becoming and beautiful in a true man. Jesus of Nazareth, the perfect man, exhibited as much of the feminine, as he did of the masculine character. And doubtless every individual, of either sex, will approach the perfection to which we all are called, just so far as he or she combines in one the virtues and graces of both. Patience, tenderness, delicacy are as needful to complete the character of a man; as firmness, enterprize and moral courage are, to complete the character of a woman.

. . . In great emergencies, at those crises which have decided the fate of nations, women have been allowed, encouraged, nay summoned to lend their aid,—both in council, and on the field of battle. Now, I believe, if they were admitted to equal advantages of education, and permitted at all times to influence the counsels, and assist in the administration of the affairs of a state—I believe those terrible emergencies, which shake nations to their centres, would much less frequently if ever arise; and the redemption of the world would be sooner accomplished. No one can deny that the peace, good order and prosperity of families are much more frequently disturbed, thrown down by the male than by the female portions of them. So too, a large proportion of the disturbers of the public peace are males. Who will not gratefully own, that the wise and virtuous mother contributes as much, nay, often more than the father to the well being of the family?

. . . Now the community, the nation ought to be as one great family. It is the intention, the tendency of Christianity so to make it. But how can it ever become so, until it shall have mothers, as well as fathers, to guide and control it? Hitherto the nations of the earth have subsisted in the condition of half-orphanage; and they have acted (have they not?) much like rude boys, too early left to their own untoward guidance.

. . . Women are coaxed, flattered, courted, but they are not respected by many men as they ought to be; neither do they respect themselves as they should. They are not regarded and treated as equals; nor do they claim to be. So long has this been the case, so long have they and we all been used to that organization of society, in which they are assigned to an inferior place, that most of us, and most too of themselves acquiesce in the wrong, as if it were right. But this does not make it so; nor avert the evil consequences, which are flowing through society, from the entire exclusion of the wisdom and virtue of half of mankind, from the councils of State, and the administrations of justice and mercy. The intellectual and moral powers of the female sex generally are not half developed, because no adequate demands are made upon them. Excluded as they are from all direct influence, in the decision of many of the greatest questions of social and national interest—they seldom take the trouble even to consider them; and so we lose the benefit we might derive from their perceptions of right, which are often clearer than our own. When we see what has been done for the redemption of mankind, by the few women, who have broken through the enclosure, in which custom would keep them, and have thought and spoken and written freely in behalf of humanity, we cannot repress the apprehension, that states and nations are suffering immeasurably, from that waste of intellect and moral sense, which are expending themselves upon the inanities of fashion, and the follies of personal or household display.

. . . Women are so often trifled with as if they were mere

toys, or used as if they were only conveniences to man's estate, that there are not a few, who always sneer when their *rights* are spoken of. But deride it who will, there is as much truth and solemnity in the claim I have set up for them, as there was in the first assertion of the right of men to govern themselves, though monarchs affected to despise it, and lordlings trampled it under their feet.

Women are too dependent upon men. We have too much power over them; and they are often cruelly oppressed. See how pitifully their labors are requited. The disclosures that have been made of the incessant, wasting toils to which they are subjected, especially in or near large cities, for a compensation utterly insufficient to provide them amply with the bare necessaries of life; the degradation of their persons to which they are often driven by the pressure of absolute want; the ease with which the base, heartless seducer escapes the condemnation which his villany deserves; and the unforgiving censure, with which his victim is pursued—these disclosures alone are enough to show how unequal, how unfair is the dealing of our race with that portion, which, if either, should be treated with the greater leniency—enough to show how false, hypocritical is much of the adulation that is bestowed on women. Can those men feel any proper respect for females, who make them their drudges from morning to night,—or who are willing to pay them the miserable pittances which they do, for labors that consume the live long day, and oft the sleepless night? Yes, about as much as the slaveholders feel for their slaves.

Again, as it respects education, that grand leveller as well as elevator of mankind,—how much more liberal are the provisions, which are made to give our sons than our daughters a generous culture, in all the arts and sciences, that open to the human soul perennial sources of high, pure satisfaction; and give to their possessor not only abilities for greater usefulness to others, but multiplied means of self subsistence. . . . But let their thirst for knowledge be ever so ardent, let their powers of acquisition be ever so good, females are no where admitted into the highest seminaries of learning.

And even as it respects property, a due portion of which is in this life convenient for all, which the majority seem to regard as "the one thing needful," our being's end and aim, which therefore ought in all fairness to be made alike accessible to all—even as it respects property, women are no where allowed the same opportunities to acquire it; nor have they the same securities for its preservation.

. . . These circumstances operate powerfully to depress, and oppress women—to make them too dependent—to leave them at the mercy of men; and I do not believe their condition will be essentially improved, until their rights are recognized as equal every way; nor until these are secured in the very framework of society.

. . . I fain would hope that, when next the people frame a Constitution for this State, the stupendous fact will not be overlooked, *that more than one half of our population are females, to whom equal rights and equal privileges ought to be accorded.*

II.

WOMEN ORGANIZED
BEFORE SENECA FALLS

"[A]bove all other causes of the 'Woman Suffrage Movement,'" Matilda Joslyn Gage wrote in *History of Woman Suffrage,* "was the Anti-Slavery struggle in this country."[1] Led by the model of black women, white women joined with them and organized for an end to the ownership of humans. In the process, they found their collective voices and the need for a parallel movement for their rights as women.

African American women formed the first female anti-slavery society in Salem, Massachusetts, in 1832.[2] Two years later, black women formed the Colored Female Anti-Slavery Society in Middletown, Connecticut, in 1834. A white teacher, Prudence Crandall, was arrested and convicted twice for the crime of teaching black girls, and forced to spend a night in a jail cell just vacated by a convict executed for murdering his wife. Doctors refused to attend her students, shopkeepers wouldn't sell to her, windows were smashed and fires started in the school, and still she and her students hung on. When intimidation failed, the Connecticut legislature passed a law under which she was arrested. The press spread the rumor that the real purpose of the school was to "train young Negro women as brides for New England bachelors." White women rose up in protest and solidarity, forming the Connecticut Female Anti-Slavery Society in 1833.[3]

The American Anti-Slavery Society (AASS) also formed in 1833. Although the Quaker abolitionist Lucretia Mott, her sister Martha Coffin Wright, and two other women took part in the organizational discussions, the women were excluded from signing the "Declaration of Sentiments and Purposes." Reverend Samuel J. May, who went on to preach the nation's first sermon on women's rights, later recalled with shame the "mortifying fact, that we men were then so blind, so obtuse, that we did not recognize those women as members of our Convention."[4]

Leaving the AASS convention, women formed their own Philadelphia Female Anti-Slavery Society. Four black women were prominent in it: Sarah Mapps Douglass (principal of the Institute for Colored Youth), Harriet Purvis, Sarah Forten, and the recording secretary, Margaretta Forten. The last three were sisters, the daughters of abolitionist leader James Forten. Reverend Samuel J. May was asked to address the new society, and James McCrummell, an African American abolitionist, was enlisted to preside over the first sessions as the women felt they knew little about "preambles and resolutions and votings."[5]

Philadelphia was a typical female anti-slavery society, focusing on circulating petitions for immediate emancipation, arranging abolition lectures, aiding schools for African American children, organizing education programs for women, boycotting products made with enslaved labor, and raising money for the anti-slavery movement with yearly bazaars.

Twelve women formed the Boston Female Anti-Slavery Society in 1834 with Susan Paul, a black woman, as one of its counselors.[6] While some of these female anti-slavery societies were integrated, it was a source of conflict in others.

Within two years the abolition movement had grown strong so quickly that the backlash descended fiercely with a "Reign of Terror," as Reverend Samuel J. May described it, "in an attempt to stem the tide."

On October 21, 1835, as though through some ordained plan, anti-slavery meetings were broken up and violently dispersed in Utica, New York, and Montpelier, Vermont.[7] In Boston the target had been members of the Female Anti-Slavery Society, who were driven from the hall adjoining the *Liberator* office of newspaper editor William Lloyd Garrison, where they were meeting. Concerned with the safety of the African American women present, they marched from the hall two by two, each white woman with a black woman. Maria Weston Chapman, known as Garrison's "right-hand woman" and an editor of anti-slavery newspapers on her own, described the mob's reaction:

> When we emerged into the open daylight there went up a roar of rage and contempt, which increased when they saw that we did not intend to separate, but walked in regular procession. They slowly gave way as we came out. As far as we could look either way the crowd extended—evidently of the so-called "wealthy and respectable"; "the moral worth"; the "influence and standing."[8]

Women faced down these violent mobs of men fearlessly. As the authors of *History of Woman Suffrage* later remarked, "Neither State officers, nor mobs in the whirlwind of passion, tempered their violence for her safety or benefit." When a mob broke up a meeting of anti-slavery women where George Thompson was speaking, he gratefully accepted the escort of three hundred women to safety. An abolitionist leader remembered a beautiful crimson shawl Maria Weston Chapman was wearing when a mob attacked Pennsylvania Hall with brickbats in 1835:

> I kept my eye on that shawl, which could be seen now here, now there, its wearer consulting with one, cheering another; and I made up my mind that until that shawl disappeared, every man must stand by his guns.[9]

The number of Female Anti-Slavery societies grew rapidly in seven years from the first, formed in 1832, to 139 societies in 1837, and they decided to hold their first national convention in New York City. More than one hundred delegates from ten states attended and hotly debated whether black women should be allowed to participate, an issue that had been a source of conflict in many of the societies. An African American delegate, Sarah Forten, addressed the following poem to the convention:

> We are thy sisters, God has truly said,
> That of one blood all nations He has made.
> O Christian woman! in a Christian land,
> Canst thou, unblushing, read this great command;
> Suffer the wrongs which wring our inmost heart
> To draw one throb of pity on thy part;
> Our skins may differ, but from thee we claim
> A sister's privilege and a sister's name"[10]

The convention responded by passing a resolution that firmly stated that "the Abandonment of prejudice is required of us as a proof of our sincerity and consistency."[11]

Writing in 1893, Monroe Alphus Majors, an African American historian, observed that this marked a turning point; all following Female Anti-Slavery Society conventions would see black and white women together as they "dealt their terrific blows at the foundation of America's disgrace."[12]

The second national convention of anti-slavery women elected black women to leadership positions. Susan Paul was one of the vice presidents and Sarah Douglass was appointed treasurer.[13]

The convention was held May 15–18, 1838, in Pennsylvania Hall, which had just recently been opened in Philadelphia. The vast crowd of five to six hundred listened to addresses, "some in behalf of the slave, others in behalf of the Indian."[14] The legacy of prejudice, not surprisingly, arose, as Sarah Grimke pointed out. Along with her sister Angelina, Sarah Grimke had abandoned their slave-holding South Carolina home and come North to join the anti-slavery movement. Sarah was "grieved," she reported, to see the prejudice against African Americans in the free states and recounted an experience of the day before at the convention.

> I came late into the assembly, and all the seats were occupied; but as soon as I was observed, effort was kindly made to procure me one; directly a colored sister came in; she was probably far more fatigued than I was, and how could you tell but that within that colored body there was a soul far more noble than mine— yet she was suffered to stand in the aisle.[15]

Mary Grew, the corresponding secretary of the Philadelphia Ladies' Anti-Slavery Society, who ran the society's school for black children, reported that throughout the convention a mob gathered and grew outside the hall. Her full report is included in this chapter.

When the session later adjourned, the men advised the women to leave by the back door. The women refused, as Laura Lovell, a delegate from the Fall River Female Anti-Slavery Society, reported. The threat was very real, for after the women's convention adjourned for the night, the mob acted. Laura Lovell wrote the story in her convention report, which is included in this chapter, following Grew's.

"On the next morning," Grew observed, "the burnt and crumbling remains of Pennsylvania Hall told the story of Philadelphia's disgrace, and the temporary triumph of the spirit of slavery." The group of black and white women, "assailed by the insults of the populace as they went," walked through the streets of Philadelphia looking for a place to meet that was not closed against them, and finally were welcomed to stay in a school run by two white women.[16]

The third national woman's anti-slavery convention was held in 1839, again in Philadelphia, and black women were once again in attendance and leadership. Sarah Douglass continued as treasurer and Grace Douglass, her mother, was a vice president. The convention incited such a threat of racial violence that the mayor of the city asked the women to hold their meetings in the daytime and avoid being seen with blacks on the streets. The women refused and responded with a resolution they passed unanimously, stating that "the moral and intellectual character of persons," and not the color of their skin, would be the determining factor in whom the women would appear with in public.[17]

A short pamphlet, or tract, was drawn up for public distribution, titled *An Appeal to American Women, on Prejudice Against Color.* The full tract is included in this chapter.

A circular distributed internally to the anti-slavery women activists by the 1839 convention ended with a plea to put themselves in the position of the enslaved women who watched their children sold into slavery, but it also asked the abolitionists to consider the wives and daughters of slaveholders who daily faced the reality of the rape their husbands and fathers had committed—slavery's "polluting touch"—through the children in the slave quarters who resembled their siblings in the big house. The courage of these women naming the rape of enslaved women embedded in the institution of slavery is highly significant. At a time when any woman who dared speak about sexuality stepped outside the bounds of respectability, this shows the degree to which the anti-slavery activists were willing to be bold to expose the "polluting touch" of the system.

> In conclusion, we have a few words to say to those who are very willing to sign an anti-slavery petition, yet excuse themselves from the labor of circulating it. You acknowledge that it is our duty to send such petitions to Congress, and, consequently, that it is the duty of some of us to procure signatures to them. You would not consent that this work should be suspended, even for one year. Yet if all were to follow your example, it would inevitably cease. The duty which we urge does not, of course, devolve upon every one of you. Each must decide for herself the question of personal obligation in the matter. It may be that from the heavy pressure of domestic duties, or from other causes, you are not able to spend even an occasional hour in pleading the cause of the slave among your friends and neighbors. We would only suggest that before making such a decision, you will, as nearly as possible, place your soul "in his soul's stead." Let the mother gather her children about her, and see them seized, sold, and driven away to southern markets and plantations, there to spend their lives in mental and moral degradation, that they may minister to the avarice and ambition of taskmasters, whose "tender mercies are cruel!" Let the daughter and the sister imagine to themselves a home made desolate by slavery's polluting touch,— let us all endeavor, for a few hours at least, to "remember those in bonds as *bound with them*," and then answer the question, Shall I circulate an anti-slavery petition?[18]

Institutionalized, legalized rape was an integral part of the system of enslavement, and that issue also was taken up by male abolitionists such as George Bourne, whose book, *Slavery Illustrated in Its Effects upon Woman and Domestic Society*, was published in 1837. "Affectionately inscribed" to "all the members of female anti slavery societies," it addressed the issue that "ought not to be named." Although the book was couched in Christian moral language, Bourne minced no words in describing the violation of female slaves by the white men who owned them.

Deeply has the conviction been rooted, during the last twenty-five years, that the condition of American colored women, and the collateral topics included in the seventh commandment [Thou shalt not commit adultery], are the most important theme in the whole controversy upon slavery; because it combines the ecclesiastical questions with all the grand moral points.

The female slave upon whom her kidnapper has fixed his "eyes full of adultery, and that cannot cease from sin," is not only unable to deliver herself by flight, but she has no means of resistance. A white woman could assume the attitude of self-defence, and if she wounded, maimed, or even killed her brutal assailant, the law would exculpate her, and she would be honored for her resistance; but she who has a colored skin dares not to resist or attempt any opposition; and if through the impulse of desperation she should inflict a wound upon her ravisher in the very attempt, she would forfeit her mortal existence if the fact was presented to one of their execrable criminal courts; and if that course was not adopted, her whole future life would be the subject of her despot's unceasing and malicious revenge.

The forcible defilement of a woman constitutes a flagitious transgression against which the divine revelation denounces its solemn condemnation; and to repress which, even our statutes declare that the conviction of the offender shall insure severe punishment. Nevertheless, in reference to the colored woman, the mandates of God are totally abrogated, and the laws of our country virtually sanctify the crime.[19]

While women could not vote, they had the legal right to petition the government. And petition they did for an end to slavery, which led the pro-slavery forces in Congress to pass a yearly set of "gag rules" tabling the petitions, forbidding them to be read or discussed. This silencing of democracy enraged northerners, and more and more people signed the anti-slavery petitions. A majority were women. More than sixty-seven thousand signatures were attached to anti-slavery petitions to Congress in 1838; about forty-five thousand of them were from women. John Quincy Adams, serving in Congress, was the champion of free speech and yearly fought the gag resolution, generally successfully, until 1840, when the House passed a standing House rule prohibiting Congress from even receiving anti-slavery petitions.[20]

Sarah and Angelina Grimke, daughters of a wealthy slave-holding planter of Charleston, South Carolina, after emancipating their slaves, were lecturing on the evils of slavery despite losing family and friends and being exiled from their home by an act of the Charleston city government because of their anti-slavery activities.[21] The American Anti-Slavery Society sent Angelina on a six-month anti-slavery speaking tour in 1836, instructing that "her appointed field of labor was among her own sex, in public or in private."[22] She spoke to female audiences, but curious men entered the rooms where she spoke, which grew progressively larger to accommodate the increasing numbers that appeared to hear her.[23] Abolitionist Wendell Phillips described the impact she had on her listeners:

> Her own hard experience, the long, lonely intellectual and moral struggle from which she came out conqueror, had ripened her power, and her wondrous faculty of laying bare her own heart to reach the hearts of others, shone forth till she carried us all captive.[24]

The General Association of Congregational Ministers of Massachusetts decided to nip this unseemly behavior of women in the bud and issued a Pastoral Letter in 1837 warning against the danger women like the Grimke sisters presented to the "unobtrusive and private" duties and influence of women that were "clearly stated in the New Testament." The power of a woman, the clerics reminded, "is her dependence, flowing from the consciousness of that weakness which God has given her for her protection." She is the vine clinging to the mighty elm and if she steps out of her God-ordained role and takes on "the independence and the overshadowing nature of the elm" that vine will "fall in shame and dishonor into the dust," they warned.

Praying, furthering religion in the home and Sunday Schools, and leading people to ministers for instruction were all appreciated, but when woman "assumes the place and tone of man as a public reformer . . . she yields the power which God has given her for her protection, and her character becomes unnatural."

The Congregational clergy especially deplored "the intimate acquaintance and promiscuous conversation of females with regard to things which ought not to be named by which that modesty and delicacy which is the charm of domestic life, and which constitutes the true influence of woman in society, is consumed, and the way opened, as we apprehend, for degeneracy and ruin." The female abolitionists were speaking openly and publicly about "slavery's polluting touch,"[25] as they called the institutionalized rape of enslaved women by their captors. In doing so, the women opened the door, the frightened ministers predicted, "for degeneracy and ruin."

Not to be silenced by the clergy, the following year, 1838, Angelina Grimke spoke before the Massachusetts Legislature, the first woman in U.S. history to address a legislative body. She brought anti-slavery petitions signed by twenty thousand people with her. She spoke so persuasively to the overflow audience that some pro-slavery legislators tried to prevent her from speaking again the following day on the pretext that such a large crowd would be attracted that the galleries would be in danger of collapsing. A member of the legislature from Salem ended the discussion by proposing that "a committee be appointed to examine the foundation of the State House of Massachusetts, to see whether it will bear another lecture from

Miss Grimke."[26] Grimke spoke with clarity and passion, and her full speech is included in this chapter.

The 1838 Woman's Anti-Slavery Convention followed with a resolution declaring that it was the Christian duty of every woman to withdraw from all churches that fellowshipped with slavery, which was a sin against God and man.[27]

The Congregational clergy weren't alone in attempting to silence women reformers with religious threats. Other members of the clergy were doing "all in their power to retard us in our work," including excommunicating women abolitionists. A resolution adopted by the 1839 national convention decried "those professed ministers of the gospel, who, while they preach the holy doctrine of 'Love thy neighbor as thyself,' exert their influence in opposition to those who endeavor to practice it."[28]

What women's rights issues led to the creation of the woman's rights movement? Knowing future generations reading the *History of Women Suffrage* would want to know, Matilda Joslyn Gage pointed to financial independence as the most immediate issue for married women:

> The discussion in several of the State Legislatures on the property rights of married women, which, heralded by the press with comments grave and gay, became the topic of general interest around many fashionable dinner-tables, and at many humble firesides. In this way all phases of the question were touched upon, involving the relations of the sexes, and gradually widening to all human interests—political, religious, civil, and social. The press and pulpit became suddenly vigilant in marking out woman's sphere, while woman herself seemed equally vigilant in her efforts to step outside the prescribed limits.[29]

Women's economic dependence on men kept them firmly in a second-class position. It was a Catch-22. If they stayed single, they maintained their financial independence, but the few jobs open to them were factory or sweat-shop, servant or nanny, and those available paid one-third to one-half of what

men in similar positions made. Unmarried women of the middle class were social pariahs, depending upon the goodwill of
others in their family for sustenance. Unless they inherited
from their father and were willing to withstand the "spinster"
label, marriage was their avenue to employment. Courtship
was a job interview, and their education, if they weren't rural
or working class, trained them to docility, obedience, and cultivated beauty—job requirements.

Women, once they married, were considered dead in the
law; this was the law of *coverture* in Blackstone's *Commentaries*, which codified British law and was adopted by the Founding Fathers:

> By marriage the husband and wife are one person in law: that is,
> the very being or legal existence of the woman is suspended dur-
> ing the marriage, or at least is incorporated and consolidated
> into that of the husband; under whose wing, protection, and
> cover, she performs every thing.[30]

Everything she brought into the marriage or acquired during
it became her husband's, to do with as he pleased. His job was
to decide and provide; hers was to obey.

The Founding Fathers had other models to follow: the Spanish code in force in Louisiana, for example, where married
women maintained property rights. Instead, when the United
States acquired Louisiana as a territory in 1803, President
Thomas Jefferson insisted upon imposing common law, which
was done by 1805. The people of Louisiana and their representatives resisted, and after a struggle, in 1806 they reinstituted
their Spanish civil law, which became the foundation of Louisiana law once Louisiana became a state.[31]

The key to woman's independence rested in controlling her
own purse strings. Financial independence was also the entering wedge in prying loose English common law, under which
women lost not only their rights, but their very identity.
Change in the law was gradual, and generally came in stages.
Married women first gained the right to control their own

property, then their income, and finally, their ability to conduct business on their own.

Mississippi passed the first married women's property act in 1839, which, according to a source quoted in the 1892 *Albany Law Journal*, was "suggested by tribal customs of the Chickasaw Indians."[32] Indeed, it was a Chickasaw woman, Betsy Love, whose lawsuit, *Fisher* v. *Allen*, established her right to keep her own property after marriage. Because Betsy was Chickasaw, the court respected the widespread Native American practice of married women retaining ownership of all property they brought into a marriage, with each spouse maintaining his or her financial independence throughout the marriage.[33]

Southern states took the lead in instituting property right laws for women. Texas, which had not yet become a state but remained an independent republic, passed an act in 1840 guaranteeing extensive financial rights to married women.[34] Maryland followed in 1843, Arkansas in 1846, and then Kentucky. Before 1848, the trend had moved north with Maine, Massachusetts, Connecticut, Rhode Island, Michigan, Indiana, and Iowa passing laws ensuring married women varying degrees of financial independence.[35]

New York could have been the first state to push aside common law and recognize a married woman's right to her own property, as Judge Thomas Hertell introduced a bill into the legislature in 1836, three years before Mississippi adopted its law. Support for the New York bill came from noted jurists. Hon. John Savage, the chief justice of the New York Supreme Court, and Hon. John C. Spencer, one of the revisers of the statutes of New York, assisted in the writing of the bill.[36]

Ernestine Rose, a Polish immigrant who had been in the country less than a year, drew up a petition in support of Hertell's bill and began circulating it. The response she received was less than enthusiastic. "Some of the ladies said the gentlemen would laugh at them; others, that they had rights enough; and the men said the women had too many rights already. After a great deal of trouble," Rose said, she obtained five signatures, and sent the petition off to the legislature.[37]

Hertell did not see his bill as "giving" married women anything; rather it would restore to them what was constitutionally theirs, being deprived, as they were, by the current law, "of the right of property without due process of law." Hertell explained why the bill was simply justice. His argument is excerpted in this chapter.

While Hertell's bill failed, married women's property bills continued to be introduced into the New York legislature, and Paulina Wright (later Davis) circulated petitions with Ernestine Rose each year such a bill was introduced. A young Elizabeth Cady Stanton was living in Albany in 1844 and joined in lobbying for the bill.[38]

The bill finally passed April 7, 1848, twelve years after its introduction. While it didn't touch a husband's right to control his wife's wages or their joint earnings, it did give her control of the real and personal property she brought into the marriage or received during it. The bill was used by other states as a model.

Leaving Quaker meeting on Sunday, July 9, 1848, five women adjourned to the spacious Federal-style mansion of Jane Hunt in Waterloo, New York, to make history, although that was not their intention at the time. Lucretia Mott was up from Philadelphia; she and her husband, James, had spent a month with the Seneca Nation as members of the Indian Committee of Philadelphia Yearly Meeting of Friends. Lucretia's sister, Martha Coffin Wright, lived in nearby Auburn. It was a good chance for local abolitionists Jane Hunt and Mary Ann McClintock to get caught up with these old friends and colleagues in the anti-slavery movement. For Jane's convenience, no doubt, they met at her house, so she could attend to her two-week-old baby.

The four women had much in common. Hicksite (progressive) Quakers, they were all veterans of the anti-slavery movement and all offered their homes as stations on the Underground Railroad. The activist and personal lives of these four women were deeply intertwined. Lucretia and her sister, Martha, had attended the founding convention of the American Anti-Slavery

Society in 1833; Lucretia and Mary Ann were at the third national convention of the Female Anti-Slavery Society with Sarah Hunt, the niece of Mary Ann's husband. When Sarah died in 1842, Richard Hunt married Jane, in whose home they were having tea.

They invited a fifth woman to join them, Elizabeth Cady Stanton, who was not a Quaker, although she sometimes attended their Junius Monthly Meeting. Committed to the antislavery cause, she was not actively involved in the movement, nor did she offer her home as a station on the Underground Railroad. Elizabeth had met Lucretia in London eight years before, when Elizabeth was on her honeymoon with her husband, Henry, who was a delegate to the World Anti-Slavery Convention. Lucretia was one of the women delegates to the convention denied her seat by the men. While Mott didn't mention it in her account of their meeting, Stanton recalled later that they vowed at the time to call a woman's rights convention in response to the discrimination.

What did each woman bring to this informal gathering? Jane's attention may have been diverted by her two-week-old baby. Mary Ann's mind was no doubt on the cause of the enslaved. Elizabeth vented her pent-up frustration at her isolation living at the end of a dirt road, her nearest neighbor a mile away, raising a growing brood (eventually seven) of sometimes sick children, with an often-absent husband. But all would have been curious to hear Lucretia's account of her month with the Seneca Nation at Cattaraugus, living with the people in this Haudenosaunee community located near the northern Pennsylvania border as they went through the painful process of deciding whether to abandon their traditional clan-based government and replace it with a U.S.-style elected system. The written record Mott left, which appears further below, gives a glimpse into what she might have shared as the women sat drinking tea that Sunday afternoon in July.

Perhaps it was this combination of energy that caused the combustion. One woman pours out her discontent at her oppression while another shares her experience of seeing empowered women, and listening are three women experienced at organizing meetings of women to change things. Whatever happened around that tea table on July 9, the result was a decision to call a meeting to discuss women's rights. They had to do it quickly to take advantage of Lucretia's presence in the area, so they tossed off a notice to run in the local *Seneca County Courier* announcing that a "convention to discuss the social, civil, and religious condition and rights of woman" would be held in ten days. A few other regional papers, like Frederick Douglass's Rochester paper, the *North Star*, also printed the notice. Anticipating a large crowd, the women secured the abolitionist-friendly Wesleyan Methodist Chapel in Seneca Falls. Recognizing the importance of women gaining their voice separate from men in the Female Anti-Slavery Societies, they called on women only to attend the first day; men could come the second day to hear Lucretia speak and take part in the proceedings.

These four Quaker friends had a dozen years of organizing themselves into action bodies; they were old hands at petitioning, speaking, and writing their feminist ideas. Jeering, insults, disdain, and violence had been thrown against them—and they'd prevailed. Their male allies—including some of the top legal minds in the country—had provided the legal foundation for challenging the foundation of their oppression; journalists had picked up their arguments and thoroughly explained to the public the unconstitutionality and immorality of the common law that defined married women as nonentities. These seasoned activists, well-schooled in theory and practice, were ready now to take all that knowledge into organizational work for their rights. They were overprepared for the task ahead of them. And they had the assistance of a newcomer, Elizabeth Cady Stanton, who was a witty, smart woman with writing skills.

Now the work began, and they were a strong team. Mary Ann McClintock was an experienced organizer; she and her husband, Thomas, were founding members of the Western New York Anti-Slavery Society and helped write its constitution. Elizabeth Cady Stanton had grown up in a legally savvy household; her father, an attorney and judge, had a string of would-be lawyers apprenticing to him, who delighted in teasing the young girl about her lack of legal rights as a female. Elizabeth had further developed her legal thinking in discussion with lawyers during the New York legislature's deliberations in 1844 over a Married Women's Property Bill. Recognizing the need for resolutions to present for the convention's approval and lacking time in a two-day convention to appoint a committee to draw them up, Mary Ann and her daughters, with the help of Elizabeth, would do the work. Using Jefferson's Declaration of Independence as a model, Elizabeth transformed the document with the addition of two words, "and women," to the famous, "all men are created equal," and the women drafted their Declaration of Sentiments along with a list of grievances and resolutions to remedy them.

Stanton took the document home to tweak, and then went further. Without consulting the other women, she added an additional grievance, that men had deprived women of the vote, and an additional resolution declaring that women had the duty to secure the ballot for themselves. While there had been a tumult of discussion around women voting for years, the issue of anyone voting was highly controversial among abolitionists. The American Anti-Slavery Society had passed the following resolution four years before, in 1844:

> Resolved: The secession from the United States government is the duty of every abolitionist; since no one can take office, or throw a vote for another to hold office, under the United States Constitution, without violating his anti-slavery principles, and rendering himself an abettor of the slaveholder in his sin.[39]

These abolitionists refused to vote because the Constitution had slavery built into it as a cornerstone. Each person held in slavery counted as three-fifths of a person in determining state population, and hence how many representatives a state would have in Congress. By voting or running for office, you recognized the legitimacy of this, along with the legitimacy of requiring enslaved people who took their freedom to be returned to their owners, which the Constitution also required. The anti-slavery activists had split over this question and many of the New Yorkers, such as Henry Stanton and Frederick Douglass, advocated political action to end slavery, voting and running for political office, as Henry Stanton was currently doing. The Boston wing, led by *Liberator* editor William Lloyd Garrison, would have nothing to do with the political system, focusing on changing people's hearts and minds instead.

Stanton had to have known this action would likely be opposed by Lucretia Mott and the other Quaker women. Lucretia was doubly opposed to voting. As a Garrisonian, she would not take part in a government that upheld slavery. Quakers were also opposed to voting or running for office. As pacifists, they recognized how the legitimacy of warfare rests on the assumption that the government has the authority to use armed force and that when a government waged war, it was entitled to act in the name of all those who voted. Mott would explain her position on woman suffrage in a speech the following year:

> Far be it from me to encourage women to vote, or to take an active part in politics in the present state of our government. Her right to the elective franchise, however, is the same and should be yielded to her, whether she exercise that right or not.[40]

It comes as no surprise, then, that when Elizabeth sprang it on the convention, suffrage was the only resolution that brought resistance and did not pass unanimously. Nor is it a surprise that Frederick Douglass, a political abolitionist, rose to its defense. The only African American in attendance, he said that he could not accept the right to vote if women didn't have it. Their inability to shape the democracy through their participation led not only to a "great injustice" and women's "degradation" but also to "the maiming and repudiation" of half the "moral and intellectual power" of the country's government.[41]

Despite the myriad conflicting reasons for opposing the Declaration of Sentiments, which created a blueprint for the women's rights movement that would emerge by identifying the political, social, religious, and economic oppression of women, one hundred of the three hundred attendees signed the document, which is included in this chapter.

Maria Weston Chapman, an active member of the Boston Female Anti-Slavery Society, added a note of levity to the convention with a reading of the poem "The Times that Try Men's Souls," which she had penned in response to the Congregational minister's attempt to silence the Grimke sisters eleven years before, in 1837. This ironic piece had become popular among anti-slavery workers and is included in full in this chapter.

When Lucretia Mott joined her Quaker friends and Elizabeth Cady Stanton for tea, she and her husband, James, had just come from an extended stay with the Seneca community at Cattaraugus. She might have first noticed the comfortable clothing the indigenous women wore, a loose-fitting dress below the knee with "leggings, richly ornamented with bead work, or coloured porcupine quills."[42] Watching the ease of movement of these Seneca women would have stood out in stark contrast to the restrictive corseted, layers and long dress of privileged white women.

Then she heard their confident, authoritative voices, speaking their opinions decisively, and also planning and carrying out the spiritual Strawberry Ceremony. Mott, as a Quaker, worshipped in silent, or "expectant waiting," meetings, where anyone—man or woman—who received a message was free to speak it. This was unlike every other Christian denomination in the United States, all of which refused to allow women to preach from the pulpit.

Members of the Friends Indian Committee of New York and Philadelphia Yearly Meetings, the Motts had come to check on things for the committee, which had maintained a relationship with the Seneca for more than fifty years. Counseling them on how to save some of their territory from a massive land grab a decade before, the Friends had now turned their attention to reforming the Seneca's social/economic system. The women, sacred like the earth as the creators of life, were traditionally the agriculturalists; the men were hunters. The Friends called a council with the Seneca Nation in 1845, advising:

... that your men ... will diligently apply themselves to the cultivation and improvement of their farms—that you will withdraw your females from the labors of the field and other employments not adapted to the delicacy of their sex.[43]

The Friends Committee had set up a school to teach the women how to sew and manage a household as a white woman would, and a model farm on the reservation to teach the men how to farm. They may not have understood that this move would undermine the authority of the Seneca women and destabilize the balance of responsibilities of men and women. As the agriculturalists, Haudenosaunee women had responsibility for the Nation's means of survival: their land, their food, and therefore their economy. Lucretia had protested that a council of the Seneca women should decide if they wanted this change, according to her biographer, Margaret Hope Bacon, but she was ignored.[44]

The Seneca were at a weak point. Much of their territory had been stolen from them by the Ogden land grab; many had died from typhus that winter; other missionaries had descended on them, selling assimilation and demanding conversion to their belief system, forcing divisions. Outside interests had set up men as chiefs; the legitimate chiefs had been bribed, kidnapped, and forced to accept the conditions of the land loss. The women were, with great difficulty, trying to keep the children fed and hold on to their position. Strong outside pressure demanded they drop their traditional gender-balanced political system in which clan mothers nominated and held in office their clan sachem (chief) and adopt a system of elected representatives. Lucretia and her husband, James, met with spokespersons, male and female, of the dissenting groups and listened to their concerns without judgment or opinion, recommending they seek the wisdom of "the Great Spirit."

What did Lucretia Mott see at Cattaraugus? There is no way of knowing. For one, she left a scanty paper trail. For another, being presented with something is not always the same as perceiving. We can surmise what came within her line of vision; we don't know if she saw it.

Mott wrote little about that summer of 1848, but if the writing that survives shows the relative importance she attached to events by how much she wrote about them, the Seneca Falls woman's rights convention had far less weight than her time with the Seneca. The writings, Lucretia Mott on the Seneca Convention and on the Seneca, from letters to the *Liberator*, August 24, 1848, are included in this chapter.

Here is the terrible irony. While the women gathered in Seneca Falls were demanding a political voice, the nearby Seneca women were losing theirs. The beleaguered Cattaraugus and Allegany Senecas decided to do away with the traditional political structure of chiefs, or sachems, whom the women nominated, counseled, and removed, if necessary. Following the United States model, the system replacing it would be a body of male representatives elected by men only. The Haudenosaunee women who had inspired the suffragists, showing them a model of women with equal political authority, lost that authority at the same time that suffragists were demanding theirs. Women did not regain their political voice in the Seneca Nation until 1964.

There was one exception, however. The women's connection to the land was too strong to be broken.[45] Section 6 of the 1848 Seneca constitution read:

> The power of making treaties shall be vested in the Council; but no treaty shall be binding upon the nation until the same shall be submitted to the people, and be approved by three fourths of all the legal voters, and also by three fourths of all the mothers in the nation.[46]

As Anna C. Johnson (who wrote under the pseudonym Minnie Myrtle), while getting the percentage wrong, reflected in her popular history, *The Iroquois; Or, The Bright Side of Indian Character*, seven years later:

> So there was peace instead of war, as there would often be if the voice of woman could be heard! and though the Senecas, in revising their laws and customs, have in a measure acceded to the

civilized barbarism of treating the opinions of women with contempt, where their interest is equal, they still cannot sign a treaty without the consent of *two thirds of the mothers!*[47]

I.
"Preceding Causes," by Matilda Joslyn Gage, published in *History of Woman Suffrage*, volume I, 1881

. . . Abigail Smith Adams, the wife of John Adams, was an American woman whose political insight was worthy of remark. She early protested against the formation of a new government in which woman should be unrecognized, demanding for her a voice and representation. She was the first American woman who threatened rebellion unless the rights of her sex were secured. In March, 1776, she wrote to her husband, then in the Continental Congress, "I long to hear you have declared an independency, and, by the way, in the new code of laws which I suppose it will be necessary for you to make, I desire you would remember the ladies, and be more generous and favorable to them than your ancestors. Do not put such unlimited power into the hands of husbands. Remember, all men would be tyrants if they could. If particular care and attention are not paid to the ladies, we are determined to foment a rebellion, and will not hold ourselves bound to obey any laws in which we have no voice or representation." Again and again did Mrs. Adams urge the establishment of an independency and the limitation of man's power over woman, declaring all arbitrary power dangerous and tending to revolution. . . . The women of the South, too, early demanded political equality. The counties of Mecklenburg and Rowan, North Carolina, were famous for the patriotism of their women. . . . In 1778, only two years after the Declaration of Independence was adopted, and while the flames of war were still spreading over the country, Hannah Lee Corbin, of Virginia, the sister of General Richard Henry Lee, wrote him, protesting against the taxation of women unless they were allowed to vote. He replied that "women were already possessed of that right," thus recognizing the fact of woman's enfranchisement as one of the results of the new government, and it is on record that women in Virginia did at an early day exercise the right of voting. New Jersey also specifically secured this right to women on the 2d of July, 1776—a right exercised by them for more than a third of a century. Thus our country started into governmental life freighted with the protests of the Revolutionary Mothers against being ruled without their consent. From that hour to the present, women have been continually raising their voices against political tyranny, and demanding for themselves equality of opportunity in every department of life.[48]

2.

Mary Grew's report of the second Female Anti-Slavery Society national convention, 1838

The second of these Conventions was held in this city, in the midst of those scenes of riot when infuriated Southern slaveholders and cowardly Northern tradesmen combined for purposes of robbery and arson, and surrounded Pennsylvania Hall with their representatives, the mob which plundered and burnt it, while the City Government looked on consenting to these crimes. That Convention was the last assembly gathered in that Hall, then just dedicated to the service of Freedom. Its fifth session, on the 17th of May, 1838, was held, calmly and deliberately, while the shouts of an infuriated mob rose around the building, mingling with the speakers' voices, and sometimes overwhelming them; while stones and other missiles crashing through the windows imperilled the persons of many of the audience. The presence of an assembly of women was supposed to be a partial protection against the fury of the rioters; and believing that the mob would not fire the building while it was thus filled, a committee of anti-slavery men sent a request to the Convention to remain in session during the usual interval between the afternoon and evening meetings, if, with their knowledge of their perilous surroundings, they felt willing to do so. The President laid the request before the Convention, and asked, Will you remain? A few minutes of solemn deliberation; a few moments' listening to the loud madness surging against the outer walls; a moment's unvoiced prayer for wisdom and strength, and the answer came: *We will*; and the business of the meeting proceeded. But before the usual hour of adjournment arrived, another message came from the committee, withdrawing their request, and stating that further developments of the spirit pervading the mob and the city, convinced them that it would be unwise for the Convention to attempt to hold possession of the Hall for the evening. The meeting adjourned at the usual hour, and, on the next morning, the burnt and crumbling remains of Pennsylvania Hall told the story of Philadelphia's disgrace, and the temporary triumph of the spirit of slavery.[49]

3.
Laura Lovell's report of the second Female Anti-Slavery Society convention, 1838

. . . Mrs. Weld proposed that we should, as far as possible, protect our colored sisters while going out, by taking each one of them by the arm. We passed out through a mob of two or three thousand, fierce, vile looking men, and large boys. They allowed us just room to walk, two abreast. We heard the worst language and saw the most hideous countenances, but I believe none were seriously molested. This was a new, and unexpected scene to me.[50]

. . . Our conversation was interrupted before 9 o'clock by the cry of "Fire!" Pennsylvania Hall was in flames! The mob had accomplished the work by breaking in the doors, and deliberately kindling a fire in the house—in view of the city of

Philadelphia! We walked out to witness the speedy destruction of that beautiful building which the diligent axe and hammer had been, for months, patiently rearing; that building, which the friends not only of abolition, but the friends of free discussion, the friends of civil and religious liberty, the true philanthropists and patriots of our land had reared.

. . . What evidence have we in the flames now rising to burnish the heavens above, and spread consternation and terror through this fair city—what melancholy evidence of the wretched state of public morals! How have vice and oppression, villany and outrage taken the rule! How are the pure and the good driven from the still lovely spot, whose foundations of beauty and order, were laid in peace, and liberty, and love! And where are the magistrates of Philadelphia? Where are the laws which should protect the children of Penn? All, all leagued with this vile mob? But I will not dwell on the distressing scene. Suffice it to say, that during the night, detachments from the mob were singing triumphant choruses through the streets, and in the morning they were still prowling around, as if their appetite for destruction was rather sharpened, than satiated by last evening's indulgence.[51]

4.
*An Appeal to American Women,
on Prejudice Against Color,* 1839

THE opposition which we have to encounter as a Convention of American Women,—the scorn which we excite in some, and the unaffected concern which we awaken in others, render it incumbent upon us to address you upon that subject, which, above all others, has drawn upon us odium and reproach—the admission of our colored sisters to that intercourse with us, which their moral worth demands. As we have been blamed without measure, we would ask a patient hearing: first "prove all things, then hold fast that which is good." Many of you, as individuals, would be incapable of denying to any human being, whatever sympathy and alleviation it was in your power to bestow in cases of corporeal suffering; then why should you be regardless of the deep wrong which you inflict by shunning the sensitive, the generous, the noble-spirited, who, though they may be qualified for the highest intellectual enjoyment, are yet too modest and retiring to contend for the advantages freely extended to all of the white race capable of appreciating them?

To a certain point, many of you encourage the colored man's efforts for improvement; you benevolently rejoice in witnessing his advancement in all those branches of education necessary to the mechanic or tradesman; but if he press still farther,—if he should aspire to indulge a refined taste, to satisfy the cravings of a cultivated mind by mingling with congenial society, you frown him back with scorn and contempt. The indignities and the outrages to which such are subjected,—the "wrongs which wring the very soul," can scarcely be credited by those who have not identified themselves with this injured people. Would it be believed that our museums, our literary and scientific lectures, our public exhibitions, which contribute so much to the intelligence of a people, are generally closed against this portion of our population? A short anecdote will prove that moral and intellectual elevation does not disarm this prejudice.

A young portrait painter of this city, actuated by a laudable desire of improvement in his favorite art, hoping to enjoy a privilege from which he was elsewhere debarred, went to the Philadelphia Artists' Exhibition. He was one whose eye

"Had been unsealed by nature, and his mind
Was full of nice perceptions; and a love,
Deep and intense, for what was beautiful,
Thrill'd like vitality around his heart
With an ennobling influence."

But even he was doomed to disappointment. He troubled the pure stream of the white man's pleasure, in thus attempting to gratify the cravings of his spirit by a draught from the same fountain, and the door-keeper was ordered instantly to eject the intruder. Now, putting "your souls in his soul's stead"—contemplate the withering blight thus shed upon a young aspiring spirit, and say whether these things should exist in a community of Christians professing to act upon the precept, "whatsoever ye would that men should do unto you, do ye even so unto them."

But our young artist found a friend in one of the members of this Convention; under her patronage he pursued his profession, until, he had realized a sufficient sum to carry him to a distant land, whence, in a letter, he thus touchingly expresses his acknowledgements for her friendship, and his sense of the advantages from which he had been debarred:—"The very few occasions which I have had of mingling in good society, where the monster prejudice was not strong enough to exclude me from the intellectual feast, and where I have had opportunities of realizing those ideas of the presence of superior minds, which, drawn from books, were floating in my imagination, vague and indefinite, were within your hospitable dwelling, and they will always be remembered by me with pleasurable emotions." Will the most fastidious say, that there is any thing "*demoralizing*" in exciting such feelings as these? Who would disdain thus to dispense "the oil of joy for mourning, the garment of praise for the spirit of heaviness."

We know that we have the sympathy and prayers of those on whose behalf we appeal: as one of them said, "I have prayed that abolitionists may not shrink from the trial; that strength may be given them to endure the scoffs and jeers which they may meet in treating us as they treat their own people."

We talk a great deal about the degradation of the free colored people. At whose door may the blame of their degradation be laid? As Jefferson has truly said, "it is the work of ourselves and our children." But let them alone, say some, and they will elevate themselves; we have nothing to do with it. Nothing to do with it, when we are trampling them in the very dust? Nothing to do with it, when we "have taken away the key of knowledge, and them that were entering in *we* hindered?"

Is it possible for them to accomplish their elevation while we retain our violent prejudices against them? And even should they succeed, will not the objector querulously exclaim, "How intrusive these people are?"

Women of America! we entreat you to ponder these things in your hearts; to consider how far you are "guilty concerning your brother." It is in your power, to roll back this cruel prejudice, which overwhelms thousands of our fellow creatures, equally gifted with ourselves by our common Father, though ruthlessly robbed of their heritage. Popular sentiment would forbid your associating, on terms of friendship, with any of the proscribed class, whatever may be their claims to your regard; for the *delicacy of woman is compromised*, it is said, by social intercourse with a colored sister, yet we find her wordly dignity increased in a wonderful ratio by every additional colored *servant* whom she can display in her train. Ought you to be surprised, then, that, unheeding the requirements of this inconsistent public opinion, unmoved by the scoffs of the jester, and unappalled by the threats of the vulgar, we entreat you to adhere to the Christian rule of right and justice. Endeavoring to apply this rule, we call, on behalf of our colored sister, for an equal participation with yourselves, in every social advantage, moral, literary and religious; assured that as we conscientiously tread the path of our duty the difficulties will disappear, and we shall each be able to say in the words of a celebrated writer, "That power which has swept from my heart the dust of prejudice, has taught me also to respect excellence wherever found."

In behalf of the Anti-Slavery Convention of American Women, assembled at Philadelphia.

SARAH LEWIS, *President.*

MARTHA V. BALL,

MARY GREW,

ANNA M. HOPPER,

SARAH G. BUFFUM.
Secretaries.[52]

5.
Angelina Grimke's address to the
Massachusetts Legislature, 1838

. . . I stand before you as a citizen, on behalf of the 20,000 women of Massachusetts, whose names are enrolled on petitions which have been submitted to the Legislature of which you are the organ. These petitions relate to the great and solemn subject of American slavery—a subject fraught with the deepest interest to this republic, whether we regard it in its political, moral, or religious aspects. And because it is a political subject, it has often been tauntingly said, that woman has nothing to do with it. Are we aliens, because we are women? Are we bereft of citizenship, because we are the mothers, wives, and daughters of a mighty people? Have women no country—no interests staked in public weal—no liabilities in common peril—no partnership in a nation's guilt and shame? Let the history of the world answer these queries. Read the denunciations of Jehovah against the follies and crimes of Israel's daughters. Trace the influence of woman as a courtezan and a mistress in the destinies of nations, both ancient and modern, and see her wielding her power too often to debase and destroy, rather than to elevate and save. It is often said that women rule the world, through their influence over men. If so, then may we well hide our faces in the dust, and cover ourselves with sackcloth and ashes.

It has not been by moral power and intellectual, but through the baser passions of man. This domination of women must be resigned—the sooner the better; in the age which is approaching, she should be something more—she should be a citizen; and this title, which demands an increase of knowledge and of reflection, opens before her a new empire! I hold, Mr. Chairman, that American women have to do with this subject, not only because it is moral and religious, but because it is political, inasmuch as we are citizens of this republic, and as such our honor, happiness, and well being, are bound up in its politics and government and laws.

I stand before you as a southerner, exiled from the land of

my birth, by the sound of the lash, and the pitious cry of the slave. I stand before you as a repentant slaveholder. I stand before you as a moral being, endowed with precious and inalienable rights, which are correlative with solemn duties and high responsibilities; and as a moral being I feel that I owe it to the suffering slave, and to the deluded master, to my country and the world, to do all that I can to overturn a system of complicated crimes, built up upon the broken hearts and prostrate bodies of my countrymen in chains, and cemented by the blood and sweat and tears of my sisters in bonds.[53]

6.
Judge Hertell's defense of his Married Women's Property Bill, 1836

Things are so arranged, knowledge, property, civil as well as political exclusions, man's public opinion, that the great majority of adult women must marry on whatever terms their masters have willed, or starve: or if not absolutely starve, they must renounce at least all the means of enjoyment monopolized by the males. . . . Woman can demand no enjoyment from man as a matter of right; she must beg it, like any of her children, or like a slave, as a favor. . . . I say emphatically the slave; for a slave is a person whose actions and earnings, instead of being under his own control, liable only to equal laws, to public opinion, and to his own calculations, under these, of his own interest, are under the arbitrary control of any other human being, by whatever name called. This is the essence of slavery, and what distinguishes it from freedom. A domestic, a civil, a political slave, in the plain unsophisticated sense of the word—in no metaphorical sense—is every married woman. . . . It needs hardly to be mentioned that the common law in question besides divesting married women of the right of private property and giving it to their husbands, also vests the latter with such absolute and irresponsible power over the person of the wife, as renders her the abject and servile slave and "servant" of her "legal lord and master!"

By virtue of existing laws, unmarried females can acquire, manage and dispose of their estate both real and personal and can exercise all the rights and powers relative thereto, as are possessed and exercised by men. This is as it ought to be. The doctrine, or just and moral principle of equal rights, cannot consistently and does not righteously justify laws, giving to one sex powers and privileges relative to property which are denied to the other. The "natural and inalienable right of life, liberty and the pursuit of happiness," is common to both sexes; and the law relative to the acquisition, possession and the management of property by unmarried females is in perfect harmony therewith. Not so with married women. . . . By marriage, the wife's personal property, whether acquired by will, deed, inheritance, or her own industry, becomes vested in her husband, and she is as fully deprived of her title to it, and her right to use or dispose of it, or to control the use and management of it, as if she instead of being married, had been sold a slave to a master.

The common law of England, by which the property of married women is taken from them, and given to their respective husbands, is not and never was constitution law in this state. . . . "all such parts of the 'common law' and such of the said acts and parts thereof, as are repugnant to the constitution, are hereby abrogated." Common laws and acts of the legislature of the colony of NY that formed the law of the colony shall continue to be law of this state unless repealed. —13th section of 7th article of State Constitution.

That "all men are born free and with equal rights," is an admitted maxim in the moral and political creed of all advocates and friends of free government. That this truth is meant to apply exclusively to the male sex, will not be urged by any who have a due regard for their reputation for common sense. "All" women are also "born free and with equal rights, among which are" not only the right of "life, liberty, and the pursuit of happiness," but also the right of private property. Those rights are possessed by all, each and every citizen, and of course, by females equally with male citizens.

If a law by which the private property of men or unmarried

women be taken from them and given to another without their free and voluntary consent [missing words], no law can be just or justifiable by which the property of married women is taken from them without their consent and given to another. Such it is true is the "common law of England", but being incompatible with the exercise and enjoyment of equal rights, repugnant to the spirit and principles of our free political institutions and to the provisions of the Constitution and totally inconceivable without them, is not, and never was adopted as common law in this state.[54]

7.
Declaration of Sentiments adopted at Seneca Falls convention, 1848

When, in the course of human events, it becomes necessary for one portion of the family of man to assume among the people of the earth a position different from that which they have hitherto occupied, but one to which the laws of nature and of nature's God entitle them, a decent respect to the opinions of mankind requires that they should declare the causes that impel them to such a course.

We hold these truths to be self-evident; that all men and women are created equal; that they are endowed by their Creator with certain inalienable rights; that among these are life, liberty, and the pursuit of happiness; that to secure these rights governments are instituted, deriving their just powers from the consent of the governed. Whenever any form of government becomes destructive of these ends, it is the right of those who suffer from it to refuse allegiance to it, and to insist upon the institution of a new government, laying its foundation on such principles, and organizing its powers in such form, as to them shall seem most likely to effect their safety and happiness. Prudence, indeed, will dictate that governments long established should not be changed for light and transient causes; and, accordingly, all experience hath shown that mankind are more disposed to suffer, while evils are sufferable, than to right themselves by abolishing the forms to which they were accustomed. But when a long train of abuses and usurpations, pursuing invariably the same object, evinces a design to reduce them under absolute despotism, it is their duty to throw off such government, and to provide new guards for their future security. Such has been the patient sufferance of the women under this government, and such is now the necessity which constrains them to demand the equal station to which they are entitled.

The history of mankind is a history of repeated injuries and usurpations on the part of man toward woman, having in direct object the establishment of an absolute tyranny over her. To prove this, let facts be submitted to a candid world.

He has never permitted her to exercise her inalienable right to the elective franchise.

He has compelled her to submit to laws, in the formation of which she had no voice.

He has withheld from her rights which are given to the most ignorant and degraded men—both natives and foreigners.

Having deprived her of this first right as a citizen, the elective franchise, thereby leaving her without representation in the halls of legislation, he has oppressed her on all sides.

He has made her, if married, in the eye of the law, civilly dead.

He has taken from her all right in property, even to the wages she earns.

He has made her, morally, an irresponsible being, as she can commit many crimes with impunity, provided they be done in the presence of her husband. In the covenant of marriage, she is compelled to promise obedience to her husband, he becoming, to all intents and purposes, her master—the law giving him power to deprive her of her liberty, and to administer chastisement.

He has so framed the laws of divorce, as to what shall be the proper causes of divorce; in case of separation, to whom the guardianship of the children shall be given; as to be wholly regardless of the happiness of women—the law, in all cases, going upon a false supposition of the supremacy of man, and giving all power into his hands.

After depriving her of all rights as a married woman, if single and the owner of property, he has taxed her to support a government which recognizes her only when her property can be made profitable to it.

He has monopolized nearly all the profitable employments, and from those she is permitted to follow, she receives but a scanty remuneration.

He closes against her all the avenues to wealth and distinction, which he considers most honorable to himself. As a teacher of theology, medicine, or law, she is not known.

He has denied her the facilities for obtaining a thorough education—all colleges being closed against her.

He allows her in Church as well as State, but a subordinate position, claiming Apostolic authority for her exclusion from the ministry, and with some exceptions, from any public participation in the affairs of the Church.

He has created a false public sentiment, by giving to the world a different code of morals for men and women, by which moral delinquencies which exclude women from society, are not only tolerated but deemed of little account in man.

He has usurped the prerogative of Jehovah himself, claiming it as his right to assign for her a sphere of action, when that belongs to her conscience and her God.

He has endeavored, in every way that he could to destroy her confidence in her own powers, to lessen her self-respect, and to make her willing to lead a dependent and abject life.

Now, in view of this entire disfranchisement of one-half the people of this country, their social and religious degradation,—in view of the unjust laws above mentioned, and because women do feel themselves aggrieved, oppressed, and fraudulently deprived of their most sacred rights, we insist that they have immediate admission to all the rights and privileges which belong to them as citizens of these United States.

In entering upon the great work before us, we anticipate no small amount of misconception, misrepresentation, and ridicule; but we shall use every instrumentality within our power to effect our object. We shall employ agents, circulate tracts, petition the State and national Legislatures, and endeavor to enlist the pulpit and the press in our behalf. We hope this Convention will be followed by a series of Conventions, embracing every part of the country.

8.
"The Times that Try Men's Souls,"
by Maria Weston Chapman, 1837

Confusion has seized us, and all things go wrong,
The women have leaped from "their spheres,"
And, instead of fixed stars, shoot as comets along,
And are setting the world by the ears!
In courses erratic they're wheeling through space,
In brainless confusion and meaningless chase.

In vain do our knowing ones try to compute
Their return to the orbit designed;
They're glanced at a moment, then onward they shoot,
And are neither "to hold nor to bind;"
So freely they move in their chosen ellipse,
The "Lords of Creation" do fear an eclipse.

They've taken a notion to speak for themselves,
And are wielding the tongue and the pen;
They've mounted the rostrum; the termagant[55] elves,
And—oh horrid!—are talking to men!
With faces unblanched in our presence they come
To harangue us, they say, in behalf of the dumb.

They insist on their right to petition and pray,
That St. Paul, in Corinthians, has given them rules
For appearing in public;[56] despite what those say
Whom we've trained to instruct them in schools;
But vain such instructions, if women may scan
And quote texts of Scripture to favor their plan.

Our grandmothers' learning consisted of yore
In spreading their generous boards;
In twisting the distaff,[57] or mopping the floor,
And *obeying the will of their lords.*
Now, misses may reason, and think, and debate,
Till unquestioned submission is quite out of date.

Our clergy have preached on the sin and the shame
Of woman, when out of "her sphere,"
And labored *divinely* to ruin her fame,
And shorten this horrid career;
But for spiritual guidance no longer they look
To Fulsom, or Winslow, or learned Parson Cook.[58]

Our wise men have tried to exorcise in vain
The turbulent spirits abroad;
As well might we deal with the fetterless main,
Or conquer ethereal essence with sword;
Like the devils of Milton,[59] they rise from each blow,
With spirit unbroken, insulting the foe.

Our patriot fathers, of eloquent fame,
Waged war against tangible forms;
Aye, *their* foes were men—and if ours were the same,
We might speedily quiet their storms;
But, ah! their descendants enjoy not such bliss—
The assumptions of Britain were nothing to this.

Could we but array all our force in the field,
We'd teach these usurpers of power
That their bodily safety demands they should yield,
And in the presence of manhood should cower;
But, alas! for our tethered and impotent state,
Chained by notions of knighthood—we can but debate.

Oh! shade of the prophet Mahomet, arise!
Place woman again in "her sphere,"

And teach that her soul was not born for the skies,
But to flutter a brief moment here.
This doctrine of Jesus, as preached up by Paul,
If embraced in its spirit, will ruin us all.

—LORDS OF CREATION.[60]

9.
Lucretia Mott on the Seneca Falls convention, from letter to the *Liberator*, August 24, 1848

While in Western New York, we attended two Conventions called to consider the relative position of woman in society—one held at Seneca Falls, the other at Rochester.[61] The "proceedings" have been published in the *North Star* and several other papers.

The attendance and interest manifested, were greatly encouraging; and give hope that this long-neglected subject will soon begin to receive the attention that its importance demands.

I have received some cheering letters upon the subject since our return home—one from Mass.: while, on the other hand, private and public testimony has been borne against the movement. This must serve to impress the necessity of repeated meetings of a similar character.[62]

10.
Lucretia Mott on the Seneca, from letter to the *Liberator*, August 24, 1848

During the summer, my husband and self have had an interesting travel among the Cattaraugus Indians, of Western New York, and the self-emancipated slaves and other colored settlers of Canada West. . . . A word for the poor Indians. The few hundreds left of the Seneca Nation at the Cattaraugus reservation, are improving in their mode of living, cultivating their land, and educating their children. They, too, are learning somewhat from the political agitations abroad; and, as man is wont, are imitating the movements of France and all Europe, in seeking larger liberty—more independence.

Their Chieftainship is therefore a subject of discussion in their councils, and important changes are demanded and expected, as to the election of their chiefs, many being prepared for a yearly appointment.

Two missionaries are settled among them, and some religious party strife is apparent. The pagans adhere, of course, to the sacred festivals of their fathers, and are not disposed to exchange them for the "bread and wine" &c., of the Christian party. We had an interesting conference with them, during which their differences were presented; but we declined to decide between them, as, if attempted, we might be found equally discountenancing each form, and recommending our Quaker non-conformity. But, as that was not our mission, we commended them to the "Great Spirit," believing that those who danced religiously, might be as nearly perfect, as were those who communed in some other chosen form—neither of these being the test of acceptance.

We witnessed their strawberry dance, and grotesque though the figures were, fantastic their appearance, and rude their measured steps, and unharmonious their music, yet, in observing the profound veneration of the hundreds present, some twenty of whom were performers, and the respectful attention paid to the speeches of their chiefs, women as well as men, it was far from me to say, that our silent, voiceless worship was better adapted to their condition, or that even the Missionary, Baptism, and Sabbath, and organ, are so much higher evidence of a civilized, spiritual and Christian state.[63]

III.

THE 1850s:
The Movement Takes Off

After its local start in Seneca Falls and Rochester, more local conventions followed in Ohio in the next few years. Then, in 1850, the movement organized nationally. The *New York Tribune* of September 11, 1850, carried a call for a national woman's rights convention to be held in Worcester, Massachusetts, during the last week of October.

National conventions followed yearly for the next decade, with one exception in 1857, and petitions to state legislatures for women's legal and political rights garnered thousands of signatures and stimulated public discussions. While there was interest in working for the vote, activism also focused on gaining property rights, education, employment opportunities, "equal pay for equal work," guardianship of their children, the right to divorce, and an end to oppression by religious dogma. The push for rights triggered a backlash, and those opposed to women's rights responded in print and legislative halls.

While women were organizing nationally for their rights, the federal government strengthened the institution of slavery by taking away any safe space on U.S. soil for enslaved people who were taking their freedom, and the two movements found common cause, with many of the same activists.

The first two major donations arrived to fund the women's rights work toward the end of the decade, both from men. Francis Jackson of Boston gave $5,000 in 1858 ($154,000.00 in purchasing power today) followed by fellow Bostonian Charles F. Hovey, who left $50,000 ($1,540,000.00 in today's currency) in a trust fund to promote social justice causes, including women's rights. Money was now available to fund paid organizers, and Susan B. Anthony quickly emerged, single, committed, and needing employment.

Free love, Freethought, and dress reform conventions spun off as women challenged the institutions of marriage and religion along with the social norms of fashion and the sexual double standard.

The woman's rights movement had been around for decades, as women and men, singly and in groups, spoke, wrote, petitioned, and legislated women's rights. Seneca Falls, followed by other local conventions, signaled a change to the beginning of organization. This buildup culminated in the first national woman's rights convention, held in 1850 in Worcester, Massachusetts, which formalized the structure to be taken by the organized work for women's rights.

The list of eighty-nine signers to the call read like a roll sheet of the most prominent reformers. More than one thousand people from eleven states crowded the halls of the convention and listened to discussions of the medical education of women (needed), their business capacity (great); and their position in the Bible (equal). Dress reform was called for and a woman new to the movement, Abby Price, argued that prostitution has economic causes and could be "cured" by opening profitable work to women. Her speech is included in this chapter.[1] William Lloyd Garrison wrote, "I doubt whether a more important movement has ever been launched, touching the destiny of the race, than this in regard to the equality of the sexes."[2] Frederick Douglass and Sojourner Truth attended, representing the interests of African Americans.[3]

Avoiding a top-down organizational structure, the convention set up a loose central steering committee of nineteen, with one or two members from each state who would serve for a year, correspond with one another, raise funds and awareness, and hold conventions in their respective regions.[4] They divided their work into areas of education, industrial avocations, civil and political rights and regulations, and social relations.

The Business Committee presented a resolution calling for "Equality before the law, without distinction of sex or color." The word "male" should be taken out of every state constitution, the committee proposed, and all occupations should be open to women equally with men. Married women should have equal rights with their husbands to their possessions, as well, since husbands controlled all their wives' property, earnings, and possessions in most states and wives couldn't inherit or pass on inheritance equally with their husbands.[5]

Lucretia Mott warned that women "would find it necessary to take an antagonistic position and to meet the prejudices and opposition of the world with directness and an earnest expression of the truth." Women, Mott urged, must "speak to tingle the ear of man for the degraded position he has kept woman under for so many ages."

The *New York Tribune* carried lengthy and respectful accounts of each day's proceedings, reprinted in the paper's European edition, which led Harriet Taylor Mill to respond in a British journal, the *Westminster Review*, sparking the woman's movement in England. The press coverage of the convention was, with the exception of the *Tribune,* generally abusive as, "From North to South the press found these reformers wonderfully ridiculous people. The 'hen convention' was served up in every variety of style,"[6] the authors of *History of Woman Suffrage* explained. For example, the *National Intelligencer* reprinted this editorial from the *Springfield* (Massachusetts) *Republican*:

> The Worcester Convention women want to be preachers, politicians, merchants, administrators of laws. It is useless to reason against such fanaticism like this, and fruitless also. Views like these can never prevail among the sex. They are too well-cultivated for such unnatural growth. . . . We are told . . . that Mrs. Davis presided with great dignity. Miss Brown, a beautiful young lady from Oberlin, in a fluent speech is understood to have floored St. Paul on a Bible argument. . . . Woman would have done much more for the advancement of the sex by staying

home tending their babies, instructing their children, and assisting their husbands, or in fitting [them]selves to assume these high duties for which no woman yet ever found herself too well qualified.[7]

A month before the birth of the national woman's rights movement, President Millard Fillmore signed the Fugitive Slave Act into law on September 18, 1850. Part of the Great Compromise between the slave-holding states and the northern free states, jerry-rigged by Kentucky congressperson Henry Clay, it was designed to put an end, once and for all, to any discussion of the issue of slavery in Congress. Fugitive slave cases would now come under federal jurisdiction; the safe zones northern states created when they abolished slavery were now illegal. No soil anywhere in the United States was safe for an African American, enslaved or free. All a white person needed to prove ownership of an African American person was a simple affidavit. Although on trial, accused black men and women were denied the right of trial by jury and were not allowed to testify on their own behalf.

Anyone preventing the arrest of a fugitive, or aiding in his or her concealment or rescue, was subject to a fine of one thousand dollars, imprisonment up to six months, and civil damages of one thousand dollars for each piece of African American "property" the purported owner lost by their actions.[8]

As the woman's movement emerged, the anti-slavery movement kicked up its activity. The two movements were now in many ways inseparable and would be until the end of the Civil War. With many of the same people active in both and the anti-slavery and women's rights conventions often held in conjunction with one another, the theory overlapped as well.

The Philadelphia Female Anti-Slavery Society spoke out against the infamous Fugitive Slave Act in its final (1870) report:

Probably no statute was ever written, in the code of a civilized nation, so carefully and cunningly devised for the purpose of depriving men of liberty.[9]

The final resolution adopted by the 1850 Worcester convention read:

> *Resolved*, That the cause we have met to advocate—the claim for woman of all her natural and civil rights—bids us remember the two millions of slave women at the South, the most grossly wronged and foully outraged of all women; and in every effort for an improvement in our civilization, we will bear in our heart of hearts the memory of the trampled womanhood of the plantation, and omit no effort to raise it to a share in the rights we claim for ourselves.[10]

The system of marriage deprived women of many of the rights denied to African Americans under the system of enslavement, as Elizabeth Cady Stanton pointed out in an address to the New York Legislature the following decade.

Ernestine Rose took a similar position. Rose was a Polish immigrant, a Jewish Freethinker and abolitionist whose feminist activism predated the Seneca Falls convention by more than a decade. She circulated petitions in the 1830s for married women's property rights and was an eloquent orator. By the 1850s Rose may have been the best-known voice of women's rights in the country, as is apparent in her address to the 1851 national women's rights convention, included in this chapter, in which she discusses the legal death of women in marriage.

When Elizabeth Cady Stanton and Ernestine Rose gathered signatures calling for married women's property rights in the 1830s, they were following the petition work model of the Female Anti-Slavery Societies. The organized movement now picked up the petition work. Stanton addressed the New York State Legislature on February 20, 1854, in support of a petition signed by 5,931 men and women, calling for the "just and equal rights of women." The Senate had also received a petition signed by 4,164 men and women in support of woman suffrage. Both measures were referred to select committees. The committees' discussion and report, which appeared in the *Albany Evening Journal,* is included in this chapter and is a classic example of the arguments prevalent at the time in opposition to women's rights.

When the Founding Fathers refused to pay taxes without representation, Hannah Lee Corbin, of Virginia, wrote her brother, General Richard Henry Lee, protesting against the taxation of women unless they were allowed to vote.[11] Others also challenged this contradiction between the revolutionary spirit and women's condition.

Once the organized woman's movement began, taxation without representation became a major rallying cry.

The first Ohio women's rights convention, held in 1850, adopted an address to the women of the state that quoted Professor Walker, "a distinguished lawyer of our own State," who, in his "Introduction to American Law," questioned, "Is the principle of taxation without representation," in regard to women, "less oppressive and tyrannical, than when our fathers expended their blood and treasure, rather than submit to its injustice?"[12] In 1851, a petition was sent from Ontario County, New York, praying the legislature to exempt women from taxation.[13] At the 1852 national convention, Lucy Stone spoke on the matter, and the full speech is included in this chapter.

Stone walked her talk, refusing to pay her taxes, explaining to the tax collector:

Orange, N. J., Dec. 18, 1858.

Mr. Mandeville, Tax Collector,

Sir:—Enclosed I return my tax bill, without paying it. My reason for doing so is, that women suffer taxation, and yet have no representation, which is not only unjust to one-half the adult population, but is contrary to our theory of government. For years some women have been paying their taxes under protest, but still taxes are imposed, and representation is not granted. The only course now left us is to refuse to pay the tax. We know well what the immediate result of this refusal must be.

But we believe that when the attention of men is called to the wide difference between their theory of government and its practice, in this particular, they can not fail to see the mistake they now make, by imposing taxes on women, while they refuse them the right of suffrage, and that the sense of justice which is in all good men, will lead them to correct it. Then we shall cheerfully pay our taxes—not till then.[14]

The authorities then seized her property, consisting of two tables, four chairs, one stand, and two steel plate likenesses of abolitionists S. P. Chase and Gerrit Smith, selling it at public auction to cover her taxes.[15]

Stone was not the first to refuse to pay her taxes; that distinction, according to the *Woman's Tribune*, goes to a Miss Wall in 1850.[16] Ernestine Rose, in a passionate speech at the 1853 national woman's rights convention, which began with an acknowledgment of the feminists imprisoned during the French Revolution, charged, "And in spite of another principle, recognized in this Republic, namely, that 'taxation without representation is tyranny,' she is taxed without being represented."[17]

When Massachusetts held a constitutional convention in 1853, suffragists sent an appeal to the citizens of the state on the equal political rights of woman:

. . . Our Revolution claimed that taxation and representation should be co-extensive. While the property and labor of women are subject to taxation, she is entitled to a voice in fixing the amount of taxes, and the use of them when collected, and is entitled to a voice in the laws that regulate punishments. It would be a disgrace to our schools and civil institutions, for any one to argue that a Massachusetts woman who has enjoyed the full advantage of all their culture, is not as competent to form an opinion on civil matters, as the illiterate foreigner landed but a few years before upon our shores—unable to read or write—by no means free from early prejudices, and little acquainted with our institutions. Yet such men are allowed to vote.[18]

Caroline Dahl circulated a suffrage petition to the Massachusetts Senate and House in 1858 reminding the elected representatives that "Governments derive their just powers from the consent of the governed" and "Taxation and representation are inseparable."[19]

Dr. Harriot K. Hunt, a woman of "wealth and position," gained notoriety by protesting every year against being compelled to pay taxes while not recognized in the government.[20] The *New York Tribune*'s report on her 1853 protest is included in this chapter.

With the creation of a national organization focusing on multiple women's rights issues, the 1850s saw an explosion of activism, well-documented in the major form of communication, the newspapers. Antioch opened, joining Oberlin as the second college to admit women and black men. Support grew in the press, and the first women's rights paper, the *Una*, "devoted to the elevation of Woman," began publication, edited by Paulina Wright Davis, the president of the 1850 Worcester convention. The *New York Tribune* welcomed the *Una* into its ranks.[21]

Women were boldly entering formerly male professions, such as medicine and religion. A sampling of writing from just the first few years in 1850 demonstrates the flurry of activity.

The last commencement of the Women's Medical College in Philadelphia nine women graduated. The faculty proffered a diploma complimentary for Harriet [*sic*] Hunt after eighteen years of practice.[22]

Antoinette Brown (later Blackwell) drew criticism from the press as she entered the pulpit as the first (irregularly) ordained woman minister.[23]

The women even began to rebel against fashion constrictions during the decade. The fashionable woman in the 1850s, strapped into stays tightly laced at the back and held in place in front by a two-inch-wide wooden "busk," sat and stood ramrod straight. These corsets exerted twenty to eighty pounds of pressure on her internal organs, causing weakness, shortness of breath, digestive problems, and sometimes broken ribs and displaced vital organs. Women died in childbirth as a result. Heavy petticoats, six to eight creating a dome shape for her heavy, long skirt, hung from this trapped waist. Delicate high heels throwing off her center of balance completed the debilitating outfit.

Women in health spas now threw away their corsets and donned a short skirt and loose-fitting trousers, while Frances Wright had stood "condemned of a violation of the unalterable laws of nature" for wearing just such an outfit for her public speeches as early as 1828.[24]

Women members of the utopian Oneida Community in 1848 created a "reform costume" with leggings, like the nearby native Oneida Nation women. Elizabeth Cady Stanton's second cousin, Elizabeth Smith Miller, introduced her to the outfit that gained the name *bloomer,* for the Seneca Falls newspaper editor, Amelia Bloomer, who popularized the idea of dress reform. Susan B. Anthony, Lucy Stone, and others in the woman's rights movement picked it up. Paulina Wright Davis, who wrote the call for the first national woman suffrage convention and started the *Una*, wore the reform dress to Washington when her husband was elected to Congress in 1853. She was initially ostracized by the other congressional wives.[25]

Ridiculed, denounced from the pulpit by ministers quoting the biblical sanction in Deuteronomy, "Woman shall not take unto herself that which pertaineth to man," threatened by mobs, and accused of taking away men's power by wearing trousers, the suffrage leaders quickly abandoned the new dress, explaining their strategic decision, but dress reform spawned a new, separate movement, which denounced the suffragists for their lack of principle. The newspapers duly reported the dress reform movement and the conflict. The *New York Tribune*, tongue-in-cheek, endorsed the new cause:

> When, in the course of passing events, it becomes necessary for the women of one nation to break off the bonds which Fashion has thrown around them, and to assume among the females of other nations a separate and distinct dress, to which the laws of Nature and a regard for their health so fully entitled them. . . . The history of the present "Tyranness Fashion" is a history of

repeated injuries both to the comfort of the women and to their pockets, having in direct object the constant soiling of their garments, and the ruination of their health.[26]

Elizabeth Cady Stanton explained how women changed the way they dressed to become healthier, and how that simple act aroused the ire of some men, in her "Reminiscences," published in the first volume of *History of Woman Suffrage* in 1881, in an excerpt that is included in this chapter.

Dress reformers publicly called out these suffragists for abandoning the movement for healthier clothing, which can be observed in the 1857 *New York Tribune* report on the "Movement for Dress Reform," included in this chapter.

These early women's rights activists saw the institution of marriage as a foundation of women's oppression. "It is in vain to look for the elevation of woman, so long as she is degraded in marriage," Elizabeth Cady Stanton wrote privately to Susan B. Anthony. "The right idea of marriage is at the foundation of all reforms."[27] Stanton in 1840 had convinced the minister marrying her to take the requirement that she promise to obey her husband out of the ceremony. Lucy Stone, who had done the same when she married, agreed with Stanton: "I very much wish that a wife's right to her own body should be pushed at our next convention."[28]

Ohio's first woman's rights convention, held at Salem April 19–20, 1850, sent a memorial to the Ohio Constitutional Convention that said in part:

We would especially direct the attention of the Convention to the legal condition of married women. . . . All that she has, becomes legally his, and he can collect and dispose of the profits of her labor without her consent, as he thinks fit, and she can own nothing, have nothing, which is not regarded by the law as belonging to her husband. Over her person he has a more limited power. Still, if he render life intolerable, so that she is forced to leave him, he has the power to retain her children, and "seize her and bring her back, for he has a right to her society which he

may enforce, either against herself or any other person who de-
tains her"). Woman by being thus subject to the control, and dependent on the will of man, loses her self-dependence; and no
human being can be deprived of this without a sense of degradation.[29]

Rape was legally institutionalized in marriage, as was wife
battering. If women fled loveless or dangerous marriages, husbands had recourse. Women were considered dead in the law;
they did not exist legally, so they were required to live with
their husbands. A runaway wife could be tracked down and
returned by the authorities. Or a husband could advertise that
his wife had fled, and he no longer had any responsibility for
her financially. In other words, she had nothing, since he legally owned everything.

Some couples took direct action. In their marriage ceremony,
Lucy Stone and her husband, Henry Blackwell, protested the
tyrannical power husbands were given, a story carried in newspapers, such as the *Syracuse Standard*, May 7, 1855:

"While we acknowledge our mutual affection, by publicly
assuming the sacred relationship of husband and wife, yet in
justice to ourselves and a great principle, we deem it a duty to
declare that this act on our part implies no sanction of, nor
promise of voluntary obedience to, such of the present laws of
marriage, as refuse to recognize the wife as an independent rational being, while they confer upon the husband an injurious
and unnatural superiority, investing him with legal powers which
no honorable man would exercise, and which no man should
possess."[30]

Stone went one step further. Before the marriage, she consulted several eminent lawyers, including Salmon P. Chase,
who would later become chief justice of the Supreme Court, to
see if there was a law requiring a woman to take her husband's
name. She learned there wasn't. So, in 1855 Lucy Stone kept
her own name.[31]

The *History of Woman Suffrage* editors applauded her and acknowledged the price she paid for her forward step:

> This was a timely protest against the whole idea of the old Blackstone code, which made woman a nonentity in marriage. Lucy Stone took an equally brave step in refusing to take her husband's name, respecting her own individuality and the name that represented it. These protests have called down on Mrs. Stone much ridicule and persecution, but she has firmly maintained her position, although at great inconvenience in the execution of legal documents, and suffering the injustice of having her vote refused. as Lucy Stone, soon after the bill passed in Massachusetts giving all women the right to vote on the school question.[32]

This was not an individual action, however, but a movement with a name. Women who kept their own name in marriage were called "Lucy Stoners." Others continued to protest the legal death of women that constituted the marriage ceremony. Augustus Harman and Ellen Beard, of Aurora, Illinois, editors of the *Reformer*, went one step further. Protesting "against every law, statute or customs making a distinction between the duties, rights, and responsibilities of the husband and wife," they married themselves in front of an attorney, taking the authority for recognizing their union out of the hands of the church and placing it in the state.[33]

Questioning the sacred institution of marriage led quickly to charges of "free lover," a position that put one far outside acceptable society. When Elizabeth Smith Miller asked her second cousin to clarify her position, Stanton replied that if by free lover she meant "woman's right to give her body to the man she loves and no other, to become a mother or not as her desire, judgment, and conscience may dictate . . . to be absolute sovereign of herself," then yes, she was a free lover.[34] Stone, in discussion with her more conservative husband, began to back away from the issue a bit, believing a convention just to discuss marriage should be held. That is exactly what happened—called not by the woman suffrage movement, but by a new movement, as the *Syracuse Standard* reported on September 18, 1857:

> A BIG-HEARTED WOMAN. —On the 4th and 5th of the present month the Spiritualists of Ohio held a Convention at Ravenna. Much was said, and it may be more was done among them. During the discussion a Mrs. Lewis of Cleveland, evidently a warm spirited woman, delivered herself by saying—
>
> That she was in favor of universal freedom, and that loving whomsoever she chose was a part of that freedom, and to confine her to love one man was an abridgement of her rights.—She said "although she had one husband in Cleveland, she considered herself married to the whole human race. All men were her husbands and she had an undying love for them." She said also "what business is it to the world whether one man is the father to my children or ten men are? I have a right to say who shall be the father of my offspring."[35]

The *Syracuse Standard* reprinted from the *New York Tribune* an incendiary attack on marriage delivered at a Rutland, Vermont, Free Convention in 1858, which is reprinted in full in this chapter.

The idea that women have an absolute right to their own bodies, to determine when and if they will birth, and to love whom they will under their own conditions is not new; it was raised in the press in 1858.

I.

Abby H. Price's speech at the first national woman's rights convention, in 1850

Mrs. Abby H. Price, of Hopedale, made an address on the injustice of excluding girls from the colleges, the trades and the professions, and the importance of training them to some profitable labor, and thus to protect their virtue, dignity, and self-respect by securing their pecuniary independence.

She thought the speediest solution of the vexed problem of prostitution was profitable work for the rising generation of girls. The best legislation on the social vice was in removing the legal disabilities that cripple all their powers. Woman, in order to be equally independent with man, must have a fair and equal chance. He is in nowise restricted from doing, in every department of human exertion, all he is able to do. If he is bold and ambitious, and desires fame, every avenue is open to him. He may blend science and art, producing a competence for his support, until he chains them to the car of his genius, and, with Fulton and Morse, wins a crown of imperishable gratitude. If he desires to tread the path of knowledge up to its glorious temple-summit, he can, as he pleases, take either of the learned professions as instruments of pecuniary independence, while he plumes his wings for a higher and higher ascent. Not so with woman. Her rights are not recognized as equal; her sphere is circumscribed—not by her ability, but by her sex. If, perchance, her taste leads her to excellence, in the way they give her leave to tread, she is worshiped as almost divine; but if she reaches for laurels they have in view, the wings of her genius are clipped because she is a woman.[36]

2.

Ernestine Rose's speech at the 1851 National Woman's Rights Convention in Worcester, Massachusetts

After having heard the letter read from our poor incarcerated sisters of France, well might we exclaim, Alas, poor France! where is thy glory? Where the glory of the Revolution of 1848, in which shone forth the pure and magnanimous spirit of an oppressed nation struggling for Freedom? Where the fruits of that victory that gave to the world the motto, "Liberty, Equality, and Fraternity"? A motto destined to hurl the tyranny of kings and priests into the dust, and give freedom to the enslaved millions of the earth. Where, I again ask, is the result of those noble achievements, when woman, ay, one-half of the nation, is deprived of her rights? Has woman then been idle during the contest between "right and might"? Has she been wanting in ardor and enthusiasm? Has she not mingled her blood with that of her husband, son, and sire? Or has she been recreant in hailing the motto of liberty floating on your banners as an omen of justice, peace, and freedom to man, that at the first step she takes practically to claim the recognition of her rights, she is rewarded with the doom of a martyr?

But right has not yet asserted her prerogative, for might rules the day; and as every good cause must have its martyrs, why should woman not be a martyr for her cause? But need we wonder that France, governed as she is by Russian and Austrian despotism, does not recognize the rights of humanity in the recognition of the rights of woman, when even here, in this far-famed land of freedom, under a Republic that has inscribed on its banner the great truth that "all men are created free and equal, and endowed with inalienable rights to life, liberty, and the pursuit of happiness"—a declaration borne, like the vision of hope, on wings of light to the remotest parts of the earth, an omen of freedom to the oppressed and down-trodden children of man—when, even here, in the very face of this eternal truth, woman, the mockingly so-called "better half" of man, has yet to plead for her rights, nay, for her life. For what is life without liberty, and what is liberty without equality of rights? And as for the pursuit of happiness, she is not allowed to choose any line of action that might promote it; she has only thankfully to accept what man in his magnanimity decides as best for her to do, and this is what he does not choose to do himself.

Is she then not included in that declaration? Answer, ye wise men of the nation, and answer truly; add not hypocrisy to oppression! Say that she is not created free and equal, and therefore (for the sequence follows on the premise) that she is not entitled to life, liberty, and the pursuit of happiness. But with all the audacity arising from an assumed superiority, you dare not so libel and insult humanity as to say, that she is not included in that declaration; and if she is, then what right has man, except that of might, to deprive woman of the rights and privileges he claims for himself? And why, in the name of reason and justice, why should she not have the same rights? Because she is woman? Humanity recognizes no sex; virtue recognizes no sex; mind recognizes no sex; life and death, pleasure and pain, happiness and misery, recognize no sex. Like man, woman comes involuntarily into existence; like him, she possesses physical and mental and moral powers, on the proper cultivation of which depends her happiness; like him she is subject to all the vicissitudes of life; like him she has to pay the penalty for disobeying nature's laws, and far greater penalties has she to suffer from ignorance of her more complicated nature; like him she enjoys or suffers with her country. Yet she is not recognized as his equal!

In the laws of the land she has no rights; in government she has no voice. And in spite of another principle, recognized in this Republic, namely, that "taxation without representation is tyranny," she is taxed without being represented. Her property may be consumed by taxes to defray the expenses of that unholy, unrighteous custom called war, yet she has no power to give her vote against it. From the cradle to the grave she is subject to the power and control of man. Father, guardian, or husband, one conveys her like some piece of merchandise over to the other.

At marriage she loses her entire identity, and her being is said to have become merged in her husband. Has nature thus merged it? Has she ceased to exist and feel pleasure and pain? When she violates the laws of her being, does her husband pay the penalty? When she breaks the moral laws, does he suffer the punishment? When he supplies his wants, is it enough to satisfy her nature? And when at his nightly orgies, in the grog-shop and the oyster-cellar, or at the gaming-table, he squanders the means she helped, by her co-operation and economy, to accumulate, and she awakens to penury and destitution, will it supply the wants of her children to tell them that, owing to the superiority of man she had no redress by law, and that as her being was merged in his, so also ought theirs to be? What an inconsistency, that from the moment she enters that compact, in which she assumes the high responsibility of wife and mother, she ceases legally to exist, and becomes a purely submissive being. Blind submission in woman is considered a virtue, while submission to wrong is itself wrong, and resistance to wrong is virtue, alike in woman as in man.

But it will be said that the husband provides for the wife, or in other words, he feeds, clothes, and shelters her! I wish I had the power to make every one before me fully realize the degradation contained in that idea. Yes! he *keeps* her, and so he does a favorite horse; by law they are both considered his property. Both may, when the cruelty of the owner compels them to, run away, be brought back by the strong arm of the law, and according to a still extant law of England, both may be led by the halter to the market-place, and sold. This is humiliating indeed, but nevertheless true; and the sooner these things are known and understood, the better for humanity. It is no fancy sketch. I know that some endeavor to throw the mantle of romance over the subject, and treat woman like some ideal existence, not liable to the ills of life. Let those deal in fancy, that have nothing better to deal in; we have to do with sober, sad realities, with stubborn facts.

Again, I shall be told that the law presumes the husband to be kind, affectionate, and ready to provide for and protect his wife. But what right, I ask, has the law to presume at all on the subject? What right has the law to entrust the interest and happiness of one being into the hands of another? And if the merging of the interest of one being into the other is a necessary consequence on marriage, why should woman always remain on the losing side? Turn the tables. Let the identity and interest of the husband be merged in the wife. Think you she would act less generously toward him, than he toward her? Think you she is not capable of as much justice, disinterested devotion, and abiding affection, as he is? Oh, how grossly you misunderstand and wrong her nature! But we desire no such undue power over man; it would be as wrong in her to exercise it as it now is in him. All we claim is an equal legal and social position. We have nothing to do with individual man, be he good or bad, but with the laws that oppress woman. We know that bad and unjust laws must in the nature of things make man so too. If he is kind, affectionate, and consistent, it is because the kindlier feelings, instilled by a mother, kept warm by a sister, and cherished by a wife, will not allow him to carry out these barbarous laws against woman.

But the estimation she is generally held in, is as degrading as it is foolish. Man forgets that woman can not be degraded without its reacting on himself. The impress of her mind is stamped on him by nature, and the early education of the mother, which no after-training can entirely efface; and therefore, the estimation she is held in falls back with double force upon him. Yet, from the force of prejudice against her, he knows it not. Not long ago, I saw an account of two offenders, brought before a Justice of New York. One was charged with stealing a pair of boots, for which offense he was sentenced to six months' imprisonment; the other crime was assault and battery upon his wife: he was let off with a reprimand from the judge! With my principles, I am entirely opposed to punishment, and hold, that to reform the erring and remove the causes of evil is much more efficient, as well as just, than to punish. But the judge showed us the comparative value which he set on these two kinds of *property*. But then you must remember that the boots were taken by a stranger, while the wife was insulted by her legal owner! Here it will be said, that such degrading cases are but few. For the sake of humanity, I hope they are. But as long as woman shall be oppressed by unequal laws, so long will she be degraded by man.

We have hardly an adequate idea how all-powerful law is in forming public opinion, in giving tone and character to the mass of society. To illustrate my point, look at that infamous, detestable law, which was written in human blood, and signed and sealed with life and liberty, that eternal stain on the statute book of this country, the Fugitive Slave Law. Think you that before its passage, you could have found any in the free States—except a few politicians in the market—base enough to desire such a law? No! no! Even those who took no interest in the slave question, would have shrunk from so barbarous a thing. But no sooner was it passed, than the ignorant mass, the rabble of the self-styled Union Safety Committee, found out that we were a law-loving, law-abiding people! Such is the magic power of Law. Hence the necessity to guard against bad ones. Hence also the reason why we call on the nation to remove the legal shackles from woman, and it will have a beneficial effect on that still greater tyrant she has to contend with, Public Opinion.

Carry out the republican principle of universal suffrage, or strike it from your banners and substitute "Freedom and Power to one half of society, and Submission and Slavery to the other." Give woman the elective franchise. Let married women have the same right to property that their husbands have; for whatever the difference in their respective occupations, the duties of the wife are as indispensable and far more arduous than the husband's. Why then should the wife, at the death of her husband, not be his heir to the same extent that he is heir to her? In this inequality there is involved another wrong. When the wife dies, the husband is left in the undisturbed possession of all there is, and the children are left with him; no change is made, no stranger intrudes on his home and his affliction. But when the husband dies, the widow, at best receives but a mere pittance, while strangers assume authority denied to the wife. The sanctuary of affliction must be desecrated by executors; everything must be ransacked and assessed, lest she should steal something out of her own house: and to cap the climax, the children must be placed under guardians. When the husband dies poor, to be sure, no guardian is required, and the children are left for the mother to care and toil for, as best she may. But when anything is left for their maintenance, then it must be placed in the hands of strangers for safe keeping! The bringing-up and safety of the children are left with the mother, and safe they are in her hands. But a few hundred or thousand dollars can not be entrusted with her!

But, say they, "in case of a second marriage, the children must be protected in their property." Does that reason not hold as good in the case of the husband as in that of the wife? Oh, no! When *he* marries again, he still retains his identity and power to act; but *she* becomes merged once more into a mere nonentity; and therefore the first husband must rob her to prevent the second from doing so! Make the laws regulating property between husband and wife, equal for both, and all these difficulties would be removed.

According to a late act, the wife has a right to the property she brings at marriage, or receives in any way after marriage. Here is some provision for the favored few; but for the laboring many, there is none. The mass of the people commence life with no other capital than the union of heads, hearts, and hands. To the benefit of this best of capital, the wife has no right. If they are unsuccessful in married life, who suffers more the bitter consequences of poverty than the wife? But if successful, she can not call a dollar her own. The husband may will away every dollar of the personal property, and leave her destitute and penniless, and she has no redress by law. And even where real estate is left she receives but a life-interest in a third part of it, and at her death, she can not leave it to any one belonging to her: it falls back even to the remotest of his relatives. This is law, but where is the justice of it? Well might we say that laws were made to prevent, not to promote, the ends of justice.

In case of separation, why should the children be taken from the protecting care of the mother? Who has a better right to them than she? How much do fathers generally do toward bringing them up? When he comes home from business, and the child is in good humor and handsome trim, he takes the little darling on his knee and plays with it. But when the wife, with the care of the whole household on her shoulders, with little or no help, is not able to put them in the best order, how much does he do for them? Oh, no! Fathers like to have children good natured, well-behaved, and comfortable, but how to put them in that desirable condition is out of their philosophy. Children always depend more on the tender, watchful care of the mother, than of the father. Whether from nature, habit, or both, the mother is much more capable of administering to their health and comfort than the father, and therefore she has the best right to them. And where there is property, it ought to be divided equally between them, with an additional provision from the father toward the maintenance and education of the children.

Much is said about the burdens and responsibilities of married men. Responsibilities indeed there are, if they but felt them; but as to burdens, what are they? The sole province of man seems to be centered in that one thing, attending to some business. I grant that owing to the present unjust and unequal reward for labor, many have to work too hard for a subsistence; but whatever his vocation, he has to attend as much to it before as after marriage. Look at your bachelors, and see if they do not strive as much for wealth, and attend as steadily to business, as married men. No! the husband has little or no increase of burden, and every increase of comfort after marriage; while most of the burdens, cares, pains, and penalties of married life fall on the wife. How unjust and cruel, then, to have all the laws in his favor! If any difference should be made by law between husband and wife, reason, justice, and humanity, if their voices were heard, would dictate that it should be in her favor.

No! there is no reason against woman's elevation, but there are deep-rooted, hoary-headed prejudices. The main cause of them is, a pernicious falsehood propagated against her being, namely, that she is inferior by her nature. Inferior in what? What has man ever done, that woman, under the same advantages, could not do? In morals, bad as she is, she is generally considered his superior. In the intellectual sphere, give her a fair chance before you pronounce a verdict against her. Cultivate the frontal portion of her brain as much as that of man is cultivated, and she will stand his equal at least. Even now, where her mind has been called out at all, her intellect is as bright, as capacious, and as powerful as his. Will you tell us, that women have no Newtons, Shakespeares, and Byrons? Greater natural powers than even those possessed may have been destroyed in woman for want of proper culture, a just appreciation, reward for merit as an incentive to exertion, and freedom of action, without which, mind becomes cramped and stifled, for it can not expand under bolts and bars; and yet, amid all blighting, crushing circumstances—confined within the narrowest possible limits, trampled upon by prejudice and injustice, from her education and position forced to occupy herself almost exclusively with the most trivial affairs—in spite of all these difficulties, her intellect is as good as his. The few bright meteors in man's intellectual horizon could well be matched by woman, were she allowed to occupy the same elevated position. There is no need of naming the De Staëls, the Rolands, the Somervilles, the Wollstonecrofts [sic], the Sigourneys, the Wrights, the Martineaus, the Hemanses, the Fullers, Jagellos, and many more of modern as well as ancient times, to prove her mental powers, her patriotism, her self-sacrificing devotion to the cause of humanity, and the eloquence that gushes from her pen, or from her tongue. These things are too well known to require repetition. And do you ask for fortitude, energy, and perseverance? Then look at woman under suffering, reverse of fortune, and affliction, when the strength and power of man have sunk to the lowest ebb, when his mind is overwhelmed by the dark waters of despair. She, like the tender ivy plant bent yet unbroken by the storms of life, not only upholds her own hopeful courage, but clings around the tempest-fallen oak, to speak hope to his faltering spirit, and shelter him from the returning blast of the storm.[37]

3.
New York State Legislature's Select Committees'
February 20, 1854, response to a petition signed by
5,931 men and women, calling for the
"just and equal rights of women"

Mr. Burnett: I hope the House will not act at all on this subject without due consideration. I hope before even this motion is put, gentlemen will be allowed to reflect upon the important question whether these individuals deserve any consideration at the hands of the Legislature. Whatever may be their pretensions or their sincerity, they do not appear to be satisfied with having unsexed themselves, but they desire to unsex every female in the land, and to set the whole community ablaze with unhallowed fire. I trust, sir, the House may deliberate before we suffer them to cast this firebrand into our midst. (Here was heard a "hiss" from some part of the chamber). True, as yet, there is nothing officially before us, but it is well known that the object of these unsexed women is to overthrow the most sacred of our institutions, to set at defiance the Divine law which declares man and wife to be one, and establish on its ruins what will be in fact and in principle but a species of legalized adultery. That this is their real object, however they may attempt to disguise it, is well known to every one who has looked, not perhaps at the intentions of all who take part in it, but at the practical and inevitable result of the movement.

It is, therefore, a matter of duty, a duty to ourselves, to our consciences, to our constituents, and to God, who is the source of all law and of all obligations, to reflect long and deliberatively before we shall even seem to countenance a movement so unholy as this. The Spartan mothers asked no such immunities as are asked for by these women. The Roman mothers were content to occupy their legitimate spheres; and our own mothers, who possessed more than Spartan or Roman virtue, asked for no repudiation of the duties, obligations, or sacred relations of the marital rite.

Are we, sir, to give the least countenance to claims so preposterous, disgraceful, and criminal as are embodied in this address? Are we to put the stamp of truth upon the libel here set forth, that men and women, in the matrimonial relation, are to be equal? We know that God created man as the representative of the race; that after his creation, his Creator took from his side the material for woman's creation; and that, by the institution of matrimony, woman was restored to the side of man, and became one flesh and one being, he being the head. But this law of God and creation is spurned by these women who present themselves here as the exponents of the wishes of our mothers, wives, and daughters. They ask no such exponents, and they repel their sacrilegious doctrines.

But again, sir, our old views of matrimony were, that it was a holy rite, having holy relations based on mutual love and confidence; and that while woman gave herself up to man, to his care, protection, and love, man also surrendered something in exchange for this confidence and love. He placed his happiness and his honor, all that belongs to him of human hopes and of human happiness, in the keeping of the being he received in the sacred relationship of wife. I say, sir, that this ordinance, sought to be practically overthrown by these persons, was established by God Himself; and was based on the mutual love and confidence of husband and wife. But we are now asked to have this ordinance based on jealousy and distrust; and, as in Italy, so in this country, should this mischievous scheme be carried out to its legitimate results, we, instead of reposing safe confidence against assaults upon our honor in the love and affection of our wives, shall find ourselves obliged to close the approaches to those assaults by the padlock. (The "hiss" was here repeated).

Mr. Lozier: Mr. Speaker, twice I have heard a hiss from the lobby. I protest against the toleration of such an insult to any member of this House, and call for proper action in view of it.

The Speaker: The chair observed the interruption, and was endeavoring to discover its source, but has been unable to do so. If, however, its author can be recognized, the chair will immediately order the person to the bar of the House.[38]

. . . The motion for the Select Committee prevailed, ayes, 84; the Committee appointed, and Mr. Wood excused from serving.

REPORT OF THE SELECT COMMITTEE.
In Assembly, Monday, *March 27, 1854.*

. . . Your Committee are well aware that the matters submitted to them have been, and still are, the subject of ridicule and jest; but they are also aware that ridicule and jest never yet effectually put down either truth or error; and that the development of our times and the progression of our age is such, that many thoughts laughed at to-day as wild vagaries, are to-morrow recorded as developed principles or embodied as experimental facts.

A higher power than that from which emanates legislative enactments has given forth the mandate that man and woman shall not be equal; that there shall be inequalities by which each in their own appropriate sphere shall have precedence to the other; and each alike shall be superior or inferior as they well or ill act the part assigned them. Both alike are the subjects of Government, equally entitled to its protection; and civil power must, in its enactments, recognize this inequality. We can not obliterate it if we would, and legal inequalities must follow.

. . . Your Committee will not attempt to prescribe, or, rather, they will not attempt to define the province and peculiar sphere which a power that we can not overrule has prescribed for the different sexes. Every well-regulated home and household in the land affords an example illustrative of what is woman's proper sphere, as also that of man. Government has its miniature as well as its foundation in the homes of our country; and as in governments there must be some recognized head to control and direct, so must there also be a controlling and directing power in every smaller association; there must be some one to act and to be acted with as the embodiment of the persons associated. In the formation of governments, the manner in which the common interest shall be embodied and represented is a matter of conventional arrangement; but in the family an influence more potent than that of contracts and conventionalities, and which everywhere underlies humanity, has indicated that the husband shall fill the necessity which exists for a head. Dissension and distraction quickly arise when this necessity is not answered. The harmony of life, the real interest of both husband and wife, and of all dependent upon them, require it. In obedience to that requirement and necessity, the husband is the head—the representative of the family.

. . . Your Committee can not regard marriage as a *mere contract*, but as something above and beyond; something more binding than records, more solemn than specialties; and the person who reasons as to the relations of husband and wife as upon an ordinary contract, in their opinion commits a fatal error at the outset; and your Committee can not recommend any action based on such a theory.

As society progresses new wants are felt, new facts and combinations are presented which constantly call for more or less of addition to the body of our laws, and often for innovations upon customs so old that "the memory of man runneth not to the contrary thereof." The marriage relation, in common with everything else, has felt the effects of this progress, and from time to time been the subject of legislative action. And while your Committee report adversely to the prayer of the petitions referred to them, they believe that the time has come when certain alterations and amendments are, by common consent, admitted as proper and necessary.

Your Committee recommend that the assent of the mother, if she be living, be made necessary to the validity of any disposition which the father may make of her child by the way of the appointment of guardian or of apprenticeship. The consent of the wife is now necessary to a deed of real estate in order to bar her contingent interest therein; and there are certainly far more powerful reasons why her consent should be necessary to the conveyance or transfer of her own offspring to the care, teaching, and control of another.

When the husband from any cause neglects to provide for the support and education of his family, the wife should have the right to collect and receive her own earnings and the earnings of her minor children, and apply them to the support and education of the family free from the control of the husband, or any person claiming the same through him.

There are many other rules of law applicable to the relation of husband and wife which, in occasional cases, bear hard upon the one or the other, but your Committee do not deem it wise that a new arrangement of our laws of domestic relations should be attempted to obviate such cases; they always have and always will arise out of every subject of legal regulation.

There is much of wisdom (which may well be applied to this and many other subjects) in the quaint remark of an English lawyer, philosopher, and statesman, that "it were well that men in their innovations would follow the example of time, which innovateth greatly but quietly, and by degrees scarcely to be perceived. It is good also in states not to try experiments, except the necessity be urgent and the utility evident; and well to beware that it be the reformation that draweth on the change, and not the desire of change that pretendeth the reformation."

In conclusion, your Committee recommend that the prayer of the petitioners be denied; and they ask leave to introduce a bill corresponding with the suggestions hereinbefore contained.[39]

4.
Lucy Stone's comments at the 1852 National Woman's Rights Convention regarding taxation

It is the duty of woman to resist taxation as long as she is not represented. It may involve the loss of friends as it surely will the loss of property. But let them all go; friends, house, garden spot, and all. The principle at issue requires the sacrifice. Resist, let the case be tried in the courts; be your own lawyers; base your cause on the admitted self-evident truth, that taxation and representation are inseparable. One such resistance, by the agitation that will grow out of it, will do more to set this question right than all the conventions in the world. There are $15,000,000 of taxable property owned by women of Boston who have no voice either in the use or imposition of the tax.[40]

5.
The New York Tribune's reporting on Harriot Hunt's tax protest, and her letter to the Boston authorities, November 16, 1853

WOMAN AND TAXATION. The following Protest of Dr. HARRIET [sic] K. HUNT, of Boston, against the repeated taxation of property by a State which denies her all Political

Franchises, will of course be answered by Conservatism with a sneer. But how else *could* it be answered?

> To the Authorities of the City of Boston, (Mass.) and the Citizens generally.
>
> Harriet [*sic*] K. Hunt, Physician, a native and permanent resident of the City of Boston, and for many years a tax-payer therein, in making payment of her taxes for the coming year, protests *again* against the injustice of levying taxes without a *right* of representation. The present system of taxation is a serious wrong, a violation of justice as well as a violation of republicanism. If of all the women in Massachusetts, who are citizens only *ten* felt this wrong, those *ten* should be redressed; but when nearly two thousand petitioners presented themselves, through their *signatures*, to your Constitutional Convention on this vital question, it was *"inexpedient"* for the Convention to take any action in relation thereto. What woman of thought can consent to be governed (for that is the argument) under the present subversive party elements, that bring into office those who are to represent her?
>
> No reasonable or satisfactory answer has ever been given to woman on this subject, only that *man* represented her, through fathers, brothers, husbands and sons. Your remonstrant has no such *representation*, and there are many in like situation. "State, county and city tax," the former the expense of the Constitutional Convention, in which she had no voice, (but petition,) and how farcical that power of petition, when she can neither express *assent* or *dissent* to its doings, but be unjustly taxed, and like an idiot, lunatic, or infant, be *compelled* to meet it. Of the "city tax" one word. The inequality and injustice of our Public School System, in having no High School for Girls, while our boys have both a Latin and High School, was spoken of in her last protest, and our privileged right of petition tested by the voice of at least 2,700, for such High School. This petition was duly presented last spring, and whatever action may have taken place in the School Committee, the public are ignorant; no High School for Girls has yet been organized.
>
> With these views which might now be fully carried out, with

the increase of her tax bill, in consequence of *your* Constitutional Convention, which can result in no permanent good, since the great central element of *Justice*, was by the Committee on our petitions winked into "*expediency,*" and no minority report, nor any act of the Convention, vindicated or even recognized the right of Woman, on the *real basis of representation*, *Humanity*.

Thus dissatisfied with city expenditures, the inequality of public school education, (*sexualizing education*,) your remonstrant pays her taxes *compulsorily*, instead of *cheerfully*, feeling within *her* that element of patriotism which inspired *her*, as well as *your* forefathers, in the utterance of that deep, full, and clear sentiment: "Taxation without *representation* is tyranny." This is respectfully submitted.

HARRIET [*sic*] K. HUNT.

No. 52 Green St., Boston, Nov. 5, 1853[41]

6.

Elizabeth Cady Stanton on "the Bloomer costume" in her "Reminiscences," published in *History of Woman Suffrage*, volume I, 1881

Quite an agitation occurred in 1852, on woman's costume. In demanding a place in the world of work, the unfitness of her dress seemed to some, an insurmountable obstacle. How can you, it was said, ever compete with man for equal place and pay, with garments of such frail fabrics and so cumbrously fashioned, and how can you ever hope to enjoy the same health and vigor with man, so long as the waist is pressed into the smallest compass, pounds of clothing hung on the hips, the limbs cramped with skirts, and with high heels the whole woman thrown out of her true equilibrium. Wise men, physicians, and sensible women, made their appeals, year after year; physiologists lectured on the subject; the press commented, until it seemed as if there were a serious demand for some decided steps, in the direction of a rational costume for women. The most casual observer could see how many pleasures young girls were continually sacrificing to their dress: In walking, running, rowing, skating, dancing, going up and down stairs, climbing trees and fences, the airy fabrics and flowing skirts were a continual impediment and vexation. We can not estimate how large a share of the ill-health and temper among women is the result of the crippling, cribbing influence of her costume. Fathers, husbands, and brothers, all joined in protest against the small waist, and stiff distended petticoats, which were always themes for unbounded ridicule. But no sooner did a few brave conscientious women adopt the bifurcated costume, an imitation in part of the Turkish style, than the press at once turned its guns on "The Bloomer," and the same fathers, husbands, and brothers, with streaming eyes and pathetic tones, conjured the women of their households to cling to the prevailing fashions. The object of those who donned the new attire, was primarily health and freedom; but as the daughter of Gerrit Smith introduced it just at the time of the early conventions, it was supposed to be an inherent element in the demand for political equality. As some of those who advocated the right of suffrage wore the dress, and had been identified with all the unpopular reforms, in the reports of our conventions, the press rung the changes on "strong-minded," "Bloomer," "free love," "easy divorce," "amalgamation." I wore the dress two years and found it a great blessing. What a sense of liberty I felt, in running up and down stairs with my hands free to carry whatsoever I would, to trip through the rain or snow with no skirts to hold or brush, ready at any moment to climb a hill top to see the sun go down, or the moon rise, with no ruffles or trails to be limped by the dew, or soiled by the grass. What an emancipation from little petty vexatious trammels and annoyances every hour of the day. Yet such is the tyranny of custom, that to escape constant observation, criticism, ridicule, persecution, mobs, one after another gladly went back to the old slavery and sacrificed freedom to repose. I have never wondered since that the Chinese women allow their daughters' feet to be encased in iron shoes, nor that the Hindoo widows walk calmly to the funeral pyre. I suppose no act of my life ever gave my cousin, Gerrit Smith, such deep sorrow, as my abandonment of the "Bloomer costume." He published an open letter to me on the subject, and when his daughter, Mrs. Miller, three years after, followed my example, he felt that women had so little courage and persistence, that for a time he almost despaired of the success of the suffrage movement; of such vital consequence in woman's mental and physical development did he feel the dress to be.

Gerrit Smith, Samuel J. May, James C. Jackson, and Charles Dudley Miller sustained the women who led in this reform unflinchingly, during the trying experiment. Let the names of those who made this protest be remembered. We knew the Bloomer costume never could be generally becoming, as it required a perfection of form, limbs, and feet, such as few possessed, and we who wore it also knew that it was not artistic. Though the martyrdom proved too much for us who had so many other measures to press on the public conscience, yet no experiment is lost, however evanescent, that rouses thought to the injurious consequences of the present style of dress, sacrificing to its absurdities so many of the most promising girls of this generation.[42]

7.

Public letter by Gerrit Smith to Elizabeth Cady Stanton criticizing her for giving up the reform dress, dated December 1, 1855, referenced in "Reminiscences"

Peterboro, *December 1, 1855.*

Elizabeth C. Stanton.—*My Dear Friend:*—The "Woman's Rights Movement" has deeply interested your generous heart, and you have ever been ready to serve it with your vigorous understanding. It is, therefore, at the risk of appearing somewhat unkind and uncivil, that I give my honest answer to your question. You would know why I have so little faith in this movement. I reply, that it is not in the proper hands; and that the proper hands are not yet to be found. The present age, although in advance of any former age, is, nevertheless, very far from being sufficiently under the sway of reason to take up the cause of woman, and carry it forward to success. A much stronger and much more widely diffused common sense than has character-ized any of the generations, must play its mightiest artillery upon the stupendous piles of nonsense, which tradition and chivalry and a misinterpreted and superstitious Christianity have reared in the way of this cause, ere woman can have the prospect of the recognition of her rights and of her confessed equality with man.

The object of the "Woman's Rights Movement" is nothing less than to recover the rights of woman—nothing less than to achieve her independence. She is now the dependent of man; and, instead of rights, she has but privileges—the mere conces-sions (always revocable and always uncertain) of the other sex to her sex. I say nothing against this object. It is as proper as it is great; and until it is realized, woman can not be half herself, nor can man be half himself. I rejoice in this object; and my sorrow in, that they, who are intent upon it, are not capable of adjusting themselves to it—not high-souled enough to consent to those changes and sacrifices in themselves, in their positions and rela-tions, essential to the attainment of this vital object.

What if a nation in the heart of Europe were to adopt, and uniformly adhere to, the practice of cutting off one of the hands of all their new-born children? It would from this cause be re-duced to poverty, to helpless dependence upon the charity of sur-rounding nations, and to just such a measure of privileges as they might see fit to allow it, in exchange for its forfeited rights. Very great, indeed, would be the folly of this strange nation. But a still greater folly would it be guilty of, should it, notwithstand-ing this voluntary mutilation, claim all the wealth, and all the rights, and all the respect, and all the independence which it en-joyed before it entered upon this systematic mutilation.

Now, this twofold folly of this one-hand nation illustrates the similar twofold folly of some women. Voluntarily wearing, in common with their sex, a dress which imprisons and cripples them, they, nevertheless, follow up this absurdity with the greater one of coveting and demanding a social position no less full of admitted rights, and a relation to the other sex no less full of independence, than such position and relation would naturally and necessarily have been, had they scorned a dress which leaves them less than half their personal power of self-subsistence and usefulness. I admit that the mass of women are not chargeable with this latter absurdity of cherishing aspirations and urging claims so wholly and so glaringly at war with this voluntary imprisonment and this self-degradation. They are content in their helplessness and poverty and destitution of rights. Nay, they are so deeply deluded as to believe that all this belongs to their natural and unavoidable lot. But the handful of women of whom I am here complaining—the woman's rights women—persevere just as blindly and stubbornly as do other women, in wearing a dress that both marks and makes their impotence, and yet, O amazing inconsistency! they are ashamed of their dependence, and remonstrate against its injustice. They claim that the fullest measure of rights and independence and dignity shall be accorded to them, and yet they refuse to place themselves in circumstances corresponding with their claim. They demand as much for themselves as is acknowledged to be due to men, and yet they refuse to pay the necessary, the never-to-be-avoided price of what they demand—the price which men have to pay for it.

I admit that the dress of woman is not the primal cause of her helplessness and degradation. That cause is to be found in the false doctrines and sentiments of which the dress is the outgrowth and symbol. On the other hand, however, these doctrines and sentiments would never have become the huge bundle they now are, and they would probably have all languished, and perhaps all expired, but for the dress. For, as in many other instances, so in this, and emphatically so in this, the cause is made more efficient by the reflex influence of the effect. Let woman give up the irrational modes of clothing her person, and these doctrines and sentiments would be deprived of their most vital aliment by being deprived of their most natural expression. In no other practical forms of folly to which they might betake themselves, could they operate so vigorously and be so invigorated by their operation.

Were woman to throw off the dress, which, in the eye of

chivalry and gallantry, is so well adapted to womanly graceful-ness and womanly helplessness, and to put on a dress that would leave her free to work her own way through the world, I see not but that chivalry and gallantry would nearly or quite die out. No longer would she present herself to man, now in the bewitching character of a plaything, a doll, an idol, and now in the degraded character of his servant. But he would confess her transmutation into his equal; and, therefore, all occasion for the display of chivalry and gallantry toward her on the one hand, and tyranny on the other, would have passed away. Only let woman attire her person fitly for the whole battle of life—that great and often rough battle, which she is as much bound to fight as man is, and the common sense expressed in the change will put to flight all the nonsensical fancies about her superiority to man, and all the nonsensical fancies about her inferiority to him. No more will then be heard of her being made of a finer material than man is made of; and, on the contrary, no more will then be heard of her being but the complement of man, and of its taking both a man and a woman (the woman, of course, but a small part of it) to make up a unit. No more will it then be said that there is sex in mind—an original sexual difference in intellect. What a pity that so many of our noblest women make this foolish admission! It is made by the great majority of the women who plead the cause of woman.

I am amazed that the intelligent women engaged in the "Woman's Rights Movement," see not the relation between their dress and the oppressive evils which they are striving to throw off. I am amazed that they do not see that their dress is indis-pensable to keep in countenance the policy and purposes out of which those evils grow. I hazard nothing in saying, that the rela-tion between the dress and degradation of an American woman, is as vital as between the cramped foot and degradation of a Chinese woman; as vital as between the uses of the inmate of the harem and the apparel and training provided for her. Moreover, I hazard nothing in saying, that an American woman will never have made her most effectual, nor, indeed, any serviceable pro-test against the treatment of her sex in China, or by the lords of the harem, so long as she consents to have her own person clothed in ways so repugnant to reason and religion, and grateful only to a vitiated taste, be it in her own or in the other sex.

Women are holding their meetings; and with great ability do they urge their claim to the rights of property and suffrage. But, as in the case of the colored man, the great needed change is in himself, so, also, in the case of woman, the great needed change is in herself. Of what comparative avail would be her exercise of the right of suffrage, if she is still to remain the victim of her present false notions of herself and of her relations to the other sex?—false notions so emphatically represented and perpetuated by her dress? Moreover, to concede to her the rights of property would be to benefit her comparatively little, unless she shall resolve to break out from her clothes-prison, and to undertake right earnestly, as right earnestly as a man, to get property. Solomon says: "The destruction of the poor is their poverty." The adage that knowledge is power, is often repeated; and there are, indeed, many instances to verify it. Nevertheless, as a general proposition, it is a thousandfold more emphatically true that property is power. Knowledge helps to get property, but property is the power. That the slaves are a helpless prey, is chiefly because they are so poor and their masters so rich. The masses almost everywhere are well-nigh powerless, because almost everywhere they are poor. How long will they consent to be poor? Just so long as they shall consent to be robbed of their God-given right to the soil. That women are helpless is no wonder, so long as women are paupers.

As long as woman shall be silly enough to learn her lessons in the schools of gallantry and chivalry, so long will it be the height of her ambition to be a graceful and amiable burden upon the other sex. But as soon as she shall consent to place herself under the instructions of reason and common sense, and to discard, as wholly imaginary, those differences between the nature of man and the nature of woman, out of which have grown innumerable nonsensical doctrines and notions, and all sorts of namby pamby sentiments, so soon will she find that, to no greater extent than men are dependent on each other, are women to foster the idea of their dependence on men. Then, and not till then, will women learn that, to be useful and happy, and to accomplish the high purposes of their being, they must, no less emphatically than men, stand upon their own feet, and work with own hands, and bear the burdens of life with their own strength, and brave its storms with their own resoluteness.

The next "Woman's Rights Convention" will, I take it for granted, differ but little from its predecessors. It will abound in righteous demands and noble sentiments, but not in the evidence that they who enunciate these demands and sentiments are prepared to put themselves in harmony with what they conceive and demand. In a word, for the lack of such preparation and of the deep earnestness, which alone can prompt to such preparation, it will be, as has been every other Woman's Rights Convention, a failure. Could I see it made up of women whose dress would indicate their translation from cowardice to courage; from slavery to freedom; from the kingdom of fancy and fashion and foolery to the kingdom of reason and righteousness, then would I hope for the elevation of woman, aye, and of man too, as perhaps I have never yet hoped. What should be the parts and particulars of such dress, I am incapable of saying. Whilst the "Bloomer dress" is unspeakably better than the common dress, it nevertheless affords not half that freedom of the person which woman is entitled and bound to enjoy. I add, on this point, that however much the dresses of the sexes should resemble each other, decency and virtue and other considerations require that they should be obviously distinguishable from each other.

I am not unaware that such views as I have expressed in this letter will be regarded as serving to break down the characteristic delicacy of woman. I frankly admit that I would have it broken down; and that I would have the artificial and conventional, the nonsensical and pernicious thing give place to the natural delicacy which would be common to both sexes. As the delicacy, which is made peculiar to one of the sexes, is unnatural, and, therefore, false, this, which would be common to both, would be natural, and, therefore, true. I would have no characteristic delicacy of woman, and no characteristic coarseness of man. On the contrary, believing man and woman to have the same nature, and to be therefore under obligation to have the same character, I would subject them to a common standard of morals and manners. The delicacy of man should be no less shrinking than that of woman, and the bravery of woman should be one with the bravery of man. Then would there be a public sentiment very unlike that which now requires the sexes to differ in character, and which, therefore, holds them amenable to different codes—codes that, in their partiality to man, allow him to commit high crimes, and that, in their cruelty to woman, make the bare suspicion of such crimes on her part the justification of her hopeless degradation and ruin.

They who advocate that radical change in her dress which common sense calls for, are infidels in the eyes of such as subscribe to this interpretation of the Bible. For if the Bible teaches that the Heaven-ordained condition of woman is so subordinate and her Heaven-ordained character so mean, then they are infidels who would have her cast aside a dress so becoming that character and condition, and have her put on a dress so entirely at war with her humble nature, as to indicate her conscious equality with man, and her purpose to assert, achieve, and maintain her independence. Alas, how misapprehended are the true objects and true uses of the Bible! That blessed book is given to us, not so much that we may be taught by it what to do, as that we may be urged by its solemn and fearful commands and won by its melting entreaties, to do what we already know we should do. Such, indeed, is the greatest value of its recorded fact that Jesus Christ died to save us from our sins. We already know that we should repent of our sins and put them away; and it is this fact which furnishes our strongest possible motive for doing so. But men run to the Bible professedly to be taught their duty in matters where their very instincts—where the laws, written in large, unmistakable, ineffaceable letters upon the very foundations of their being—teach them their duty. I say *professedly*, for generally it is only so. They run to the Bible, not to learn the truth, but to make the Bible the minister to folly and sin. They run from themselves to the Bible, because they can more easily succeed in twisting its records into the service of their guilty passions and guilty purposes than they can their inflexible convictions. They run to the Bible for a paramount authority that shall override and supplant these uncomfortable convictions. They run from the teachings of their nature and the remonstrances of their consciences to find something more palatable. Hence, we find the rum-drinker, and slaveholder, and polygamist, and other criminals going to the Bible. They go to it for the very purpose of justifying their known sins. But not only may we not go to the Bible to justify what we ourselves have already condemned, but we must not take to the judicature of that book, as an open question, any of the wrongs against which nature and common sense cry out—any of the wrongs which nature and common sense call on us to condemn.

So fraught with evil, and ruinous evil, is this practice, on the part of the Church as well as the world, of inquiring the judgment of the Bible in regard to sins, which the natural and universal conscience condemns, but which the inquirer means to persist in, if only he can get the Bible to testify against his conscience and in favor of his sins; so baleful, I say, is this practice, as to drive me to the conclusion that the Bible can not continue to be a blessing to mankind in spite of it. The practice, in its present wide and well-nigh universal extent, turns the heavenly volume into a curse. Owing to this practice, the Bible is, this day, a hindrance rather than a help to civilization.

But if woman is of the same nature and same dignity with man, and if as much and as varied labor is needed to supply her wants as to supply the wants of man, and if for her to be, as she so emphatically is, poor and destitute and dependent, is as fatal to her happiness and usefulness and to the fulfillment of the high purposes of her existence, as the like circumstances would be to the honor and welfare of man, why then put her in a dress which compels her to be a pauper—a pauper, whether in ribbons or rags? Why, I ask, put her in a dress suited only to those occasional and brief moods, in which man regards her as his darling, his idol, and his angel; or to that general state of his mind in which he looks upon her as his servant, and with feelings certainly much nearer contempt than adoration. Strive as you will to elevate woman, nevertheless the disabilities and degradation of this dress, together with that large group of false views of the uses of her being and of her relations to man, symbolized and perpetuated, as I have already said, by this dress, will make your striving vain.

Woman must first fight against herself—against personal and mental habits so deep-rooted and controlling, and so seemingly inseparable from herself, as to be mistaken for her very nature. And when she has succeeded there, an easy victory will follow. But where shall be the battle-ground for this indispensable self-conquest? She will laugh at my answer when I tell her, that her dress, aye, her dress, must be that battle-ground. What! no wider, no sublimer field than this to reap her glories in! My further answer is, that if she shall reap them anywhere, she must first reap them there. I add, that her triumph there will be her triumph everywhere; and that her failure there will be her failure everywhere.

Affectionately yours,
Gerrit Smith.[43]

8.
Public letter by Elizabeth Cady Stanton to Gerrit Smith as counterargument, December 21, 1855

My Dear Cousin:—Your letter on the "Woman's Right Movement" I have thoroughly read and considered. I thank you, in the name of woman, for having said what you have on so many vital points. You have spoken well for a man whose convictions on this subject are the result of reason and observation; but they alone whose souls are fired through personal experience and suffering can set forth the height and depth, the source and center of the degradation of women; they alone can feel a steadfast faith in their own native energy and power to accomplish a final triumph over all adverse surroundings, a speedy and complete success. You say you have but little faith in this reform, because the changes we propose are so great, so radical, so comprehensive; whilst they who have commenced the work are so puny, feeble, and undeveloped. The mass of women are developed at least to the point of discontent, and that, in the dawn of this nation, was considered a most dangerous point in the British Parliament, and is now deemed equally so on a Southern plantation. In the human soul, the steps between discontent and action are few and short indeed. You, who suppose the mass of women contented, know but little of the silent indignation, the deep and settled disgust with which they contemplate our present social arrangements. You claim to believe that in every sense, thought, and feeling, man and woman are the same. Well, now, suppose yourself a woman. You are educated up to that point where one feels a deep interest in the welfare of her country, and in all the great questions of the day, in both Church and State; yet you have no voice in either. Little men, with little brains, may pour forth their little sentiments by the hour, in the forum and the sacred desk, but public sentiment and the religion of our day teach us that silence is most becoming in woman. So to solitude you betake yourself, and read for your consolation the thoughts of dead men; but from the Bible down to Mother Goose's Melodies, how much complacency, think you, you would feel in your womanhood? The philosopher, the poet, and the saint, all combine to make the name of woman synonymous with either fool or devil. Every passion of the human soul, which in manhood becomes so grand and glorious in its results, is fatal to womankind. Ambition makes a Lady Macbeth; love, an Ophelia; none but those brainless things, without will or passion, are ever permitted to come to a good end. What measure of content could you draw from the literature of the past?

Again, suppose yourself the wife of a confirmed drunkard. You behold your earthly possessions all passing away; your heart is made desolate; it has ceased to pulsate with either love, or hope, or joy. Your house is sold over your head, and with it every article of comfort and decency; your children gather round you, one by one, each newcomer clothed in rags and crowned with shame; is it with gladness you now welcome the embrace of that beastly husband, feel his fevered breath upon your cheek, and inhale the disgusting odor of his tobacco and rum? Would not your whole soul revolt from such an union? So do the forty thousand drunkards' wives now in this State. They, too, are all discontented, and but for the pressure of law and gospel would speedily sunder all these unholy ties. Yes, sir, there are women, pure and virtuous and noble as yourself, spending every day of all the years of their existence in the most intimate association with infamous men, kept so by that monstrous and unnatural artifice, baptized by the sacred name of marriage. I might take you through many, many phases of woman's life, into those sacred relations of which we speak not in our conventions, where woman feels her deepest wrongs, where in blank despair she drags out days, and weeks, and months, and years of silent agony. I might paint you pictures of real life so vivid as to force from you the agonized exclamation, How can women endure such things!

We who have spoken out, have declared our rights, political and civil; but the entire revolution about to dawn upon us by the acknowledgment of woman's social equality, has been seen and felt but by the few. The rights, to vote, to hold property, to speak in public, are all-important; but there are great social rights, before which all others sink into utter insignificance. The cause of woman is, as you admit, a broader and a deeper one than any with which you compare it; and this, to me, is the very reason why it must succeed. It is not a question of meats and drinks, of money and lands, but of human rights—the sacred right of a woman to her own person, to all her God-given powers of body and soul. Did it ever enter into the mind of man that woman too had an inalienable right to life, liberty, and the pursuit of her individual happiness? Did he ever take in the idea that to the mother of the race, and to her alone, belonged the right to say when a new being should be brought into the world? Has he, in the gratification of his blind passions, ever paused to think whether it was with joy and gladness that she gave up ten or twenty years of the heyday of her existence to all the cares and sufferings of excessive maternity? Our present laws, our religious teachings, our social customs on the whole question of marriage and divorce, are most degrading to woman; and so long as man continues to think and write, to speak and act, as if maternity was the one and sole object of a woman's existence—so long as children are conceived in weariness and disgust—you must not look for high-toned men and women capable of accomplishing any great and noble achievement. But when woman shall stand on an even pedestal with man—when they shall be bound together, not by withes of law and gospel, but in holy unity and love, then, and not till then, shall our efforts at minor reforms be crowned with complete success. Here, in my opinion, is the starting-point; here is the battle-ground where our independence must be fought and won. A true marriage relation has far more to do with the elevation of woman than the style and cut of her dress. Dress is a matter of taste, of fashion; it is changeable, transient, and may be doffed or donned at the will of the individual; but institutions, supported by laws, can be overturned but by revolution. We have no reason to hope that pantaloons would do more for us than they have done for man himself. The negro slave enjoys the most unlimited freedom in his attire, not surpassed even by the fashions of Eden in its palmiest days; yet in spite of his dress, and his manhood, too, he is a slave still. Was the old Roman in his toga less of a man than he now is in swallow-tail and tights? Did the flowing robes of Christ Himself render His life less grand and beautiful? In regard to dress, where you claim to be so radical, you are far from consistent.

Believing, as you do, in the identity of the sexes, that all the difference we see in tastes, in character, is entirely the result of education—that "man is woman and woman is man"—why keep up these distinctions in dress? Surely, whatever dress is convenient for one sex must be for the other also. Whatever is necessary for the perfect and full development of man's physical being, must be equally so for woman. I fully agree with you that woman is terribly cramped and crippled in her present style of dress. I have not one word to utter in its defense; but to me, it seems that if she would enjoy entire freedom, she should dress just like man. Why proclaim our sex on the house-tops, seeing that it is a badge of degradation, and deprives us of so many rights and privileges wherever we go? Disguised as a man, the distinguished French woman, "George Sand," has been able to see life in Paris, and has spoken in political meetings with great applause, as no woman could have done. In male attire, we could travel by land or sea; go through all the streets and lanes of our cities and towns by night and day, without a protector; get seven hundred dollars a year for teaching, instead of three, and ten dollars for making a coat, instead of two or three, as we now do. All this we could do without fear of insult, or the least sacrifice of decency or virtue. If nature has not made the sex so clearly defined as to be seen through any disguise, why should we make the difference so striking? Depend upon it, when men and women in their every-day life see and think less of sex and more of mind, we shall all lead far purer and higher lives.

Your letter, my noble cousin, must have been written in a most desponding mood, as all the great reforms of the day seem to you on the verge of failure. What are the experiences of days and months and years in the lifetime of a mighty nation? Can one man in his brief hour hope to see the beginning and end of any reform? When you compare the public sentiment and social customs of our day with what they were fifty years ago, how can you despair of the temperance cause? With a Maine Law and divorce for drunkenness, the rum-seller and drunkard must soon come to terms. Let woman's motto be, "No union with Drunkards," and she will soon bring this long and well-fought battle to a triumphant close.

Neither should you despair of the anti-slavery cause; with its martyrs, its runaway slaves, its legal decisions in almost every paper you take up, the topic of debate in our national councils, our political meetings, and our literature, it seems as if the nation were all alive on this question. True, four millions of slaves groan in their chains still, but every man in this nation has a higher idea of individual rights than he had twenty years ago.

As to the cause of woman, I see no signs of failure. We already have a property law, which in its legitimate effects must elevate the *femme covert* into a living, breathing woman, a wife into a property-holder, who can make contracts, buy and sell. In a few years we shall see how well it works. It needs but little forethought to perceive that in due time these large property-holders must be represented in the Government; and when the mass of women see that there is some hope of becoming voters and lawmakers, they will take to their rights as naturally as the negro to his heels when he is sure of success. Their present seeming content is very much like Sambo's on the plantation. If you truly believe that man is woman, and woman is man; if you believe that all the burning indignation that fires your soul at the sight of injustice and oppression, if suffered in your own person, would nerve you to a life-long struggle for liberty and independence, then know that what you feel, I feel too, and what I feel the mass of women feel also. Judge by yourself, then, how long the women of this nation will consent to be deprived of their social, civil, and political rights; but talk not to us of failure. Talk not to us of chivalry, that died long ago. Where do you see it? No gallant knight presents himself at the bar of justice to pay the penalty of our crimes. We suffer in our own persons, on the gallows, and in prison walls. From Blackstone down to Kent, there is no display of gallantry in your written codes. In social life, true, a man in love will jump to pick up a glove or bouquet for a silly girl of sixteen, whilst at home he will permit his aged mother to carry pails of water and armfuls of wood, or his wife to lug a twenty-pound baby, hour after hour, without ever offering to relieve her. I have seen a great many men priding themselves on their good breeding—gentlemen, born and educated—who never manifest one iota of spontaneous gallantry toward the women of their own household.

Divines may preach thanksgiving sermons on the poetry of the arm-chair and the cradle; but when they lay down their newspapers, or leave their beds a cold night to attend to the wants of either, I shall begin to look for the golden age of chivalry once more. If a short dress is to make the men less gallant than they now are, I beg the women at our next convention to add at least two yards more to every skirt they wear. And you mock us with dependence, too. Do not the majority of women in every town support themselves, and very many their husbands, too? What father of a family, at the loss of his wife, has ever been able to meet his responsibilities as woman has done? When the mother dies the house is made desolate, the children are forsaken—scattered to the four winds of heaven—to the care of any one who chooses to take them. Go to those aged widows who have reared large families of children, unaided and alone, who have kept them all together under one roof, watched and nursed them in health and sickness through all their infant years, clothed and educated them, and made them all respectable men and women, ask them on whom they depended. They will tell you on their own hands, and on that never-dying, never-failing love, that a mother's heart alone can know. It is into hands like these—to these who have calmly met the terrible emergencies of life—who, without the inspiration of glory, or fame, or applause, through long years have faithfully and bravely performed their work, self-sustained and cheered, that we commit our cause. We need not wait for one more generation to pass away, to find a race of women worthy to assert the humanity of women, and that is all we claim to do.

Affectionately yours,
Elizabeth Cady Stanton. [44]

9.
Dress reformers criticize suffragists for abandoning the movement in a *New York Tribune* article,
January 20, 1857

A WORD FOR BACKSLIDERS. *The Woman's Advocate* takes us to task for our strictures on the course pursued by Mrs. Blackwell [Lucy Stone], Miss Anthony, Mrs. Stanton, and others, for renouncing the Reform Dress. The writer indites for our benefit a long homily upon "acting from principle," which sounds very like hundreds of others of a like nature that have been circulated through the conservative press for years past, and which amounts simply to this: The writer is fully convinced that there is such a thing as "acting from principle," yet where found, or in what it consists, she seems entirely ignorant. For instance, if a woman is convinced that the physical being of the race is suffering and diseased by fashion's demands, and she turns to a better way of life in the hope of strengthening her weak and prostrate powers, and by her example trusting to lead others in a better path, *The Advocate* sees no "principle" involved, but merely a "matter of convenience...."

> "They are charged with being recreant to principle, and doing great damage to the cause of women generally."

We repeat the charge, for these women said they adopted the Reform Dress from principle; hence, in laying it off, they have proved recreant to principle. They said a change must be made in woman's dress, else she could never accomplish the desired good. They knew there must be pioneers in this cause, and their weak effort at sustaining it speaks but little for their powers to triumph over error, if opposition assails them. It is very heroic to dwell in admiring language over the heroes and martyrs of the past, who have endured persecution for conscience sake, but quite another thing to witness the doings of the present strugglers in the ranks of reform, who are willing to meet persecution for the truth's sake. And an established truth it is that fashion's requirements are dwarfing woman's powers and crushing her physical being. This is well sustained by the evidence of many of our first physicians, and by the acknowledgment of hundreds of sufferers —as any woman knows who is at all acquainted with the weakness and debility under which thousands labor—stimulated, if not wholly caused, by the curse of fashion.

> "They have tried the Bloomer dress to their satisfaction. They adopted it, as they thought, as a matter of 'principle.' They found, after a trial, that it was a question of convenience. It was to strike a balance between the annoyance of long dresses and the annoyance of constant observation, remark and insult for wearing an unusual costume. We do not deny the right of a woman to wear such a dress."

We do not believe they were satisfied the old costume was half as good, or that they were doing right in returning to it, else Lucy Stone Blackwell would not have alluded to the

Reform Dress in such strong terms of approbation as she did at the late convention in New York. It is not merely the annoyance of the long dress which makes us so bitter in our denunciation of it, but the physical curse which it imposes upon our sex, entailing disease, pain and death, and at the same time unfitting her to equally mingle with men in the political, professional and business relations which these ladies mentioned are striving so hard that she may do. No, it is all folly to imagine that she can stand on an equal footing with man, thus cramped, while he enjoys such unfettered freedom. Every one who enters the tilt-ground of reform, which must necessarily be that of change, must make calculations to meet the attendant annoyance, else they should never show sign of battle; but this making a great flourish of arms, and then retiring from the arena at the first onset of the foe, shows a cowardice for which they should blush.[45]

10.
Speech by "Mrs. Branch" on Free Love printed in the *Syracuse Standard*, July 1858

"FREE LOVE." It is no more than fair, after our comments on the speech of Mrs. BRANCH, at the Rutland convention, that we should give her remarks in full, which we do in this day's STANDARD.—Those who feel interested in the subject will find food for digestion in this speech, which contains a bold attack upon the institution of marriage, and a frank avowal of Free Love doctrines. However abhorrent these licentious views may be, no one will question the ability with which they are enunciated by this "strong-minded woman." The *Tribune* correspondent, who furnished a report of the speech, says it was the ablest one made during the Convention.

THE RUTLAND CONVENTION. Free Love Speech of Mrs. Branch. Woman's Rights in a new Aspect.

I am aware that I have chosen almost a forbidden subject; forbidden from the fact that any one that can and *dare* look the marriage question in the face, and openly denounce the marriage institution as the sole cause of woman's degradation and misery, is an object of scorn, of suspicion and opprobrious epithets.—I ask of *that* now, as I did formerly of the church, is it so sacred that it cannot be questioned? Lucy Stone said to me at the recent Woman's Rights Convention held in New York, "The marriage question must and will some day be discussed." I asked, "Why are you not willing that it should be discussed now and here?" She did not think it a proper place; their platform was not a free one; they wished the rights of woman in regard to voting settled then, and there, and *that* would settle all other rights—I asked: "How can she have the right to vote, when she had not even the right to her name in the marriage bonds?" She said: "It is a mistaken idea that woman is obliged to give up her name and take that of her husband by the ceremony. I have not given up mine and no law can compel me to. I call myself Lucy Stone, and shall always."—How would it have been with Mrs. Blackwell if she had kept the fact of the marriage ceremony a secret, and gone to a hotel with the intention of stopping a few days, with Mr. Blackwell signing her name Lucy Stone, would they have been permitted to occupy one room?—What do you suppose would have been the astonishment of the virtuous landlord at such a proceeding, and what would have been his answer? Mrs. Lucy Stone Blackwell, and every one else, knows the act would be sufficient to denounce her in the eyes of society an infamous woman. The marriage ceremony is necessary to keep woman virtuous and respectable, and all intercourse with man, out of its holy rites, renders her an outcast and a thing to be despised. Is it because she is naturally vicious and wicked that bonds are placed upon her? Has she no nature that may not be proscribed and estimated by man law-makers? Has she no inborn right that belongs to herself? As she stands here before the world she has none. She has not even that kind compliment that is paid to man in the Constitution of the United States, "that man is endowed with certain inalienable rights." And to the marriage ceremony I say she is indebted for her wrongs, for her aching heart, her chains, her slavery. Woman must strike the blow if she would be free, and become the equal of man. You speak of her right to labor, her right to teach, her right to vote, and lastly, though not least, her right to get married; but do you say anything about *her right to love when she will, where she will, and whom she will?* Yes, here is a stipulation for her in this resolution.

She is to have an isolated household with an exclusive conjugal love. This is very pretty in sentiment; and Moore beautifully expresses it in his "Fire Worshippers:"

"Oft in my fancy's wanderings
I've wished that little isle had wings,
    And we within its fairy bowers,
Were wafted off to seas unknown,
    Where not a pulse would beat but ours,
And we might *live, love, die* alone;
    Where the bright eyes of angels only
Should come around us to behold,
A Paradise so pure and lonely."[46]

But this will not do for practical life, where man and woman work from ten to eighteen hours out of the twenty-four. The working class are by far the larger class, and the isolated household is the worst place in the world for them. The man comes home to his meals, which are set on the table amid crying children and the sickly, despairing face of his wife; there is no social life. Even the exclusive conjugal love that bound them together in the marriage ceremony has long since settled into the mildest form of friendship. The enthusiasm and ardor, and poetry, and sacredness, are forever destroyed by constant familiarity in the isolated household. Just as woman is isolated and confined within the isolated and confined limits of a home, just so will her off-spring be narrow-minded, bigoted and selfish. Just as she is free in her thoughts, her affections, making her home wherever she chooses, just so will her children be brave and expansive in their ideas, noble and great, and honorable in virtuous deeds, benevolent in heart, and tolerant in all things, however opposite to them, because they feel within that they have not only the perfection, but the imperfections of humanity. . . . Let me draw a picture of the isolated home, and one that came under my own observation. See the woman with a careworn face—long lines of grief have made deep furrows. Her thin hand and shriveled figure; her dejected, weary air; her desponding tones, tell of something that lies heavy at her heart. Surely, never Christ, bearing the great heavy cross up to crucifixion, could feel the deep woe that presses against her soul. "Ah, me!"— comes with a sad sigh as we lay our hand upon her head. "Tell us," we say; and she throws open the inmost recesses of her soul, and tells the story of her life—how she aspired to be great from childhood; how noble thoughts took possession of her; how she loved, and married the object of her love; how dear the first-born of her heart grew to her; how it died, and she clothed herself in the habiliments of woe, and shut out the light of day in her heart, and sat down alone at home, without friends or hope or consolation; how other children came to her, but they did not fill the void—the black veil was drawn down from between her and happiness, and pinned to the soul by the arrow of affliction. There was no sympathy in the world, and she longed to lie down in the grave and rest. She brushed away the tears and hid her hope; hope has died out; we speak of husbands and children; they have no sympathy. "Are you willing," we ventured to ask, "to look for one moment into your own soul?" "I have always tried to do right, but circumstances were against me. My husband has long since ceased to love me, although he presses upon me the necessity of bearing children whenever he pleases. My children are perverse and wayward, and I don't know what to do with them. Some people go right through the world, and always light hearted and happy. I never saw an unhappy day till I was married." "But of yourself, have you never thought of a plan whereby you might be relieved from these troubles." "Oh, yes, of many, but I have no right to think or speak my sentiments, for I am married; if I do, my husband says it is better for me to attend to the domestic affairs, and he will do the thinking. He deprives me of female friends because women love to gossip; of male friends, for the world might talk about it; besides, he says a mother ought always to be at home taking care of her home and children, and providing for her husband's wants; and

I have nothing but death; when that comes, I shall go where everything will be bright and happy, and my soul's longings will be satisfied." Now, I ask, what is that woman's life? Is she what God intended she should be? No! she was made fair and beautiful in childhood; given those noble aspirations to cultivate in the garden of her soul, given as seeds for the truth. What did she do with them? *Sold them* with herself, at sixteen, when she entered into the marriage contract, and thus bowed down her soul forever. In her isolated household she threw away her life, and added to the too many already children thrust into the world half made up—children of chance, children of lust, abortions who feel that they have no right to existence; children of disease whose tainted flesh and running sores are a disgrace and an everlasting reproach to the morals and purity of any community. Byron cursed his mother for his deformed feet, and there are thousands and thousands of children cursing the sacred name of mother for their deformed bodies and moral conditions.[47]

Mrs. [Matilda Joslyn] Gage, Mrs. [Ernestine] Rose, Mr. [Henry C.] Wright[48] and others, go back to the mother's influence, and go a step further back, and say it is the marriage institution that is at fault. It is the binding marriage ceremony that keeps woman degraded in mental and moral Slavery. She must demand her freedom, her right to receive the equal wages of man for her labor—*her right to bear children when she will, and by whom she will.* Woman is not totally depraved. She will never abuse one right that is given to her, and she will never step aside from her own nature. If she desires to go to the ballot-box, it is because there is a wrong somewhere, and she takes that way to right it. If she desires to become a lawyer, it is because there are laws to be redressed and made better. If she desires to preach, it is because she feels the woes and afflictions of humanity. If she desires rights, it is because she needs them. I believe in the absolute freedom of the affections, and it is woman's privilege, aye her right, to accept or refuse any love that comes to her. *She should be the ruling power in all matters of love;* and when her love has died out for the man who has taken her to his heart, she is living a lie to herself, her own nature and to him, if she continues to hold an intimate relation with him. And so is man's relative position to woman. When his love has died out, and he continues to live with his wife, on any consideration, he strikes a blow at the morality of his nature, and lives a life of deception, not only to her and society, but he is responsible for all the crimes that his children, born under those circumstances, are liable to commit. A gentleman said to me a little time ago: "My wife is a Woman's Rights woman; she talks about her rights, and I allow it, but she really has none. I am her husband, she is my property; and if I do not like a thing, I say so, and I do not consider she has any right to dispute it. I do not hold any argument, for I consider my will law.—And if I loved a woman, and was not bound to her by the marriage ceremony, I should not think of disputing her will or wishes, for fear she would show me the door, and I should have no alternative but to go out of it. Her will is absolute, for I have no claim upon her, and she is justified in all she does; so it is necessary to guard myself and movements in order to retain the love and respect of the woman I love." What a pleasing prospect is this for the wife, who is rearing her children in her isolated household, and imagining the husband immaculate in that as well as other actions, and respecting her in the sacred office of wife and mother. Why should woman tame herself into calm submission, and be the slave and toy and plaything of man? What is marriage? Is it the linking together of two loving hearts in holy, sacred union? No! Seldom the case when compared to the many thousands upon thousands of marriages of convenience. Women are bought and paid for as the negro slave is. She is estimated as a thing of barter; for a man counts the cost of his intended wife as deliberately as if he thought of keeping a cow, a dog, or a pig. Now, what are the rights and privileges of women in the marriage institution? It gives us the privilege to become *Mrs.* Brown instead of *Mrs.* Smith. That is an honor, no doubt, as it relieves woman from the stigma of *old maid.* It gives us the privilege of being supported and attending to domestic affairs; the privilege to see that the dinner is served at proper hours for a hungry husband; the privilege oftentimes, to sit up alone half the night to let that husband in from a delightful concert and oyster supper that he has enjoyed with Mr. Jones and his beautiful wife. Then we have a right; and—listen, women of the Nineteenth Century—the marriage institution gives you one right; one right that you have not perhaps, hitherto valued; *it gives you the right to bear children.* It is not a privilege; it is not an inheritance that your nature craves; but it is the law of wise men, who know very much better than you do when *you want a child, and when you ought to become a mother.* Love is not dependent on reason, or judgment, or education, or mental acquirements, or society, or control of any kind. It is a holy, sacred emanation from the most vital part of our natures, and to say when or where it shall be limited or restricted, is a violation of our individual rights.[49]

IV.

THE 1860s:
In Full Stride, the War's Setback, and Regrouping After

WORKING ON THE POLITICAL AND THE PERSONAL ISSUES

After a full decade of organized work, the women's rights movement had found its stride by 1860 and was celebrating its victories while pushing forward on all fronts, as demonstrated in the November 1860 Appeal to the Women of New York that is the first reading in this chapter.

While pushing for legal and political rights, these foremothers had also discovered within the first decade of their movement that THE PERSONAL IS POLITICAL, a lesson feminists would have to rediscover a century later, having lost that knowledge. When the women raised the issue of marriage and divorce at the 1860 national women's rights convention, they slipped across the boundary from legal to personal and raised a backlash that was played out in the press between Elizabeth Cady Stanton and Horace Greeley, editor of the *New York Tribune*, an excerpt of which is included following the "Appeal."

ALL IN FOR THE WAR EFFORT, 1861–1865

The national women's rights conventions held yearly (except 1857) during the 1850s saw victory after victory as these

forward-looking women and their male allies began the transformation of society. Then suddenly everything came to a
screeching halt. Shortly after President Abraham Lincoln's inauguration, Confederates attacked South Carolina's Fort Sum-
ter in April 1861. Seven southern slave states seceded from the
United States to form the Confederate States of America; four
more states would later join. A third of the thirty-four states
had left the United States and the nation was at war.

Setting aside their own struggle for freedom, the members of
the organized women's movement suspended their yearly conventions and brought their organized power to assisting the
war effort in myriad ways.

Some women disguised themselves as men to serve the
armies on both sides, while other women openly served militarily. Harriet Tubman, for example, used her extensive knowledge of southern geography, gathered over her years of guiding
enslaved people to freedom in the North, to fight for the Union
as a spy and scout. She planned and led a military expedition,
the first woman in U.S. history to do so. Clara Barton minis-
tered to the wounded on the battlefield, and Dorothea Dix
served as the government superintendent of women nurses. Josephine S. Griffing, while gathering signatures in the Northwest for the Woman's Loyal National League, saw the need of
"a comprehensive system of protection, help, and education,
for the slaves in the trying transition of freedom," according to
History of Woman Suffrage.[1] She came to Washington and
lobbied for a bill to establish the Freedman's Bureau, which
finally passed in March 1865, and was signed by President
Lincoln just before his assassination.

Dr. Elizabeth Blackwell, the first U.S. woman to earn a medical degree, started the Sanitary Commission in 1861 to aid
sick and wounded soldiers. Under government authorization,
women in the seven thousand chapters throughout the Union
raised more than $92 million, the largest private philanthropic
effort in the country to that point. The *History of Woman Suffrage* editors described how women came together to support
the war effort, "from the girl of tender years, to the aged matron of ninety, whose trembling hands scraped lint or essayed

to knit socks and mittens for 'the boys in blue.'" Their Sanitary Fairs, held in all the cities, "were the wonders of the world in the variety and beauty of their exhibits and the vast sums realized from them."[2]

Trained by her father, a Maryland governor, Anna Ella Carroll became a political operative at a young age, influencing policy at the national level, and was reputed to "scheme, connive, and maneuver as well as any man."[3] She gave back their freedom to the people she held in enslavement and lobbied hard to keep Maryland in the Union through editorials and personal correspondence. As a woman she was able to travel without arousing suspicion, so President Lincoln sent her, accompanied by an army officer, on a reconnaissance mission to the western front. Her reports resulted in major military strategies. The president and his cabinet, however, decided to keep secret her authorship of the critical Tennessee campaign. They feared it would undermine the war effort were the public to know that plans for this campaign, which turned the tide of the war to the Union, were formulated by not only a civilian, but a civilian woman. Learning the story from Carroll, Matilda Joslyn Gage wrote this account and printed it in pamphlet form for distribution in 1880, with another form of it published in the second volume of *History of Woman Suffrage*.[4]

Colonel Thomas A. Scott, assistant secretary of war under Secretary of War Edwin Stanton, was among the men in the know who also confirmed Carroll's account of her war work, as Gage cited:

COL. THOMAS A. SCOTT'S LETTER TO THE SENATE MILITARY COMMITTEE.

Hon. Jacob M. Howard, United States Senate:—

On or about the 30th of November, 1861, Miss Carroll, as stated in her memorial, called on me as Assistant Secretary of War, and suggested the propriety of abandoning the expedition which was then preparing to descend the Mississippi River, and to adopt instead, the Tennessee River, and handed to me the plan of the campaign as appended to her memorial, which plan I submitted to the Secretary of War, and its general ideas were adopted. On my return from the south-west in 1862, I informed Miss Carroll, as she states in her memorial, that through the adoption of this plan, the country had been saved millions, and that it entitled her to the kind consideration of Congress.

Thos. A. Scott[5]

Gage concluded in *"Who Planned the Tennessee Campaign?"*:

. . . But during the war, all officials of the government were opposed to having it made known that the government was proceeding according to the advice and under the plan of a civilian, and that civilian a *woman*. Judge Wade [Benjamin F. Wade, chairman of the Committee on the conduct of the War and, after Lincoln's assassination, acting vice president] at one time said, "I have sometimes reproached myself that I had not made known the author when they were discussing the resolution in Congress to find out, *but Mr. Lincoln and Mr. Stanton were* opposed to its being known that the armies were moving under the plan of a civilian, directed by the President as Commander-in-chief. Mr. Lincoln said it was that which made him hesitate to inaugurate the movement against the opinion of the military commanders and he did not wish to risk the effect it might have upon the armies if they found out some outside party had originated the campaign; that he wanted the country and the armies to believe they were doing the whole business of saving the country."

Judge Evans conversed with Col. Scott upon this subject, Scott urging the absolute necessity of Miss Carroll's making no claim to the campaign while the struggle continued.

In the plenitude of her self-sacrificing patriotism, Miss Carroll remained obscurely in the back-ground, though the country was indebted to her for its salvation. While thousands of men have in the past years received thanks and rewards from the country for work done under her plan, she is still to-day, fifteen years after the close of the war, left to struggle for recognition from that country, which is indebted to her for its salvation.[6]

Suffragists launched a campaign for Carroll to be recognized by Congress and given a pension compensated at the rate appropriate to her war service. House Bill 7256 was introduced in 1881 with Carroll's pension to be at the rate awarded to major generals. However, with the assassination of President Garfield the bill disappeared. Congress finally did put Carroll on the pension roll, with $50.00 ($1,240.00) a month for life for the "important military service rendered by her during the late Civil War."[7]

While serving as a Union contract surgeon, Dr. Mary Walker was captured as a spy, imprisoned in a Confederate POW jail, and became the first woman awarded the Congressional Medal of Honor. She continued to wear the trousers and short skirt she had adopted out of necessity during her war work, and as she was walking down the street in New York City one day in 1866, according to the *New York Times*, an unruly crowd gathered to view her garb. Instead of dispersing the mob, Officer Johnson of the Seventh Precinct arrested Walker for appearing in male costume and disorderly conduct.[8]

An immense audience from many states answered the call for a national convention in May 1863 to discuss how women could "do everything in their power to aid the Government in the prosecution of this war to the glorious end of freedom." The convention president, Lucy Stone, introduced Angelina Grimke Weld, whose convention speech is included in this chapter.[9]

Following Grimke's speech, the convention expressed interest in forming a Woman's Loyal National League and adopted the following resolution:

> *Resolved*, That we, loyal women of the nation, assembled in convention in New York, this 14th day of May, 1863, do hereby pledge ourselves one to another in a Loyal League, to give support to the Government in so far as it makes the war for freedom.[10]

The call went out for women across the country to gather signatures on the Woman's Loyal National League petitions to abolish slavery, which were distributed by the organization's secretary, Susan B. Anthony, in 1863.

> With us, *the people*, is the power to achieve the work by our agents in Congress. On us, therefore, rests the momentous responsibility.
>
> Shall we not all join then in one loud, earnest, *effectual* prayer to Congress, which will swell on its ear like the voice of many waters, that this bloody, desolating war shall be arrested and ended, by the immediate and final removal, by Statue Law and amended Constitution, of that crime and curse which alone has brought it upon us?
>
> Now surely is our accepted time.
>
> On our own heads will be the blood of our thousands slain, if, with the power in our own hands, we do not end that system for ever, which is so plainly autographed all over with the Divine displeasure.
>
> In the name of justice and of freedom then let us rise and decree the destruction of our destroyer. Let us with myriad voice *compel* Congress to
>
> "Consign it to remorseless fire!
>
> Watch till the last faint spark expire,
>
> Then strew its ashes on the wind
>
> Nor leave one atom wreck behind."
>
> In behalf of the Women's League.
>
>   SUSAN B. ANTHONY, *Secretary*.[11]

In less than a year, the Woman's Loyal National League (WLNL) gathered 265,314 signatures from twenty-two of the twenty-three Union states on its petitions in support of the newly proposed Thirteenth Amendment to formally abolish slavery. While proclaiming 100,000 signatures, when counting the names, Senator Charles Sumner's clerk found there were actually more than twice that many, including a sprinkling of names from New Brunswick and New Orleans. Senator Sumner presented these petitions, joined together by state into one enormous roll, to Congress on February 9, 1864. There were two forms of the petition: one for both men and women to sign and one specifically for women. Both petitions are included in this chapter, along with the address Sumner delivered upon presenting the petitions to Congress.

Elizabeth Cady Stanton, now president of the WLNL, sent out an appeal cheering on the five thousand members to continue working toward their goal of gathering one million signatures. When the Senate passed the Thirteenth Amendment the following day, on April 8, 1864, the work became even more imperative, to ensure the amendment's passage. In Stanton's message, which is included in this chapter, you'll note that she only acknowledges 100,000 signatures, not the final count of two-and-a-half times as many.

The WLNL sent out twenty thousand emancipation petitions circulated by two thousand men and women, boys and girls, who collected 400,000 signatures in the brief two and a half years from the beginning of their campaign until the House endorsed the Thirteenth Amendment on January 31, 1865. The amendment was ratified quickly by the required number of states on December 6, 1865, after the conclusion of the Civil War. That number of petition signatures, undoubtedly the largest gathered that quickly in U.S. history to that point, had a major impact on Congress and the states to abolish slavery. The amendment legally ended enslavement, with one exception that would lead to the rise of the prison-industrial complex in the twentieth century:

Section 1. Neither slavery nor involuntary servitude, *except as a punishment for crime whereof the party shall have been duly convicted*, shall exist within the United States, or any place subject to their jurisdiction.

With the passage of the Thirteenth Amendment the WLNL achieved its goal and disbanded. The organization had set the stage for the work to be done after the abolition of slavery with two resolutions at its 1864 convention:

Resolved, That until the old union with slavery be broken, and the Constitution so amended as to secure the elective franchise to all citizens who bear arms, or are taxed to support the Government, we have no foundations on which to build a true Republic.

Resolved, That we demand for the new nation a new Constitution, in which the guarantee of liberty and equality to every human being shall be so plainly and clearly written as never again to be called in question.[12]

The women's rights organization came back to life after suspending its yearly conventions to focus on ending slavery. It immediately gathered ten thousand signatures sent to the 1865–66 session of Congress demanding woman suffrage. This was a decisive moment in history. The Constitution was about to be changed.

Abolitionist William Lloyd Garrison declared this document a "covenant with death and an agreement with hell," as he put a match to the Constitution at a July 4 celebration in 1854. The founding document of the United States was a slave-owner's dream, legalizing slavery in two places: the requirement of the return of enslaved people who had taken their freedom and the counting of the enslaved as three-fifths of a person when counting population to determine how many representatives a state could send to Congress. The federal government had just created a new class of citizens, freed blacks, who were no longer three-fifths of a person. How would they change the Constitution to reflect this fact?

Congress now had to clarify what black citizenship meant. Further, if the federal government, which had just proclaimed humans could no longer be property, was to ensure that the newly freed blacks could protect themselves from their former owners, how could it do that without cloaking African Americans in the protection of the ballot? And if voting privileges were to be extended to all blacks, why not also to women? The *History of Woman Suffrage* editors explained:

The first point, his emancipation, settled, the political status of the negro was next in order; and to this end various propositions were submitted to Congress. But to demand his enfranchisement on the broad principle of natural rights, was hedged about with difficulties, as the logical result of such action must be the enfranchisement of all ostracised classes; not only the white women of the entire country, but the slave women of the South. Though our Senators and Representatives had an honest aversion to any proscriptive legislation against loyal women, in view of their varied and self-sacrificing work during the war, yet the only way they could open the constitutional door just wide enough to let the black *man* pass in, was to introduce the word "male" into the national Constitution. After the generous devotion of such women as Anna Carroll and Anna Dickinson[13] in sustaining the policy of the Republicans, both in peace and war, they felt it would come with an ill-grace from that party, to place new barriers in woman's path to freedom. But how could the amendment be written without the word "male"? was the question.[14]

The tradition of yearly woman's rights conventions, begun in 1850 and suspended during the war, started up again in May 1866, but with a startling departure. The door of freedom had swung open; women and African American men could walk through arm in arm and finally create the vision of democracy the Founding Fathers had imperfectly achieved: a government based on the consent of all the governed. If this vision was to be achieved, it was time for the women's rights movement to absorb the abolition movement and join forces for universal suffrage. At this 1866 women's rights convention, Susan B. Anthony presented a resolution, which is included in this chapter, calling for a new organization that would work for universal suffrage. This organization, the American Equal Rights Association (AERA)—the first organization in the country to demand universal suffrage—was subsequently established.

Not all abolitionists were in agreement, however. The American Anti-Slavery Society, under the leadership of Wendell Phillips, decided to continue, rebranding its organization now that enslavement was abolished, to work for gaining the vote for African American men only.

The AERA, on the other hand, would fight for full voting

rights for women and African American men, and the battle
would be fought at both the state and national levels. The first
campaign was the District of Columbia, with the introduction
of a bill in Congress (which controls D.C.) to extend voting
rights to African American males in the District. Despite a
massive petition campaign to also include woman suffrage,
what happened next foreshadowed the ultimate outcome of the
nonviolent war for universal suffrage in this transformational
moment, as told in the *History of Woman Suffrage*.

> The second session of the Thirty-ninth Congress is memorable
> for an able debate in the Senate on the enfranchisement of
> woman. On Monday, December 10, 1866, Senator Cowan, of
> Pennsylvania, moved to amend the amendment by striking out
> the word "male" before the word person. This debate in the Sen-
> ate lasted three entire days, and during that time the comments
> of the press were as varied as they were multitudinous. Even
> [*New York Tribune* editor] Horace Greeley, who had ever been
> a true friend to woman, in favor of all her rights, industrial, edu-
> cational, and political, said the time had not yet come for her
> enfranchisement.[15]

Senator Cowan's amendment failed in the Senate committee
37 to 9, while a similar attempt in the House failed 74 to 49
with 68 not voting. At the same time, Congress was considering extending the vote to the recently freed African American
men in the former Confederacy. The *New York Times* suggested one reason the Republican-controlled Congress was de-
liberating the action.

> The Philadelphia Press characterizes it as a "stupendous delu-
> sion to expect Congress and the Executive to do that for the un-
> educated freedmen of the South, which the independent States of
> the North have failed or refused to do for the better trained and
> more experienced free colored men in their section." In the
> main, we believe this is true. Still it is evident that negro suffrage
> in the Southern States is pressed upon public favor by many con-
> siderations which do not affect it at the North.

A large portion of our people fear that in the political reorganization of the South, the power will fall again into the hands of those who were foremost in the rebellion; and they seek a remedy for this in giving the suffrage to the enfranchised slaves. They assume that these slaves would naturally vote with the anti-slavery men of the North,—that they would constitute an offset to the vote of those who were recently rebels, and that their admission to the ballot-box would, therefore, afford a safeguard against the return of the Southern States into rebel hands. Whether right or wrong, this is the motive which leads very many Northern men to advocate negro suffrage at the South; and this reason does not apply at the North.[16]

During this heated time, abolitionist and women's rights supporter Henry Blackwell stepped forward in 1867 with a racist argument for woman suffrage, "What the South Can Do," which he sent to the legislators of the South. Your white women, Blackwell pointed out, outnumber both male and female African Americans, so giving women the vote would be a sure-fire way to maintain your institution of white supremacy.[17]

The Radical Republicans, who gained control of Congress in 1866, were contesting President Andrew Johnson's conciliatory attitude toward the South. At the same time, they were backing down from their solid commitment to women's right to vote as they began limiting their work to obtaining it for African American men. The second annual convention of the AERA met in May 1867 with a solid repudiation of the Republican backsliding on universal suffrage. The Republican Party's call for the vote for black men only, endorsed by the American Anti-Slavery Society, "is a cruel abandonment of the slave women of the South, a fraud on the tax-paying women of the North, and an insult to the civilization of the nineteenth century," the convention charged. The resolution ended with a pledge "to renewed and untiring exertions, until equal suffrage and citizenship are acknowledged throughout our entire country, irrespective of sex or color."[18]

Charles Remond, who had refused to take part in the 1840 World Anti-Slavery Convention proceedings when women

were excluded, again came to the front for women's rights as
an African American ally, saying, "In an hour like this I repudiate the idea of expediency. All I ask for myself I claim for my
wife and sister." Robert Purvis, a black vice president of the
AERA who chaired the convention in the absence of President
Lucretia Mott, echoed Remond's words:

> I can not agree that this or any hour is 'especially the negro's.' I
> am an anti-slavery man because I hate tyranny and in my nature
> revolt against oppression, whatever its form or character. As an
> abolitionist, therefore, I am for the equal rights movement, and
> as one of the confessedly oppressed race, how could I be other-
> wise? With what grace could I ask the women of this country to
> labor for my enfranchisement, and at the same time be unwilling
> to put forth a hand to remove the tyranny, in some respects
> greater, to which they are subjected?[19]

The year's work had been extensive, and also expensive, as
Anthony reported to the convention, noting a debt of $617.33.

Undaunted by defeat and debt, the AERA had moved on to
the next contest, petitioning the New York Constitutional
Convention to amend the state constitution so "as to secure the
right of suffrage to all citizens, without distinction of race or
sex." The AERA appointed Henry Ward Beecher, Elizabeth
Cady Stanton, and Frederick Douglass as representatives to the
Constitutional Convention, directing them to argue for the
elimination of the twenty-five-dollar property qualification for
African American men and the extension of the elective franchise to women. The Constitutional Convention assembled in
Albany on June 4, 1867. The *History of Woman Suffrage* editors recounted what happened, describing the use of two tactics that would prove divisive: humiliating their opponent and
the use of class, race, and native-born supremacy in claiming
women's rights.[20]

The final vote was 19 for and 125 against. Meanwhile, the
next major effort for universal suffrage was taking place in
Kansas, where voters faced a constitutional amendment for

universal suffrage. "Bleeding Kansas," as Horace Greeley coined it, had been the precursor to the Civil War when, under the Kansas-Nebraska Act of 1854, settlers were to decide if the state should be slave or free. Pro-slavery settlers flocked to the territory, as did abolitionists who relocated from the East to keep the state free. Their differences quickly became violent and an undeclared war continued until 1861, when Kansas finally was admitted to the Union as a free state. Women from the East who had settled in Kansas had been organizing for their rights all this time, as Susan E. Wattles later reminisced in a letter to Susan B. Anthony, which is included in this chapter.

Victory quickly proved to be elusive, as the *History of Woman Suffrage* editors explained.

> Eastern politicians warned the Republicans of Kansas that "negro suffrage" was a party measure in national politics, and that they must not entangle themselves with the "woman question." On all sides came up the cry, this is "the negro's hour." Though the Republican State Central Committee adopted a resolution leaving all their party speakers free to express their individual sentiments, yet they selected men to canvass the State, who were known to be unscrupulous and disreputable, and violently opposed to woman suffrage. The Democratic party was opposed to both amendments and to the new law on temperance, which it was supposed the women would actively support.[21]

George Francis Train, a charismatic, wealthy financial speculator from New York, who had ambitions to be president of the United States, joined the Kansas campaign in the last two weeks, offering personal and financial support. Touring with Susan B. Anthony, his populist message drew in the working class, while his uncensored racism appealed to "the prejudices of the ignorant."[22] Abandoned by the eastern press and the Republicans, Stanton and Anthony made a drastic and ultimately damaging decision, which they justified in *History of Woman Suffrage*:

Seeing that the republican vote must be largely against the woman's amendment, the question arose what can be done to capture enough democratic votes to outweigh the recalcitrant republicans. At this auspicious moment George Francis Train appeared in the State as an advocate of woman suffrage. He appealed most effectively to the chivalry of the intelligent Irishmen, and the prejudices of the ignorant; conjuring them not to take the word "white" out of their constitution unless they did the word "male" also; not to lift the negroes above the heads of their own mothers, wives, sisters, and daughters. The result was a respectable democratic vote in favor of woman suffrage.[23]

. . . Abolitionists were severe in their denunciations against these ladies, because, while belonging to anti-slavery associations, they affiliated with the bitter enemies of the negro and all his defamers. To which they replied: "So long as opposition to slavery is the only test for a free pass to your platform and membership of your association, and you do not shut out all persons opposed to woman suffrage, why should we not accept all in favor of woman suffrage to our platform and association, even though they be rabid pro-slavery Democrats? Your test of faithfulness is the negro, ours is the woman; the broadest platform, to which no party has as yet risen, is humanity." Reformers can be as bigoted and sectarian and as ready to malign each other, as the Church in its darkest periods has been to persecute its dissenters.[24]

So utterly had the women been deserted in the Kansas campaign by those they had the strongest reason to look to for help, that at times all effort seemed hopeless. The editors of the New York *Tribune* and the *Independent* can never know how wistfully, from day to day, their papers were searched for some inspiring editorials on the woman's amendment, but naught was there; there were no words of hope and encouragement, no eloquent letters from an Eastern man that could be read to the people; all were silent. Yet these two papers, extensively taken all over Kansas, had they been as true to woman as to the negro, could have revolutionized the State. But with arms folded, Greeley, Curtis, Tilton, Beecher, Higginson, Phillips, Garrison,

Frederick Douglass, all calmly watched the struggle from afar, and when defeat came to both propositions, no consoling words were offered for woman's loss, but the women who spoke in the campaign were reproached for having "killed negro suffrage."[25]

When the votes were counted, suffrage for women and African American men were both defeated; each receiving about ten thousand votes.

George Francis Train now held out a carrot to Stanton and Anthony. He would fund a woman's rights paper for them, provided they would allow him to editorialize in it. Plus, he would fund a lecture tour for the three of them at cities all the way home to New York from Kansas. Fully aware of Train's racism, they agreed. In a characteristic speech Train had delivered in England a few years earlier he argued that blacks were intellectually, culturally, and morally inferior to whites, and slavery had actually improved their lot by introducing them to the superior white world.[26]

Stanton and Anthony came under increasing criticism from the movement for their alliance with Train, which grew as they began publication of their newspaper in January 1868. Train named the paper the *Revolution*. He was joined in funding the enterprise by his fellow Democrat David Melliss, the financial editor of the *World*. Susan B. Anthony served as owner and publisher, while Stanton was joined in editorial duties by Parker Pillsbury, their long-time ally.[27] Creating more criticism, Anthony took over the AERA offices for the newspaper's use and kicked out Lucy Stone, while Stanton, along with Train, advocated applying an educational test for voters on its pages in direct violation of the AERA's universal suffrage stand. They defended their alliance with Democrats, which at the time was the party of southern whites:

But Democrats seeing the inconsistency of Republicans, did advocate our cause, present our petitions in Congress, and frank our documents to all parts of the country. And because these women, denied help and encouragement from other sources, accepted aid from the Democrats, they were called "Copperheads"; disloyal to the Government. Women who had been complimented by the Republican press as "wise," "prudent," "noble," while rolling up 300,000 petitions for emancipation, were now said to be "selfish," "impracticable," "unreasonable," because forsooth they demanded some new liberties for themselves. Moreover said the Republicans, "these Democrats are hypocritical, they do not believe in the extension of suffrage to any class." To this the women replied, "If the Democrats advocate a grand measure of public policy which they do not believe, they occupy much higher ground than Republicans who refuse to press the same measure which they claim to believe. At all events the hypocrisy of Democrats serves us a better purpose in the present emergency than does the treachery of Republicans."[28]

At the AERA annual meeting in May 1868, Lucy Stone introduced two petitions to Congress; one to extend suffrage to women in the District of Columbia and the territories, the other for a Sixteenth Amendment to prohibit the states from disenfranchising citizens on account of sex. Frederick Douglass spoke in favor of both.[29]

On July 28, 1868, the Fourteenth Amendment to the Constitution was ratified, with the legislatures in every former Confederate state except Tennessee voting against its adoption. They weren't the only opponents. A section of the AERA stood with Stanton and Anthony and their male allies, Robert Purvis, Parker Pillsbury, and Reverend Samuel J. May in seeing the political danger it presented to women. Its adoption would not just ignore women, it would injure them. While Section 1 promised that women and African American men would now, finally, be recognized as citizens, Section 2 took away the protection of citizenship from women:

Section 1. All persons born or naturalized in the United States, and subject to the jurisdiction thereof, are citizens of the United States and of the State wherein they reside. No State shall make or enforce any law which shall abridge the privileges or immunities of citizens of the United States; nor shall any state deprive any person of life, liberty, or property, without due process of law; nor deny to any person within its jurisdiction the equal protection of the laws.[30]

Section 2. Representatives shall be apportioned among the several states according to their respective numbers, counting the whole number of persons in each state, excluding Indians not taxed. But when the right to vote at any election for the choice of electors for President and Vice President of the United States, representatives in Congress, the executive and judicial officers of a state, or the members of the legislature thereof, is denied to any of the male inhabitants of such state being of twenty-one years of age, and citizens of the United States, or in any way abridged, except for participation in rebellion or other crime, the basis of representation therein shall be reduced in the proportion which the number of such male citizens shall bear to the whole number of male citizens twenty-one years of age in such state.

There it was, not once but three times. Citizens were identified as male, implying that women were not citizens. It was a smart way to ensure that southern whites wouldn't deny the vote to black men. Each state's representation in the House was based on the number of people living there, women included. If they denied any of their male citizens voting rights, the state's number of representatives would be reduced by the number of voters they denied voting rights. In threatening the South with consequences if African Americans were denied the vote, Congress made punishment apply only when men were denied the vote. Without the word "male," women would have been implicitly granted voting rights. The purpose of including "male" was to avoid that possibility, because the Fourteenth Amendment was the carrot/threat to the South to approve the pending Fifteenth Amendment, which would extend voting rights to African American men.

In the process of protecting southern black men, the Fourteenth Amendment introduced gender into the U.S. Constitution three times, specifically denying women the protection of citizenship. Up until this point the Constitution had been silent about gender, so presumably a simple enabling act could have been passed to bring women in as voters. Further, if the Fourteenth Amendment had included women, it would have protected the voting rights of all women, since states would be at risk of losing representation in Congress if they denied black women, as well as white women, the vote. But with the word "male" specifically defining citizenship, this amendment seemed to declare that women, black and white, were excluded from voting or experiencing the benefits of citizenship. Declared "dead in the law" by Blackstone's code, with the Fourteenth Amendment, women would be declared suffrage-dead in the Constitution. Many women pointed out the hypocrisy of counting women in the basis of representation but denying them "a voice in the rulers whose election their numbers helped to secure."[31]

Women across the North took matters into their own hands and resisted. They broke the law to claim their right of citizenship. They voted. In a separate ballot box, 120 women voted in a prohibition referendum in Sturgis, Michigan. Between 50 and 80 women voted in Topeka, Kansas. In Passaic, New Jersey, women voted at an election for commissioner of streets and sidewalks; women also voted on erecting waterworks in Schenectady, New York, and in a school meeting in Sturgis, Michigan. A woman who demanded that her ballot be accepted instead of her Democratic husband's voted for Grant in Lawrence, Massachusetts. Having provided their own ballots and box, 172 African American and white women voted in a federal election in Vineland, New Jersey. In eleven cities altogether during 1868, women claimed the right to vote by voting. This would be just the beginning.[32]

Not all the Republican congressional representatives abandoned the women. Massachusetts senator Henry Wilson introduced a bill to extend the elective franchise in the District of Columbia to women, while Indiana representative George Julian introduced a similar bill in the House, along with one to grant woman suffrage in the territories. Congress had enacted African American male suffrage in the territories in 1867; why not women?

Julian also introduced an amendment in the House for universal suffrage. Kansas senator Pomeroy, who had stumped the state for woman suffrage during the Kansas campaign, introduced a similar amendment in the Senate. This constitutional amendment, had it been adopted in 1868, would have created full voting rights for all citizens, women and men, black and white. Congress—made up entirely of white males—ignored this historic opportunity, not even debating the proposed amendment. Congressmen had made up their minds to turn their back on women. They would open the door only a crack, wide enough to let through African American men, who were sure to vote Republican. The Fifteenth Amendment, which would soon pass Congress, read:

> Section 1. The right of citizens of the United States to vote shall not be denied or abridged by the United States or by any State on account of race, color, or previous condition of servitude.
>
> Section 2. The Congress shall have power to enforce this article by appropriate legislation.

Only eight northern states had black male suffrage at the time and the amendment would enfranchise them. Protected by the Union army from the poll taxes and other measures designed to keep them from voting, southern black men made their way to the polls. The amendment, however, contained nothing to prevent widespread attempted voter suppression, nor did it guarantee African American men the right to hold office.

Some women and their male allies—black and white—opposed the Fifteenth Amendment, holding out for universal suffrage. Stanton editorialized this stance in the *Revolution*, in editorials that are included in this chapter.[33]

Women regrouped with a national woman's suffrage convention in January 1869, the first they had ever held in Washington,

D.C. Kansas senator Pomeroy opened the convention, declaring to an overflow crowd that "suffrage is a natural, inalienable right, it must, of necessity, belong to every citizen of the republic, black and white, male and female."[34] Delegates from more than twenty states from Maine to California elected Lucretia Mott president. The convention report is printed in part in this chapter.

The House passed the Fifteenth Amendment on February 25, 1869, and the Senate followed the next day. On March 15, 1869, Representative George W. Julian submitted a simple "Joint Resolution" to Congress for a Sixteenth Amendment to the federal Constitution for universal suffrage, with a provision that nullified the "male" citizenship requirement of the Fourteenth Amendment, ensuring women's right to vote. Petitions for the Sixteenth Amendment were immediately printed and sent throughout the nation. The woman suffrage amendment read:

> Art. 16. The Right of Suffrage in the United States shall be based on citizenship, and shall be regulated by Congress; and all citizens of the United States, whether native or naturalized, shall enjoy this right equally without any distinction or discrimination whatever founded on sex.[35]

Beyond universal suffrage, the *Revolution* was calling for educated suffrage. If enacted, this would be another form of voter suppression, since it had been illegal to educate enslaved people. Stanton used racist terms and went further. She seemed to endorse the lynching of a black man in Tennessee who had been accused of raping a white woman. Suffrage for black men, she suggested, could "culminate in fearful outrages on womanhood, especially in the southern states."[36] Questions began to emerge about Anthony's use of the organization's funds as well. Stanton and Anthony were challenged for their racism and potential misappropriation of funds at the AERA annual May meeting two months later. The exchange is published in this chapter.

Congress had passed the Fifteenth Amendment and sent it to the states for ratification. The discussion turned to the question of whether the AERA should endorse it. Should the organization back down from its founding principle of universal suffrage and accept the half-measure of the Fifteenth Amendment?

These were seasoned abolitionists who had seen the strength of holding to their principles. From the 1830s, when they were hated outliers, mobbed and reviled, accused of being godless criminals, they had held tight, calling for unconditional emancipation. Enslaved people will never be freed unconditionally, general wisdom said, so accept a compromise measure. Compensate the slaveholders for their lost property. Free the enslaved, but then send them back to Africa, to live in Liberia. The abolitionists held out, slowly converting people to the rightness of their cause until finally they had won a complete victory. Should they abandon this all-or-nothing strategy or give in to expediency and support a partial victory? The debate, included in this chapter, was fierce enough to tear the organization apart.

After this lengthy debate, the AERA voted to endorse the Fifteenth Amendment. Stanton, Anthony, and Gage explained what resulted.

Out of these broad differences of opinion on the amendments, as shown in the debates, divisions grew up between Republicans and Abolitionists on the one side, and the leaders of the Woman Suffrage movement on the other. The constant conflict on the Equal Rights platform proved the futility of any attempt to discuss the wrongs of different classes in one association. A general dissatisfaction had been expressed by the delegates from the West at the latitude of debate involved in an Equal Rights Association. Hence, a change of name and more restricted discussions were strenuously urged by them. Accordingly, at the close of Anniversary week, a meeting was called at the Woman's Bureau, which resulted in reorganization under the name of "The National Woman Suffrage Association."

There had been so much trouble with men in the Equal Rights

Society, that it was thought best to keep the absolute control henceforth in the hands of women. Sad experience had taught them that in trying emergencies they would be left to fight their own battles, and therefore it was best to fit themselves for their responsibilities by filling the positions of trust exclusively with women. This was not accomplished without a pretty sharp struggle. As it was, they had to concede the right of membership to men, in order to carry the main point, as several ladies would not join unless men also could be admitted. All preliminaries discussed and amicably adjusted, a list of officers was chosen and an organization completed, making a XVIth Amendment the special object of its work and consideration.[37]

The Massachusetts contingent regrouped and formed their own organization. Lucy Stone explained that two national associations for woman's suffrage were needed to restore harmony. She pointed to the radical abolitionists and the Republicans as an example. While they could not work together, separately they did good work, as two woman's organizations could do.[38]

The Executive Committee of the New England Woman Suffrage Association followed up with a letter by five abolitionist women's rights activists: Lucy Stone; two Unitarian ministers, Thomas Wentworth Higginson and George H. Vibbert; and two founders of the New England's Women's Club, Caroline Severance and Julia Ward Howe, author of "The Battle Hymn of the Republic." The new "truly National and representative" organization would be named the American Woman Suffrage Association, they wrote. Theirs would be "at once more comprehensive and more widely representative" than any other suffrage groups, with delegates chosen by state associations.[39]

Fundamental differences between the two groups arose as they organized. The National Woman Suffrage Association (NWSA) would work toward a federal amendment while the American Woman Suffrage Association (AWSA) took the states' rights position and would ask states to grant woman suffrage. Membership reflected the difference in strategy.

Members of the NWSA directly joined the organization, while the AWSA set up a delegate system, where members joined through a state chapter, with delegates appointed through these state organizations. The NWSA practiced direct democracy, while the AWSA set up a representative system. The NWSA would have women officers; the AWSA had men as well.[40]

History belongs to those who write it, and the NWSA authors of *History of Woman Suffrage* described the split this way:

> During the Autumn of this year there was a secession from our ranks, and the preliminary steps were taken for another organization. Aside from the divisions growing out of a difference of opinion on the amendments, there were some personal hostilities among the leaders of the movement that culminated in two Societies, which were generally spoken of as the New York and Boston wings of the Woman Suffrage reform. The former, as already stated, called the "National Woman Suffrage Association," with Elizabeth Cady Stanton for President, organized in May; the latter called "The American Woman Suffrage Association," with Henry Ward Beecher for President, organized the following November. Most of those who inaugurated the reform remained in the National Association—Lucretia Mott, Martha C. Wright, Ernestine Rose, Clarina Howard Nichols, Paulina Wright Davis, Sarah Pugh, Amy Post, Mary H. Hallowell, Lydia Mott, Catharine A. F. Stebbins, Adeline Thomson, Josephine S. Griffing, Clemence S. Lozier, Rev. Olympia Brown, Matilda Joslyn Gage, Elizabeth Cady Stanton, Susan B. Anthony—and continued to work harmoniously together.[41]

This momentous decade in United States history ended with a suffrage victory on December 10, 1869. The Council and House of Representatives of Wyoming Territory determined that women could vote. It was a partial victory, since territorial residents, unlike those living in states, can't vote for president and have no representation in Congress. The next year the men in Utah Territory followed Wyoming's lead and gave the vote, limited as it was, to women.

I.

"Appeal to the Women of New York and Petition" from Elizabeth Cady Stanton, President; Lydia Mott, Secretary and Treasurer; Ernestine L. Rose; Martha C. Wright; and Susan B. Anthony, on behalf of the New York State Woman Suffrage Committee, November 1860

Women of New York:—Once more we appeal to you to make renewed efforts for the elevation of our sex. In our marital laws we are now in advance of every State in the Union. Twelve years ago New York took the initiative step, and secured to married women their property, received by gift or inheritance. Our last Legislature passed a most liberal act, giving to married women their rights, to sue for damages of person or property, to their separate earnings and their children; and to the widow, the possession and control of the entire estate during the minority of the youngest child. Women of New York! You can no longer be insulted in the first days of your widowed grief by the coarse minions of the law at your fireside, coolly taking an inventory of your household goods, or robbing your children of their natural guardian.

While we rejoice in this progress made in our laws, we see also a change in the employment of women. They are coming down from the garrets and up from the cellars to occupy more profitable posts in every department of industry, literature, science, and art. In the church, too, behold the spirit of freedom at work. Within the past year, the very altar has been the scene of well-fought battles; women claiming and exercising their right to vote in church matters, in defiance of precedent, priest, or Paul.

Another evidence of the importance of our cause is seen in

the deep interest men of wealth are manifesting in it. Three great bequests have been given to us in the past year. Five thousand dollars from an unknown hand, a share in the munificent fund left by that noble man of Boston, Charles F. Hovey, and four hundred thousand dollars by Mr. Vassar, of Poughkeepsie, to found a college for girls, equal in all respects to Yale and Harvard. Is it not strange that women of wealth are constantly giving large sums of money to endow professorships and colleges for boys exclusively—to churches and to the education of the ministry, and yet give no thought to their own sex—crushed in ignorance, poverty, and prostitution—the hopeless victims of custom, law, and Gospel, with few to offer a helping hand, while the whole world combine to aid the boy and glorify the man?

Our movement is already felt in the Old World. The nobility of England, with Lord Brougham at their head, have recently formed a "Society for Promoting the Employments of Women."

All this is the result of the agitation, technically called "Woman's Rights," through conventions, lectures, circulation of tracts and petitions, and by the faithful word uttered in the privacy of home. The few who stand forth to meet the world's cold gaze, its ridicule, its contumely, and its scorn, are urged onward by the prayers and tears, crushed hopes and withered hearts of the sad daughters of the race. The wretched will not let them falter; and they who seem to do the work, ever and anon draw fresh courage and inspiration from the noblest women of the age, who, from behind the scene, send forth good words of cheer and heartfelt thanks.

Six years hence, the men of New York purpose to revise our State Constitution. Among other changes demanded, is the right of suffrage for women—which right will surely be granted, if through all the intervening years every woman does her duty. Again do we appeal to each and all—to every class and condition—to inform themselves on this question, that woman may no longer publish her degradation by declaring herself satisfied in her present position, nor her ignorance by asserting that she has "all the rights she wants."

Any person who ponders the startling fact that there are

four millions of African slaves in this republic, will instantly put the question to himself, "Why do these people submit to the cruel tyranny that our government exercises over them?" The answer is apparent—"simply because they are ignorant of their power." Should they rise *en masse*, assert and demand their rights, their freedom would be secure. It is the same with woman. Why is it that one-half the people of this nation are held in abject dependence—civilly, politically, socially, the slaves of man? Simply because woman knows not her power. To find out her natural rights, she must travel through such labyrinths of falsehood, that most minds stand appalled before the dark mysteries of life—the seeming contradictions in all laws, both human and divine. But, because woman can not solve the whole problem to her satisfaction, because she can not prove to a demonstration the rottenness and falsehood of our present customs, shall she, without protest, supinely endure evils she can not at once redress? The silkworm, in its many wrappings, knows not it yet shall fly. The woman, in her ignorance, her drapery, and her chains, knows not that in advancing civilization, she too must soon be free, to counsel with her conscience and her God.

The religion of our day teaches that in the most sacred relations of the race, the woman must ever be subject to the man; that in the husband centers all power and learning; that the difference in position between husband and wife is as vast as that between Christ and the church; and woman struggles to hold the noble impulses of her nature in abeyance to opinions uttered by a Jewish teacher, which, alas! the mass believe to be the will of God. Woman turns from what she is taught to believe are God's laws to the laws of man; and in his written codes she finds herself still a slave. No girl of fifteen could read the laws, concerning woman, made, executed, and defended by those who are bound to her by every tie of affection, without a burst of righteous indignation. Few have ever read or heard of the barbarous laws that govern the mothers of this Christian republic, and fewer still care, until misfortune brings them into the iron grip of the law. It is the imperative duty of educated women to study the Constitution and statutes under which they live, that when they shall have a voice in the government, they may bring wisdom and not folly into its councils.

We now demand the ballot, trial by jury of our peers, and an equal right to the joint earnings of the marriage copartnership. And, until the Constitution be so changed as to give us a voice in the government, we demand that man shall make all his laws on property, marriage, and divorce, to bear equally on man and woman.

		E. CADY STANTON, *President.*
		LYDIA MOTT, *Sec. and Treas.*
New York State	{	ERNESTINE L. ROSE.
Woman's Rights Committee.		MARTHA C. WRIGHT.
		SUSAN B. ANTHONY.

November, 1860.

N. B.—Let every friend commence to get signatures to the petition without delay, and send up to Albany early in January, either to your representative or to Lydia Mott.

How can any wife or mother, who to-day rejoices in her legal right to the earnings of her hands, and the children of her love, withhold the small pittance of a few hours or days in getting signatures to the petition, or a few shillings or dollars to carry the work onward and upward, to a final glorious consummation.

A New York State Woman's Rights Convention will be held at Albany, the first week in February. Let there be a large attendance from all parts of the state.

PETITION.

To the Senate and Assembly of the State of New York:

We, the undersigned, citizens of _____New York, respectfully ask that the word "Male" shall be stricken from our State Constitution, that henceforth our Representatives may legislate for humanity, and not for privileged classes.[42]

2.
"Marriage and Divorce," Elizabeth Cady Stanton's letter
to Horace Greeley, the editor of the *New York Tribune*,
May 8, 1860

From The New York Tribune *of May 8.*

MARRIAGE AND DIVORCE.

To the Editor of the New York Tribune:

SIR:—At our recent National Woman's Rights Convention
many were surprised to hear Wendell Phillips object to the question of Marriage and Divorce, as irrelevant to our platform. He
said: "We had no right to discuss there any laws or customs but
those where inequality existed in the sexes; that the laws on
Marriage and Divorce rested equally on man and woman; that
he suffered, as much as she possibly could, the wrongs and
abuses of an ill-assorted marriage."

Now, it must strike every careful thinker, that an immense
difference rests in the fact, that man has made the laws, cunningly and selfishly, for his own purpose. From Coke down to
Kent, who can cite one clause of the marriage contract where
woman has the advantage? When man suffers from false legislation, he has his remedy in his own hands. Shall woman be denied the right of protest against laws in which she has had no
voice—laws which outrage the holiest affections of her nature—
laws which transcend the limits of human legislation—in a Convention called for the express purpose of considering her
wrongs? He might as well object to a protest against the injustice
of hanging a woman, because capital punishment bears equally
on man and woman.

The contract of marriage is by no means equal. The law permits the girl to marry at twelve years of age, while it requires
several years more of experience on the part of the boy. In entering this compact, the man gives up nothing that he before
possessed—he is a man still; while the legal existence of the
woman is suspended during marriage, and henceforth she is

known but in and through the husband. She is nameless, purseless, childless—though a woman, an heiress, and a mother.

Blackstone says: "The husband and wife are one, and that one is the husband." Kent says: "The legal effects of marriage are generally deducible from the principle of the common law, by which the husband and wife are regarded as one person, and her legal existence and authority lost or suspended during the continuance of the matrimonial union."—Vol. 2, p. 109. Kent refers to Coke on Littleton, 112, a. 187, B. Litt. sec. 168, 291.

The wife is regarded by all legal authorities as a "*feme-covert*," placed wholly *sub potestate viri*. Her moral responsibility, even, is merged in the husband. The law takes it for granted that the wife lives in fear of her husband; that his command is her highest law: hence a wife is not punishable for theft committed in presence of her husband.—Kent, vol. 2, p. 127. An unmarried woman can make contracts, sue and be sued, enjoy the rights of property, to her inheritance—to her wages—to her person—to her children; but, in marriage, she is robbed by law of all and every natural and civil right. "The disability of the wife to contract, so as to bind herself, arises not from want of discretion, but because she has entered into an indissoluble connection, by which she is placed under the power and protection of her husband."—Kent, vol. 2, p. 127. She is possessed of certain rights until she is married; then all are suspended, to revive again the moment the breath goes out of the husband's body.—See "Cowen's Treatise," vol. 2, p. 709.

If the contract be equal, whence come the terms "marital power"—"marital rights"—"obedience and restraint"—"dominion and control"—"power and protection," etc., etc.? Many cases are stated, showing the exercise of a most questionable power over the wife, sustained by the courts.—See Bishop on Divorce, p. 489.

The laws on Divorce are quite as unequal as those on Marriage; yes, far more so. The advantages seem to be all on one side, and the penalties on the other. In case of divorce, if the husband be the guilty party, he still retains the greater part of the property. If the wife be the guilty party, she goes out of the partnership penniless.—Kent, vol. 2, p. 33; Bishop on Divorce, p. 492.

In New York and some other States, the wife of the guilty husband can now sue for a divorce in her own name, and the costs come out of the husband's estate; but, in the majority of the States, she is still compelled to sue in the name of another, as she has no means of paying costs, even though she may have brought her thousands into the partnership. "The allowance to the innocent wife of *ad interim* alimony and money to sustain the suit, is not regarded as strict right in her, but of sound discretion in the court."—Bishop on Divorce, p. 581.

"Many jurists," says Kent, vol. 2, p. 88, "are of opinion that the adultery of the husband ought not to be noticed or made subject to the same animadversions as that of the wife, because it is not evidence of such entire depravity, nor equally injurious in its effects upon the morals, good order, and happiness of domestic life. Montesquieu, Pothier, and Dr. Taylor all insist that the cases of husband and wife ought to be distinguished, and that the violation of the marriage vow, on the part of the wife, is the most mischievous, and the prosecution ought to be confined to the offense on her part.—"Esprit des Loix," tom. 3, 186; "Traité du Contrat de Mariage," No. 516; "Elements of Civil Law," p. 254.

Say you, "These are but the opinions of men"? On what else, I ask, are the hundreds of women depending, who this hour demand in our courts a release from burdensome contracts? Are not these delicate matters left wholly to the discretion of courts? Are not young women from the first families dragged into the public courts—into assemblies of men exclusively—the judges all men, the jurors all men?—no true woman there to shield them by her presence from gross and impertinent questionings, to pity their misfortunes, or to protest against their wrongs?

The administration of justice depends far more on the opinions of eminent jurists, than on law alone, for law is powerless when at variance with public sentiment.

Do not the above citations clearly prove inequality? Are not the very letter and spirit of the marriage contract based on the idea of the supremacy of man as the keeper of woman's virtue—her sole protector and support? Out of marriage, woman asks nothing at this hour but the elective franchise. It is only in marriage that she must demand her rights to person, children, property, wages, life, liberty, and the pursuit of happiness. How can we discuss all the laws and conditions of marriage, without perceiving its essential essence, end, and aim? Now, whether the institution of marriage be human or divine, whether regarded as indissoluble by ecclesiastical courts, or dissoluble by civil courts, woman, finding herself equally degraded in each and every phase of it, always the victim of the institution, it is her right and her duty to sift the relation and the compact through and through, until she finds out the true cause of her false position. How can we go before the Legislatures of our respective States, and demand new laws, or no laws, on divorce, until we have some idea of what the true relation is?

We decide the whole question of slavery by settling the sacred rights of the individual. We assert that man can not hold property in man, and reject the whole code of laws that conflicts with the self-evident truth of that assertion.

Again I ask, is it possible to discuss all the laws of a relation, and not touch the relation itself?

Yours respectfully,
ELIZABETH CADY STANTON.

3.
Horace Greeley's response in the *New York Tribune*, May 14, 1860

Whether the Woman's Rights Convention will finally succeed or not in enlarging the sphere of woman, they have certainly been very successful in enlarging that of their platform. Having introduced easy Divorce as one of the reforms which the new order of things demands, we can see no good reason why the platform should not be altogether replanked. We respectfully suggest that with this change of purpose there shall also be a change in name, and that hereafter these meetings shall be called not by name of Woman, but in the name of Wives Discontented. Hitherto we have supposed that the aim of this movement related to wrongs which woman suffered as woman, political and social inequalities, and disabilities with which she was mightily burdened. A settlement of the marriage relation, we conceive, does not come within this category. As there can be no wives without husbands, the subject concerns the latter quite as much as it does the former. One of the wrongs which it is charged woman suffers from man, is that he legislates for her when she is not represented. We acknowledge the justice of that plea, and, for that very reason, complain that she, under the name of Woman's Rights, should attempt to settle a question of such vital importance to him where he is supposed to be admitted only on sufferance. We believe in woman's rights; we have some conclusions on the rights of husbands and wives; we are not yet, we confess, up to that advanced state which enables us to consider the rights of wives as something apart from that of husbands.

On the subject of marriage and divorce we have some very positive opinions, and what they are is pretty generally known. But even were they less positive and fixed, we should none the less protest against the sweeping character of the resolutions introduced at the Woman's Rights Convention on Friday by Mrs. Elizabeth Cady Stanton. We can not look upon the marriage relation as of no more binding force than that which a man may make with a purchaser for the sale of dry-goods, or an engagement he may contract with a schoolmaster or governess. Such doctrine seems to us simply shocking.

The intimate relation existing between one man and one woman, sanctified by, at least, the memory of an early and sincere affection, rendered more sacred by the present bond of dependent children, the fruit of that love, hallowed by many joys and many sorrows, though they be only remembered joys and sorrows, with other interests that can be broken in upon only to be destroyed—such a relation, we are very sure, has elements of quite another nature than those which belong to the shop or the counting-house. In our judgment, the balance of duty can not be struck like the balance of a mercantile statement of profit and loss, or measured with the calculations we bestow on an account current. Such a doctrine we regard as pernicious and debasing. We can conceive of nothing that would more utterly sap the foundations of sound morality, or give a looser rein to the most licentious and depraved appetites of the vilest men and women. Upon the physiological and psychological laws which govern generation, we do not care here to enter, even if Mrs. Stanton leads the way; but we believe that the progress of the world, springing out of connections formed under such a dispensation of humanity as is here indicated, with so little of duty or conscience, with so little hope or expectation of abiding affection, with so little intention of permanency as must necessarily belong to them, would be more monstrous than the world has ever dreamed of. For such a rule of married life contemplates no married life at all, and no parental relation. It destroys the family; it renders the dearest word in the Saxon tongue (home) a vague and unmeaning term; it multiplies a thousand-fold and renders universal all the evils which in the imperfections of human nature are now occasional under the binding force of a moral sense, the duty of continency, and the remnant of nothing else is left of love.

There are some other things besides in these resolutions to which we might object on the score of truth, some things which we rather marvel, modest women should say, and that modest women, in a mixed assembly, should listen to with patience. But these are secondary matters. The thought—more than them all—that the marriage tie is of the same nature as a mere business relation, is so objectionable, so dangerous, that we do not care to draw attention from that one point.[43]

4.

The *History of Woman Suffrage* editors' conclusion to the divorce debate between Elizabeth Cady Stanton and Horace Greeley in the *New York Tribune*

In asserting that marriage is an equal relation for husbands and wives, Mr. Greeley, like Mr. Phillips, begs the whole question. If it is legitimate to discuss all laws that bear unequally on man and woman in woman's rights conventions, surely those that grow out of marriage, which are the most oppressive and degrading on the statute-book, should command our first consideration. There could be no slaveholders without slaves; the one relation involves the other, and yet it would be absurd to say that slaves might not hold a convention to discuss the inequality of the laws sustaining that relation, and incidentally the whole institution itself, because the slaveholder shared in the evils resulting from it. There never has been a woman's convention held in which the injustice suffered by wives and mothers has not been a topic for discussion, and legitimately so. And if the only way of escape from the infamous laws by which all power is placed in the hands of man, is through divorce, then that is the hospitable door to open for those who wish to escape. No proposition contained in Mrs. Stanton's speech on divorce, viewed in any light, can be a tenth part so shocking as the laws on the statute-books, or the opinions expressed by many of the authorities in the English and American systems of jurisprudence.

It is difficult to comprehend that the release of the miserable from false relations, would necessarily seduce the contented from happy ones, or that the dearest word in the Saxon tongue (home) should have no significance, after drunkards and villains were denied the right to enter it. It is a pleasant reflection, in view of the dolorous results Mr. Greeley foresees from the passage of a divorce law, that the love of men and women for each other and their children in no way depends on the Statutes of New York. In the State of Indiana, where the laws have been very liberal for many years, family life is as beautiful and permanent as in South Carolina and New York, where the tie can be dissolved for one cause only. When we consider how little protection the State throws round the young and thoughtless in entering this relation, stringent laws against all escape are cruel and despotic, especially to woman, for if home life, which is everything to her, is discordant, where can she look for happiness?[44]

5.
Angelina Grimke Weld's speech at the
Woman's Loyal National League convention, May 1863

I came here with no desire and no intention to speak; but my heart is full, my country is bleeding, my people are perishing around me. But I feel as a South Carolinian, I am bound to tell the North, go on! go on! Never falter, never abandon the principles which you have adopted. I could not say this if we were now where we stood two years ago. I could not say thus when it was proclaimed in the Northern States that the Union was all that we sought. No, my friends, such a Union as we had then, God be praised that it has perished. Oh, never for one moment consent that such a Union should be re-established in our land. There was a time when I looked upon the Fathers of the Revolution with the deepest sorrow and the keenest reproach. I said to their shadows in another world, "Why did you leave this accursed system of slavery for us to suffer and die under? why did you not, with a stroke of the pen, determine—when you acquired your own independence—that the principles which you adopted in the Declaration of Independence should be a shield of protection to every man, whether he be slave or whether he be free?" But, my friends, the experience of sixty years has shown me that the fruit grows slowly. I look back and see that great Sower of the world, as he traveled the streets of Jerusalem and dropped the precious seed, "Do unto others as ye would that others should do unto you." I look at all the contests of different nations, and see that, whether it were the Patricians of Rome, England, France, or any part of Europe, every battle fought gained something to freedom. Our fathers, driven out by the oppression of England, came to this country and planted that little seed of liberty upon the soil of New England. When our Revolution took place, the seed was only in the process of sprouting. You must recollect that our Declaration of Independence was the very first National evidence of the great doctrine of brotherhood and equality. I verily believe that those who were the true lovers of liberty did all they could at that time. In their debates in the Convention they denounced slavery—they protested against the hypocrisy and inconsistency of a nation declaring such glorious truths, and then trampling them underfoot by enslaving the poor and oppressed, because he had a skin not colored like their own; as though a man's skin should make any difference in the recognition of his rights, any more than the color of his hair or of his eyes. This little blade sprouted as it were from the precious seeds that were planted by Jesus of Nazareth. But, my friends, if it took eighteen hundred years to bring forth the little blade which was seen in our Declaration, are we not unreasonable to suppose that more could have been done than has been done, looking at the imperfections of human nature, looking at the selfishness of man, looking at his desire for wealth and his greed for glory?

Had the South yielded at that time to the freemen of the North, we should have had a free Government; but it was impossible to overcome the long and strong prejudices of the South in favor of slavery. I know what the South is. I lived there the best part of my life. I never could talk against slavery without making my friends angry—never. When they thought the day was far off, and there was no danger of emancipation, they were willing to admit it was an evil; but when God in His providence raised up in this country an Anti-slavery Society, protesting against the oppressions of the colored man, they began to feel that truth which is more powerful than arms—that truth which is the only banner under which we can successfully fight. They were comparatively quiet till they found, in the election of Mr. Lincoln, the scepter had actually departed from them. His election took place on the ground that slavery was not to be extended—that it must not pass into the Territories. This was what alarmed them. They saw that if the National Government should take one such step, it never would stop there; that this principle had never before been acknowledged by those who had any power in the nation.

God be praised. Abolitionists never sought place or power. All they asked was freedom; all they wanted was that the white man should take his foot off the negro's neck. The South determined to resist the election of Mr. Lincoln. They determined if Fremont was elected, they would rebel. And this rebellion is like their own Republic, as they call it; it is founded upon slavery. As I asked one of my friends one day, "What are you rebelling for? The North never made any laws for you that they have not cheerfully obeyed themselves. What is the trouble between us?" Slavery, slavery is the trouble. Slavery is a "divine institution." My friends, it is a fact that the South has incorporated slavery into her religion; that is the most fearful thing in this rebellion. They are fighting, verily believing that they are doing God service. Most of them have never seen the North. They understand very little of the working of our institutions; but their politicians are stung to the quick by the prosperity of the North. They see that the institution which they have established can not make them wealthy, can not make them happy, can not make them respected in the world at large, and their motto is, "Rule or ruin."[45]

6.

The Woman's Loyal National League petitions presented to Congress on February 9, 1864, calling for an end to the institution of slavery

Petition presented to Congress to abolish slavery,
February 9, 1864

FORM OF PETITION.

To the Senate and House of Representatives of the United States in Congress assembled:

The undersigned, citizens of _____, believing slavery the great cause of the present rebellion, and an institution fatal to the life of Republican Government, earnestly pray your honorable bodies to immediately abolish it throughout the United States; and to adopt measures for so amending the Constitution, as forever to prohibit its existence in any portion of our common country.

MEN | WOMEN

Petition for women's signature presented to Congress to
abolish slavery, February 9, 1864

WOMEN'S EMANCIPATION PETITION

Put no signatures on the back of the Petition
  When this sheet is full, paste another at the bottom.
  If possible, send contributions to help pay the heavy ex-
penses incurred.
  Do not copy the names—return the original signatures no
matter if the paper is worn or soiled.
  When your district is thoroughly canvassed, return the peti-
tions and donations to this office.
  W. L. National League, Room 20, Cooper Institute, New
York.
To the Senate and House of Representatives of the United States:
  The undersigned, Women of the United States above the age
of eighteen years, earnestly pray that your Honorable Body
will pass at the earliest practicable day an Act emancipating all
persons of African descent held to involuntary service or labor
in the United States.

NAME | RESIDENCE

Senator Sumner's address to Congress upon delivering the
petitions to abolish slavery, February 9, 1864

THE PRAYER OF
ONE HUNDRED THOUSAND.

*Speech of Hon. Chas. Sumner on the
Presentation of the First
Installment of the Emancipation Petition
of the Women's National League.*

In the Senate of the United States, Tuesday, February 9th, 1864.
  MR. SUMNER—Mr. President: I offer a petition which is

now lying on the desk before me. It is too bulky for me to take up. I need not add that it is too bulky for any of the pages of this body to carry.

This petition marks a stage of public opinion in the history of slavery, and also in the suppression of the rebellion. . . .

It will be perceived that the petition is in rolls. Each roll represents a State. For instance, here is New York with a list of seventeen thousand seven hundred and six names; Illinois with fifteen thousand three hundred and eighty; and Massachusetts with eleven thousand six hundred and forty-one. [The exact number of signatures, as ascertained by Senator Sumner's clerk, was 265,314.] These several petitions are consolidated into one petition, being another illustration of the motto on our coin—*E pluribus unum.*

This petition is signed by one hundred thousand men and women, who unite in this unparalleled number to support its prayer. They are from all parts of the country and from every condition of life. They are from the sea-board, fanned by the free airs of the ocean, and from the Mississippi and the prairies of the West, fanned by the free airs which fertilize that extensive region. They are from the families of the educated and uneducated, rich and poor, of every profession, business, and calling in life, representing every sentiment, thought, hope, passion, activity, intelligence which inspires, strengthens, and adorns our social system. Here they are, a mighty army, one hundred thousand strong, without arms or banners; the advance-guard of a yet larger army.

But though memorable for their numbers, these petitioners are more memorable still for the prayer in which they unite. They ask nothing less than universal emancipation; and this they ask directly at the hands of Congress. No reason is assigned. The prayer speaks for itself. It is simple, positive. So far as it proceeds from the women of the country, it is naturally a petition, and not an argument. But I need not remind the Senate that there is no reason so strong as the reason of the heart. Do not all great thoughts come from the heart?

It is not for me, on presenting this petition, to assign reasons which the army of petitioners has forborne to assign. But I may not improperly add that, naturally and obviously, they all feel in their hearts, what reason and knowledge confirm: not only that slavery *as a unit,* one and indivisible, is the guilty origin of the rebellion, but that its influence everywhere, even outside the rebel States, has been hostile to the Union, always impairing loyalty, and sometimes openly menacing the national government. It requires no difficult logic to conclude that such a monster, wherever it shows its head, is a *national enemy,* to be pursued and destroyed as such, or at least a nuisance to the national cause to be abated as such. The petitioners know well that Congress is the depository of those supreme powers by which rebellion, alike in its root and in its distant offshoots, may be surely crushed, and by which unity and peace may be permanently secured. They know well that the action of Congress may be with the co-operation of the slave-masters, or even without the co-operation, under the overruling law of military necessity, or the commanding precept of the Constitution "to guarantee to every State a Republican form of government." Above all, they know well that to save the country from peril, especially to save the national life, there is no power, in the ample arsenal of self-defense, which Congress may not grasp; for to Congress, under the Constitution, belongs the prerogative of the Roman Dictator to see that the Republic receives no detriment. Therefore to Congress these petitioners now appeal. I ask the reference of the petition to the Select Committee on Slavery and Freedmen.[46]

7.
Elizabeth Cady Stanton's follow-up petition call of April 7, 1864, on behalf of the Woman's Loyal National League

OFFICE OF THE WOMAN'S LOYAL NATIONAL LEAGUE ⎫
Room No. 20, Cooper Institute, N. Y., *April 7, 1864.* ⎭

Dear Friend:—With this you will receive a Form of a Petition to Congress, the object of which you can not mistake nor regard with indifference. To procure on it the largest possible number of adult names, at the earliest practicable moment, it is hoped you will regard as less a duty than a pleasure. Already we have sent one installment of our petition forward, signed by one hundred thousand persons; the presentation of which, by Senator Sumner, produced a marked effect on both Congress and the country. We hope to send a million before the adjournment of Congress, which we shall easily do and even more, if you and the twenty thousand others to whom we have sent petitions will promptly, generously co-operate with us. For nearly three years has the scourge of war desolated us; sweeping away at least three hundred thousand of the strength, bloom, and beauty of our nation. And the war-chariot still rolls onward, its iron wheels deep in human blood! The God, at whose justice Jefferson long ago trembled, has awaked to the woes of the bondmen.

"For the sighing of the oppressed, and for the crying of the needy, now will I arise, saith the Lord." The redemption of that pledge we now behold in this dread Apocalypse of war. Nor should we expect or hope the calamity will cease while the fearful cause of it remains. Slavery has long been our national sin. War is its natural and just retribution. But the war has made it the constitutional right of the Government, as it always has been the moral duty of the people, to abolish slavery. We are, therefore, without excuse, if the solemn duty be not now performed. With us, the people, is the power to achieve the work by our agents in Congress. On us, therefore, rests the momentous responsibility. Shall we not all join then in one loud, earnest, effectual prayer to Congress, which will swell on its ear like the voice of many waters, that this bloody, desolating war shall be arrested and ended, by the immediate and final removal, by Statute Law and amended Constitution, of that crime and curse which alone has brought it upon us? Now surely is our accepted time. On our own heads will be the blood of our thousands slain, if, with the power in our own hands, we do not end that system forever, which is so plainly autographed all over with the Divine displeasure. In the name of justice and of freedom then let us rise and decree the destruction of our destroyer. Let us with myriad voice *compel* Congress to

"Consign it to remorseless fire!
Watch till the last faint spark expire;
Then strew its ashes on the wind,
Nor leave one atom wreck behind."

Susan B. Anthony, *Secretary*.
In behalf of the Women's League,

FORM OF PETITION.

*To the Senate and House of Representatives of the United
States in Congress assembled:*
    The undersigned, citizens of _____, believing slavery the
great cause of the present rebellion, and an institution fatal to
the life of Republican Government, earnestly pray your Honorable Bodies to immediately abolish it throughout the United
States; and to adopt measures for so amending the Constitution, as forever to prohibit its existence in any portion of our
common country.

MEN. | WOMEN.[47]

8.
Susan B. Anthony's proposal for the creation of an
organization to work for universal suffrage at the
eleventh National Woman's Rights Convention, held
May 10, 1866

Whereas, By the act of Emancipation and the Civil Rights bill,
the negro and woman now hold the same civil and political
status, alike needing only the ballot; and whereas the same arguments apply equally to both classes, proving all partial legislation fatal to republican institutions, therefore,
    Resolved, That the time has come for an organization that
shall demand Universal Suffrage, and that hereafter we shall
be known as the "American Equal Rights Association."
    Miss Anthony said: Our friend Mrs. Mott desires me to

explain the object of this change, which she would gladly do but for a severe cold, which prevents her from making herself heard. For twenty years we have pressed the claims of woman to the right of representation in the government. The first National Woman's Rights Convention was held in Worcester, Mass., in 1850, and each successive year conventions were held in different cities of the Free States—Worcester, Syracuse, Cleveland, Philadelphia, Cincinnati, and New York—until the rebellion. Since then, till now, we have held no conventions. Up to this hour, we have looked to State action only for the recognition of our rights; but now, by the results of the war, the whole question of suffrage reverts back to Congress and the U. S. Constitution. The duty of Congress at this moment is to declare what shall be the basis of representation in a republican form of government. There is, there can be, but one true basis; and that is that taxation must give representation; hence our demand must now go beyond woman—it must extend to the farthest bound of the principle of the "consent of the governed," as the only authorized or just government. We, therefore, wish to broaden our Woman's Rights platform, and make it in *name*—what it ever has been in *spirit*—a Human Rights platform. It has already been stated that we have petitioned Congress the past winter to so amend the Constitution as to prohibit disfranchisement on account of sex. We were roused to this work by the several propositions to prohibit negro disfranchisement in the rebel States, which at the same time put up a new bar against the enfranchisement of women. As women we can no longer *seem* to claim for ourselves what we do not for others—nor can we work in two separate movements to get the ballot for the two disfranchised classes—the negro and woman—since to do so must be at double cost of time, energy, and money.

New York is to hold a Constitutional Convention the coming year. We want to make a thorough canvass of the entire State, with lectures, tracts, and petitions, and, if possible, create a public sentiment that shall send genuine Democrats and Republicans to that Convention who shall strike out from our Constitution the two adjectives *"white male,"* giving to every citizen, over twenty-one, the right to vote, and thus make the Empire State the first example of a true republican form of government. And what we propose to do in New York, the coming eighteen months, we hope to do in every other State so soon as we can get the men, and the women, and the money, to go forward with the work. Therefore, that we may henceforth concentrate all our forces for the practical application of our one grand, distinctive, national idea— Universal Suffrage—I hope we will unanimously adopt the resolution before us, thus resolving this Eleventh National Woman's Rights Convention into the "American Equal Rights Association."

The Resolution was unanimously adopted.[48]

9.
Susan E. Wattles's letter to Susan B. Anthony on Kansas's struggle to become a free (non-slave) state and achieve universal suffrage, December 30, 1881

Mound City, *December 30, 1881.*

My Dear Miss Anthony:—Here, as in New York, the first in the woman suffrage cause were those who had been the most earnest workers for freedom. They had come to Kansas to prevent its being made a slave State. The most the women could do was to bear their privations patiently, such as living in a tent in a log cabin, without any floor all winter, or in a cabin ten feet square, and cooking out of doors by the side of a log, giving up their beds to the sick, and being ready, night or day, to feed the men who were running for their lives. Then there was the ever present fear that their husbands would be shot. The most obnoxious had a price set upon their heads. A few years ago a man said: "I could have got $1,000 once for shooting Wattles, and I wish now I had done it." When in Ohio, our house was often the temporary home of the hunted slave; but in Kansas it was the *white* man who ran from our door to the woods because he saw strangers coming.

After the question of a free State seemed settled, we who had thought and talked on woman's rights before we came to Kansas, concluded that now was the woman's hour. We determined to strive to obtain Constitutional rights, as they would be more secure than Legislative enactments. On the 13th of February, 1858, we organized the Moneka Woman's Rights Society. There were only twelve of us, but we went to work circulating petitions and writing to every one in the Territory whom we thought would aid us. Our number was afterwards increased to forty; fourteen of them were men. We sent petitions to Territorial Legislatures, Constitutional Conventions, State Legislatures, and Congress. Many of the leading men were advocates of women's rights. Governor Robinson, S. N. Wood, and Erastus Heath, with their wives, were constant and efficient workers. Mrs. Robinson wrote a book on "Life in Kansas." "Allibone's Dictionary of Authors" says: "Mrs. Robinson is an accomplished lady, the wife of Governor Robinson. She possessed the knowledge of events and literary skill necessary to produce an interesting and trustworthy book, and one which will continue to have a permanent value. The women of Kansas suffered more than the men, and were not less heroic. Their names are not known; they were not elected to office; they had none of the exciting delights of an active out-door life on these attractive prairies; they endured in silence; they took care of the home, of the sick. If 'home they brought her warrior dead, she nor swooned nor uttered sigh.' It is fortunate that a few of these truest heroes have left a printed record of pioneer life in Kansas."

The last vigorous effort we made in circulating petitions was when Congress was about extending to the colored men the right to vote. Many signed then for the first time. One woman said, "I know my husband does not believe in women voting, but he hates the negroes, and would not want them placed over me." I saw in *The Liberator* that a bequest to the woman's rights cause had been made by a gentleman in Boston, and I asked Wendell Phillips if we could have some of it in Kansas. He directed me to Susan B. Anthony, and you gave us $100. This small sum we divided between two lecturers, and paying for tracts. John O. Wattles lectured and distributed tracts in Southern Kansas. We were greatly rejoiced when we found, by corresponding with Mrs. Nichols, that she intended to work for our cause whether she had any compensation or not. Kansas women can never be half thankful enough for what she did for them. There has never been a time since, when the same amount of effort would have accomplished as much; and the little money we gave her could scarcely have paid her stage fare.

When the question was submitted in 1867, and the men were to decide whether women should be allowed to vote, we felt very anxious about the result. We strongly desired to make Kansas the banner State for Freedom. We did all we could to secure it, and some of the best speakers from the East came to our aid. Their speeches were excellent, and were listened to by large audiences, who seemed to believe what they heard; but when voting day came, they voted according to their prejudices, and our cause was defeated. My work has been very limited. I have only been able to talk and circulate tracts and papers. I took *The Una, The Lily, The Sybil, The Pittsburg Visitor, The Revolution, Woman's Journal, Ballot Box,* and *National Citizen*; got all the subscribers I could, and scattered them far and near. When I gave away *The Revolution*, my husband said, "Wife, that is a very talented paper; I should think you would preserve that." I replied: "They will continue to come until our cause is won, and I must make them do all the good they can." I am delighted with the "Suffrage History." I do not think you can find material to make the second volume as interesting. I knew of most of the incidents as they transpired, yet they are full of interest and significance to me now. My book is now lent where I think it will be highly appreciated.[49]

10.

Elizabeth Cady Stanton's editorials opposing the Fifteenth Amendment in the *Revolution*, October 21, 1869, and June 3, 1869

All wise women should oppose the Fifteenth Amendment for two reasons. 1st. Because it is invidious to their sex. Look at it from what point you will and in every aspect, it reflects the old idea of woman's inferiority, her subject condition. And yet the one need to secure an onward step in civilization is a new dignity and self-respect in women themselves. No one can think that the pending proposition of "manhood suffrage" exalts woman, either in her own eyes or those of the man by her side, but it does degrade her practically and theoretically, just as black men were more degraded when all other men were enfranchised.

2d. We should oppose the measure, because men have no right to pass it without our consent. When it is proposed to change the constitution or fundamental law of the State or Nation, all the people have a right to say what that change shall be.

If women understood this pending proposition in all its bearings, theoretically and practically, there would be an overwhelming vote against the admission of another man to the ruling power of this nation, until they themselves were first enfranchised. There is no true patriotism, no true nobility in tamely and silently submitting to this insult. It is mere sycophancy to man; it is licking the hand that forges a new chain for our degradation; it is indorsing the old idea that woman's divinely ordained position is at man's feet, and not on an even platform by his side.

By this edict of the liberal party, the women of this Republic are now to touch the lowest depths of their political degradation.

JUNE 3, 1869.

The Fifteenth Amendment.—*It is not to be believed that the nation which is now engaged in admitting the newly liberated*

negro to the plenitude of all political franchise, will much lon-
ger retain woman in a state of helotage, which is more degrad-
ing than ever, because being no longer shared by any of the
male sex, it constitutes every woman the inferior of every
man.—John Stuart Mill.

It is this thought, so clearly seen and concisely stated by this
distinguished English philosopher and statesman, that I have
endeavored to press on the hearts of American reformers for
the last four years. I have seen and felt, with a vividness and
intensity that no words could express, the far-reaching consequences of this degradation of one-half the citizens of the
republic, on the government, the Saxon race, and woman herself, in all her political, religious, and social relations. It is
sufficiently humiliating to a proud woman to be reminded ever
and anon in the polite world that she's a political nonentity; to
have the fact gracefully mourned over, or wittily laughed at, in
classic words and cultured voice by one's superiors in knowledge, wisdom and power; but to hear the rights of woman
scorned in foreign tongue and native gibberish by everything in
manhood's form, is enough to fire the souls of those who think
and feel, and rouse the most lethargic into action.

If, with weak and vacillating words and stammering tongue,
our bravest men to-day say freedom to woman, what can we
hope when the millions educated in despotism, ignorant of
the philosophy of true government, religion and social life,
shall be our judges and rulers? As you go down in the scale of
manhood, the idea strengthens at every step, that woman was
created for no higher purpose than to gratify the lust of man.
Every daily paper heralds some rape on flying, hunted girls;
and the pitying eyes of angels see the holocaust of womanhood
no journal ever notes. In thought I trace the slender threads
that link these hideous, overt acts to creeds and codes that
make an aristocracy of sex. When a mighty nation, with a
scratch of the pen, frames the base ideas of the lower orders
into constitutions and statute laws, and declares every serf,
peasant and slave the rightful sovereigns of all womankind,
they not only degrade every woman in her own eyes, but in
that of every man on the footstool. A cultivated lady in

Baltimore writes us a description of a colored republican reunion, held in that city a few evenings since, in which a colored gentleman offered the following toast: "Our wives and daughters —May the women of our race never unsex themselves by becoming strong-minded."

E. C. S.[50]

II.

The *Revolution*'s reporting of the first National Woman's Suffrage Convention, held in Washington in January 1869

Washington, January 22, 1869.

Dear Revolution:—The first National Woman's Suffrage Convention ever held in Washington, closed on Wednesday night. There were representatives from about twenty States, and the deepest interest was manifested through all the sessions, increasing to the end. On the morning of the Convention the business committee assembled in the ante-room of Carroll Hall, to discuss resolutions, officers, etc. As Senator Pomeroy, of Kansas, was present, it was decided that he should open the meeting and preside as long as his public duties would permit. This gave us assurance of a healthy repose in the chair, which greatly helps to take off the chill in opening a convention. After a grave discussion of resolutions, permanent officers, etc., Mr. Pomeroy led the way to the platform, called the meeting to order, and made an able speech, taking the broad ground that as suffrage is a natural, inalienable right, it must, of necessity, belong to every citizen of the republic, black and white, male and female. Mrs. Mott was chosen President, resolutions were reported, and when everything was in fine working order (except the furnace) Mr. Pomeroy slipped off to his senatorial duties, to watch the grand Kansas swindle now on the tapis, and to protect, if possible, the interests of the people.

Whatever elements or qualities combine to render any popular convention every way successful, were most felicitously blended in this gathering in Washington. In numbers, interest, earnestness, variety and especially ability, there was surely little left to be desired. As to numbers in attendance, from Maine, California, and all the way between, it is sufficient to say that although the first session was most encouragingly large, there was a constant increase till the last evening, when the spacious hall was crowded in every part, until entrance was absolutely impossible, long before people ceased coming. Of the interest in the proceedings, it may be said that it was proposed to hold three sessions each day, with a brief recess at noon. But twelve o'clock and all o'clock were forgotten, and the day session continued until after four; the only regret seeming then to be that there were not more hours, and that human nature had not greater power of endurance.

The harmony that prevailed was all that could reasonably have been expected (if not even desired), considering the nature of the questions in hand, and the large number and variety of opinions entertained and expressed in the different sessions. On the one vital point, that suffrage is the inalienable right of every intelligent citizen who is held amenable to law, and is taxed to support the government, there was no difference expressed. The issue that roused the most heated debate was whether the colored man should be kept out of the right of suffrage until woman could also be enfranchised. One young, but not ineffectual speaker, declared he considered the women the bitterest enemies of the negro; and asked, with intense emotion, shall they be permitted to prevent the colored man from obtaining his rights? But it was not shown that women, anywhere, were making any effort toward that result. One or two women present declared they were unwilling that any more men should possess the right of suffrage until women had it also. But these are well known as most earnest advocates of universal suffrage, as well as the long-tried and approved friends of the colored race.

The discussion between colored men on the one side and women on the other, as to whether it was the duty of the women of the nation to hold their claims in abeyance, until all colored men are enfranchised, was spicy, able and affecting. When that noble man, Robert Purvis of Philadelphia, rose, and, with the loftiest sense of justice, with a true Roman grandeur, ignored his race and sex, rebuked his own son for his narrow position, and demanded for his daughter all he asked for his son or himself, he thrilled the noblest feelings in his audience. Is has been a great grief to the leading women in our cause that there should be antagonism with men whom we respect, whose wrongs we pity, and whose hopes we would fain help them to realize. When we contrast the condition of the most fortunate women at the North, with the living death colored men endure everywhere, there seems to be a selfishness in our present position. But remember we speak not for ourselves alone, but for all womankind, in poverty, ignorance and hopeless dependence, for the women of that oppressed race too, who, in slavery, have known a depth of misery and degradation that no man can ever appreciate.

That there were representatives of both political parties present, was very apparent, and sometimes forms of expression betrayed a little unnecessary partisan preference; but there was not one who bore any part in the long and intensely exciting discussions, who could be justly charged with any wish, however remote, to hold personal prejudice or party preference above principle and religious regard to justice and right. There was one feature in the convention that we greatly deplore, and that was an impatience, not only with the audience, but with some on the platform whenever any man arose to speak. We must not forget that men have sensibilities as well as women, and that our strongest hold to-day on the public mind is the fact that men of eloquence and power on both continents are pleading for our rights. While we ask justice for ourselves, let us at least be just to the noble men who advocate our cause. It is certainly generous in them to come to our platforms, to help us maintain our rights, and share the ridicule that attends every step of progress, and it is clearly our duty to defend their rights, at least when speaking in our behalf.

We had a brief interview with Senator Roscoe Conkling. We gave him a petition signed by 400 ladies of Onondaga County, and urged him to make some wise remarks on the subject of woman's suffrage when he presented it. We find all the New York women are sending their petitions to Senator Pomeroy. He seems to be immensely popular just now. We think our own Senators need some education in this direction. It would be well for the petitions of the several States to be placed in the hands of their respective Senators, that thus the attention of all of them might be called to the important subject. It is plain to see that Mr. Conkling is revolving this whole question in his mind. His greatest fear is that coarse and ignorant women would crowd the polls and keep the better class away.

Parker Pillsbury's speech on "The Mortality of Nations," was one of the best efforts of his life, and as grand an argument on the whole question of Republican government as was ever made on the woman suffrage platform. Although he had been one of the earliest and most enthusiastic Abolitionists, yet the enfranchisement of woman had always in his mind seemed of equal importance to that of the black man. In Mr. Pillsbury's philosophy on both questions, the present was ever the time for immediate and absolute justice.

One great charm in the convention was the presence of Lucretia Mott, calm, dignified, clear and forcible as ever. Though she is now seventy-six years old, she sat through all the sessions, and noted everything that was said and done. It was a satisfaction to us all that she was able to preside over the first National Woman's Suffrage Convention ever held at the Capitol. Her voice is stronger and her step lighter than many who are her juniors by twenty years. She preached last Sunday in the Unitarian Church to the profit and pleasure of a highly cultivated and large audience. We were most pleased to meet ex-Governor Robinson, the first Governor of Kansas, in the convention. He says there is a fair prospect that an amendment to strike out the word "male" from the Constitution will be submitted again in that State, when, he thinks, it will pass without doubt. Mrs. Minor, President of the Woman's Suffrage Association of Missouri, and Mrs. Starrett of Lawrence, Kansas, gave us a pleasant surprise by their appearance at the convention. They took an active part in the deliberations, and spoke with great effect. Senator Wilson was present, though he did not favor us with a speech. We urged him to do so, but he laughingly said he had no idea of making himself a target for our wit and sarcasm. We asked him, as he would not speak, to tell us the "wise, systematic, and efficient way" of pressing woman's suffrage. He replied, "You are on the right track, go ahead." So we have decided to move "on this line" until the inauguration of the new administration, when, under the dynasty of the chivalrous soldier, "our ways will, no doubt, be those of pleasantness, and all our paths be peace." New Jersey was represented by Deborah Butler of Vineland, the only live spot in that benighted State, and we thought her speech quite equal to what we heard from Mr. Cattell in the Senate. During the evening sessions, large numbers of women from the several departments were attentive listeners. Lieutenant-Governor Root of Kansas read the bill now before Congress demanding equal pay for women in the several departments where they perform equal work with the men by their side. He offered a resolution urging Congress to pass the bill at once, that justice might be done the hundreds of women in the District, for their faithful work under government.

Mrs. Stanton's speech the first evening of the convention gave a fair statement of the hostile feelings of women toward the amendments; we give the main part of it. Of all the other speeches, which were extemporaneous, only meagre and unsatisfactory reports can be found.

Mrs. Stanton said:—A great idea of progress is near its consummation, when statesmen in the councils of the nation propose to frame it into statutes and constitutions; when Reverend Fathers recognize it by a new interpretation of their creeds and canons; when the Bar and Bench at its command set aside the legislation of centuries, and girls of twenty put their heels on the Cokes and Blackstones of the past.

Those who represent what is called "the Woman's Rights Movement," have argued their right to political equality from every standpoint of justice, religion, and logic, for the last twenty years. They have quoted the Constitution, the Declaration of Independence, the Bible, the opinions of great men and women in all ages; they have plead the theory of our government; suffrage a natural, inalienable right; shown from the lessons of history, that one class can not legislate for another; that disfranchised classes must ever be neglected and degraded; and that all privileges are but mockery to the citizen, until he has a voice in the making and administering of law. Such arguments have been made over and over in conventions and before the legislatures of the several States. Judges, lawyers, priests, and politicians have said again and again, that our logic was unanswerable, and although much nonsense has emanated from the male tongue and pen on this subject, no man has yet made a fair, argument on the other side. Knowing that we hold the Gibraltar rock of reason on this question, they resort to ridicule and petty objections. Compelled to follow our assailants, wherever they go, and fight them with their own weapons; when cornered with wit and sarcasm, some cry out, you have no logic on your platform, forgetting that we have no use for logic until they give us logicians at whom to hurl it, and if, for the pure love of it, we now and then rehearse the logic that is like a, b, c, to all of us, others cry out—the same old speeches we have heard these twenty years. It would be safe to say a hundred years, for they are the same our fathers used when battling old King George and the British Parliament for their right to representation, and a voice in the laws by which they were governed. There are no new arguments to be made on human rights, our work to-day is to apply to ourselves those so familiar to all; to teach man that woman is not an anomalous being, outside all laws and constitutions, but one whose rights are to be established by the same process of reason as that by which he demands his own.

When our Fathers made out their famous bill of impeachment against England, they specified eighteen grievances. When the women of this country surveyed the situation in their first convention, they found they had precisely that number, and quite similar in character; and reading over the old revolutionary arguments of Jefferson, Patrick Henry, Otis, and Adams, they found they applied remarkably well to their case. The same arguments made in this country for extending suffrage from time to time, to white men, native born citizens, without property and education, and to foreigners; the same used by John Bright in England, to extend it to a million new voters, and the same used by the great Republican party to enfranchise a million black men in the South, all these arguments we have to-day to offer for woman, and one, in addition, stronger than all besides, the difference in man and woman. Because man and woman are the complement of one another, we need woman's thought in national affairs to make a safe and stable government.

The Republican party to-day congratulates itself on having carried the Fifteenth Amendment of the Constitution, thus securing "manhood suffrage" and establishing an aristocracy of sex on this continent. As several bills to secure Woman's Suffrage in the District and the Territories have been already presented in both houses of Congress, and as by Mr. Julian's bill, the question of so amending the Constitution as to extend suffrage to all the women of the country has been presented to the nation for consideration, it is not only the right but the duty of every thoughtful woman to express her opinion on a Sixteenth Amendment. While I hail the late discussions in Congress and the various bills presented as so many signs of progress, I am especially gratified with those of Messrs. Julian and Pomeroy, which forbid any State to deny the right of suffrage to any of its citizens on account of sex or color.

This fundamental principle of our government—the equality of all the citizens of the republic—should be incorporated in the Federal Constitution, there to remain forever. To leave this question to the States and partial acts of Congress, is to defer indefinitely its settlement, for what is done by this Congress may be repealed by the next; and politics in the several States differ so widely, that no harmonious action on any question can ever be secured, except as a strict party measure. Hence, we appeal to the party now in power, everywhere, to end this protracted debate on suffrage, and declare it the inalienable right of every citizen who is amenable to the laws of the land, who pays taxes and the penalty of crime. We have a splendid theory of a genuine republic, why not realize it and make our government homogeneous, from Maine to California. The Republican party has the power to do this, and now is its only opportunity. Woman's Suffrage, in 1872, may be as good a card for the Republicans as Gen. Grant was in the last election. It is said that the Republican party made him President, not because they thought him the most desirable man in the nation for that office, but they were afraid the Democrats would take him if they did not. We would suggest, there may be the same danger of Democrats taking up Woman Suffrage if they do not. God, in his providence, may have purified that party in the furnace of affliction. They have had the opportunity, safe from the turmoil of political life and the temptations of office, to study and apply the divine principles of justice and equality to life; for minorities are always in a position to carry principles to their logical results, while majorities are governed only by votes. You see my faith in Democrats is based on sound philosophy. In the next Congress, the Democratic party will gain thirty-four new members, hence the Republicans have had their last chance to do justice to woman. It will be no enviable record for the Fortieth Congress that in the darkest days of the republic it placed our free institutions in the care and keeping of every type of manhood, ignoring womanhood, all the elevating and purifying influences of the most virtuous and humane half of the American people. . . .

I urge a speedy adoption of a Sixteenth Amendment for the following reasons:

1.   A government, based on the principle of caste and class, can not stand. The aristocratic idea, in any form, is opposed to the genius of our free institutions, to our own declaration of rights, and to the civilization of the age. All artificial distinctions, whether of family, blood, wealth, color, or sex, are equally oppressive to the subject classes, and equally destructive to national life and prosperity. Governments based on every form of aristocracy, on every degree and variety of inequality, have been tried in despotisms, monarchies, and republics, and all alike have perished. In the panorama of the past behold the mighty nations that have risen, one by one, but to fall. Behold their temples, thrones, and pyramids, their gorgeous palaces and stately monuments now crumbled all to dust. Behold every monarch in Europe at this very hour trembling on his throne. Behold the republics on this Western continent convulsed, distracted, divided, the hosts scattered, the leaders fallen, the scouts lost in the wilderness, the once inspired prophets blind and dumb, while on all sides the cry is echoed, "Republicanism is a failure," though that great principle of a government "by the people, of the people, for the people," has never been tried. Thus far, all nations have been

built on caste and failed. Why, in this hour of reconstruction, with the experience of generations before us, make another experiment in the same direction? If serfdom, peasantry, and slavery have shattered kingdoms, deluged continents with blood, scattered republics like dust before the wind, and rent our own Union asunder, what kind of a government, think you, American statesmen, you can build, with the mothers of the race crouching at your feet, while iron-heeled peasants, serfs, and slaves, exalted by your hands, tread our inalienable rights into the dust? While all men, everywhere, are rejoicing in new-found liberties, shall woman alone be denied the rights, privileges, and immunities of citizenship? While in England men are coming up from the coal mines of Cornwall, from the factories of Birmingham and Manchester, demanding the suffrage; while in frigid Russia the 22,000,000 newly-emancipated serfs are already claiming a voice in the government; while here, in our own land, slaves, but just rejoicing in the proclamation of emancipation, ignorant alike of its power and significance, have the ballot unasked, unsought, already laid at their feet—think you the daughters of Adams, Jefferson, and Patrick Henry, in whose veins flows the blood of two Revolutions, will forever linger round the campfires of an old barbarism, with no longings to join this grand army of freedom in its onward march to roll back the golden gates of a higher and better civilization? Of all kinds of aristocracy, that of sex is the most odious and unnatural; invading, as it does, our homes, desecrating our family altars, dividing those whom God has joined together, exalting the son above the mother who bore him, and subjugating, everywhere, moral power to brute force. Such a government would not be worth the blood and treasure so freely poured out in its long struggles for freedom. . . .

2. I urge a Sixteenth Amendment, because "manhood suffrage" or a man's government, is civil, religious, and social disorganization. The male element is a destructive force, stern, selfish, aggrandizing, loving war, violence, conquest, acquisition, breeding in the material and moral world alike discord, disorder, disease, and death. See what a record of blood and cruelty the pages of history reveal! Through what slavery, slaughter, and

sacrifice, through what inquisitions and imprisonments, pains and persecutions, black codes and gloomy creeds, the soul of humanity has struggled for the centuries, while mercy has veiled her face and all hearts have been dead alike to love and hope! The male element has held high carnival thus far, it has fairly run riot from the beginning, overpowering the feminine element everywhere, crushing out all the diviner qualities in human nature, until we know but little of true manhood and womanhood, of the latter comparatively nothing, for it has scarce been recognized as a power until within the last century. Society is but the reflection of man himself, untempered by woman's thought, the hard iron rule we feel alike in the church, the state, and the home. No one need wonder at the disorganization, at the fragmentary condition of everything, when we remember that man, who represents but half a complete being, with but half an idea on every subject, has undertaken the absolute control of all sublunary matters.

People object to the demands of those whom they choose to call the strong-minded, because they say, "the right of suffrage will make the women masculine." That is just the difficulty in which we are involved to-day. Though disfranchised we have few women in the best sense, we have simply so many reflections, varieties, and dilutions of the masculine gender. The strong, natural characteristics of womanhood are repressed and ignored in dependence, for so long as man feeds woman she will try to please the giver and adapt herself to his condition. To keep a foothold in society woman must be as near like man as possible, reflect his ideas, opinions, virtues, motives, prejudices, and vices. She must respect his statutes, though they strip her of every inalienable right, and conflict with that higher law written by the finger of God on her own soul. She must believe his theology, though it pave the highways of hell with the skulls of newborn infants, and make God a monster of vengeance and hypocrisy. She must look at everything from its dollar and cent point of view, or she is a mere romancer. She must accept things as they are and make the best of them. To mourn over the miseries of others, the poverty of the poor, their hardships in jails, prisons, asylums, the horrors of war, cruelty, and brutality in every form, all this would be mere sentimentalizing. To protest against the intrigue, bribery, and corruption of public life, to desire that her sons might follow some business that did not involve lying, cheating, and a hard, grinding selfishness, would be arrant nonsense. In this way man has been moulding woman to his ideas by direct and positive influences, while she, if not a negation, has used indirect means to control him, and in most cases developed the very characteristics both in him and herself that needed repression. And now man himself stands appalled at the results of his own excesses, and mourns in bitterness that falsehood, selfishness and violence are the law of life. The need of this hour is not territory, gold mines, railroads, or specie payments, but a new evangel of womanhood, to exalt purity, virtue, morality, true religion, to lift man up into the higher realms of thought and action.

We ask woman's enfranchisement, as the first step toward the recognition of that essential element in government that can only secure the health, strength, and prosperity of the nation. Whatever is done to lift woman to her true position will help to usher in a new day of peace and perfection for the race. In speaking of the masculine element, I do not wish to be understood to say that all men are hard, selfish, and brutal, for many of the most beautiful spirits the world has known have been clothed with manhood; but I refer to those characteristics, though often marked in woman, that distinguish what is called the stronger sex. For example, the love of acquisition and conquest, the very pioneers of civilization, when expended on the earth, the sea, the elements, the riches and forces of Nature, are powers of destruction when used to subjugate one man to another or to sacrifice nations to ambition. Here that great conservator of woman's love, if permitted to assert itself, as it naturally would in freedom against oppression, violence, and war, would hold all these destructive forces in check, for woman knows the cost of life better than man does, and not with her consent would one drop of blood ever be shed, one life sacrificed in vain. With violence and disturbance in the natural world, we see a constant effort to maintain an equilibrium of forces. Nature, like a loving mother, is ever trying to keep land and sea, mountain and valley, each in its place, to hush the angry winds and waves, balance the extremes of heat and cold, of rain and drought, that peace, harmony, and beauty may reign supreme. There is a striking analogy between matter and mind, and the present disorganization of society warns us, that in the dethronement of woman we have let loose the elements of violence and ruin that she only has the power to curb. If the civilization of the age calls for an extension of the suffrage, surely a government of the most virtuous, educated men and women would better represent the whole, and protect the interests of all than could the representation of either sex alone. But government gains no new element of strength in admitting all men to the ballot-box, for we have too much of the man-power there already. We see this in every department of legislation, and it is a common remark, that unless some new virtue is infused into our public life the nation is doomed to destruction. Will the foreign element, the dregs of China, Germany, England, Ireland, and Africa supply this needed force, or the nobler types of American womanhood who have taught our presidents, senators, and congressmen the rudiments of all they know?

3. I urge a Sixteenth Amendment because, when "manhood suffrage" is established from Maine to California, woman has reached the lowest depths of political degradation. So long as there is a disfranchised class in this country, and that class its women, a man's government is worse than a white man's government with suffrage limited by property and educational qualifications, because in proportion as you multiply the rulers, the condition of the politically ostracised is more hopeless and degraded. John Stuart Mill, in his work on "Liberty," shows that the condition of one disfranchised man in a nation is worse than when the whole nation is under one man, because in the latter case, if the one man is despotic, the nation can easily throw him off, but what can one man do with a nation of tyrants over him? If American women find it hard to bear the oppressions of their own Saxon fathers, the best orders of manhood, what may they not be called to endure when all the lower orders of foreigners now crowding our shores legislate for them and their daughters. Think of Patrick and Sambo and Hans and Yung Tung, who do

not know the difference between a monarchy and a republic, who can not read the Declaration of Independence or Webster's spelling-book, making laws for Lucretia Mott, Ernestine L. Rose, and Anna E. Dickinson. Think of jurors and jailors drawn from these ranks to watch and try young girls for the crime of infanticide, to decide the moral code by which the mothers of this Republic shall be governed? This manhood suffrage is an appalling question, and it would be well for thinking women, who seem to consider it so magnanimous to hold their own claims in abeyance until all men are crowned with citizenship, to remember that the most ignorant men are ever the most hostile to the equality of women, as they have known them only in slavery and degradation.

Go to our courts of justice, our jails and prisons; go into the world of work; into the trades and professions; into the temples of science and learning, and see what is meted out everywhere to women—to those who have no advocates in our courts, no representatives in the councils of the nation. Shall we prolong and perpetuate such injustice, and by increasing this power risk worse oppressions for ourselves and daughters? It is an open, deliberate insult to American womanhood to be cast down under the iron-heeled peasantry of the Old World and the slaves of the New, as we shall be in the practical working of the Fifteenth Amendment, and the only atonement the Republican party can make is now to complete its work, by enfranchising the women of the nation. I have not forgotten their action four years ago, when Article XIV., Sec. 2, was amended by invidiously introducing the word "male" into the Federal Constitution, where it had never been before, thus counting out of the basis of representation all men not permitted to vote, thereby making it the interest of every State to enfranchise its male citizens, and virtually declaring it no crime to disfranchise its women. As political sagacity moved our rulers thus to guard the interests of the negro for party purposes, common justice might have compelled them to show like respect for their own mothers, by counting woman too out of the basis of representation, that she might no longer swell the numbers to legislate adversely to her interests. And this desecration of the last will and testament of the fathers, this retrogressive legislation for woman, was in the face of the earnest protests of thousands of the best educated, most refined and cultivated women of the North.

Now, when the attention of the whole world is turned to this question of suffrage, and women themselves are throwing off the lethargy of ages, and in England, France, Germany, Switzerland, and Russia are holding their conventions, and their rulers are everywhere giving them a respectful hearing, shall American statesmen, claiming to be liberal, so amend their constitutions as to make their wives and mothers the political inferiors of unlettered and unwashed ditch-diggers, boot-blacks, butchers, and barbers, fresh from the slave plantations of the South, and the effete civilizations of the Old World? While poets and philosophers, statesmen and men of science are all alike pointing to woman as the new hope for the redemption of the race, shall the freest Government on the earth be the first to establish an aristocracy based on sex alone? to exalt ignorance above education, vice above virtue, brutality and barbarism above refinement and religion? Not since God first called light out of darkness and order out of chaos, was there ever made so base a proposition as "manhood suffrage" in this American Republic, after all the discussions we have had on human rights in the last century. On all the blackest pages of history there is no record of an act like this, in any nation, where native born citizens, having the same religion, speaking the same language, equal to their rulers in wealth, family, and education, have been politically ostracised by their own countrymen, outlawed with savages, and subjected to the government of outside barbarians. Remember the Fifteenth Amendment takes in a larger population than the 2,000,000 black men on the Southern plantation. It takes in all the foreigners daily landing in our eastern cities, the Chinese crowding our western shores, the inhabitants of Alaska, and all those western isles that will soon be ours. American statesmen may flatter themselves that by superior intelligence and political sagacity the higher orders of men will always govern, but when the ignorant foreign vote already holds the balance of power in all the large cities by sheer force of numbers, it is simply a question of impulse or passion, bribery or fraud, how our elections will be carried. When the highest offices in the gift of the people are bought and sold in Wall Street, it is a mere chance who will be our rulers. Whither is a nation tending when brains count for less than bullion, and clowns make laws for queens? It is a startling assertion, but nevertheless true, that in none of the nations of modern Europe are the higher classes of women politically so degraded as are the women of this Republic to-day. In the Old World, where the government is the aristocracy, where it is considered a mark of nobility to share its offices and powers, women of rank have certain hereditary lights which raise them above a majority of the men, certain honors and privileges not granted to serfs and peasants. There women are queens, hold subordinate offices, and vote on many questions. In our Southern States even, before the war, women were not degraded below the working population. They were not humiliated in seeing their coachmen, gardeners, and waiters go to the polls to legislate for them; but here, in this boasted Northern civilization, women of wealth and education, who pay taxes and obey the laws, who in morals and intellect are the peers of their proudest rulers, are thrust outside the pale of political consideration with minors, paupers, lunatics, traitors, idiots, with those guilty of bribery, larceny, and infamous crimes.

Would those gentlemen who are on all sides telling the women of the nation not to press their claims until the negro is safe beyond peradventure, be willing themselves to stand aside and trust all their interests to hands like these? The educated women of this nation feel as much interest in republican institutions, the preservation of the country, the good of the race, their own elevation and success, as any man possibly can, and we have the same distrust in man's power to legislate for us, that he has in woman's power to legislate wisely for herself.

4. I would press a Sixteenth Amendment, because the history of American statesmanship does not inspire me with confidence in man's capacity to govern the nation alone, with justice and mercy. I have come to this conclusion, not only from my own observation, but from what our rulers say of themselves.

Honorable Senators have risen in their places again and again, and told the people of the wastefulness and corruption of the present administration. Others have set forth, with equal clearness, the ignorance of our rulers on the question of finance. . . .

The following letters were received and read in the Convention:

New York, Jan. 14, 1869.

Mrs. Josephine S. Griffing,—*Dear Madam*:—Your favor of the 6th inst. is received. Permit me to assure you it would give me great pleasure to be present at your important convention of the 19th, but indisposition will not allow me that gratification.

Looking at all the circumstances; the position, the epoch, and the efforts now being made to extend the right to the ballot, your Convention is perhaps the most important that was ever held. It is a true maxim, that it is easier to do justice than injustice; to do right than wrong; and to do it at once, than by small degrees. How much better and easier it would have been for Congress, when they enfranchised all the men of the District of Columbia, had they included the women also; but better late than never. Let the National government, to which the States have a right to look for good example, do justice to woman now, and all the States will follow. . . .

It was a terrible mistake and a fundamental error, based upon ignorance and injustice, ever to have introduced the word "male" into the Federal Constitution. The terms "male" and "female" simply designate the physical or animal distinction between the sexes, and ought be used only in speaking of the lower animals. Human beings are men and women, possessed of human faculties and understanding, which we call mind; and mind recognizes no sex, therefore the term "male," as applied to human beings—to citizens—ought to be expunged from the constitution and laws as a last remnant of barbarism—when the animal, not mind, when might, not right, governed the world. Let your Convention, then, urge Congress to wipe out that purely animal distinction from the national constitution. That noble instrument was destined to govern intelligent, responsible human beings—men and women—not sex. The childish argument that all women don't ask for the franchise would hardly deserve notice were it not sometimes used by men of sense. To all such I would say, examine ancient and modern history, yes, even of your own times, and you will find there never has been a time when all men of any country—white or black—have ever asked for a reform. Reforms have to be claimed and obtained by the few, who are in advance, for the benefit of the many who lag behind. And when once obtained and almost forced upon them, the mass of the people accept and enjoy their benefits as a matter of course. Look at the petitions now pouring into Congress for the franchise for women, and compare their thousands of signatures with the few isolated names that graced our first petitions to the Legislature of New York to secure to the married woman the right to hold in her own name the property that belonged to her, to secure to the poor, forsaken wife the right to her earnings, and to the mother the right to her children. "All" the women did not ask for those rights, but all accepted them with joy and gladness when they were obtained; and so it will be with the franchise. But woman's claim for the ballot does not depend upon the numbers that demand it, or would exercise the right; but upon precisely the same principles that man claims it for himself. Chase, Sumner, Stevens, and many of both Houses of Congress have, time after time, declared that the franchise means "Security, Education, Responsibility, Self-respect, Prosperity, and Independence." Taking all these assertions for granted and fully appreciating all their benefits, in the name of security, of education, of responsibility, of self-respect, of liberty, of prosperity and independence we demand the franchise for woman.

Please present this hastily-written contribution to your Convention with best wishes.

Yours, dear madam, very truly,

Ernestine L. Rose.

William Lloyd Garrison writes: Unable to attend the Convention, I can only send you my warm approval of it, and the object it is designed to promote. It is boastingly claimed in behalf of the Government of the United States that it is "of the people, by the people, and for the people." Yet reckoning the whole number at thirty-eight millions, no less than one-half—that is, nineteen millions—are political ciphers. A single male voter, on election day, outweighs them all!

Aaron M. Powell writes: I have no doubt that if a fair and honest vote can be had upon the question, submitted upon its own merits, in the Senate and House of Representatives, both the friends and opponents of the measure here, as in Great Britain when John Stuart Mill's proposition was first voted upon in Parliament, will be surprised at the revelation of its real strength.

Mrs. Caroline H. Dall writes: It mitigates my regret in declining your invitation to remember that these are not the dark days of the cause.

Senator Fowler, of Tenn., writes: It is not possible that the people who have so enlarged the boundaries of the political rights of another race just emerged from slavery, will fail to recognize the claims of the women of the United States to equal rights in all the relations of life.

Wm. H. Sylvis says: I am in favor of universal suffrage, universal amnesty, and universal liberty.

Abby Hopper Gibbons says: My father, Isaac T. Hopper, was an advocate for woman and her work, he believed in her thoroughly. His life long he was associated with many of the best women of his day. With the help of good men, we shall ere long stand side by side with ballot in hand.

Paulina Wright Davis: If women are the only unrecognized class as a part of the people, then woe to the nation! for there will be no noble mothers; frivolity, folly, and madness will seize them, for all inverted action of the faculties becomes intense in just the ratio of its earnestness.

Harriet Beecher Stowe writes: I am deeply interested in the work, and hopeful that a broader sphere is opening for woman, that as a class they may be trained in early life more as men are in education and business.

Gen. Oliver O. Howard answers: Please express to the Committee my thanks for the invitation. I should be pleased to accept, but a lecture engagement in the West will compel me to be absent from the city.

James M. Scovill, of New Jersey, says: I deeply desire to come.

Go on in your great work. The Convention tells on the public mind.

Gerrit Smith replies: I thank you for your invitation, though it is not in my power to attend the Convention. God hasten the day when the civil and political rights of woman shall be admitted to be equal to those of man.

Simeon Corley, M.C., of South Carolina, writes: Having been an advocate of woman suffrage for a quarter of a century, I had the pleasure yesterday of enrolling my name and that of my wife on your list of delegates. To-day Hon. James H. Goss, M.C., of South Carolina, requested me to have you insert his name. I think you may safely count on the South Carolina delegation.

This Convention was the first public occasion when the women opposed to the XIV Amendment, measuring their logic with Republicans, Abolitionists, and colored men, ably maintained their position. The division of opinion was marked and earnest, and the debate was warm between Messrs. Douglass, Downing, Hinton, Dr. Purvis, and Edward M. Davis on one side, and the ladies, with Robert Purvis and Parker Pillsbury on the other. Edward M. Davis, the son-in-law of Lucretia Mott, was so hostile to the position of the women on the XIV Amendment that he refused to enroll his name as a member of the Convention. Nevertheless, Mrs. Mott in the chair, allowed him to criticise most severely the resolutions and the position of those with whom she stood. She answered his attacks with her usual gentleness, and advocated the resolutions. Robert Purvis, differing with his own son and other colored men, denounced their position with severity. Yet good feeling prevailed throughout, and the Convention adjourned in order and harmony.[51]

12.
The American Equal Rights Association's debate on the Fifteenth Amendment, May 1869

The Executive Committee of the Equal Rights Association issued a call for the anniversary in New York, early in the spring of 1869. Never for any Convention were so many letters written to distinguished legislators and editors, nor so many promptly and fairly answered.

The anniversary commenced on Wednesday morning at Steinway Hall, New York. The opening session was very largely attended, the spacious hall being nearly full, showing that the era of anniversaries of important and useful societies, had by no means passed away. In the absence of the president, Mrs. Lucretia Mott, the chair was taken by Mrs. Elizabeth Cady Stanton, First Vice-President. Rev. Mrs. Hanaford, of Massachusetts, opened the meeting with prayer.

Lucy Stone presented verbally the report of the Executive Committee for the past year, running over the petitions in favor of woman suffrage presented during the year to Congress and State Legislatures and the various conventions held in different parts of the country, and remarked upon the greater respect now shown to the petitions. Formerly, she said, they were laughed at, and frequently not at all considered. This last year they were referred to committees, and often debated at great length in the legislatures, and in some cases motions to submit to the people of the State an amendment to the State Constitution doing away with the distinction of sex in the matter of suffrage was rejected by very small majorities. In one State, that of Nevada, such a motion was carried; and the question will shortly be submitted to the people of the State. A number of important and very successful conventions have been held in the Western States, and have made a decided impression. But what is most significant is, that newspapers of all shades of opinion are giving a great deal of space to this subject. It is recognized as among the great questions of the age, which can not be put down until it is settled upon the basis of immutable justice and right. The report was unanimously accepted and adopted.

Rev. O. B. Frothingham.—I am not here this morning thinking that I can add any thing to the strength of the cause, but thinking that perhaps I may gain something from the generous, sweet atmosphere that I am sure will prevail. This is a meeting, if I understand it, of the former Woman's Rights

Association, and the subjects which come before us properly are the subjects which concern woman in all her social, civil, and domestic life. But the one question which is of vital moment and of sole prominence, is that of suffrage. All other questions have been virtually decided in favor of woman. She has the *entrée* to all the fields of labor. She is now the teacher, preacher, artist, she has a place in the scientific world—in the literary world. She is a journalist, a maker of books, a public reader; in fact, there is no position which woman, as woman, is not entitled to hold. But there is one position that woman, as woman, does not occupy, and that is the position of a voter. One field alone she does not possess, and that is the political field; one work she is not permitted, and that is the work of making laws. This question goes down to the bottom—it touches the vital matter of woman's relation to the State. . . . Is there anything in the constitution of the female mind, to disqualify her for the exercise of the franchise. As long as there are fifty, thirty, ten, or even one woman who is capable of exercising this trust or holding this responsibility it demonstrates that sex, as a sex, does not disfranchise, and the whole question is granted. (Applause.) Here our laws are made by irresponsible people—people who demoralize and debauch society; people who make their living in a large measure by upholding the institutions that are inherently, forever, and always corrupt. (Applause.) Laws that are made by the people who own dramshops, who keep gambling-saloons, who minister to the depraved passions and vices of either sex, laws made by the idler, the dissipated, by the demoralized—are they laws? It is true that this government is founded upon caste. Slavery is abolished, but the aristocracy of sex is not. One reason that the suffrage is not conceded to woman is that those who refuse to do so, do not appreciate it themselves. (Applause.) As long as the power of suffrage means the power to steal, to tread down the weak, and get the rich offices into their own hands, those who have the key of the coffers will wish to keep it in their own pockets. (Applause.)

The Committee on Organization reported the officers of the society for the ensuing year.

Stephen Foster laid down the principle that when any persons on account of strong objections against them in the minds of some, prevented harmony in a society and efficiency in its operations, those persons should retire from prominent positions in that society. He said he had taken that course when, as agent of the Anti-Slavery Society, he became obnoxious on account of his position on some questions. He objected, to certain nominations made by the committee for various reasons. The first was that the persons nominated had publicly repudiated the principles of the society. One of these was the presiding officer.

Mrs. Stanton:—I would like you to say in what respect.

Mr. Foster:—I will with pleasure; for, ladies and gentlemen, I admire our talented President with all my heart, and love the woman. (Great laughter.) But I believe she has publicly repudiated the principles of the society.

Mrs. Stanton:—I would like Mr. Foster to state in what way.

Mr. Foster:—What are these principles? The equality of men—universal suffrage. These ladies stand at the head of a paper which has adopted as its motto Educated Suffrage. I put myself on this platform as an enemy of educated suffrage, as an enemy of white suffrage, as an enemy of man suffrage, as an enemy of every kind of suffrage except universal suffrage. *The Revolution* lately had an article headed "That Infamous Fifteenth Amendment." It is true it was not written by our President, yet it comes from a person whom she has over and over again publicly indorsed. I am not willing to take George Francis Train on this platform with his ridicule of the negro and opposition to his enfranchisement.

Mrs. Mary A. Livermore:—Is it quite generous to bring George Francis Train on this platform when he has retired from *The Revolution* entirely?

Mr. Foster:—If *The Revolution*, which has so often indorsed George Francis Train, will repudiate him because of his course in respect to the negro's rights, I have nothing further to say. But it does not repudiate him. He goes out; it does not cast him out.

Miss Anthony:—Of course it does not.

Mr. Foster:—My friend says yes to what I have said. I thought it was so. I only wanted to tell you why the Massachusetts society can not coalesce with the party here, and why we want these women to retire and leave us to nominate officers who can receive the respect of both parties. The Massachusetts Abolitionists can not co-operate with this society as it is now organized. If you choose to put officers here that ridicule the negro, and pronounce the Amendment infamous, why I must retire; I can not work with you. You can not have my support, and you must not use my name. I can not shoulder the responsibility of electing officers who publicly repudiate the principles of the society.

Henry B. Blackwell said: In regard to the criticisms on our officers, I will agree that many unwise things have been written in *The Revolution* by a gentleman who furnished part of the means by which that paper has been carried on. But that gentleman has withdrawn, and you, who know the real opinions of Miss Anthony and Mrs. Stanton on the question of negro suffrage, do not believe that they mean to create antagonism between the negro and the woman question. If they did disbelieve in negro suffrage, it would be no reason for excluding them. We should no more exclude a person from our platform for disbelieving negro suffrage than a person should be excluded from the anti-slavery platform for disbelieving woman suffrage. But I know that Miss Anthony and Mrs. Stanton believe in the right of the negro to vote. We are united on that point. There is no question of principle between us.

The vote on the report of the Committee on Organization was now taken, and adopted by a large majority.

Mr. Douglass:—I came here more as a listener than to speak, and I have listened with a great deal of pleasure to the eloquent address of the Rev. Mr. Frothingham and the splendid address of the President. There is no name greater than that of Elizabeth Cady Stanton in the matter of woman's rights and equal rights, but my sentiments are tinged a little against *The Revolution*. There was in the address to which I allude the employment of certain names, such as "Sambo," and the gardener, and the bootblack, and the daughters of Jefferson and

Washington, and all the rest that I can not coincide with. I have asked what difference there is between the daughters of Jefferson and Washington and other daughters. (Laughter.) I must say that I do not see how any one can pretend that there is the same urgency in giving the ballot to woman as to the negro. With us, the matter is a question of life and death, at least, in fifteen States of the Union. When women, because they are women, are hunted down through the cities of New York and New Orleans; when they are dragged from their houses and hung upon lamp-posts; when their children are torn from their arms, and their brains dashed out upon the pavement; when they are objects of insult and outrage at every turn; when they are in danger of having their homes burnt down over their heads; when their children are not allowed to enter schools; then they will have an urgency to obtain the ballot equal to our own. (Great applause.)

A Voice:—Is that not all true about black women?

Mr. Douglass:—Yes, yes, yes; it is true of the black woman, but not because she is a woman, but because she is black. (Applause.) Julia Ward Howe at the conclusion of her great speech delivered at the convention in Boston last year, said: "I am willing that the negro shall get the ballot before me." (Applause.) Woman! why, she has 10,000 modes of grappling with her difficulties. I believe that all the virtue of the world can take care of all the evil. I believe that all the intelligence can take care of all the ignorance. (Applause.) I am in favor of woman's suffrage in order that we shall have all the virtue and vice confronted. Let me tell you that when there were few houses in which the black man could have put his head, this woolly head of mine found a refuge in the house of Mrs. Elizabeth Cady Stanton, and if I had been blacker than sixteen midnights, without a single star, it would have been the same. (Applause.)

Miss Anthony:—The old anti-slavery school say women must stand back and wait until the negroes shall be recognized. But we say, if you will not give the whole loaf of suffrage to the entire people, give it to the most intelligent first. (Applause.) If intelligence, justice, and morality are to have precedence in the Government, let the question of woman be brought up first and that of the negro last. (Applause.) While I was canvassing the State with petitions and had them filled with names for our cause to the Legislature, a man dared to say to me that the freedom of women was all a theory and not a practical thing. (Applause.) When Mr. Douglass mentioned the black man first and the woman last, if he had noticed he would have seen that it was the men that clapped and not the women. There is not the woman born who desires to eat the bread of dependence, no matter whether it be from the hand of father, husband, or brother; for any one who does so eat her bread places herself in the power of the person from whom she takes it. (Applause.) Mr. Douglass talks about the wrongs of the negro; but with all the outrages that he to-day suffers, he would not exchange his sex and take the place of Elizabeth Cady Stanton. (Laughter and applause.)

Mr. Douglass:—I want to know if granting you the right of suffrage will change the nature of our sexes? (Great laughter.)

Miss Anthony:—It will change the pecuniary position of woman; it will place her where she can earn her own bread. (Loud applause.) She will not then be driven to such employments only as man chooses for her.

Mrs. Norton said that Mr. Douglass's remarks left her to defend the Government from the inferred inability to grapple with the two questions at once. It legislates upon many questions at one and the same time, and it has the power to decide the woman question and the negro question at one and the same time. (Applause.)

Mrs. Lucy Stone:—Mrs. Stanton will, of course, advocate the precedence for her sex, and Mr. Douglass will strive for the first position for his, and both are perhaps right. If it be true that the government derives its authority from the consent of the governed, we are safe in trusting that principle to the uttermost. If one has a right to say that you can not read and therefore can not vote, then it may be said that you are a woman and therefore can not vote. We are lost if we turn away from the middle principle and argue for one class. I was once a teacher among fugitive slaves. There was one old man, and every tooth was gone, his hair was white, and his face was full of wrinkles, yet, day after day and hour after hour, he came up to the school-house and tried with patience to learn to read, and by-and-by, when he had spelled out the first few verses of the first chapter of the Gospel of St. John, he said to me, "Now, I want to learn to write." I tried to make him satisfied with what he had acquired, but the old man said, "Mrs. Stone, somewhere in the wide world I have a son; I have not heard from him in twenty years; if I should hear from him, I want to write to him, so take hold of my hand and teach me." I did, but before he had proceeded in many lessons, the angels came and gathered him up and bore him to his Father. Let no man speak of an educated suffrage. The gentleman who addressed you claimed that the negroes had the first right to the suffrage, and drew a picture which only his great word-power can do. He again in Massachusetts, when it had cast a majority in favor of Grant and negro suffrage, stood upon the platform and said that woman had better wait for the negro; that is, that both could not be carried, and that the negro had better be the one. But I freely forgave him because he felt as he spoke. But woman suffrage is more imperative than his own; and I want to remind the audience that when he says what the Ku-Kluxes did all over the South, the Ku-Kluxes here in the North in the shape of men, take away the children from the mother, and separate them as completely as if done on the block of the auctioneer. Over in New Jersey they have a law which says that *any* father—he might be the most brutal man that ever existed—*any* father, it says, whether he be under age or not, may by his last will and testament dispose of the custody of his child, born or to be born, and that such disposition shall be good against all persons, and that the mother may not recover her child; and that law modified in form exists over every State in the Union except in Kansas. Woman has an ocean of wrongs too deep for any plummet, and the negro, too, has an ocean of wrongs that can not be fathomed. There are two great oceans; in the one is the black man, and in the other is the woman. But I thank God for that XV. Amendment, and hope that it will be adopted in every State. I will be thankful in my soul if *any* body can get out of the terrible pit. But I believe that the safety of the government would be more promoted by the admission of woman as an element of restoration and harmony than the negro. I believe that the influence of woman will save the country before every other power. (Applause.) I see the signs of the times pointing to this consummation, and I believe that in some parts of the country women will vote for the President of these United States in 1872. (Applause.)

At the opening of the evening session Henry B. Blackwell presented a series of resolutions. Antoinette Brown Blackwell spoke, and was followed by Olive Logan.

Miss Logan said:—I stand here to-night full of faith, inborn faith, in the rights of woman to advance boldly in all ennobling paths. . . . In my former sphere of life, the equality of woman was fully recognized so far as the kind of labor and the amount of reward for her labor are concerned. As an actress, there was no position in which I was not fully welcomed if I possessed the ability and industry to reach it. If I could become a Ristori, my earnings would be as great as hers, and if I was a man and could become a Kean, a Macready, or a Booth, the same reward would be obtained. If I reach no higher rank than what is called a "walking lady," I am sure of the same pay as a man who occupies the position of a "walking gentleman." In that sphere of life, be it remembered, I was reared from childhood; to that place I was so accustomed that I had no idea it was a privilege denied my sex to enter into almost every other field of endeavor.

In literature also I found myself on an equality with man. If I wrote a good article, I got as good pay; and heaven knows the pay to man or woman was small enough. (Applause). In that field, for a long time, I did not feel an interest in the subject of women's rights, and stood afar off, looking at the work of those revolutionary creatures, Mrs. Stanton and Miss Anthony. The idea of identifying myself with them was as far removed from my thoughts as becoming a female gymnast and whirling upon a trapeze. But once I wrote a lecture, and one night I delivered it. Adhering to my practice of speaking about that which was most familiar, my lecture was about the stage.

I lectured, simply because I thought the pay would be better in that department; the idea that I was running counter to anybody's prejudice, never entered my head. And I was so far removed that I never read a page of *The Revolution* in my life, and, what is more, I did not want to; and when Miss Anthony passed down Broadway and saw the bills announcing my lecture she knew nothing about me, and what is more, she did not want to. (Laughter). She made a confession to me afterwards. She said to herself, "Here is a lady going to lecture about the stage," looking through her blessed spectacles, as I can see her (laughter)—and I can hear her muttering "a woman's rights woman." (Laughter). That is not so very long ago, a little over a year. Since this great question of woman's rights was thrust upon me, I am asked to define my position; wherever I have traveled in the fifteen months I have had to do so. A lady of society asked me, "Are you in favor of woman's rights?" I had either to answer yes or no, and "Yes," I said. (Applause). . . .

I met, in my travels, in a New England town, an educated woman, who found herself obliged to earn her livelihood, after living a life of luxury and ease. Her husband, who had provided her with every material comfort, had gone to the grave. All his property was taken to pay his debts, and she found herself penniless. What was that woman to do? She looks abroad among the usual employments of women, and her only resource seems to be that little bit of steel around which cluster so many associations—the needle—and by the needle, with the best work and the best wages, the most she can get is two dollars a day. With this, poor as it is, she will be content; but she finds an army of other women looking for the same, and most of them looking in vain. These things have opened my eyes to a vista such as I never saw before. They have touched my heart as it never before was touched. They have aroused my conscience to the fact that this woman question is the question of the hour, and that I must take part in it. I take my stand boldly, proudly, with such earnest, thoughtful women as Susan B. Anthony, Mrs. Stanton, and Anna Dickinson, to work together with them for the enfranchisement of woman, for her elevation personally and socially, and above all for her right and opportunity to work at such employments as she can follow, with the right to such pay as men get. (Applause). There are thousands of women who have no vital interest in this question. They are happy wives and daughters, and may they ever be so; but they can not tell how soon their husbands and brothers may be lost to them, and they will find themselves destitute and penniless with no resources in themselves against misfortune. Then it will be for such that we labor. Our purpose is to help those who need help, widows and orphan girls. There is no need to do battle in this matter. In all kindness and gentleness we urge our claims. There is no need to declare war upon man, for the best of men in this country are with us heart and soul. These are with us in greater numbers even than our own sex. (A Voice—"That is true." Great applause). Do not say that we seek to break up family peace and fireside joy; far from it. (Applause). We interfere not with the wife or daughter who is happy in the strong protection thrown around her by a father or husband, but it is cowardice for such to throw obstacles in the way of those who need help. More than this, for the sake of the helpless woman, to whose unhappiness in the loss of beloved ones is added the agony of hard and griping want. For the sake of the poor girl who has no power to cope with the hard actualities of a desolate life, while her trembling feet tread the crumbling edge of the dark abyss of infamy. For the sake of this we are pleading and entertaining this great question, withhold your answer till at least you have learned to say, "God speed."

The next speaker was Miss Phoebe Couzins, a young law student from St. Louis, who spoke in a most agreeable and forcible manner.

Miss Couzins said:—Mrs. President and Ladies: I deem it the duty of every earnest woman to express herself in regard to the XVth Amendment to our Federal Constitution. I feel deeply the humiliation and insult that is offered to the women of the United States in this Amendment, and have always publicly protested against its passage. During a recent tour through the Eastern States I became still more (if that were possible) firmly fixed in my convictions. Its advocates are unwilling to have it publicly discussed, showing that they know there is an element of weakness in it which will not bear a thorough investigation.

While feeling entirely willing that the black man shall have all the rights to which he is justly entitled, I consider the claims of the black woman of paramount importance. I have had opportunities of seeing and knowing the condition of both sexes, and will bear my testimony, that the black women are, and always have been, in a far worse condition than the men. As a class, they are better, and more intelligent than the men, yet they have been subjected to greater brutalities, while compelled to perform exactly the same labor as men toiling by their side in the fields, just as hard burdens imposed upon them, just as severe punishments decreed to them, with the added cares of maternity and household work, with their children taken from them and sold into bondage; suffering a thousandfold more than any man could suffer. Then, too, the laws for women in the Southern States, both married and single, degrade them still further. The black men, as a class, are very tyrannical in their families; they have learned the lesson of brute force but too well, and as the marriage law allows the husband entire control over his wife's earnings and her children, she is in worse bondage than before; because in many cases the task of providing for helpless children and an idle, lazy, husband, is imposed on the patient wife and mother; and, with this sudden elevation to citizenship, which the mass of stupid, ignorant negroes look upon as entitling them to great honor, I regard the future state of the negro woman, without the ballot in her hand, as deplorable. And what is said of the ignorant black man can as truthfully be said of the ignorant white man; they all regard woman as an inferior being. She is their helpless, household slave. He is her ruler, her law-giver, her conscience, her judge and jury, and the prisoner at the bar has no appeal. This XVth Amendment thrusts all women still further down in the scale of degradation, and I consider it neither praiseworthy nor magnanimous for women to assert that they are willing to hold their claims in abeyance, until all shades and types of men have the franchise. It is admitting a false principle, which all women, who are loyal to truth and justice, should immediately reject. For over twenty-five years, the advocates of woman suffrage have been trying to bring this vital question before the country. They have accomplished herculean tasks and still it is up-hill work. Shall they, after battling so long with ignorance, prejudice and unreasoning customs, stand quietly back and obsequiously say they are willing that the floodgates shall be opened and a still greater mass of ignorance, vice and degradation let in to overpower their little army, and set this question back for a century? Their solemn duty to future generations forbids such a compromise.

The advocates of the XVth Amendment tell us we ought to accept the half loaf when we can not get the whole. I do not see that woman gets any part of the loaf, not even a crumb that falls from the rich man's table. It may appear very magnanimous for men, who have never known the degradation of being thrust down in the scale of humanity by reason of their sex, to urge these yielding measures upon women, they can not and do not know our feelings on the subject, and I regard it as neither just nor generous to eternally compel women to yield on all questions (no matter how humiliating), simply because they are women.

The Anti-Slavery party declares that with the adoption of the XVth Amendment their work is done. Have they, then, been battling for over thirty years for a fraction of a principle? If so, then the XVth Amendment is a fitting capstone to their labors. Were the earnest women who fought and endured so heroically with them, but tools in the hands of the leaders, to place "manhood suffrage" on the highest pinnacle of the temple dedicated to Truth and Justice? And are they now to bow down, and worship in abject submission this fractional part of a principle, that has hitherto proclaimed itself, as knowing neither bond nor free, male nor female, but one perfect humanity?

The XV. Amendment virtually says that every intelligent, virtuous woman is the inferior of every ignorant man, no matter how low he may be sunk in the scale of morality, and every instinct of my being rises to refute such doctrine, and God speaking within me says, No! eternally No!

Rev. Gilbert Haven, editor of *Zion's Herald*, was introduced, and said—Ladies and Gentlemen: As I believe that is the way to address you, or shall I merge you into one and call you fellow citizens—

Miss Anthony—Let me tell you how to say it. It is perfectly right for a gentleman to say "ladies and gentlemen," but a lady should say, "gentlemen and ladies." (Great applause.) You mention your friend's name before you do your own. (Applause.) I always feel like rebuking any woman who says, "ladies and gentlemen." It is a lack of good manners. (Laughter and great applause.)

Mr. Haven—I thank the lady for the rule she has laid down. Now, Mr. Beecher has said that a minister is composed of the worst part of man and woman, and there are wealthy men who say that the pulpit should be closed against the introduction of politics, but I am glad this sentiment is not a rule; I rejoice that the country has emancipated the ministry so that a minister can speak on politics. I go further than saying that it is the mere right of the women to achieve suffrage. I say that it is an obligation imposed upon the American people to grant the demands of this large and influential class of the commonwealth. The legislation of the country concerns the woman as much as the man. Is not the wife as much interested in the preservation of property as her husband? Another reason is, that the purity of politics depends upon the admission of woman to the franchise, for without her influence morality in politics can not be secured. (Applause.)

Henry B. Blackwell presented the following resolution:

Resolved, That in seeking to remove the legal disabilities which now oppress woman as wife and mother, the friends of woman suffrage are not seeking to undermine or destroy the sanctity of the marriage relation, but to ennoble marriage, making the obligations and responsibilities of the contract mutual and equal for husband and wife.

Mary A. Livermore said that that was introduced by her permission, but the original resolution was stronger, and she having slept over it, thought that it should be introduced instead of that one, and offered the following:

> *Resolved,* That while we recognize the disabilities which the legal marriage imposes upon woman as wife and mother, and while we pledge ourselves to seek their removal by putting her on equal terms with man, we abhorrently repudiate Free Loveism as horrible and mischievous to society, and disown any sympathy with it.

Mrs. Livermore said that the West wanted some such resolution as that in consequence of the innuendoes that had come to their ears with regard to their striving after the ballot.

Mrs. Hanaford spoke against such inferences not only for the ministers of her own denomination, but the Christian men and women of New England everywhere. She had heard people say that when women indorsed woman suffrage they indorsed Free Loveism, and God knows they despise it. Let me carry back to my New England home the word that you as well as your honored President, whom we love, whose labor we appreciate, and whose name has also been dragged into this inference, scout all such suggestions as contrary to the law of God and humanity.

Lucy Stone: I feel it is a mortal shame to give any foundation for the implication that we favor Free Loveism. I am ashamed that the question should be asked here. There should be nothing said about it at all. Do not let us, for the sake of our own self-respect, allow it to be hinted that we helped forge a shadow of a chain which comes in the name of Free Love. I am unwilling that it should be suggested that this great, sacred cause of ours means anything but what we have said it does. If any one says to me, "Oh, I know what you mean, you mean Free Love by this agitation," let the lie stick in his throat. You may talk about Free Love, if you please, but we are to have the right to vote. To-day we are fined, imprisoned, and hanged, without a jury trial by our peers. You shall not cheat us by getting us off to talk about something else. When we get the suffrage, then you may taunt us with anything you please, and we will then talk about it as long as you please.

Ernestine L. Rose: We are informed by the people from the West that they are wiser than we are, and that those in the East are also wiser than we are. If they are wiser than we, I think it strange that this question of Free Love should have been brought upon this platform at all. I object to Mrs. Livermore's resolution, not on account of its principles, but on account of its pleading guilty. When a man comes to me and tries to convince me that he is not a thief, then I take care of my coppers. If we pass this resolution that we are not Free Lovers, people will say it is true that you are, for you try to hide it. Lucretia Mott's name has been mentioned as a friend of Free Love, but I hurl back the lie into the faces of all the ministers in the East and into the faces of the newspapers of the West, and defy them to point to one shadow of a reason why they should connect her name with that vice. We have been thirty years in this city before the public, and it is an insult to all the women who have labored in this cause; it is an insult to the thousands and tens of thousands of men and women that have listened to us in our Conventions, to say at this late hour that we are not Free Lovers.

Susan B. Anthony repudiated the resolution on the same ground as Mrs. Rose, and said this howl came from those men who knew that when women got their rights they would be able to live honestly: no longer be compelled to sell themselves for bread, either in or out of marriage.

Mrs. Dr. L. S. Batchelder, a delegate appointed by the Boston Working Women's Association, said that she represented ten thousand working women of New England, and they had instructed her as their representative to introduce a resolution looking to the amelioration of the condition of the working women.

Senator Wilson spoke as follows: This is a rather new place for me to stand, and yet I am very glad to say that I have no new views in regard to this question. I learned fifteen or twenty years ago something about this reform in its earliest days, when the excellent people, who have labored so long with so much earnestness and fidelity, first launched it before the country. I never knew the time in the last fifteen or twenty years that I was not ready to give my wife the right to vote if she wanted it. I believe in the Declaration of Independence in its full scope and meaning; believing it was born of Christianity; that it came from the teachings of the New Testament; and I am willing to trust the New Testament and the Declaration of Independence anywhere on God's earth, and to adopt their doctrine in the fullest and broadest manner. I do not know that all the good in the world will be accomplished when the women of the United States have the right to vote. But it is sure to come. Truth is truth, and will stand.

Mrs. Ernestine L. Rose referred to the assertion of the Rev. Mr. Haven, that the seeds of the Woman's Rights reform were sown in Massachusetts, and proceeded to disprove it. Thirty-two years ago she went round in New York city with petitions to the Legislature to obtain for married women the right to hold property in their own names. She only got five names the first year, but she and others persevered for eleven years, and finally succeeded. Who, asked Mrs. Rose, was the first to call a National Convention of women—New York or Massachusetts? [Applause.] I like to have justice done and honor given where it is due.

Mrs. Sarah F. Norton, of the New York Working Woman's Association, referring to the former attempt to exclude the discussion of the relations of capital and labor, argued that the question was an appropriate one in any Woman's Rights Convention, and proposed that some member of the New York Working Women's Association be heard on that point.

Mrs. Eleanor Kirk accordingly described the beginning, progress, and operations of the Association. She also replied to the recent criticism of the *World* upon the semi-literary, semi-Woman's Rights nature of the meetings of their associations, and contended that they had a perfect right to debate and read essays, and do anything else that other women might do.

Mrs. Mary F. Davis spoke in behalf of the rights of her own sex, but expressed her willingness to see the negro guaranteed in his rights, and would wait if only one question could be disposed of. But she thought they would not have to wait long, for the Hon. Mr. Wilson had assured them that their side is to be strongly and successfully advocated. Every step in the great cause of human rights helps the next one forward. In 1848 Mrs. Stanton called the first Convention at Seneca Falls.

Miss Anthony: And Lucretia Mott.

Mrs. Davis: Yes, and Lucretia Mott; and I love to speak of them in association. Mrs. Rose has alluded to the primary steps she took, and there were Susan B. Anthony, Lucy Stone, Antoinette Brown Blackwell, and Paulina Wright Davis, and a great galaxy who paved the way; and we stand here to proclaim the immortal principle of woman's freedom. [Great applause.] The lady then referred to the great work that lay before them in lifting out of misery and wretchedness the numbers of women in this city and elsewhere, who were experiencing all the fullness of human degradation. Even when they had finished their present work, a large field was still before them in the elevation of their sex. [Applause.]

Mrs. Paulina W. Davis said she would not be altogether satisfied to have the XVth Amendment passed without the XVIth, for woman would have a race of tyrants raised above her in the South, and the black women of that country would also receive worse treatment than if the Amendment was not passed. Take any class that have been slaves, and you will find that they are the worst when free, and become the hardest masters. The colored women of the South say they do not want to get married to the negro, as their husbands can take their children away from them, and also appropriate their earnings. The black women are more intelligent than the men, because they have learned something from their mistresses. She then related incidents showing how black men whip and abuse their wives in the South. One of her sister's servants whipped his wife every Sunday regularly. [Laughter.] She thought that sort of men should not have the making of the laws for the government of the women throughout the land. [Applause.]

Mr. Douglass said that all disinterested spectators would concede that this Equal Rights meeting had been pre-eminently a Woman's Rights meeting. [Applause.] They had just heard an argument with which he could not agree—that the suffrage to the black men should be postponed to that of the women. I do not believe the story that the slaves who are enfranchised become the worst of tyrants. [A voice, "Neither do I." Applause.] I know how this theory came about. When a slave was made a driver, he made himself more officious than the white driver, so that his master might not suspect that he was favoring those under him. But we do not intend to have any master over us. [Applause.]

The President, Mrs. Stanton, argued that not another man should be enfranchised until enough women are admitted to the polls to outweigh those already there. [Applause.] She did not believe in allowing ignorant negroes and foreigners to make laws for her to obey. [Applause.]

Mrs. Harper (colored) asked Mr. Blackwell to read the fifth resolution of the series he submitted, and contended that that covered the whole ground of the resolutions of Mr. Douglass. When it was a question of race, she let the lesser question of sex go. But the white women all go for sex, letting race occupy a minor position. She liked the idea of working women, but she would like to know if it was broad enough to take colored women?

Miss Anthony and several others: Yes, yes.

Mrs. Harper said that when she was at Boston there were sixty women who left work because one colored woman went to gain a livelihood in their midst. [Applause.] If the nation could only handle one question, she would not have the black women put a single straw in the way, if only the men of the race could obtain what they wanted. [Great applause.]

Mr. C. C. Burleigh attempted to speak, but was received with some disapprobation by the audience, and confusion ensued.

Miss Anthony protested against the XVth Amendment because it wasn't Equal Rights. It put two million more men in position of tyrants over two million women who had until now been the equals of the men at their side.

Mr. Burleigh again essayed to speak. The confusion was so great that he could not be heard.

Mrs. Stone appealed for order, and her first appearance

caused the most respectful silence, as did the words of every one of the ladies who addressed the audience. Mr. Burleigh again ventured, but with no better result, and Miss Anthony made another appeal to the audience to hear him. He tried again to get a word in, but was once more unsuccessful.

Mrs. Livermore, after protesting against the disorderly behavior of the audience, said a few words in advocacy of the resolutions of Mr. Douglass, when a motion was made to lay them upon the table, and Mr. Blackwell moved the "previous question."

Miss Anthony hoped that this, the first attempt at gagging discussion, would not be countenanced. (Applause.) She made a strong protest against this treatment of Mr. Burleigh. Sufficient silence was obtained for that gentleman to say that he had finished; but he was determined that they should hear the last word. (Hisses and laughter.) He now took his seat. The motion to lay the resolutions upon the table for discussion in the evening was then carried, and the Association adjourned till the evening, to meet in the large hall of the Cooper Institute. A letter from Jules Favre, the celebrated French advocate and *litterateur*, was read, after which addresses were delivered by Madam Anneke, of Milwaukee (in German), and by Madame de Hericourt, of Chicago (in French). Both of these ladies are of revolutionary tendencies, and left their native countries because they had rendered themselves obnoxious by a too free expression of their political opinions.

Madam Anneke said—*Mrs. President*: Nearly two decades have passed since, in answer to a call from our co-workers, I stood before a large assembly, over which Mrs. Mott presided, to utter, in the name of suffering and struggling womanhood, the cry of my old Fatherland for freedom and justice. At that time my voice was overwhelmed by the sound of sneers, scoffs, and hisses—the eloquence of tyranny, by which every outcry of the human heart is stifled. Then, through the support of our friends Mrs. Rose and Wendell Phillips, who are ever ready in the cause of human rights, I was allowed, in my native tongue, to echo faintly the cry for justice and freedom. What a change has been wrought since then! To-day they greet us with deferential respect. Such giant steps are made by public opinion! What they then derided, and sought, through physical power and rough ignorance, to render wholly impossible, today they greet with the voice of welcome and jubilee. Such an expression of sentiment is to us the most certain and joyful token of a gigantic revolution in public opinion—still more gratifying is it, that the history of the last few years proves that under the force of an universal necessity, reason and freedom are being consistently developed. Such is the iron step of time, that it brings forward every event to meet its rare fulfillment. Under your protection I am once more permitted, in this dawning of a new epoch which is visible to all eyes that will see, and audible to all ears that will hear, to express my hopes, my longing, my striving, and my confidence. And now, permit me to do so in the language of my childhood's play, as well as that of the earnest and free philosophy of German thinkers and workers. Not that I believe it is left to me to interest the children of my old Fatherland, here present, in the new era of truth and freedom, as if these glorious principles were not of yore implanted in their hearts—as if they could not take them up in a strange idiom—but because I am urged from my deepest soul to speak out loud and free, as I have ever felt myself constrained to do, and as I can not do in the language of my beloved adopted land. The consciousness and the holy conviction of our inalienable human rights, which I have won in the struggle of my own strangely varied life, and in the wrestling for independence which has carried me through the terrors of bloody revolution, and brought me to this effulgent shore where *Sanita Libertas* is free to all who seek it—this sacred strand, of which our German poet says: *Dich halte ich!* (I have gained thee and will not leave thee.) So I turn to you, my dear compatriots, in the language of our Fatherland—to you who are accustomed to German ways of thinking—to you who have grown up in the light which flows from thinking brains—to you whose hearts warmly cherish human rights and human worth—who are not afraid of truth when it speaks of such deep, clear, and universally important subjects as human rights and human duties. He who fears truth will find hiding places, but he who combats for it is worthy of it. The method of its adversaries is to address themselves to thoughtless passion, and thus arouse mockery and abuse against those who search for scientific knowledge to appeal to easily moved feelings and kindle sentiments of hatred and contempt. They can do this only while truth is in the minority—only until right shall become might.

You will learn to judge of woman's strength when you see that she persists strenuously in this purpose, and secures, by her energy, the rights which shall invest her with power. That which you can no longer suppress in woman—that which is free above all things—that which is pre-eminently important to mankind, and must have free play in every mind, is the natural thirst for scientific knowledge—that fountain of all peacefully progressing amelioration in human history. This longing, this effort of reason seeking knowledge of itself, of ideas, conclusions, and all higher things, has, as far as historical remembrance goes back never been so violently suppressed in any human being as in woman. But, so far from its having been extinguished in her, it has, under the influence of this enlightened century, become a gigantic flame which shines most brightly under the protection of the star-spangled banner. There does not exist a man-made doctrine, fabricated expressly for us, and which we must learn by heart, that shall henceforth be our law. Nor shall the authority of old traditions be a standard for us—be this authority called Veda, Talmud, Koran, or Bible. No. Reason, which we recognize as our highest and only law-giver, commands us to be free. We have recognized our duty—we have heard the rustling of the golden wings of our guardian angel—we are inspired for the work!

We are no longer in the beginning of history—that age which was a constant struggle with nature, misery, ignorance, helplessness, and every kind of bondage. The moral idea of the State struggles for that fulfillment in which all individuals shall be brought into a union which shall augment a million-fold both its individual and collective force. Therefore, don't exclude us—don't exclude woman—don't exclude the whole half of the human family. Receive us—begin the work in which a new era shall dawn. In all great events we find that woman has a guiding hand—let us stay near you now, when humanity is concerned. Man has the spirit of truth, but woman alone has passion for it. All creations need love—let us, therefore, celebrate a union from which shall spring the morning of freedom for humanity. Give us our rights in the State. Honor us as your equals, and allow us to use the rights which belong to us, and which reason commands us to use. Whether it be prudent to enfranchise woman, is not the question—only whether it be right. What is positively right, must be prudent, must be wise, and must, finally, be useful. Give the lie to the monarchically disposed statesman, who says the republic of the United States is only an experiment, which earlier or later will prove a failure. Give the lie to such hopes, I say, by carrying out the whole elevated idea of the republic—by calling the entire, excluded half of mankind and every being endowed with reason, to the ballot-box, which is the people's holy palladium.

Madame de Hericourt said: I wish to ask if rights have their source in ability, in functions, in qualities? No, certainly; for we see that all men, however they may differ in endowments, have equal rights. What, then, is the basis of rights? Humanity. Consequently, even if it be true that woman is inferior to man in intelligence and social ability, it is not desirable that she shut herself within what is called woman's sphere. In a philosophical light, the objections brought against her have no bearing on this question. Woman must have equal rights with man, because she is, like him, a human being; and only in establishing, through anatomical or biological proof, that she does not belong to the human race, can her rights be withheld. When such demonstration is made, my claims shall cease. In the mean time, let me say that woman—whether useful or useless—belonging to humanity, must have the rights of humanity.

But is it true that the equality of man and woman would not be useful to society? We might answer this question in the affirmative were the sexes alike, but for the very reason that they differ in many respects, is the presence of woman by the side of man, if we desire order and justice, everywhere necessary. Is it graceful, I ask, to walk on one leg? Men, since the beginning of history, have had the bad taste to prefer a lame society to one that is healthy and beautiful. We women have really too much taste to yield longer to such deformity. In law, in institutions, in every social and political matter, there are two sides. Up to the present day, man has usurped what belongs to woman. That is the reason why we have injustice, corruption, international hatred, cruelty, war, shameful laws—man assuming, in regard to woman, the sinful relation of slaveholder. Such relation must and will change, because we women have decided that it shall not exist. With you, gentlemen, we will vote, legislate, govern—not only because it is our right, but because it is time to substitute order, peace, equity, and virtue, for the disorder, war, cruelty, injustice, and corruption which you, acting alone, have established. You doubt our fitness to take part in government because we are fickle, extravagant, etc., etc., as you say. I answer, there is an inconsiderable minority which deserve such epithets; but even if all women deserved them, who is in fault? You not only prefer the weak-minded, extravagant women to the strong-minded and reasonable ones, but as soon as a woman attempts to leave her sphere, you, cowardlike, throw yourselves before her, and secure to your own profit all remunerative occupations. I could, perhaps, forgive your selfishness and injustice, but I can not forgive your want of logic nor your hypocrisy. You condemn woman to starvation, to ignorance, to extravagance, in order to please yourselves, and then reproach her for this ignorance and extravagance, while you heap blame and ridicule on those who are educated, wise, and frugal. You are, indeed, very absurd or very silly. Your judgment is so weak that you reproach woman with the faults of a slave, when it is you who have made and who keep her a slave, and who know, moreover, that no true and virtuous soul can accept slavery. You reproach woman with being an active agent in corruption and ruin, without perceiving that it is you who have condemned her to this awful work, in which only your bad passions sustain her. Whatever you may do, you can not escape her influence. If she is free, virtuous, and worthy, she will give you free, virtuous, and worthy sons, and maintain in you republican virtues. If she remain a slave, she will debase you and your sons; and your country will come under the rule of tyranny. Insane men can not understand that where there is one slave there are always two—he who wears the chain and he who rivets it. Unreasonable, short-sighted men can not understand that to enfranchise woman is to elevate man; to give him a companion who shall encourage his good and noble aspirations, instead of one who would debase and draw him down into an abyss of selfishness and dishonesty. Gentlemen, will you be just, will you preserve the republic, will you stop the moral ruin of your country; will you be worthy, virtuous, and courageous for the welfare of your nation, and, in spite of all obstacles, enfranchise your mothers, wives, daughters, and sisters? Take care that you be not too late! Such injustice and folly would be at the cost of your liberty, in which event you could claim no mercy, for tyrants deserve to be the victims of tyrants.

After her brief address, Madame de Hericourt submitted to the Convention a series of resolutions for the organization of Women's Leagues.

Ernestine L. Rose said—*Mrs. Chairman, Ladies and Gentlemen*: What we need is to arouse both men and women to the great necessity of justice and of right. The world moves. We need not seek further than this Convention assembled here to-night to show that it moves. We have assembled here delegates from the East and the West, from the North and the South, from all over the United States, from England, from France, and from Germany—all have come to give us greeting and well-wishes, both in writing and in speech. I only wish that this whole audience might have been able to understand and appreciate the eloquent speeches which have been delivered here to-night. They have been uttered in support of the claim— the just demand—of woman for the right to vote. Why is it, my friends, that Congress has enacted laws to give the negro of the South the right to vote? Why do they not at the same time protect the negro woman? If Congress really means to protect the negro race, they should have acknowledged woman just as much as man; not only in the South, but here in the North, the only way to protect her is by the ballot. We have often heard from this platform, and I myself have often said, that with individual man we do not find fault. We do not war with man; we war with bad principles. And let me ask whether we have not the right to war with these principles which stamp the degradation of inferiority upon women.

This Society calls itself the Equal Rights Association. That I understand to be an association which has no distinction of sex, class, or color. Congress does not seem to understand the meaning of the term universal. I understand the word universal to include All. Congress understood that Universal Suffrage meant the white man only. Since the war we have changed the name for Impartial Suffrage. When some of our editors, such as Mr. Greeley and others, were asked what they meant by impartial suffrage, they said, "Why, man, of course; the man and the brother." Congress has enacted resolutions for the suffrage of men and brothers. They don't speak of the women and sisters. [Applause.] They have begun to change their tactics, and call it manhood suffrage. I propose to call it Woman Suffrage; then we shall know what we mean. We might commence by calling the Chinaman a man and a brother, or the Hottentot, or the Calmuck, or the Indian, the idiot or the criminal, but where shall we stop? They will bring all these in before us, and then they will bring in the babies—the *male* babies. [Laughter.] I am a foreigner. I had great difficulty in acquiring the English language, and I never shall acquire it. But I am afraid that in the meaning of language Congress is a great deal worse off than I have ever been. I go for the change of name; I will not be construed into a man and a brother. I ask the same rights for women that are extended to men—the right to life, liberty, and the pursuit of happiness; and every pursuit in life must be as free and open to me as any man in the land. [Applause.] But they will never be thrown open to me or to any of you, until we have the power of the ballot in our own hands. That little paper is a great talisman. We have often been told that the golden key can unlock all the doors. That little piece of paper can unlock doors where golden keys fail. Wherever men are— whether in the workshop, in the store, in the laboratory, or in the legislative halls—I want to see women. Wherever man is, there she is needed; wherever man has work to do—work for the benefit of humanity—there should men and women unite and co-operate together. It is not well for man to be alone or work alone; and he can not work for woman as well as woman can work for herself. I suggest that the name of this society be changed from Equal Rights Association to Woman's Suffrage Association.

Lucy Stone said she must oppose this till the colored man gained the right to vote. If they changed the name of the association for such a reason as it was evident it was proposed, they would lose the confidence of the public. I hope you will not do it.

A Gentleman: Mrs. President, I hope you will do it. I move that the name of the association be changed to the "Universal Franchise Association."

Mrs. Stanton: The question is already settled by our constitution, which requires a month's notice previous to the annual meeting before any change of name can be made. We will now have a song. [Laughter.]

Mr. Blackwell said that he had just returned from the South, and that he had learned to think that the test oath required of white men who had been rebels must be abolished before the vote be given to the negro. He was willing that the negro should have the suffrage, but not under such conditions that he should rule the South. [At the allusion of Mr. Blackwell to abolishing the test oath, the audience hissed loudly.]

Mrs. Stanton said—Gentlemen and Ladies: I take this as quite an insult to me. It is as if you were invited to dine with me and you turned up your nose at everything that was set on the table.

Mrs. Livermore said: It certainly requires a great amount of nerve to talk before you, for you have such a frankness in expressing yourselves that I am afraid of you. [Laughter and applause.] If you do not like the dish, you turn up your nose at it and say, "Take it away, take it away." [Laughter.] I was brought up in the West, and it is a good place to get rid of any superfluous modesty, but I am afraid of you. [Applause.] It seems that you are more willing to be pleased than to hear what we have to say. [Applause.] Throughout the day the men who have attended our Convention have been turbulent. [Applause.] I say it frankly, that the behavior of the majority of men has not been respectful. [Applause.] She then gave a pathetic narration of the sorrow she had seen among the depraved and destitute of our great cities, and said the work of the coming year would be to get up a monster petition of a million of names asking the Legislature for suffrage. [Applause.]

After a song from the Hutchinson Family, who had come from Chicago to entertain the audiences of the Association, the meeting adjourned.[52]

This section of the convention proceedings was deleted by the editors of *History of Woman Suffrage* in their reprinting of the convention report.

Mr. Foster: Then I have other objections to these women being officers of this Society. When we organized this Society, we appointed a committee for the purpose of having a body which would be responsible for the funds of the Society and we appointed a treasurer to take care of the funds. But if you look into that committee's report, you will find that it shirked its duty. That committee put its funds in the hands of an individual person, and let her run the machine.

Miss ANTHONY: That is true.

Mr. FOSTER: And she never kept any books or account of the expenditures.

Miss ANTHONY: That is false. Every dollar ever received by me and every dollar expended, item by item, was presented to the trust fund committee of Boston, of which this gentleman is a member. The account was audited, and has been reported to me, by Wendell Phillips, Parker Pillsbury, Abby Kelly Foster, and Charles F. Whipple, and they voted me a check of $1000 to balance the account.

Mr. FOSTER: I would be glad to believe Miss Anthony, but her statement is not reliable for Wendell Phillips and Abby Kelly Foster told me so.[53]

Mr. FOSTER: I only wanted to tell you why the Massachusetts society can not coalesce with the party here, and why we want these women to retire and leave us to nominate officers who can receive the respect of both parties. The Massachusetts Abolitionists can not co-operate with this society as it is now organized. If you choose to put officers here that ridicule the negro, and pronounce the Amendment infamous, why I must retire; I can not work with you. You can not have my support, and you must not use my name. I can not shoulder the responsibility of electing officers who publicly repudiate the principles of the society.

HENRY B. BLACKWELL said: The facts of the case are these. During the early portion of the Society Miss Anthony was given full power over the funds of the Society to spend them as she thought best. Some of us thought her expenditures were not judicious; no one doubted the purity of her motives. The whole financial matter, however, has been settled in this way. Miss Anthony brought in a statement of her expenditures to the Society. No one doubts that all the expenditures were exactly made as she reported. Her statement made due to herself from the society $1000. Now, Miss Anthony, for the sake of harmony and the good of the cause has given up her claim for this $1000. In regard to this we have to say that we are entirely satisfied with the settlement thus made. When a person for the good of a cause will make a pecuniary sacrifice of expenditures made, which expenditures many might consider perfectly wise, although some of us did not, it shows such a spirit that I think this question might well have been kept back.[54]

V.

THE 1870s:
A Decade of Progress, Loss, and Refining Tactics

The Fifteenth Amendment was ratified in 1870, ensuring the vote for African American men, and Representative Julian's resolution, a Sixteenth Amendment to enfranchise women, was set aside. All men could now vote except Native American men, who were citizens of their own sovereign nations. While women could vote in two territories, no woman had a voice in national elections. The United States of America had officially become a government based on the consent of men only.

The two suffrage organizations followed separate paths. A federal amendment to the constitution was the only way to ensure woman suffrage, the National American Woman Suffrage Association (NWSA) contended, while the rival American Woman Suffrage Association (AWSA) took a states' rights position, arguing that states might decide who could vote. The AWSA strategy had the indirect effect of strengthening the southern states, which were eager to immediately disenfranchise the new black male voters. If states gave women the vote, why couldn't they take it away from black men?

The AWSA established its own newspaper, the *Woman's Journal,* to counter the NWSA's *Revolution.* The *Journal*'s first issue announced that the paper would focus exclusively on woman suffrage, as the AWSA was committed to do.[1] This stance contrasted sharply with the *Revolution*'s history of addressing a wide spectrum of women's issues and, as the NWSA developed, the practice of its organization. Henry Blackwell introduced the following resolution into the 1870 AWSA convention and it was unanimously adopted:

> *Resolved*, That the American Woman Suffrage Association heartily invites the cooperation of all individuals and all State societies who feel the need of a truly National Association on a delegated basis, which shall avoid side issues, and devote itself to the main question of suffrage. Adopted unanimously.[2]

Other issues emerged for the NWSA. Stanton supported the Working Woman's Association when it came to the defense of Hester Vaughn, a servant whose employer coerced her into having intercourse with him and fired her when she became pregnant. Arrested for infanticide when she was found critically ill with her dead newborn beside her, Vaughn was found guilty and sentenced to death. The Working Woman's Association sent Dr. Clemence S. Lozier, one of the early wave of woman's rights physicians, to examine Vaughn. These working women then called a mass meeting to demand Vaughn's pardon, an end to capital punishment, and women's right to vote for the laws that ruled them and sit on the juries that sentenced them. Through the movement's direct action, Vaughn was pardoned.[3]

Dr. Lozier, who was an NWSA member, came to realize, through this and other cases she saw, how reproductive education also was needed, and she set out to write a series of tracts. The first, "Child-Birth Made Easy," advocated a diet of whole grains, fresh fruit, and vegetables, loose clothing, and two hours' exercise daily, along with sitz baths. The full tract is included in this chapter.

The AWSA also heard from working women. The president of the parasol-makers, "who had been forced out of employment by their employers," dropped in on their 1873 convention, "not as women suffragists but as women suffering, to ask of the audience their sympathetic support":

My Worthy Friends, Ladies and Gentlemen: I was not prepared
to meet an audience like this. In consequence of being oppressed
by our employers we were obliged to leave their employ, because
we can not earn our bread. Consequently we held a meeting up
stairs to-night, and knowing that you were here we thought we
would let you know that there are hundreds of women suffering,
not for the ballot but for bread. I have never wanted the ballot. I
believe it belongs to the men who have it; but I come to ask you
in the name of humanity if there can be any society organized
that will repress the unscrupulous employers and let the public
know they are oppressing the poor girls. Men are strong; they
can get together and ask what they want; they can organize in
large bodies, but the working women are the most oppressed
race in the United States. I am thankful to you, gentlemen and
ladies (I should have put the ladies first), for giving me your attention. I don't intend to detain you long, because your meeting
is here for a different purpose, but I hope you will give me your
sympathies. I can not make you an eloquent speech, for I, as a
working woman, have had to labor eighteen hours a day for my
bread, and therefore have had no time to educate myself as an
orator.[4]

While focusing on state suffrage, the AWSA resolutions in
1872 also supported the NWSA's federal suffrage work and
recognized the civil disobedience women were committing
when they voted:

Resolved, That we call upon Congress to enact a law establishing impartial suffrage for all citizens irrespective of sex, in the
District of Columbia and the Territories; also to declare woman
eligible to all offices under Government, with equal pay for
equal work: also to submit a XVI Constitutional Amendment
prohibiting political distinctions on account of sex.

. . . 5. *Resolved*, That we demand from the State Legislatures
laws establishing equal suffrage for women in choosing electors
of President and Vice-President of the United States, also in
choosing municipal and State officers, in every case where the
qualifications of voters are not restricted by the State

Constitutions; also to amend the State Constitutions so as to establish equal rights for all.

6. And Whereas, many women have recently applied for registration as voters, and in some cases, have actually voted, and are now being prosecuted on the charge of having voted illegally; therefore,

Resolved, That we call upon the State and Federal courts to interpret all legal provisions that will admit of such a construction in favor of the equality of women.

8. Resolved, That the Executive Committee be instructed to address memorials to Congress, and State Legislatures, and National Conventions of every political party, in behalf of the legal and political equality of woman.[5]

In this moment when the question of who can vote was on the national table, Francis Minor came up with a new legal strategy. The husband of NWSA officer Virginia Minor, he was a strong ally and a Missouri attorney. The Constitution, Francis Minor reasoned, leaves it to the states to decide the qualification of voters, but it does not give them the right to deny citizens the right to vote. And since the Fourteenth amendment expressly declares, "No State shall make or enforce any laws that shall abridge the privileges or immunities of citizens of the United States,"[6] any state constitutions denying women suffrage "are violative alike of the spirit and letter of the Federal Constitution."[7] Women were actually enfranchised by the Fourteenth Amendment, Minor therefore reasoned. Picking up the new strategy, the NWSA now argued that the Fourteenth Amendment was the grounds for woman suffrage.

The concept that rights were protected at the federal level of the government was critical during the 1870s, when southern states were trying every means to deny African American men their right to vote, and the federal government had to stand firmly against states' rights if the rights of formerly enslaved citizens were to be protected. When Congress passed legislation empowering citizens who were refused their voting rights by local election officials to take their cases to federal court, another door opened. While the Enforcement Acts of 1870 and 1871 were clearly designed to protect the ballot for African American men, they also meant women could test the law by bringing legal action against registrars refusing to register them or officials refusing to take their ballots.[8]

The NWSA affirmed its commitment to federal suffrage in the St. Louis Adoptions ratified at the 1869 national convention in St. Louis, included in this chapter.

This became the argument the NWSA would use for the next five years. Women already had the right to vote, if the Constitution were interpreted correctly. Ten thousand extra copies of the *Revolution* containing Francis Minor's resolutions making this argument were published and "sent to friends throughout the country, laid on every member's desk in Congress, and circulated at the Washington Convention of 1870."[9]

Women continued to vote, breaking the state laws that denied them the right, but claiming they were entitled to it by federal law. Sojourner Truth joined other women in Michigan at the polls. More than seventy women in Washington, D.C., including Josephine Griffing, Belva Lockwood, and the popular writer Grace Greenwood and her eighty-year-old mother, "marched in solid phalanx to the registrar's office, but were repulsed." Among them was Mary Ann Shadd Cary, a member of the D.C. Universal Franchise Society and their spokesperson at the Colored National Labor Union convention in 1869. Appointed chair of the Colored National Labor Union's Committee on Female Suffrage, she was joined by suffragists Lockwood and Griffing (both white NWSA members), who served on her committee. The first African American woman to publish a weekly newspaper in North America, Cary went on to become an attorney and active member of the NWSA-affiliated Universal Franchise Society. Cary was also a founder of the Colored Woman's Progressive Franchise Association.

Vineland, New Jersey, was another hotbed of activity; women attempted to vote there as early as 1868 and within four years the number of resisters in the town had grown to 183. From Maryland to Washington Territory, from Fayetteville, New York, to South Newbury, Ohio, women exercised their inherent right to vote. These were not isolated acts. No one knew how many cases there were, since there was no national clearinghouse for information, but the newspapers were full of stories of women voting. Susan B. Anthony was arrested along with twelve Rochester, New York, women, and the judge instructed the jury to find her guilty. Fined one hundred dollars, she refused to pay it.[10]

African American women voted in South Carolina, where the four suffragist Rollin sisters wielded such influence that their home was called the unofficial Republican Party headquarters. Charlotte "Lottie" Rollin was secretary of the state affiliate of the AWSA. Chairing the first convention of this South Carolina Woman's Rights Association, which was held in Columbia on December 20, 1870, Rollin said:

> It had been so universally the custom to treat the idea of woman suffrage with ridicule and merriment that it becomes necessary in submitting the subject for earnest deliberation that we assure the gentlemen present that our claim is made honestly and seriously. We ask suffrage not as a favor, not as a privilege, but as a right based on the ground that we are human beings, and as such, entitled to all human rights. While we concede that woman's ennobling influence should be confined chiefly to home and society, we claim that public opinion has had a tendency to limit woman's sphere to too small a circle, and until woman has the right of representation this will last, and other rights will be held by an insecure tenure.[11]

Matilda Joslyn Gage produced a treatise that put forth the new strategy in concise terms, combining the Minors' argument with application of the Enforcement Acts, which Congress had passed to implement the Fourteenth Amendment's voter protection. Reprinted widely, her "Woman's Rights Catechism" quickly became a valuable campaign document.[12] Gage's logic was relentless: The women who voted were not breaking the law; the lawbreakers were those denying women the vote. The full "Catechism" is included in this chapter.

The suffragists had created a win-win strategy. If arrested

for voting, women would use the inherent right argument in their defense. If not allowed to vote, they would use the Enforcement Acts in bringing suit against the registrar who had refused to accept their ballot.

Attorney Carrie S. Burnham brought her well-reasoned, 112-page case before the Pennsylvania Supreme Court. A portion of the suit is included in this chapter.

Despite the differences between the two suffrage organizations, pressure was mounting from a number of sources requesting a unification of forces and Theodore Tilton, influential Republican editor of the *Independent,* called for a meeting of the AWSA and the NWSA in 1870 to see if they could merge. When the NWSA representatives insisted at the meeting that any new organization must support a potential Sixteenth Amendment for woman suffrage, the AWSA volunteers withdrew. Those remaining were left to create a new organization, the Union Woman Suffrage Association (UWSA), which was essentially the NWSA's vision and strategy.

At dueling AWSA and NWSA conventions held just two months later in New York City on the same day in May, the NWSA determined in a business meeting session to merge into the UWSA, with Tilton as president and passage of the proposed Sixteenth Amendment the primary work to be done. With two men as presidents of the opposing organizations, Tilton heading the UWSA and his friend Reverend Henry Ward Beecher as the head of the AWSA, the NWSA leaders created the illusion of merger. Controlling the UWSA, they had put the AWSA into a position of having to succumb to the NWSA's leadership or refuse merger. Tilton, Stanton, and Anthony then took over a meeting of the old AERA's executive committee, voting that that society merge with the UWSA.

It was a brilliant move. The NWSA thereby consolidated its authority, brought the AERA under its wing, and exposed the irresolvable difference between the two suffrage associations, while taking the moral high ground by seemingly demonstrating a willingness to merge. Outmaneuvered, the AWSA refused the merger attempt. The two groups would work independently for twenty years.[13]

A further gap now developed between the two suffrage organizations in the person of stockbroker and newspaper editor Victoria Woodhull, who secured a hearing before the Judiciary Committee of the House in 1871 with a memorial "praying for the passage of such laws as may be necessary and proper for carrying into execution the right vested by the Constitution in the citizens of the United States to vote without regard to sex."[14] The NWSA strategy, developed out of Minor's analysis, was to bypass the legislative branch of government, commit civil disobedience by voting, then take the cases to court and let the judiciary affirm women's voting rights. Woodhull threw it back to the legislative branch of government, calling on Congress to pass enabling legislation like that they had provided black male voters to protect their voting rights.

The Union Woman Suffrage Association (the old NWSA) met shortly after Woodhull's testimony, and the leadership, impressed with Woodhull's logic, invited her to attend the convention and present her congressional speech. Convinced by Woodhull's argument that a Supreme Court decision or a constitutional amendment might not be necessary, the organization enthusiastically picked up Woodhull's strategy.[15]

Woodhull's congressional testimony was part of a larger plan. The previous year she had announced on the pages of the *New York Herald* that she would form a new progressive third party, the Equal Rights Party, and run for president of the United States.[16] She had the backing of Free Thinkers, marriage and reproductive-rights reformers, labor unions, and free lovers. She and her sister had published the first U.S. English printing of Marx and Engels's *Communist Manifesto* in their newspaper, *Woodhull and Claflin's Weekly*, and headed the woman's section of Marx's International Workingmen's Association.[17]

Woodhull quickly butted heads with Susan B. Anthony at the conclusion of her UWSA convention speech. Woodhull announced a meeting to form her new Equal Rights Party the following day. Although the UWSA was scheduled to meet at that time, Stanton suggested they attend the organizational meeting of the Equal Rights Party instead, but Anthony announced that would not happen. When the convention-goers demanded a vote, Anthony adjourned the meeting and turned out the lights, angering the UWSA members.[18]

The sparsely attended UWSA meeting the next day voted to dissolve itself into the old National Woman Suffrage Association with Anthony as its president. At the same time, drawing the crowds, was the meeting to form the Equal Rights Party with Woodhull as its United States presidential candidate. Woodhull, without obtaining his endorsement, accepted Frederick Douglass as her vice-presidential running mate.

The press immediately picked up scandalous news that the woman suffragists had endorsed an acknowledged free lover as their presidential candidate. The AWSA quickly separated itself from the NWSA's support of Woodhull at its May 10, 1871, convention. A resolution was introduced and discussed:

> 8. *Resolved*, That the claim of woman to participate in making the laws she is required to obey, and to equality of rights in all directions, has nothing to do with special social theories, and that the recent attempts in this city and elsewhere to associate the woman suffrage cause with the doctrines of free love, and to hold it responsible for the crimes and follies of individuals, is an outrage upon common sense and decency, and a slander upon the virtue and intelligence of the women of America.[19]
>
> The eighth resolution was then discussed, to which Mr. Kilgore also objected, offering a motion that all the resolution coming after the words "special social theories," be stricken out. He was opposed, especially, to the introduction of the words "free love." What was meant by them?
>
> Mr. Blackwell said the Convention meant by the use of that phrase exactly what the New York *Tribune* of that morning meant, in its statement that the woman suffrage movement was one for free love.
>
> The President said this great movement was not responsible for the freaks and follies of individuals. The resolutions simply denied that this association indorsed free love, which certain papers charged them with. After considerable discussion, the

resolution was adopted by the strong, decided and united voices of nearly a thousand people, voting in the affirmative.[20]

On a rainy evening the following November, 1871, Woodhull delivered a speech to an overflow crowd of three thousand in New York City's Steinway Hall. Introduced by Theodore Tilton, Woodhull began by detailing the history of the struggle for religious and political freedom in the Western world, then explained that social freedom would be the next stage of the battle for individual liberty. The abridged speech is reprinted in this chapter.

In her speech, Woodhull directly challenged the AWSA's newspaper, the *Woman's Journal*, "whose conductors have felt called upon to endeavor to convince the people that it has no affiliation with those" who advocate free love. The newspaper was lying. Woodhull and the AWSA's former president, Reverend Henry Ward Beecher, had been lovers. Woodhull practiced what she preached, while Reverend Henry Ward Beecher preached against what he practiced.

Beecher used his position of power as the most famous minister in the country to sexually coerce female members of his congregation. Elizabeth Tilton was one. And here was the kicker. Elizabeth Tilton was an officer in the NWSA, and her husband, Theodore Tilton, had been president of the short-lived Union Woman Suffrage Association when Beecher was president of the AWSA. The AWSA, denouncing free love and distancing itself from the NWSA because of its association with Woodhull, had been formed with a president who practiced free love. Not only that, he did it with an officer of the NWSA.

The hypocrisy was too much for Woodhull. Woodhull spoke truth to power, exposing in her paper, *Woodhull and Claflin's Weekly*, the hypocrisy of Beecher's publicly pious persona hiding a minister who used his position to sexually violate his female parishioners. She was surprisingly kind and focused, condemning not the man but the social conditions that created him.

. . . I assumed at once and got a sufficient admission that his real life was something very different from the awful "virtue" he was

preaching . . . that the dreadful suzz was merely a bogus senti-
mentality, pumped in his imagination, because our sickly religious literature, and Sunday School morality, and pulpit
phariseeism had humbugged him all his life into the belief that
he ought to act and feel in this harlequin and absurd way.[21]

In the same issue, her coeditor sister Tennessee Claflin revealed that Luther C. Challis, a model of Wall Street integrity,
along with a friend, had gotten two young girls, fifteen and
sixteen years old, drunk and sexually violated them.

These newspaper editors sent a warning that they were prepared to expose other "respectable" sexual violators in high
places.

Whenever a person whom we know to be a hypocrite stands up
and denounces us because of our doctrines . . . we shall unmask
him. . . . That is plain, terse and impossible of misconception. . . . We are prepared to take all the responsibility for libel
suits and imprisonment.[22]

Little did they know how soon that last sentence would
prove a dire prediction. The paper containing the exposé of the
sexual violation of teenagers and the hypocrisy of Beecher hit
the newsstands on October 28, 1872, and immediately sold out
the first run of one hundred thousand copies, with thousands
more selling out as soon as they could be printed. The furor
grabbed the attention of Anthony Comstock, a one-man morality campaigner working under the auspices of the YMCA.
In June, he had lobbied through Congress a bill making it illegal to send obscene publications through the mail. This was
his opportunity to enforce the law. On November 2, the sisters
were arrested under Comstock's law. George Francis Train offered to put up the sixteen-thousand-dollar bail to release
them, but Woodhull and Claflin chose to remain in jail until
their hearing two days later. Discharged, they were immediately rearrested on grand jury indictments.

The following day, November 5, the country's first female
presidential candidate sat out the election in jail, arrested for

publicly proclaiming a woman's right to not be violated, and calling men to a level of honesty about their exploitive sexual behavior.

Over the next year, the sisters would be arrested several times. When their case was finally heard in June 1873, the charges were dismissed because the federal law did not include newspapers as a medium in which obscene matter could be prosecuted. Comstock had already taken measures to close the loophole with an "Act of the Suppression of Trade in, and Circulation of, Obscene Literature and Articles of Immoral Use."

The Comstock law gave Anthony Comstock the ability to decide what was obscene. For Comstock, that was anything to do with sex and reproduction. His goal was to stop the practice of birth control and abortion.

Methods of birth control were known and widely available at the time; some of them had been for years. Dr. Charles Knowlton described one form in his 1833 birth control guide, *Fruits of Philosophy*:

> Another check which the old idea of conception has led some to recommend with considerable confidence, consists in introducing into the vagina, previous to connection, a very delicate piece of sponge, moistened with water, to be immediately afterward withdrawn by means of a very narrow ribbon attached to it. . . . [A]s there are many little ridges or folds in the vagina, we can not suppose the withdrawal of the sponge would dislodge all the semen in every instance. If, however, it were well moistened with some liquid which acted chemically upon the semen, it would be pretty likely to destroy the fecundating property of what might remain.[23]

The sponge and "pessaries" (forms of diaphragms and cervical caps) were available, as well as the "baudruche" (condom), which functioned also "to secure from syphilitic affections."[24] Newspapers secured a whopping one hundred thousand dollars a year advertising birth control pills and abortifacients made of natural herbs—some real, many bogus—"as a preventive of irregularities and as a monthly regulator, thus relieving

those suffering with anguish and anxiety," the cryptic adver-
tisements read.[25]

The Comstock laws, picked up by many states in an even
more repressive form, may have had a far deeper effect on
women's lives than the absence of voting rights. With the legal
blackout on birth control and abortion, many women would
be forced into unwanted births for nearly a hundred years until
the laws' final overturning by the Supreme Court's 1965 ruling
in *Griswold* v. *Connecticut.*

The upshot of Woodhull's exposé was this. Beecher was
fully exonerated; the lives of Elizabeth and Theodore Tilton
were shattered; Stanton and Anthony found themselves on opposite sides of a critical issue; and Woodhull and Claflin eventually sought respectability. The AWSA and the NWSA were
further divided but a new organization championing woman's
body right soon emerged.

Freethinkers who opposed established religion formed the
Liberal League in July 1876. One of the organization's primary
goals was to fight the Comstock Acts, which they did with petitions, court cases, and public opinion but with little success.
The organization presented a petition calling for the repeal of
the Comstock law with seventy thousand signatures to the
House of Representatives in 1878, but Congress upheld the law.

Some NWSA officials, most notably Matilda Joslyn Gage
and Elizabeth Cady Stanton, connected with the Freethought
movement. The more conservative Christian AWSA leadership
did not.

The Freethinkers fearlessly fought for a woman's right to her
body, as well as exposing sexual violation. Defying the Comstock laws, E. H. Heywood included a firsthand account of sex
trafficking in his 1877 book, *Sexual Indulgence and Denial:
Uncivil Liberty. An Essay to Show the Injustice and Impolicy
of Ruling Woman Without Her Consent.*

CHINESE GIRLS PROSTITUTION . . . A remarkable spectacle
was the landing of the women and girls, of whom there were two
hundred and forty on board. It was like landing a drove of sheep
or cows. At all points of the compass were men to drive them,

and they came off the boat in squads of fifteen or twenty each. The policemen and Chinese "bosses" kept each squad together and drove the entire crowd into a corner under a shed, where they stood watched as closely as ever was guarded a gang of slaves in the South. If a Chinawoman, resident here, approached too near, she was seized and pushed away; and if any of the new comers left the crowd, she was driven back, or seized by the back of the neck and shoved to her place again.

Most of those who come are young girls, many not over twelve or fifteen years of age, and nine-tenths, at least, for purposes of prostitution. Into seven or eight cars, reserved to transport them to the Chinese quarters, these creatures were driven in squads and hauled to a point on Jackson street. The women then ran the gauntlet again. The alley, which is one of the narrowest and filthiest in the city, was lined with Chinamen and women, as the strangers were driven through it, up some old rickety steps into the Dupont street theatre, and in the pit of that wretched place were again herded. Here they were assorted, marked over, and sent to the "six companies" to which they were consigned.[26]

Heywood was arrested and convicted of violating the 1873 Comstock Act and sentenced to two years' hard labor. Massive protests led to his pardon, and, although arrested four more times, he continued to publish his free love paper, *The Word*, until his death in 1893.

Having practiced nonviolent civil disobedience for decades by illegally voting, the NWSA launched another campaign of civil disobedience, a tax protest which it launched, appropriately, on the centennial of the Boston Tea Party, December 16, 1873. Dr. Clemence S. Lozier, president of the New York Woman Suffrage Association (an affiliate of the NWSA), issued a call for a mass meeting on that day inviting the tax-paying women of New York to protest against the tyranny of taxation without representation. That call appears in this chapter.

Matilda Joslyn Gage questioned in a *Syracuse Journal* article on May 7, 1871:

Oh, wise men, can you tell why he means she, when taxes are to
be assessed, and does not mean she, when taxes are to be voted
upon? The whole question of a woman's demand for a vote
along with taxation is a simple question of justice.[27]

Gage also corrected history, telling readers of several newspapers for which she wrote articles that the original tax pro-
testers were the Founding Mothers, not the Fathers.

In 1770, six years before the Declaration of Independence, the
women of New England made a public, combined protest
against taxation without representation; and as tea was the article upon which Great Britain was then expending her strength,
these women of the American Colonies united themselves into a
league, and bound themselves, to use no more tea in their families until the tax upon it was repealed. This league was formed
by the married women, but three days afterwards the young ladies held an anti-tax meeting. These young ladies publicly declared they did not take this step for themselves alone, but they
protested against this taxation as a matter of principle, and with
a view to benefit their posterity.

These public protests against taxation were made more than
five years before the commencement of the Revolutionary War.
They, also, were the real origin of the famous Tea Party in Boston Harbor, which did not take place until three years after the
public protest of the women. The women of today are the direct
posterity of the women of the Revolution, and as our foremothers protested against "taxation without representation,"
so, do we, their descendants, protest against being taxed without being represented.[28]

Tax Protest Leagues sprang up around the country, from
New York to Chicago to San Francisco, and as news of the resistance grew, individual women joined those who had gone
before and refused to pay their taxes.

Women of means, who were beginning to fund women's issues, also joined the tax protest, sending petitions to the New
York Legislature in the summer of 1877. One woman was

Susan A. King, the head of a New York firm composed of women with a capital of $1 million. King made her fortune, appropriately, in the tea trade, and then invested smartly in real estate. Her petition was signed by a few other wealthy women, who together held $9 million in assets, which represents $217 million in purchasing power today.[29]

With women voting illegally, suing the registrars who refused to register them to vote, and protesting their taxes, the stage was sent to bring the burning question of woman suffrage to the highest court in the land.

Virginia Minor, NWSA officer and president of the Missouri Woman Suffrage Association, and her attorney husband, who developed the argument that women possessed the vote under the Fourteenth Amendment, would now be the ones to test it in the Supreme Court. Reese Happersett, the St. Louis registrar of voters, refused to place Virginia Minor's name on the voting list because "she was not a 'male' citizen, but a woman," and therefore ineligible to vote in the state of Missouri, he said. In association with her husband (married women under the common law were unable to bring suit independently of their husbands), Virginia Minor sued for damages and lost both in the circuit court and then on appeal to the Missouri Supreme Court.

The Minors carried the case to the United States Supreme Court, with Francis Minor acting as the chief attorney arguing this landmark woman suffrage case in 1874. Since their task was to decide "what the law is, not to declare what it should be," the judges had to rely on precedent, they determined, which over time established that the Constitution never meant citizenship to confer the right of suffrage. "Certainly," these nine white men ruled, "if the courts can consider any question settled, this is one." Unanimously they decided "that the Constitution of the United States does not confer the right of suffrage upon any one," so the state constitutions and laws that denied women the right to vote were legal. If people thought the laws were wrong, they should change them, the Supreme Court added.[30]

Gage, in a speech at the next NWSA convention, showed that the Supreme Court was wrong in asserting that the federal government did not determine suffrage; the states did. The full speech is included in this chapter.

Meanwhile, at the AWSA, a stronger religious tone was emerging. Bishop Gilbert Haven of the Methodist Episcopal Church was elected president of the organization in 1875.[31] While the NWSA was battling in the Supreme Court, the 1874 AWSA convention applauded the victories in religious and labor bodies. Hailing recent endorsements of woman suffrage by the Methodist Convention of Michigan, the Conferences of Iowa, and other state religious bodies around the country, the AWSA "cordially" invited the support "of Christians of all denominations" in the woman suffrage effort.

The AWSA also claimed the Patrons of Husbandry's Granges, the Sovereigns of Industry's Councils, and the Good Templars' Lodges as "practical auxiliaries of the woman suffrage movement" because of their recent recognition of the right of women to vote and hold office in their societies.[32]

The Supreme Court setback was echoed at the state level. Just as the New York constitutional convention had considered and discarded women's suffrage in 1867, thirteen other states throughout the nation followed suit during the late 1860s and throughout the 1870s. New Jersey, Vermont, Pennsylvania, and Ohio were joined by Louisiana, Texas, and Arkansas to the South; Missouri, Illinois, Nebraska, and Colorado in the heartland, and California and Washington Territory in the West.

While the right was consistently denied, the very fact that it was being considered meant progress. Woman suffrage was now on everybody's mind. From the halls of Congress to state legislatures, this essential question was hotly debated by the all-male elected representatives.

The struggle for women's voting rights was now being waged internationally as well, as the call for the 1873 NWSA Convention rejoiced:

Woman Suffrage Anniversary.—National Woman Suffrage Association.—The Twenty-fifth Woman Suffrage Anniversary will be held in Apollo Hall, New York, Tuesday, May 6, 1873. Lucretia Mott and Elizabeth Cady Stanton, who called the first Woman's Rights convention at Seneca Falls, 1848, will be present to give their reminiscences. That Convention was scarcely mentioned by the local press; now, over the whole world, equality for woman is demanded. In the United States, woman suffrage is the chief political question of the hour. Great Britain is deeply agitated upon the same topic; Germany has a princess at the head of its National Woman's Rights organization. Portugal, Spain, and Russia have been roused. In Rome an immense meeting, composed of the representatives of Italian democracy, was recently called in the old Coliseum; one of its resolutions demanded a reform in the laws relating to woman and a re-establishment of her natural rights. Turkey, France, England, Switzerland, Italy, sustain papers devoted to woman's enfranchisement. A Grand International Woman's Rights Congress is to be held in Paris in September of this year, to which the whole world is invited to send delegates, and this Congress is to be under the management of the most renowned liberals of Europe. Come up, then, friends, and celebrate the Silver Wedding of the Woman Suffrage movement. Let our Twenty-fifth Anniversary be one of power; our reform is everywhere advancing, let us redouble our energies and our courage.[33]

While individual men had long been allies, men were now developing organized support, as Lillie Devereux Blake explained. The recently-formed "Young Men's Woman Suffrage League" brought together members between eighteen and forty-five in New York City for well-attended weekly meetings of speeches and debates. Playfully arguing the affirmative side, many young men saw the logic and "have become warm supporters of the measure," Blake reported.[34]

Massachusetts men stepped up as allies as well, with "thirty-five eminent and representative men of the state" presenting a memorial to the Massachusetts Legislature calling for legislation to allow women citizens to vote in all elections and be elected or appointed to any office.[35]

And then came an opportunity to point out to the country

the government's hypocrisy in a dramatic way. In 1876 the country prepared to celebrate one hundred proud years of existing as a republic, based on the consent of the governed. How would the suffragists seize the moment?

The president of the NWSA, Matilda Joslyn Gage, penned a protest that the organization adopted at its January 1876 convention and then widely circulated:

> We, the undersigned women of the United States, asserting our faith in the principles of the Declaration of Independence and in the constitution of the United States, proclaiming it as the best form of government in the world, declare ourselves a part of the people of the nation unjustly deprived of the guaranteed and reserved rights belonging to citizens of the United States; because we have never given our consent to this government; because we have never delegated our rights to others; because this government is false to its underlying principles; because it has refused to one-half its citizens the only means of self-government—the ballot; because it has been deaf to our appeals, our petitions and our prayers;
>
> Therefore, in presence of the assembled nations of all the world, we protest against this government of the United States as an oligarchy of sex, and not a true republic; and we protest against calling this a centennial celebration of the independence of the people of the United States.[36]

The convention resolved that the women in 1876 "have greater cause for discontent, rebellion and revolution, than the men of 1776," because the Founding Fathers were ruled by a monarch, upheld in a system based on the "divine right of kings," not one claiming to be "of the people, by the people, and for the people." Women felt the injustice even more deeply, "because our masters, instead of dwelling in a foreign land, are our husbands, our fathers, our brothers and our sons."

They were in solidarity, they claimed, with Abigail Adams, who in 1776 declared that "the passion for liberty cannot be strong in the breasts of those who are accustomed to deprive

their fellow-creatures of liberty." And, just as Adams predicted, "We are determined to foment a rebellion, and will not
hold ourselves bound by laws in which we have no voice or
representation."[37]

Stanton and Gage, the NWSA authors, set to work on a
Declaration of Rights of Women, since the original Declaration needed revision. Then they made plans to present it at the
government's official July 4 celebration in Philadelphia. Denied
at each level of request, all the way up to the office of the vice
president of the United States, they faced a tough decision.
Would they present it illegally, risking arrest? The NWSA leadership was divided. Stanton and Mott said no. Gage explained
the decision she and a few others came to, as well as what un-
folded. The account is included in this chapter, followed by the
declaration the women penned.

The NWSA regrouped after the Supreme Court defeat with an
admirable agility and changed tactics with the changing conditions. The *History of Woman Suffrage* editors explained that,
having been defeated "at the polls, in the courts, in the national celebration, and in securing a plank in the platforms of
the Republican and Democratic parties," the NWSA saw the
writing on the wall. If, in fact, the Constitution and the Fourteenth Amendment didn't protect their voting rights, they
would go back to their original strategy, to fight for, and win,
a suffrage amendment.

Their work had not been in vain, however. The courtroom
arguments and congressional debates had created "a wide-
spread agitation" and the question of women's rights was now
a public issue.[38]

Gage also introduced a new tactic, which quickly spread
when picked up by the NWSA members. Congress had the authority to pass legislation restoring voting rights to men who
had been convicted of crimes—even treason—as well as granting citizenship and the ballot to immigrants who had fought
for the country. This seemed like an entering wedge, and Gage
sent an individual petition to Congress. Her representative,

Elias W. Leavenworth, responded by introducing a bill into the House of Representatives on February 5, 1877, to "relieve the political disabilities of Matilda Joslyn Gage," granting her full citizenship and voting rights.[39]

While the bills did not pass Congress, the point was made. If southern men who had committed treason against the United States government were relieved of their political disabilities and allowed once again the voting privilege of citizens, why not the loyal women of the North?

California senator A. A. Sargent, whose wife, Ellen Clark, was an officer in the NWSA, introduced a constitutional amendment to enfranchise women in 1878, similar to the Sixteenth Amendment joint resolution introduced by George Julian in 1869. Senator Sargent's joint resolution read exactly as did the suffrage amendment finally adopted forty-one years later in 1920:

Joint Resolution *proposing an Amendment to the Constitution of the United States.*—

Resolved by the Senate and House of Representatives of the United States of America in congress assembled, two-thirds of each House concurring therein, That the following article be proposed to the legislatures of the several States as an amendment to the Constitution of the United States, which, when ratified by three-fourths of the said legislatures, shall be valid as part of the said constitution, namely:

Article 16, Sec. 1.—The right of citizens of the United States to vote shall not be denied or abridged by the United States or by any State on account of sex.

Sec. 2.—Congress shall have power to enforce this article by appropriate legislation.

The bill was referred to The Committee on Privileges and Elections, which granted two days of testimony to the NWSA.

There were distractions, however, to the focus of the struggle. One was in the form of a temperance petition, presented by the Woman's Christian Temperance Union (WCTU), an "organized army of Mother love for God, Home, and Country," which had been formed in 1874 to end the consumption of liquor in the United States. The meeting notes stated that immediately after the suffrage hearing in the House, Maine representative Frye presented, "with glowing remarks," a WCTU petition containing thirty thousand signatures asking for women to be permitted to vote on the question of temperance. WCTU president Frances E. Willard and ex-president Annie T. Wittenmyer were then given a hearing. This timing, along with Representative Frye's remarks, linked the two issues of suffrage and temperance.[40]

The second weakening of the suffrage amendment's position came from the AWSA, which reiterated state, not national, suffrage, as the *History of Woman Suffrage* editors explained. While the AWSA also circulated petitions for a federal amendment, the executive committee chair, Lucy Stone, reminded AWSA members of "the far greater importance of petitioning the State legislatures." Despite the fact that the federal government had demonstrated its ability to enfranchise its citizens by the Fifteenth Amendment, which secured the vote for African American men, Stone argued that the Constitution gives that right to the states. If Congress is made up solely of states that deny women suffrage, she maintained, their representatives are not going to support an amendment that their own states haven't approved. Circulate both petitions together for signatures, she counseled, but "give special prominence" to the ones calling for state suffrage.[41]

Not all women wanted the vote; some women actively worked against their rights. When attorney Belva A. Lockwood presented a memorial and petition to Congress asking suffrage for the women of D.C. in 1871, Mrs. Admiral Dahlgren and Mrs. General Sherman (they assumed their husband's titles in their own names) presented a memorial with an almost equal number of signatures on an anti-suffrage petition.[42]

Mrs. H. C. Spencer responded to Dahlgren with a widely circulated pamphlet,[43] and Gage, as chair of the Committee on

Arrangements, invited Dahlgren and her anti-suffrage friends to attend the next NWSA convention and explain their position.[44]

Dahlgren declined the invitation. She was back in all her anti-suffrage glory in 1879, memorializing the Senate Committee on Privileges and Elections against the submission of the Sixteenth Amendment. Ironically, in pointing to the supposed oppressive condition of Native American women as evidenced by the burden they carry, she did not recognize that these women were carrying their own belongings, which they never lost ownership of when they married, as women did in the United States.[45]

Despite the opposition, the NWSA had gathered more than forty thousand signatures of men and women from thirty-five states and five territories in 1879, which led to the first favorable report woman suffrage had received in the Senate. The full report is included in this chapter, and while it was the minority report, it claimed it had the power of logic and reason on its side.

A contentious resolution for educated suffrage, the position the *Revolution* had taken the previous decade, was introduced to the 1877 NWSA convention, and although it caused prolonged discussion, it finally passed with a few dissenting voices. Arguing the need for an educated citizenry in a government based on the consent of the governed, the resolution called for a constitutional amendment that would "make education compulsory," allowing "all citizens of legal age, without distinction of sex, who can read and write the English language," to vote.

It had been illegal for enslaved people to learn to read and write, and, if enacted, this amendment would have blocked most former slaves, men and women, from voting while enfranchising most white women. This issue would emerge later as some suffragists argued that immigrants should not be allowed to vote for the same reason.[46]

Mary Ann Shadd Cary entered the discussion at the 1878 NWSA convention about whether to support a political party. Described in the convention report as "a worthy representative of the District of Columbia, the first colored woman that ever edited a newspaper in the United States, and who had been a worker in the cause for twenty years," Cary reported for the Colored Woman's Progressive Franchise Association that "the colored women would support whatever party would allow them their rights, be it Republican or Democratic. An active member of the NWSA-affiliated Universal Franchise Society in D.C., Cary attended NWSA conventions as a delegate and member of the press and served on the Business Committee in 1876.[47]

The May 1878 convention of the NWSA passed several remarkably progressive resolutions, introduced by Gage. Unlike the racist resolution of the previous year, this year's NWSA resolutions declared that the judicial refusal to naturalize Chinese and the attempt to force citizenship on Native Americans were synonymous with refusing women the vote: all "class legislation, dangerous to the stability of our institutions." Women's voices were needed in every aspect of governmental decision-making, continued the resolutions, which went on to challenge the religious doctrine that provided the underpinning for women's second-class position. The full report is included in this chapter.

The NWSA was now officially on record declaring that the church was the foundation of women's oppression and analyzing the problem not as individual men but as an institution of power that Gage and Stanton would come to call the Patriarchate. Frances Willard, the shining light of the Woman's Christian Temperance Union, immediately disassociated from the NWSA, vowing to work only with Christian women from now on.

The following year the NWSA held its May convention in St. Louis because of the proposition to reestablish there a "social evil" law outlawing prostitution, the convention devoting a whole day to the discussion. The laws called for the arrest of any woman in the streets at night on the assumption that only prostitutes would be outside alone after dark. Homeless women were arrested along with any woman out alone for whatever reason. Parker Pillsbury years before in an editorial in the *Revolution* had questioned why prostitutes, and not their clients, should be arrested. Recalling an arrest of six women arrested just for being in a park at eleven o'clock one night, Pillsbury asked if the police would similarly arrest the male "gamblers, thieves, drunkards, and panders" in the park. Even if the women were prostitutes, why arrest them and not the men who are the real criminals, the ones who hire them? At least, Pillsbury reasoned, arrest them equally. If you really want to solve the "social evil," he concluded, don't worry about the women. Deal with the men who create the trade. "Prostitution will cease when men become sufficiently pure to make no demand for prostitutes," he believed.[48]

The NWSA took on this issue of the social evil laws. The convention charged that the proposed legislation that would keep women who were not accompanied by men off the streets after dark was "based upon the presumption that woman's freedom must be forever sacrificed to man's licence." The problem was those men who "make our streets and highways dangerous" to women, and the ballot the only means to restrain them, and "secure the freedom that belongs to her by day and by night," the NWSA resolved.[49]

An editorial by Matilda Joslyn Gage in the May 1879 issue of her *National Citizen and Ballot Box* addressed the question of why "women are so silent on the subject of public trials in cases of seduction and rape."

We know that these crimes go unpunished and are therefore multiplied fearfully, because the victims of them are usually prevented from entering complaint by the certain knowledge that if they do they will themselves be ordered into open court, and there, day after day, in the face of a low-lived, staring crowd, be compelled to live over again mentally all the horrors of the first outrage. Compelling them to come into open court is but a second outrage inflicted by the State, especially as the law provides that the punishment of the criminal shall depend, not so much upon the proof of his guilt, as upon his inability to hire others to swear that her previous character had been hurt. If he can hire anyone to swear to this, and to other lies to substantiate it, then he is, according to law, quite innocent of all offence.[50]

I.
"Child-Birth Made Easy,"
by Dr. Clemence S. Lozier, 1870

Having been a mother forty years, and for the last thirty years engaged in a large obstetrical practice, I beg leave to publish in a series of tracts, a few plain, practical hints to parents.

Much is being said on the social evil, or ante-natal infanticide, its moral aspect justly portrayed, but little or no instruction in a clear, physiological sense has been given to mothers. Many cases occur from sheer ignorance; and much real pain and alarm may be averted by the right kind of information on this vital topic.

Young women have convinced me, in plain conversation that they did not know the first truth in regard to their own formation, or the laws of generation. It seems to me extremely cruel to hold up to scorn and public disgrace such ignorant, helpless beings. Public opinion, or prevailing custom, has made it quite impossible for women to obtain proper knowledge of these important matters.

While men have had physicians of their own sex, with whom they could converse freely, we have been shut out from all opportunities for medical instruction, until recently a few medical colleges have been established in this country and some others in Europe which have opened their doors to women.

In no way can the masses of young mothers or daughters be taught so quickly and properly as by educated, benevolent, female physicians.

Feeling the need of short, practical advice in printed form, to distribute among my patients, and also believing it will be the means of lessening the crime of infanticide, I propose to publish this as one of a series of tracts to parents.

My object in this is to teach a process of diet, dress, exercise and bathing, which will obviate alarm and make childbearing safe and comparatively easy.

Osseous or bony structures are always at the beginning cartilaginous and yielding. Even a hard piece of bone steeped in acid may be made pliable, and so elastic as to tie into knots like a string.

When the human form in embryo first becomes distinctly visible, it is almost wholly a fluid, consisting only of a soft, gelatinous pulp. In this soft mass a solid substance begins to appear, which gradually increases, and organs are formed. These organs, in their rudimentary state, are soft and tender; but in the progress of their development, constantly acquiring a greater number of solid particles, the cohesion of which progressively increases, the organs at length become dense and firm. As the soft solids augment in bulk and density, bony particles are deposited, sparingly at first, and in detached masses, but accumulated by degrees; these, too, are at length fashioned into distinct osseous structures, which, extending in various directions until they touch at every point, ultimately form the connected bony frame work of the human being. This bony fabric although soft, solid, and yielding at first, becomes by degrees firm and resisting.

The mother's blood is the source of this newly moulded being; its bones and tissues. It builds, supports, and nourishes it as her own body. And is not the mother's blood derived from her food and drink, and, according to the proportion of bony material existing in them, will not the newly-forming child become more or less firm and osseous? It is quite right to suppose that nutritious food is necessary to support and nourish both mother and foetus, but nutritious food can be had without the constituents of hard, bony material, which is so largely a proportion of wheat flour, entering into our bread, pies, puddings, and all kinds of pastries.

The West Indian grains, sago, tapioca, rice, etc., which are very nutritious, have very little of lime or bony matter. La Grange says: "A person who eats one pound of farina a day for one year, will have taken three ounces, four drachms and forty-four grains of phosphate of lime into the system."

Beans, rye, oats, barley, have not so much earthy matter as wheat. Potatoes and peas not more than half as much. Flesh of fowls and young animals, one-tenth. Rice, sago, fish, eggs, still less. Cheese, one-twentieth; cabbage, endives, broccoli, artichokes, coleworts, asparagus, savoy, rhubarb, cauliflower, celery, turnips, carrots, onions, radishes, garlic, parsley, spinage, small salad, lettuce, cucumbers, leeks, beets, parsnips, mangelwurzel, mushroom, tomatoes, vegetable marrow, and fresh vegetables generally, contain less than one-fifth of osseous nutriment. Apples, pears, plums, cherries, strawberries, gooseberries, raspberries, cranberries, blackberries, huckleberries, currants, melons, olives, peaches, apricots, pineapples, nectarines, pomegranates, dates, prunes, raisins, figs, lemons, limes, oranges and grapes, on the average, are two hundred times less ossifying than bread, or anything else prepared of wheat flour. Some articles, as honey, molasses, sugar, butter, oil, vinegar, and alcohol, if unadulterated, are quite free from earthy matter. But still worse than wheat flour is common salt, cloves, and heating spices, especially, black pepper, as they derange the nervous system. With regard to drink, no water except rain or snow water, as it falls, or melted ice, is free from earthy matter, unless filtered; or better far is distilled water; it removes all earthy matter. A distilling apparatus is not very expensive, and every family should own one, if they wish pure, soft water, free from earthy material—filtering water only removes such particles as are mechanically mixed, and mere boiling it produces no beneficial change.

Spring water, pure and limpid as it appears to the eye, is found, upon chemical examination, to contain a very large proportion of calcareous earthy matter; so much, indeed, that it has been calculated that "a person drinking an average quantity of hard water per day for forty years, will, in that time, take into his body as much as would form a pillar of marble as large as an average-sized man." As it evaporates from the body, it leaves behind the earthy matter which it holds in solution, and thus tends to choke up or incrust the internal surfaces, blood-vessels and nerves, in short, to harden and petrify the whole system, in the same manner as we find it incrust vessels from which water is evaporated (for this incrusting only goes on where the water evaporates in the form of steam or vapor). Water from rivers and pits, in addition to calcareous earthy matter, generally contains putrid or vegetable substances, which are dangerous and often fatal to health. We should only drink after meals as little as will satisfy thirst. Indeed, if we ate every day as much ripe fruit as we ought, we would drink but little.

Reasoning from the above scientific theory, I have invariably found that when I could persuade my patients to adopt this system of diet, with one bath a day, either towel or sitz bath, of pleasantly cold temperature, for from five to twenty minutes, they have had comparatively easy childbirths and frequently painless. Many mothers who have had children in great pain and peril, following my advice in subsequent child-birth's, have marked the change as almost miraculous. Mrs. B., about two years since, was delivered of her first child. Both herself and husband are of mental vital temperament, with large, broad heads in the coronal region. The father thirty-five, the mother twenty-six years of age. The labor was protracted and severe, the presentation quite natural. After twenty-four hours most terrible suffering, the child was delivered by instruments and crushed, in the efforts to save the mother's life. The child weighed eleven pounds, well formed and mature, the bones of both mother and child hard and unyielding.

About eight months afterward she came to consult me. I measured the pelvic straits, found a full development and no obstruction to child-bearing, and encouraged her to venture another time, as children seemed very necessary to her complete happiness.

About two months since, I had the pleasure to deliver her of a boy of beautiful form, large head, broad shoulders, and weighing ten pounds, with only three hours labor and no need of instruments. The bones of both mother and child had been partially softened and made elastic by the daily use of lemon juice and acid fruits. Trusting to a more liberal diet after birth, no rare, inflaming, uncooked, or underdone animal food had been eaten to overstimulate and irritate the nervous system. One full towel bath before breakfast and a sitz bath at bedtime, of pleasantly cold temperature for five minutes, had been taken and two hours out-door exercise daily. Having the whole weight of the clothing on the shoulders, suspended by comfortable under-waist or suspenders, giving entire release to the venous circulation and freedom in the action of the diaphragm to assist the lungs. Thus the pure oxygen of the air imparted vitality to the blood and system that no food or medicine can ever supply. I am quite sure that in proportion as a mother, during her pregnancy, will be persuaded to live on food and drinks which are free from earthy and bony material, she will avoid pain and danger in delivery; hence the more ripe fruit, acid fruit in particular, and the less of other kinds of food, but particularly of wheat bread, or cake, or pastry of any kind is consumed, the less will be her danger and sufferings in childbirth.

Mrs. F., one of the first cases I controlled, many years ago, had suffered extremely in two previous births, so that her health, which before marriage had been perfect, gave way; and at the time of her first consultation with me, she seemed dejected and foreboding. Her lower limbs were exceedingly swoolen and painful, the veins full and varicose, almost bursting. She was full seven months pregnant. I prescribed pears, either boiled as a vegetable or ripe to be eaten at meals only (as they were plentiful at that time in our country place), and lemons and acid apples, with a towel bath once daily—of vinegar, one cupfull, salt, one teaspoonful, water (hot or cold), one pint; having a dread of cold, she took it hot, followed by gentle friction. In a few days, she felt the benefit so marked, that she became quite willing to make an entire change in her diet and dress, taking exercise freely in the open air at least two hours daily. Before breakfast, she took the juice of a lemon, mixed in a little water, or an acid orange, and at breakfast, three or four roasted apples, avoiding fine wheat bread as much as possible. The dinner consisted of the flesh of young animals, or fish, well cooked, and in small quantities, with a good supply of fresh vegetables, potatoes, peas, sweet corn and a variety of fruits—figs, prunes and dates are admissible where nutrition is desirable. The acid fruits dissolve the earthy substance of the bones and make them yielding in both mother and child. For constipation, I allowed her to take a teaspoonful, two or three times a day when needed, of a compound made of the juice of two oranges, one lemon, half-pound of Isabella grapes, and half-a-cup of good molasses, express the juices and mix in the half-cup of common molasses. She continued this course till her full term expired. The swelling of the limbs had entirely subsided. She had become so light and active, she could run up and down a flight of stairs with ease. Her health became restored, and, at the time of her delivery, she was perfectly well. Even the soreness and pain in the breasts, which at the time of my first advice, as well as during her former pregnancies, were sore and tender, became entirely free from pain, and remained in the very best condition during her period of nursing. The morning of her delivery she awakened her husband, asking him to call a lady friend, sleeping in the room above them, and before half-an-hour she was delivered, without the aid of medical skill, and when I arrived, she was nursing her child, and declared she had "no feeling of languor or sickness whatever." The child was not quite as large as the former children, but was symmetrical and perfectly healthy. After the birth she discontinued the acids and resumed a more liberal diet of bread and farinaceous food.

How different from her two former births and after results. She had been obliged to use nursing rubber shields because her nipples were so very tender, and then the children had such sore mouths and became so poor and thin. This time the nipples gave no trouble, no poison rubber shields were required, consequently the babe was not made sick with sore mouth— and just here let me enter my protest against the white rubber for children's bottles or toys. It is the source of most of the diarrhœas, sore mouths, decayed teeth, spinal curvatures, and often death itself, of babies brought up by hand. The sale of it is being prohibited in Germany. Very young babies can be taught to drink from a cup or glass, and if a nipple of any kind is requisite, one of silver or glass can easily be procured.

I could give many hundred descriptions of cases similar to the above, but I fear a lengthy treatise on the subject will defeat my object, which is, to give instruction which will be read and remembered by mothers and fathers everywhere. I would like to say something of the mental and moral aspects of maternity, but must defer it to another time, saying to parents: Do try to be yourselves what you desire your children to be. A sound mind can only be expected in a sound body. See to it that you give your children the best possible opportunities to be born of pure, healthy parents. Your duties toward your children can only be estimated in the light of a truly attentive conscience toward God, the Author of Life and Source of Truth.

DR. CLEMENCE S. LOZIER,
361 West Thirty-fourth Street, N. Y.

[TRACT NO. 2 WILL BE ON THE CARE OF INFANTS AND NURSING.][51]

2.

The St. Louis Resolutions proposed by Francis Minor and adopted by the NWSA, October 1869

Whereas, In the adjustment of the question of suffrage now before the people of this country for settlement, it is of the highest importance that the organic law of the land should be so framed and construed as to work injustice to none, but secure as far as possible perfect political equality among all classes of citizens; and,

Whereas, All persons born or naturalized in the United States, and subject to the jurisdiction thereof, are citizens of the United States, and of the State wherein they reside; be it

Resolved, 1. That the immunities and privileges of American citizenship, however defined, are National in character and paramount to all State authority.

2. That while the Constitution of the United States leaves the qualification of electors to the several States, it nowhere gives them the right to deprive any citizen of the elective franchise which is possessed by any other citizen—to regulate, not including the right to prohibit the franchise.

3. That, as the Constitution of the United States expressly declares that no State shall make or enforce any laws that shall abridge the privileges or immunities of citizens of the United States, those provisions of the several State Constitutions that exclude women from the franchise on account of sex, are violative alike of the spirit and letter of the Federal Constitution.

4. That, as the subject of naturalization is expressly withheld from the States, and as the States clearly would have no right to deprive of the franchise naturalized citizens, among whom women are expressly included, still more clearly have they no right to deprive native-born women citizens of this right.

5. That justice and equity can only be attained by having the same laws for men and women alike.

6. That having full faith and confidence in the truth and justice of these principles, we will never cease to urge the claims of women to a participation in the affairs of government equal with men.[52]

3.
"Woman's Rights Catechism,"
by Matilda Joslyn Gage, 1871

Q: From whence do governments derive their just powers?

A: Governments derive their just powers from the consent of the governed. (Declaration of Independence.)

Q: Are rights granted people by governments or through constitutions?

A: No. Rights existed before governments are founded or constitutions created.

Q: Of what use then are governments and institutions?

A: *To protect people in the exercise and enjoyment of their natural and fundamental rights, which existed before governments or constitutions were made.* (Declaration of Independence and Constitution). . . .

Q: What is a citizen?

A: *In the United States, a citizen is a person, native or naturalized, who has the privilege of exercising the elective franchise.* (Webster)

Q: What persons are citizens of the United States?

A: *All persons born or naturalized in the United States, and subject to the jurisdiction thereof, are citizens of the United States, and of the State wherein they reside.* (14th Amendment)

Q: What right has a citizen of the United States?

A: *The right to vote.* . . .

Q: What law of the United States especially enforces the recognition of the political rights of its citizens?

A: *A law passed by the 42d Congress of the United States, and signed by the President, April 19, 1871, which declares that "any person, who under color of any law, statute, ordinance, regulation, custom or usage of any State, shall subject, or cause to be subjected, any person within the jurisdiction of the United States, to the deprivation of any rights, privileges, or immunities secured by the Constitution of the United States, shall, any law to the contrary notwithstanding, be liable to the penalty required in any action at law or equity.* . . .

Q: Are those persons who, under color of law, forbid woman the ballot, law-keepers or law-breakers?

A: *They are law-breakers, acting in defiance to both National and State law, in thus refusing to women citizens the exercise of a right secured to them by the Constitution of the United States; and they render themselves liable to prosecution thereby.*[53]

4.

"Woman Suffrage. The Argument of Carrie S. Burnham
before Chief Justice Reed, and Associate Justices Agnew,
Sharswood and Mercur of the Supreme Court of
Pennsylvania, on the Third and Fourth of April, 1878"

MAY IT PLEASE THE COURT:

Have women citizens the right of suffrage under the Constitution of the United States and of this particular State of Pennsylvania? This is the direct question before your Honors to-day
for consideration and decision.

To state the proposition more generally, shall the State and
National Constitutions be so interpreted as to secure a republican, an aristocratic or a monarchical form of government?—
Having discussed this question before his Honor Mr. Justice
Sharswood and Nisi Prius, and having received an adverse decision, I should be daunted in my purpose, were I not painfully
impressed with the magnitude of the issues involved in this
cause. Were it a question involving the rights of only one individual, it might well challenge the learning and the conscience
of this Court to remedy the wrong and vindicate the right. But
it is not simply whether I shall be protected in the exercise of
my inalienable right and duty of self-government, but whether
a government, the mere agent of the people, based upon the
equality of all mankind, and which "derives its just powers
from the consent of the governed," can deny to any portion of
its intelligent, adult citizens participation therein and still hold
them amenable to its laws; and, if so, what shall be the proportion and qualification of rulers and ruled, and by what tribunal
shall these be determined?

Upon the 16th day of September, A.D. 1871, I was duly assessed by the canvassers of the Fourteenth Ward, of the city of
Philadelphia, as a resident of the eleventh division of said ward,
and two days thereafter paid to the Receiver of Taxes the
amount of county tax assessed upon me for that year. Upon
the 10th day of October following, being the second Tuesday
of October, 1871, at the general election, I presented to these

defendants, at the proper time and place of voting, my ballot in legal form, which ballot these defendants refused. Being a citizen of the United States and of the State of Pennsylvania, and having complied with all the requirements of the law in this Commonwealth for the regulation of the elective franchise, including assessment, registration, (my name being upon the canvassers' printed list of voters in the above-named precinct,) and taxation, I claim I was legally entitled to exercise my rights as an elector, under both the State and National Constitutions, wherefore I have brought this suit.[54]

5.
Victoria C. Woodhull, "And the Truth Shall Make You Free," speech, Steinway Hall, November 20, 1871

... If life, liberty and the pursuit of happiness are inalienable rights in the individual, and government is based upon that inalienability, then it must follow as a legitimate sequence that the functions of that government are to guard and protect the right to life, liberty and the pursuit of happiness, to the end that every person may have the most perfect exercise of them. And the most perfect exercise of such rights is only attained when every individual is not only fully protected in his rights, but also strictly restrained to the exercise of them within his own sphere, and positively prevented from proceeding beyond its limits, so as to encroach upon the sphere of another: unless that other first agree thereto.

... We have arrived where the very foundation of all that has been must be analyzed and understood—and this foundation is the relation of the sexes. These are the bases of society—the very last to secure attention, because the most comprehensive of subjects.

... Over the sexual relations, marriages have endeavored to preserve sway and to hold the people in subjection to what has been considered a standard of moral purity. Whether this has been successful or not may be determined from the fact that there are scores of thousands of women who are denominated prostitutes, and who are supported by hundreds of thousands of men who should, for like reasons, also be denominated prostitutes, since what will change a woman into a prostitute must also necessarily change a man into the same.

This condition, called prostitution, seems to be the great evil at which religion and public morality hurl their special weapons of condemnation, as the sum total of all diabolism; since for a woman to be a prostitute is to deny her not only all Christian, but also all humanitarian rights.

But let us inquire into this matter, to see just what it is; not in the vulgar or popular, or even legal sense, but in a purely scientific and truly moral sense.

. . . If there is *anything* in the whole universe that should enlist the earnest attention of everybody, and their support and advocacy to secure it, it is that upon which the true Welfare and happiness of everybody depends. Now to what more than to anything else do humanity owe their welfare and happiness? Most clearly to being born into earthly existence with a sound and perfect physical, mental and moral beginning of life, with no taint or disease attaching to them, either mentally, morally or physically. To be so born involves the harmony of conditions which will produce such results. To have such conditions involves the existence of such relations of the sexes as will in themselves produce them.

. . . All the relations between the sexes that are recognized as *legitimate* are denominated marriage. *But of what does marriage consist?* . . . Where is the point before reaching which it is not marriage, but having reached which it is marriage? Is it where two meet and realize that the love elements of their nature are harmonious, and that they blend into and make *one* purpose of life? or is it where a *soulless form* is pronounced over two who know *no* commingling of life's hopes? Or are *both* these processes required—first, the marriage union *without* the law, to be afterward solemnized *by* the law? If *both* terms are required, does the marriage continue after the *first* departs? or if the restrictions of the law are removed and the love continues, does marriage continue? or if the law unite two who *hate* each other, is that marriage?

... The courts hold if the law solemnly pronounce two married, *that they are married, whether love is present or not. But is this really such a marriage as this enlightened age should demand? No! It is a stupidly arbitrary law, which can find no analogies in nature. Nature proclaims in broadest* terms, and all her subjects re-echo the same *grand* truth, that sexual unions, which result in reproduction, are marriage. And sex exists wherever there is reproduction.

Law cannot change what nature has already determined. Neither will love obey if law command. Law cannot compel two to love. It has nothing to do either *with* love or with its absence. Love is superior to all law, and so also is hate, indifference, disgust and all other human sentiments which are evoked in the relations of the sexes. It legitimately and logically follows, if *love have anything* to do with marriage, that *law* has *nothing* to do with it. And on the contrary, if *law* have anything to do with marriage, that *love* has nothing to do with it. And there is no escaping the deduction.

If the test of the rights of the individual be applied to determine which of these propositions is the true one, what will be the result?

Two persons, a male and a female, meet, and are drawn together by a *mutual* attraction—a *natural* feeling unconsciously arising within their natures of which *neither* has any control—which is denominated love. This is a matter that concerns *these two*, and *no* other living soul has *any human* right to say aye, yes or no, since it is a matter in which none except the two have any right to be involved, and from which it is the duty of these two to exclude every other person, since no one can love for another or determine why another loves.

If true, mutual, natural attraction be sufficiently strong to be the *dominant* power, then it decides marriage; and if it be so decided, no law which may be in force can *any more* prevent the union than a *human* law could prevent the transformation of water into vapor, or the confluence of two streams; and for *precisely* the same reasons: that it is a *natural* law which is obeyed; which law is as *high above human law* as perfection is high above imperfection. They marry and obey this higher law than man can make—a law as old as the universe and as immortal as the elements, and for which there is no substitute.

They are sexually united, to be which is to be married by nature, and to be thus married is to be united by God. This marriage is performed without special mental volition upon the part of either, although the intellect *may* approve what the affections determine; this is to say, they marry because they love, and they love because they can neither *prevent* nor *assist* it. Suppose after this marriage has continued an indefinite time, the *unity* between them departs, could they any more prevent it than they can prevent the love? It *came* without their bidding, may it not also go without their bidding? And if it go, does not the marriage cease, and should any third persons or parties, either as *individuals* or *government*, attempt to compel the *continuance* of a unity wherein *none* of the elements of the union remain?

At no point in the process designated has there been *any* other than an exercise of the right of the two individuals to pursue happiness in their *own* way, *which* may have neither *crossed* nor interfered with *any one else's* right to the *same* pursuit; therefore, there is *no* call for a law to change, modify, protect or punish this exercise. It must be concluded, then, if individuals have the Constitutional right to pursue happiness in their *own* way, that all compelling laws of marriage and divorce are despotic, being *remnants* of the barbaric ages in which they were originated, and *utterly unfitted* for an age so *advanced* upon that, and so *enlightened* in the general principles of freedom and equality, as is this.

. . . The proper sphere of government in regard to the relations of the sexes, is to enact such laws as in the present conditions of society are necessary to *protect each individual* in the *free* exercise of his or her *right* to love, and also to protect each individual from the forced interference of *every other* person, that would compel him or her to submit to *any* action which is against their *wish* and *will*. If the law do this it fulfills its duty. If the law do not afford this protection, *and worse still*, if it *sanction* this *interference* with the rights of an individual, then it is *infamous* law and worthy only of the *old time* despotism; since individual tyranny forms no part of the guarantee of, or the right to, individual freedom.

. . . Having determined that marriage consists of a union resulting from love, without any regard whatever to the sanction of law, and consequently that the sexual relations resulting therefrom are strictly legitimate and natural, it is a very simple matter to determine what part of the sexual relations which are maintained are prostitutions of the relations.

. . . I do not care where it is that sexual commerce results from the dominant power of one sex over the other, compelling him or her to submission against the instincts of love, and where hate or disgust is present, whether it be in the gilded palaces of Fifth avenue or in the lowest purlieus of Greene street, there is prostitution, and all the law that a thousand State Assemblies may pass cannot make it otherwise.

I know whereof I speak; I have seen the most damning misery resulting from legalized prostitution. Misery such as the most degraded of those against whom society has shut her doors never know.

Thousands of poor, weak, unresisting wives are yearly murdered, who stand in spirit-life looking down upon the sickly, half made-up children left behind, imploring humanity for the sake of honor and virtue to look into this matter, to look into it to the very bottom, and bring out into the fair daylight all the blackened, sickening deformities that have so long been hidden by the screen of public opinion and a sham morality.

I would not be understood to say that there are no good conditions in the present marriage state. By no means do I say this; on the contrary, a very large proportion of present social relations are commendable—are as good as the present status of society makes possible. But what I do assert, and, that most positively, is, that all which is good and commendable, now existing, would continue to exist if all marriage laws were repealed to-morrow. Do you not perceive that law has nothing to do in continuing the relations which are based upon

continuous love? These are not results of the law to which, perhaps, their subjects yielded a willing or unwilling obedience.
Such relations exist in spite of the law; would have existed had
there been no law, and would continue to exist were the law
annulled.

. . . Should people, then, voluntarily entering legal marriage
be held thereby "till death do them part"? Most emphatically
no, if the desire to do so do not remain. How can people who
enter upon marriage in utter ignorance of that which is to render the union happy or miserable be able to say that they will
always "love and live together." They may take these vows
upon them in perfect good faith and repent of them in sackcloth and ashes within a twelve-month.

. . . Marriage laws that would be consistent with the theory of
individual rights would be such as would regulate these relations,
such as regulate all other associations of people. They should
only be obliged to file marriage articles, containing whatever
provisions may be agreed upon, as to their personal rights, rights
of property, of children, or whatever else they may deem proper
for them to agree upon. And whatever these articles might be,
they should in all cases be equally entitled to public respect and
protection. Should separation afterward come, nothing more
should be required than the simple filing of counter articles.

. . . I know of no higher, holier love than that described, and
of no more beautiful expression of it than was given in the col-
umns of the *Woman's Journal*, of Boston, whose conductors
have felt called upon to endeavor to convince the people that it
has no affiliation with those who hold to no more radical doctrine of Free Love than they proclaim as follows:

"The love that I cannot command is not mine; let me not
disturb myself about it, nor attempt to filch it from its rightful
owner. A heart that I supposed mine has drifted and gone.
Shall I go in pursuit? Shall I forcibly capture the truant and
transfix it with the barb of my selfish affections, pin it to the
wall of my chamber? God forbid! Rather let me leave my doors
and windows open, intent only on living so nobly that the best
cannot fail to be drawn to me by an irresistible attraction."

... It can now be asked: What is the legitimate sequence of Social Freedom? To which I unhesitatingly reply: Free Love, or freedom of the affections. "And are you a Free Lover?" is the almost incredulous query.

I repeat a frequent reply: "I am; and I can honestly, in the fullness of my soul, raise on my voice to my Maker, and thank Him that I am, and that I have had the strength and the devotion to truth to stand before this traducing and vilifying community in a manner representative of that which shall come with healing on its wings for the bruised hearts and crushed affections of humanity."

And to those who denounce me for this I reply: "Yes, I am a Free Lover. I have an inalienable, constitutional and natural right to love whom I may, to love as long or as short a period as I can; to change that love every day if I please, and with that right neither you nor any law you can frame have any right to interfere. And I have the further right to demand a free and unrestricted exercise of that right, and it is your duty not only to accord it, but, as a community, to see that I am protected in it. I trust that I am fully understood, for I mean just that, and nothing less!

To speak thus plainly and pointedly is a duty I owe to myself.

... It is not only usual but also just, when people adopt a new theory, or promulgate a new doctrine, that they give it a name significant of its character. There are, however, exceptional cases to be found in all ages. The Jews coined the name of Christians, and, with withering contempt, hurled it upon the early followers of Christ. It was the most opprobrious epithet they could invent to express their detestation of those humble but honest and brave people. That name has now come to be considered as a synonym of all that is good, true and beautiful in the highest departments of our natures, and is revered in all civilized nations.

In precisely the same manner the Pharisees of to-day, who hold themselves to be representative of all there is that is good and pure, as did the Pharisees of old, have coined the word Free-Love, and flung it upon all who believe not alone in

Religious and Political Freedom, but in that larger Freedom, which includes both these, Social Freedom.

For my part, I am extremely obliged to our thoughtful Pharisaical neighbors for the kindness shown us in the invention of so appropriate a name. If there is a more beautiful word in the English language than love, that word is freedom, and that these two words, which, with us, attach or belong to everything that is pure and good, should have been joined by our enemies, and handed over to us already coined, is certainly a high consideration, for which we should never cease to be thankful.

Until women come to hold men to equal account as they do the women with whom they consort; or until they regard these women as just as respectable as the men who support them, society will remain in its present scale of moral excellence. A man who is well known to have been the constant visitor to these women is accepted into society, and if he be rich is eagerly sought both by mothers having marriageable daughters and by the daughters themselves. But the women with whom they have consorted are too vile to be even acknowledged as worthy of Christian burial, to say nothing of common Christian treatment. I have heard women reply when this difficulty was pressed upon them, "We cannot ostracise men as we are compelled to women, since we are dependent on them for support." Ah! here's the rub. But do you not see that these other sisters are also dependent upon men for their support, and mainly so because you render it next to impossible for them to follow any legitimate means of livelihood? And are only those who have been fortunate enough to secure legal support entitled to live?

When I hear that argument advanced, my heart sinks within me at the degraded condition of my sisters. They submit to a degradation simply because they see no alternative except self-support, and they see no means for that. To put on the semblance of holiness they cry out against those who, for like reasons, submit to like degradation; the only difference between the two being in a licensed ceremony, and a slip of printed paper costing twenty-five cents and upward.

. . . The false and hollow relations of the sexes are thus resolved into the mere question of the dependence of women upon men for support, and women, whether married or single, are supported by men because they are women and their opposites in sex. I can see no moral difference between a woman who marries and lives with a man because he can provide for her wants, and the woman who is not married, but who is provided for at the same price.

. . . The sexual relation, must be rescued from this insidious form of slavery. Women must rise from their position as ministers to the passions of men to be their equals. Their entire system of education must be changed. They must be trained to be like men, permanent and independent individualities, and not their mere appendages or adjuncts, with them forming but one member of society. They must be the companions of men from choice, never from necessity.

. . . I protest against this form of slavery, I protest against the custom which compels women to give the control of their maternal functions over to anybody. It should be theirs to determine when, and under what circumstances, the greatest of all constructive processes—the formation of an immortal soul—should be begun. It is a fearful responsibility with which women are intrusted by nature, and the very last thing that they should be compelled to do is to perform the office of that responsibility against their will, under improper conditions or by disgusting means.

. . . Promiscuity in sexuality is simply the anarchical stage of development wherein the passions rule supreme. When spirituality comes in and rescues the real man or woman from the domain of the purely material, promiscuity is simply impossible. As promiscuity is the analogue to anarchy, so is spirituality to scientific selection and adjustment. Therefore I am fully persuaded that the very highest sexual unions are those that are monogamic, and that these are perfect in proportion as they are lasting. Now if to this be added the fact that the highest kind of love is that which is utterly freed from and devoid of selfishness, and whose highest gratification comes from rendering its object the greatest amount of happiness, let that happiness depend upon whatever it may, then you have my ideal of the highest order of love and the most perfect degree of order to which humanity can attain. An affection that does not desire to bless its object, instead of appropriating it by a selfish possession to its own uses, is not worthy the name of love. Love is that which exists to do good, not merely to get good, which is constantly giving instead of desiring.

. . . Oh! my brothers and sisters, let me entreat you to have more faith in the self-regulating efficacy of freedom. Do you not see how beautifully it works among us in other respects? In America everybody is free to worship God according to the dictates of his own conscience, or even not to worship anything, notwithstanding you or I may think that very wicked or wrong. The respect for freedom we make paramount over our individual opinions, and the result is peace and harmony, when the people of other countries are still throttling and destroying each other to enforce their individual opinions on others. Free Love is only the appreciation of this beautiful principle of freedom. One step further I entreat you to trust it still, and though you may see a thousand dangers, I see peace and happiness and steady improvement as the result.

. . . I believe in love with liberty; in protection without slavery; in the care and culture of offspring by new and better methods, and without the tragedy of self-immolation on the part of parents. I believe in the family, spiritually constituted, expanded, amplified, and scientifically and artistically organized, as a unitary home. I believe in the most wonderful transformation of human society as about to come, as even now at the very door, through general progress, science and the influential intervention of the spirit world. I believe in more than all that the millennium has ever signified to the most religious mind; and I believe that in order to prepare minds to contemplate and desire and enact the new and better life, it is necessary that the old and still prevalent superstitious veneration for the legal marriage tie be relaxed and weakened; not to pander to immorality, but as introductory to a nobler manhood and a more glorified womanhood; as, indeed, the veritable gateway to a paradise regained.[55]

6.
Dr. Clemence S. Lozier, president of the New York Woman Suffrage Association, call for a mass tax protest meeting, 1873

One hundred years ago our ancestors precipitated a rebellion by refusing to pay a tax on Tea, imposed against their will. At the end of a century 20,000,000 of their daughters are suffering precisely the same wrong; taxation without representation; and it behooves us as their descendants to demand that the freedom for which our forefathers struggled shall be given to us also! And to demand of right that the coming Centennial of "American Independence" shall find us enfranchised, or freed from taxation and responsibility to a government which denies us personality and Citizenship.[56]

7.
Matilda Joslyn Gage's argument against the Supreme Court decision in *Minor v. Happersett* at the 1875 NWSA convention

The court maintained that the United States Constitution does not confer the right of suffrage on any person, and that the matter is regulated by State Constitutions, and that when provision is made in them extending the right of suffrage to men only, such provisions are binding. It also declared that the United States had no voters in the States of its own creation. But this assertion was false upon the very face of it.

. . . Thus at the time of Chief-Justice Waite's decision asserting National want of power over the ballot, and declaring the United States possessed no voters of its own creation in the States (where else would it have them?), the country already possessed eight classes of voters, or persons whose right to the ballot was in some form under the control or sanction of the United States. The black man, the amnestied man, the naturalized man, the foreigner honorably discharged from the Union army, voters for the lower House of Congress, voters for Presidential

electors, pardoned civil and military criminals. Further research may bring still other classes to light.[57]

8.
Matilda Joslyn Gage's description of the NWSA 1876 Centennial protest, chapter XXVII, "The Centennial Year—1876," *History of Woman Suffrage*

Though refused by their own countrymen a place and part in
the centennial celebration, the women who had taken this presentation in hand were not to be conquered. They had respectfully asked for recognition; now that it had been denied, they
determined to seize upon the moment when the reading of the
Declaration of Independence closed, to proclaim to the world
the tyranny and injustice of the nation toward one-half its people. Five officers of the National Woman Suffrage Association,
with that heroic spirit which has ever animated lovers of liberty
in resistance to tyranny, determined, whatever the result, to
present the woman's declaration of rights at the chosen hour.
They would not, they dared not sacrifice the golden opportunity to which they had so long looked forward; their work was
not for themselves alone, nor for the present generation, but for
all women of all time. The hopes of posterity were in their
hands and they determined to place on record for the daughters
of 1976, the fact that their mothers of 1876 had asserted their
equality of rights, and impeached the government of that day
for its injustice toward woman. Thus, in taking a grander step
toward freedom than ever before, they would leave one bright
remembrance for the women of the next centennial.[58]

That historic Fourth of July dawned at last, one of the most
oppressive days of that terribly heated season. Susan B. Anthony, Matilda Joslyn Gage, Sara Andrews Spencer, Lillie
Devereux Blake and Phoebe W. Couzins made their way
through the crowds under the broiling sun to Independence
Square, carrying the Woman's Declaration of Rights. This declaration had been handsomely engrossed by one of their number, and signed by the oldest and most prominent advocates of

woman's enfranchisement. Their tickets of admission proved open sesame through the military and all other barriers, and a few moments before the opening of the ceremonies, these women found themselves within the precincts from which most of their sex were excluded.

The declaration of 1776 was read by Richard Henry Lee, of Virginia, about whose family clusters so much of historic fame. The close of his reading was deemed the appropriate moment for the presentation of the woman's declaration. Not quite sure how their approach might be met—not quite certain if at this final moment they would be permitted to reach the presiding officer—those ladies arose and made their way down the aisle. The bustle of preparation for the Brazilian hymn covered their advance. The foreign guests, the military and civil officers who filled the space directly in front of the speaker's stand, courteously made way, while Miss Anthony in fitting words presented the declaration. Mr. Ferry's face paled, as bowing low, with no word, he received the declaration, which thus became part of the day's proceedings; the ladies turned, scattering printed copies, as they deliberately walked down the platform. On every side eager hands were stretched; men stood on seats and asked for them, while General Hawley, thus defied and beaten in his audacious denial to women the right to present their declaration, shouted, "Order, order!"

Passing out, these ladies made their way to a platform erected for the musicians in front of Independence Hall. Here on this old historic ground, under the shadow of Washington's statue, back of them the old bell that proclaimed "liberty to all the land, and all the inhabitants thereof," they took their places, and to a listening, applauding crowd, Miss Anthony read the Declaration of Rights for Women by the National Woman Suffrage Association, July 4, 1876:

THE 1876 DECLARATION
OF RIGHTS OF WOMEN

While the nation is buoyant with patriotism, and all hearts are attuned to praise, it is with sorrow we come to strike the one discordant note, on this one-hundredth anniversary of our country's birth. When subjects of kings, emperors, and czars, from the old world join in our national jubilee, shall the women of the republic refuse to lay their hands with benedictions on the nation's head? Surveying America's exposition, surpassing in magnificence those of London, Paris, and Vienna, shall we not rejoice at the success of the youngest rival among the nations of the earth? May not our hearts, in unison with all, swell with pride at our great achievements as a people; our free speech, free press, free schools, free church, and the rapid progress we have made in material wealth, trade, commerce and the inventive arts? And we do rejoice in the success, thus far, of our experiment of self-government. Our faith is firm and unwavering in the broad principles of human rights proclaimed in 1776, not only as abstract truths, but as the corner stones of a republic. Yet we cannot forget, even in this glad hour, that while all men of every race, and clime, and condition, have been invested with the full rights of citizenship under our hospitable flag, all women still suffer the degradation of disfranchisement.

The history of our country the past hundred years has been a series of assumptions and usurpations of power over woman, in direct opposition to the principles of just government, acknowledged by the United States as its foundation, which are:

First—The natural rights of each individual.

Second—The equality of these rights.

Third—That rights not delegated are retained by the individual.

Fourth—That no person can exercise the rights of others without delegated authority.

Fifth—That the non-use of rights does not destroy them.

And for the violation of these fundamental principles of our government, we arraign our rulers on this Fourth day of July, 1876,—and these are our articles of impeachment:

Bills of attainder have been passed by the introduction of the word "male" into all the State constitutions, denying to women the right of suffrage, and thereby making sex a crime—an exercise of power clearly forbidden in article I, sections 9, 10, of the United States constitution.

The writ of habeas corpus, the only protection against *lettres de cachet* and all forms of unjust imprisonment, which the constitution declares "shall not be suspended, except when in cases of rebellion or invasion the public safety demands it," is held inoperative in every State of the Union, in case of a married woman against her husband—the marital rights of the husband being in all cases primary, and the rights of the wife secondary.

The right of trial by a jury of one's peers was so jealously guarded that States refused to ratify the original constitution until it was guaranteed by the sixth amendment. And yet the women of this nation have never been allowed a jury of their peers—being tried in all cases by men, native and foreign, educated and ignorant, virtuous and vicious. Young girls have been arraigned in our courts for the crime of infanticide; tried, convicted, hanged—victims, perchance, of judge, jurors, advocates— while no woman's voice could be heard in their defense. And not only are women denied a jury of their peers, but in some cases, jury trial altogether. During the war, a woman was tried and hanged by military law, in defiance of the fifth amendment, which specifically declares: "No person shall be held to answer for a capital or otherwise infamous crime, unless on a presentment or indictment of a grand jury, except in cases . . . of persons in actual service in time of war." During the last presidential campaign, a woman, arrested for voting, was denied the protection of a jury, tried, convicted, and sentenced to a fine and costs of prosecution, by the absolute power of a judge of the Supreme Court of the United States.

Taxation without representation, the immediate cause of the rebellion of the colonies against Great Britain, is one of the grievous wrongs the women of this country have suffered during the century. Deploring war, with all the demoralization that follows in its train, we have been taxed to support standing armies, with their waste of life and wealth. Believing in temperance, we have been taxed to support the vice, crime and pauperism of the liquor traffic. While we suffer its wrongs and abuses infinitely more than man, we have no power to protect our sons against this giant evil. During the temperance crusade, mothers were arrested, fined, imprisoned, for even praying and singing in the streets, while men blockade the sidewalks with impunity, even on Sunday, with their military parades and political processions. Believing in honesty, we are taxed to support a dangerous army of civilians, buying and selling the offices of government and sacrificing the best interests of the people. And, moreover, we are taxed to support the very legislators and judges who make laws, and render decisions adverse to woman. And for refusing to pay such unjust taxation, the houses, lands, bonds, and stock of women have been seized and sold within the present year, thus proving Lord Coke's assertion, that "The very act of taxing a man's property without his consent is, in effect, disfranchising him of every civil right."

Unequal codes for men and women. Held by law a perpetual minor, deemed incapable of self-protection, even in the industries of the world, woman is denied equality of rights. The fact of sex, not the quantity or quality of work, in most cases, decides the pay and position; and because of this injustice thousands of fatherless girls are compelled to choose between a life of shame and starvation. Laws catering to man's vices have created two codes of morals in which penalties are graded according to the political status of the offender. Under such laws, women are fined and imprisoned if found alone in the streets, or in public places of resort, at certain hours. Under the pretense of regulating public morals, police officers seizing the occupants of disreputable houses, march the women in platoons to prison, while the men, partners in their guilt, go free. While making a show of virtue in forbidding the importation of Chinese women on the Pacific coast for immoral purposes, our rulers, in many States, and even under the shadow of the national capitol, are now proposing to legalize the sale of American womanhood for the same vile purposes.

Special legislation for woman has placed us in a most anomalous position. Women invested with the rights of citizens in one section—voters, jurors, office-holders—crossing an imaginary line, are subjects in the next. In some States, a married woman may hold property and transact business in her own name; in others, her earnings belong to her husband. In some States, a woman may testify against her husband, sue and be sued in the courts; in others, she has no redress in case of damage to person, property, or character. In case of divorce on account of adultery in the husband, the innocent wife is held to possess no right to children or property, unless by special decree of the court. But in no State of the Union has the wife the right to her own person, or to any part of the joint earnings of the co-partnership during the life of her husband. In some States women may enter the law schools and practice in the courts; in others they are forbidden. In some universities girls enjoy equal educational advantages with boys, while many of the proudest institutions in the land deny them admittance, though the sons of China, Japan and Africa are welcomed there. But the privileges already granted in the several States are by no means secure. The right of suffrage once exercised by women in certain States and territories has been denied by subsequent legislation. A bill is now pending in congress to disfranchise the women of Utah, thus interfering to deprive United States citizens of the same rights which the Supreme Court has declared the national government powerless to protect anywhere. Laws passed after years of untiring effort, guaranteeing married women certain rights of property, and mothers the custody of their children, have been repealed in States where we supposed all was safe. Thus have our most sacred rights been made the football of legislative caprice, proving that a power which grants as a privilege what by nature is a right, may withhold the same as a penalty when deeming it necessary for its own perpetuation.

Representation of woman has had no place in the nation's thought. Since the incorporation of the thirteen original States, twenty-four have been admitted to the Union, not one of which has recognized woman's right of self-government. On this birthday of our national liberties, July Fourth, 1876, Colorado, like all her elder sisters, comes into the Union with the invidious word "male" in her constitution.

Universal manhood suffrage, by establishing an aristocracy of sex, imposes upon the women of this nation a more absolute and cruel despotism than monarchy; in that, woman finds a political

master in her father, husband, brother, son. The aristocracies of
the old world are based upon birth, wealth, refinement, education, nobility, brave deeds of chivalry; in this nation, on sex
alone; exalting brute force above moral power, vice above virtue, ignorance above education, and the son above the mother
who bore him.

The judiciary above the nation has proved itself but the echo
of the party in power, by upholding and enforcing laws that are
opposed to the spirit and letter of the constitution. When the
slave power was dominant, the Supreme Court decided that a
black man was not a citizen, because he had not the right to
vote; and when the constitution was so amended as to make all
persons citizens, the same high tribunal decided that a woman,
though a citizen, had not the right to vote. Such vacillating interpretations of constitutional law unsettle our faith in judicial authority, and undermine the liberties of the whole people.

These articles of impeachment against our rulers we now
submit to the impartial judgment of the people. To all these
wrongs and oppressions woman has not submitted in silence
and resignation. From the beginning of the century, when Abigail Adams, the wife of one president and mother of another,
said, "We will not hold ourselves bound to obey laws in which
we have no voice or representation," until now, woman's discontent has been steadily increasing, culminating nearly thirty
years ago in a simultaneous movement among the women of
the nation, demanding the right of suffrage. In making our just
demands, a higher motive than the pride of sex inspires us; we
feel that national safety and stability depend on the complete
recognition of the broad principles of our government. Woman's degraded, helpless position is the weak point in our institutions to-day; a disturbing force everywhere, severing family
ties, filling our asylums with the deaf, the dumb, the blind; our
prisons with criminals, our cities with drunkenness and prostitution; our homes with disease and death. It was the boast of
the founders of the republic, that the rights for which they contended were the rights of human nature. If these rights are ignored in the case of one-half the people, the nation is surely

preparing for its downfall. Governments try themselves. The recognition of a governing and a governed class is incompatible with the first principles of freedom. Woman has not been a heedless spectator of the events of this century, nor a dull listener to the grand arguments for the equal rights of humanity. From the earliest history of our country woman has shown equal devotion with man to the cause of freedom, and has stood firmly by his side in its defense. Together, they have made this country what it is. Woman's wealth, thought and labor have cemented the stones of every monument man has reared to liberty.

And now, at the close of a hundred years, as the hour-hand of the great clock that marks the centuries points to 1876, we declare our faith in the principles of self-government; our full equality with man in natural rights; that woman was made first for her own happiness, with the absolute right to herself—to all the opportunities and advantages life affords for her complete development; and we deny that dogma of the centuries, incorporated in the codes of all nations—that woman was made for man—her best interests, in all cases, to be sacrificed to his will. We ask of our rulers, at this hour, no special favors, no special privileges, no special legislation. We ask justice, we ask equality, we ask that all the civil and political rights that belong to citizens of the United States, be guaranteed to us and our daughters forever.[59]

9.
The minority report of the Senate Committee on Privileges and Elections, February 1, 1879

The undersigned, a minority of the Committee on Privileges and Elections, to whom were referred the resolution proposing an amendment to the constitution prohibiting discrimination in the right of suffrage on account of sex, and certain petitions in aid of the same, submit the following minority report:

The undersigned dissent from the report of the majority of the committee. The demand for the extension of the right of suffrage to women is not new. It has been supported by many persons in this country, in England and on the continent, famous in public life, in literature and in philosophy. But no single argument of its advocates seems to us to carry so great a persuasive force as the difficulty which its ablest opponents encounter in making a plausible statement of their objections. We trust we do not fail in deference to our esteemed associates on the committee when we avow our opinion that their report is no exception to this rule.

The people of the United States and of the several States have founded their political institutions upon the principle that all men have an equal right to a share in the government. The doctrine is expressed in various forms. The Declaration of Independence asserts that "all men are created equal" and that "governments derive their just powers from the consent of the governed." The Virginia bill of rights, the work of Jefferson and George Mason, affirms that "no man or set of men are entitled to exclusive or separate emoluments or privileges from the rest of the community but in consideration of public services." The Massachusetts bill of rights, the work of John Adams, besides reaffirming these axioms, declares that "all the inhabitants of this commonwealth, having such qualifications as they shall establish by their frame of government, have an equal right to elect officers, and to be elected for public employment." These principles, after full and profound discussion by a generation of statesmen whose authority upon these subjects is greater than that of any other that ever lived, have been accepted by substantially the whole American people as the dictates alike of practical wisdom and of natural justice. The experience of a hundred years has strengthened their hold upon the popular conviction. Our fathers failed in three particulars to carry these principles to their logical result. They required a property qualification for the right to vote and to hold office. They kept the negro in slavery. They excluded women from a share in the government. The first two of these inconsistencies have been remedied. The property test no longer exists. The fifteenth amendment provides that race, color, or previous servitude shall no longer be a disqualification.

There are certain qualifications of age, of residence, and, in some instances of education, demanded; but these are such as all sane men may easily attain.

This report is not the place to discuss or vindicate the correctness of this theory. In so far as the opponents of woman suffrage are driven to deny it, for the purpose of an argument addressed to the American people, they are driven to confess that they are in the wrong. This people are committed to the doctrine of universal suffrage by their constitutions, their history and their opinions. They must stand by it or fall by it. The poorest, humblest, feeblest of sane men has the ballot in his hand, and no other man can show a better title to it. Those things wherein men are unequal—intelligence, ability, integrity, experience, title to public confidence by reason of previous public service—have their natural and legitimate influence under a government wherein each man's vote is counted, to quite as great a degree as under any other form of government that ever existed.

We believe that the principle of universal suffrage stands today stronger than ever in the judgment of mankind. Some eminent and accomplished scholars, alarmed by the corruption and recklessness manifested in our great cities, deceived by exaggerated representations of the misgovernment of the Southern States by a race just emerging from slavery, disgusted by the extent to which great numbers of our fellow-citizens have gone astray in the metaphysical subtleties of financial discussion, have uttered their eloquent warnings of the danger of the failure of universal suffrage. Such utterances from such sources have been frequent. They were never more abundant than in the early part of the present century. They are, when made in a serious and patriotic spirit, to be received with the gratitude due to that greatest of public benefactors—he who points out to the people their dangers and their faults.

But popular suffrage is to be tried not by comparison with ideal standards of excellence, but by comparison with other forms of government. We are willing to submit our century of it to this test. The crimes that have stained our history have come chiefly from its denial, not from its establishment. The

misgovernment and corruption of our great cities have been
largely due to men whose birth and training have been under
other systems. The abuses attributed by political hostility to
negro governments at the South—governments from which the
intelligence and education of the State held themselves sulkily
aloof—do not equal those which existed under the English or
French aristocracy within the memory of living men. There
have been crimes, blunders, corruptions, follies in the history
of our republic. Aristides has been banished from public employment, while Cleon has been followed by admiring throngs.
But few of these things have been due to the extension of the
suffrage. Strike out of our history the crimes of slavery, strike
out the crimes, unparalleled for ferocity and brutality, committed by an oligarchy in its attempt to overthrow universal suffrage, and we may safely challenge for our national and State
governments comparison with monarchy or aristocracy in
their best and purest periods.

Either the doctrines of the Declaration of Independence and
the bills of rights are true, or government must rest on no principle of right whatever, but its powers may be lawfully taken
by force and held by force by any person or class who have
strength to do it, and who persuade themselves that their rule
is for the public interest. Either these doctrines are true, or you
can give no reason for your own possession of the suffrage except that you have got it. If this doctrine be sound, it follows
that no class of persons can rightfully be excluded from their
equal share in the government, unless they can be proved to
lack some quality essential to the proper exercise of political
power.

A person who votes helps, first, to determine the measures of
government; second, to elect persons to be intrusted with public administration. He should therefore possess, first, an honest
desire for the public welfare; second, sufficient intelligence to
determine what measure or policy is best; third, the capacity to
judge of the character of persons proposed for office; and,
fourth, freedom from undue influence, so that the vote he casts
is his own, and not another's. That person or class casting his
or their own vote, with an honest desire for the public welfare,

and with sufficient intelligence to judge what measure is advisable and what person may be trusted, fulfill every condition that the State can rightfully impose.

We are not now dealing with the considerations which should affect the admission of citizens of other countries to acquire the right to take part in our government. All nations claim the right to impose restrictions on the admission of foreigners trained in attachment to other countries or forms of rule, and to indifference to their own, whatever they deem the safety of the State requires. We take it for granted that no person will deny that the women of America are inspired with a love of country equal to that which animates their brothers and sons. A capacity to judge of character, so sure and rapid as to be termed intuitive, is an especial attribute of woman. One of the greatest orators of modern times has declared:

> I concede away nothing which I ought to assert for our sex when I say that the collective womanhood of a people like our own seizes with matchless facility and certainty on the moral and personal peculiarities and character of marked and conspicuous men, and that we may very wisely address ourselves to such a body to learn if a competitor for the highest honors has revealed that truly noble nature that entitled him to a place in the hearts of a nation.

We believe that in that determining of public policies by the collective judgment of the State which constitutes self-government, the contribution of woman will be of great importance and value. To all questions into the determination of which considerations of justice or injustice enter, she will bring a more refined moral sense than that of man. The most important public function of the State is the provision for the education of youths. In those States in which the public school system has reached its highest excellence, more than ninety per cent of the teachers are women. Certainly the vote of the women of the State should be counted in determining the policy that shall regulate the school system which they are called to administer.

It is seldom that particular measures of government are decided by direct popular vote. They are more often discussed before the people after they have taken effect, when the party responsible for them is called to account. The great measures which go to make up the history of nations are determined not by the voters, but by their rulers, whether those rulers be hereditary or elected. The plans of great campaigns are conceived by men of great military genius and executed by great generals. Great systems of finance come from the brain of statesmen who have made finance a special study. The mass of the voters decide to which party they will intrust power. They do not determine particulars. But they give to parties their general tone and direction, and hold them to their accountability. We believe that woman will give to the political parties of the country a moral temperament which will have a most beneficent and ennobling effect on politics.

Woman, also, is specially fitted for the performance of that function of legislative and executive government which, with the growth of civilization, becomes yearly more and more important—the wise and practical economic adjustment of the details of public expenditures. It may be considered that it would not be for the public interest to clothe with the suffrage any class of persons who are so dependent that they will, as a general rule, be governed by others in its exercise. But we do not admit that this is true of women. We see no reason to believe that women will not be as likely to retain their independence of political judgment, as they now retain their independence of opinion in regard to the questions which divide religious sects from one another. These questions deeply excite the feelings of mankind, yet experience shows that the influence of the wife is at least as great as that of the husband in determining the religious opinion of the household. The natural influence exerted by members of the same family upon each other would doubtless operate to bring about similarity of opinion on political questions as on others. So far as this tends to increase the influence of the family in the State, as compared with that of unmarried men, we deem it an advantage. Upon all questions which touch public morals, public education, all which concern the interest of the household, such a united exertion of political influence cannot be otherwise than beneficial.

Our conclusion, then, is that the American people must extend the right of suffrage to woman or abandon the idea that suffrage is a birthright. The claim that universal suffrage will work mischief in practice is simply a claim that justice will work mischief in practice. Many honest and excellent persons, while admitting the force of the arguments above stated, fear that taking part in politics will destroy those feminine traits which are the charm of woman, and are the chief comfort and delight of the household. If we thought so we should agree with the majority of the committee in withholding assent to the prayer of the petitioners. This fear is the result of treating the abuses of the political function as essential to its exercise. The study of political questions, the forming an estimate of the character of public men or public measures, the casting a vote, which is the result of that study and estimate, certainly have in themselves nothing to degrade the most delicate and refined nature. The violence, the fraud, the crime, the chicanery, which, so far as they have attended masculine struggles for political power, tend to prove, if they prove anything, the unfitness of men for the suffrage, are not the result of the act of voting, but are the expressions of coarse, criminal and evil natures, excited by the desire for victory. The admission to the polls of delicate and tender women would, without injury to them, tend to refine and elevate the politics in which they took a part. When, in former times, women were excluded from social banquets, such assemblies were scenes of ribaldry and excess. The presence of women has substituted for them the festival of the Christian home.

The majority of the committee state the following as their reasons for the conclusion to which they come:

First—If the petitioners' prayer be granted it will make several millions of female voters.

Second—These voters will be inexperienced in public affairs.

Third—They are quite generally dependent on the other sex.

Fourth—They are incapable of military duty.

Fifth—They are without the power to enforce the laws which their numerical strength may enable them to make.

Sixth—Very few of them wish to assume the irksome and responsible duties which this measure thrusts upon them.

Seventh—Such a change should only be made slowly and in obedience to a general public demand.

Eighth—There are but thirty thousand petitioners.

Ninth—It would be unjust to impose "the heavy burden of governing, which so many men seek to evade, on the great mass of women who do not wish for it, to gratify the few who do."

Tenth—Women now have the sympathy of judges and juries "to an extent which would warrant loud complaint on the part of their adversaries of the sterner sex."

Eleventh—Such a change should be made, if at all, by the States. Three-fourths of the States should not force it on the others. In any State in which "any considerable part of the women wish for the right to vote, it will be granted without the intervention of congress."

The first objection of the committee is to the large increase of the number of the voting population. We believe on the other hand, that to double the numbers of the constituent body, and to compose one-half that body of women, would tend to elevate the standard of the representative both for ability and manly character. Macaulay in one of his speeches on the Reform bill refers to the quality of the men who had for half a century been members for the five most numerous constituencies in England—Westminster, Southwark, Liverpool, Bristol and Norwich. Among them were Burke, Fox, Sheridan, Romilly, Windham, Tierney, Canning, Huskisson. Eight of the nine greatest men who had sat in parliament for forty years sat for the five largest represented towns. To increase the numbers of constituencies diminishes the opportunity for corruption. Size is itself a conservative force in a republic. As a permanent general rule the people will desire their own best interest. Disturbing forces, evil and selfish passions, personal ambitions, are necessarily restricted in their operation. The larger the field of operation, the more likely are such influences to neutralize each other.

The objection of inexperience in public affairs applies, of course, alike to every voter when he first votes. If it be valid, it would have prevented any extension of the suffrage, and would exclude from the franchise a very large number of masculine voters of all ages.

That women are quite generally dependent on the other sex is true. So it is true that men are quite generally dependent on the other sex. It is impossible so to measure this dependence as to declare that man is more dependent on woman or woman upon man. It is by no means true that the dependence of either on the other affects the right to the suffrage.

Capacity for military duty has no connection with capacity for suffrage. The former is wholly physical. It will scarcely be proposed to disfranchise men who are unfit to be soldiers by reason of age or bodily infirmity. The suggestion that the country may be plunged into wars by a majority of women who are secure from military dangers is not founded in experience. Men of the military profession, and men of the military age are commonly quite as eager for war as non-combatants, and will hereafter be quite as indifferent to its risks and hardships as their mothers and wives.

The argument that women are without the power to enforce the laws which their numerical strength may enable them to make, proceeds from the supposition that it is probable that all the women will range themselves upon one side in politics and all the men on the other. Such supposition flatly contradicts the other arguments drawn from the dependence of women and from their alleged unwillingness to assume political burdens. So men over fifty years of age are without the power to enforce obedience to laws against which the remainder of the voters forcibly rebel. It is not physical power alone, but power aided by the respect for law of the people, on which laws depend for their enforcement.

The sixth, eighth and ninth reasons of the committee are the same proposition differently stated. It is that a share in the government of the country is a burden, and one which, in the judgment of a majority of the women of the country, they ought not to be required to assume. If any citizen deem the exercise of this franchise a burden and not a privilege, such person is under no constraint to exercise it. But if it be a birthright, then it is obvious that no other power than that of the individual concerned can rightfully restrain its exercise. The committee concede that women ought to be clothed with the ballot in any State where any considerable part of the women desire it. This is a pretty serious confession. On the vital, fundamental question whether the institutions of this country shall be so far changed that the number of persons in it who take a part in the government shall be doubled, the judgment of women is to be and ought to be decisive. If woman may fitly determine this question, for what question of public policy is she unfit? What question of equal importance will ever be submitted to her decision? What has become of the argument that women are unfit to vote because they are dependent on men, or because they are unfit for military duty, or because they are inexperienced, or because they are without power to enforce obedience to their laws?

The next argument is that by the present arrangement the administration of justice is so far perverted that one-half the citizens of the country have an advantage from the sympathies of juries and judges which "would warrant loud complaint" on the part of the other half. If this be true, it is doubtless due to an instinctive feeling on the part of juries and judges that existing laws and institutions are unjust to women, or to the fact that juries composed wholly of men are led to do injustice by their susceptibility to the attractions of women. But certainly it is a grave defect in any system of government that it does not administer justice impartially, and the existence of such a defect is a strong reason for preferring an arrangement which would remove the feeling that women do not have fair play, or for so composing juries that, drawn from both sexes, they would be impartial between the two.

The final objection of the committee is that "such a change should be made, if at all, by the States. Three-fourths of the States should not force it upon the others. Whenever any considerable part of the women in any State wish for the right to vote, it will be granted without the intervention of congress." Who can doubt that when two thirds of congress and three-fourths of the States have voted for the change, a considerable number of women in the other States will be found to desire it, so that, according to the committee's own belief, it can never be forced by a majority on unwilling communities? The prevention of unjust discrimination by States against large classes of people in respect to suffrage is even admitted to be a matter of national concern and an important function of the national constitution and laws. It is the duty of congress to propose amendments to the constitution whenever two-thirds of both houses deem them necessary. Certainly an amendment will be deemed necessary, if it can be shown to be required by the principles on which the constitution is based, and to remove an unjust disfranchisement from one-half the citizens of the country. The constitutional evidence of general public demand is to be found not in petitions, but in the assent of three-fourths of the States through their legislatures or conventions.

The lessons of experience favor the conclusion that woman is fit for a share in government. It may be true that in certain departments of intellectual effort the greatest achievements of women have as yet never equaled the greatest achievements of men. But it is equally true that in those same departments women have exhibited an intellectual ability very far beyond that of the average of men and very far beyond that of most men who have shown very great political capacity. But let the comparison be made in regard to the very thing with which we have to deal. Of men who have swayed chief executive power, a very considerable proportion have attained it by usurpation or by election, processes which imply extraordinary capacity on their part as compared with other men. The women who have held such power have come to it as sovereigns by inheritance, or as regents by the accident of bearing a particular relation to the lawful sovereign when he was under some incapacity. Yet it is an undisputed fact that the number of able and successful female sovereigns bears a vastly greater proportion to the whole number of such sovereigns, than does the number of able and successful male sovereigns to the whole number of men who have reigned. An able, energetic, virtuous king or emperor is the exception and not the rule in the history of modern Europe. With hardly an exception the female sovereigns or regents have been wise and popular. Mr. Mill, who makes this point, says:

> We know how small a number of reigning queens history presents in comparison with that of kings. Of this small number a far larger proportion have shown talents for rule, though many of them have occupied the throne in difficult periods. When to queens and empresses we add regents and viceroys of provinces, the list of women who have been eminent rulers of mankind swells to a great length. . . . Especially is this true if we take into consideration Asia as well as Europe. If a Hindoo principality is strongly, vigilantly and economically governed; if order is preserved without oppression; if cultivation is extending and the people prosperous, in three cases out of four that principality is under a woman's rule. This fact, to me an entirely unexpected one, I have collected from a long official knowledge of Hindoo governments.

Certainly history gives no warning that should deter the American people from carrying out the principles upon which their government rests to this most just and legitimate conclusion. Those persons who think that free government has anywhere failed, can only claim that this tends to prove, not the failure of universal suffrage, but the failure of masculine suffrage. Like failure has attended the operation of every other great human institution, the family, the school, the church, whenever woman has not been permitted to contribute to it her full share. As to the best example of the perfect family, the perfect school, the perfect church, the love, the purity, the truth of woman are essential, so they are equally essential to the perfect example of the self-governing State.

GEO. F. HOAR,

JOHN H. MITCHELL,

ANGUS CAMERON.[60]

10.
Resolutions adopted by the National Woman Suffrage Association convention, May 1878

Resolved, That a government of the people, by the people and for the people is yet to be realized; for that which is formed, administered and controlled only by men, is practically nothing more than an enlarged oligarchy, whose assumptions of natural superiority and of the right to rule are as baseless as those enforced by the aristocratic powers of the old world.

Resolved, That in celebrating our third decade we have reason to congratulate ourselves on the marked change in woman's position—in her enlarged opportunities for education and labor, her greater freedom under improved social customs and civil laws, and the promise of her speedy enfranchisement in the minor political rights she has already secured.

Resolved, That the International Congress called in Paris, July 20, to discuss the rights of woman—the eminent Victor Hugo, its presiding officer—is one of the most encouraging events of the century, in that statesmen and scholars from all parts of the world, amid the excitement of the French Exposition, propose to give five days to deliberations upon this question.

Resolved, That the majority report of the chairman of the Committee on Privileges and Elections, Senator Wadleigh of New Hampshire, against a sixteenth amendment to secure the political rights of woman in its weakness, shows the strength of our reform.

Resolved, That the national effort to force citizenship on the Indians, the decision of Judge Sawyer in the United States Circuit Court of California against the naturalization of the Chinese, and the refusal of congress to secure the right of suffrage to women, are class legislation, dangerous to the stability of our institutions.

Whereas, Woman's rights and duties in all matters of legislation are the same as those of man.

Resolved, That the problems of labor, finance, suffrage, international rights, internal improvements, and other great questions, can never be satisfactorily adjusted without the enlightened thought of woman, and her voice in the councils of the nation.

Resolved, That the question of capital and labor is one of special interest to us. Man, standing to woman in the position of capitalist, has robbed her through the ages of the results of her toil. No just settlement of this question can be attained until the right of woman to the proceeds of her labor in the family and elsewhere is recognized, and she is welcomed into every industry on the basis of equal pay for equal work.

Resolved, That as the first duty of every individual is self-development, the lessons of self-sacrifice and obedience taught woman by the Christian church have been fatal, not only to her own vital interests, but through her, to those of the race.

Resolved, That the great principle of the Protestant Reformation, the right of individual conscience and judgment heretofore exercised by man alone, should now be claimed by woman; that, in the interpretation of Scripture, she should be guided by her own reason, and not by the authority of the church.

Resolved, That it is through the perversion of the religious element in woman—playing upon her hopes and fears of the future, holding this life with all its high duties in abeyance to that which is to come—that she and the children she has trained have been so completely subjugated by priestcraft and superstition.[61]

VI.

THE 1880s:
A Decade of Progress and Danger

Delegates to the January 1880 National Woman Suffrage Association (NWSA) convention were greeted with a stage "tastefully decorated with flags and flowers" while on the walls surrounding them hung their usual mottoes:

> "True labor reform: the ballot for woman, the unpaid laborer of the whole earth."

> "Man's work is from sun to sun, but woman's work is never done."

> "Taxation without representation is tyranny. Woman is taxed to support pauperism and crime, and is compelled to feed and clothe the law-makers who oppress her."

> "Women are voting on education, the bulwark of the republic, in Kansas, Michigan, Minnesota, Colorado, Oregon, New Hampshire and Massachusetts."

> "Women are voting on all questions in Wyoming and Utah. The vote of women transformed Wyoming from barbarism to civilization."

> "The financial problem for woman: equal pay for equal work, and one hundred cents on the dollar."

> "When a woman *Will*, she Will, and you may depend on it, she WILL vote."[1]

While the speeches and resolutions adopted by the convention focused primarily on passage of the suffrage amendment, the additional issues of the NWSA were well represented. Women, "the great unpaid and unrecognized laborer and producer of the whole earth" should receive equal pay. While fathers now legally had sole right to the children they sired, the mother should have custody of her children, who should carry her surname, and not their father's. Excluding women from the ministry, a practice of most Christian denominations, was denounced as "theocratic tyranny." Elected U.S. president twice and crowned with glory and honor, Ulysses S. Grant achieved his military victories through the "plans and rare genius" of Anna Ella Carroll, while she had "for fifteen years been suffering in poverty unrecognized and unrewarded," a convention resolution charged.[2]

Victories were incremental at the national level, as slowly the NWSA chipped-away at the resistance of the men who served in Congress. In 1881 Congress created a special committee on woman suffrage.[3] Although the NWSA wanted a permanent standing committee, not a special committee, which had to be decided upon at the opening of each Congress, this was a partial victory. Two years later, this special committee sent a report to the House of Representatives proposing a woman suffrage amendment to the Constitution. The full report is included in this chapter.

Small victories are cause for small celebration, as *History of Woman Suffrage* acknowledged.

Thus closed the forty-seventh congress, and although with so little promise of any substantial good for women, yet this slight recognition in legislation was encouraging to those who had so long appealed in vain for the attention of their representatives. A committee to even consider the wrongs of woman was more than had ever been secured before, and one to propose some measures of justice, sustained by the votes of a few statesmen awake to the degradation of disfranchisement, gave some faint hope of more generous action in the near future. The tone of the debates in these later years even, on the nature and rights of

women, is wholly unworthy the present type of developed womanhood and the age in which we live.[4]

In 1880, the NWSA sent a delegate to each of the presidential
nominating conventions asking each party to adopt the following plank in its platform: *Resolved*, That the right to use the
ballot *inheres* in the citizen of the United States, and we pledge
ourselves to secure protection in the exercise of this right to all
citizens irrespective of sex.[5]

The NWSA delegates attended the nominating conventions,
made their argument, and failed to receive a woman suffrage
endorsement from any of the three major parties: Republican,
Democratic, and Greenback. The one ally on the Republican
platform committee, an African American delegate from
Michigan, moved its adoption without success. The fringe Prohibition Party, however, in its eleventh plank endorsed woman
suffrage, "for their own protection, and as a rightful means for
a proper settlement of the liquor question," linking the vote
and temperance.[6]

The Republican Party disappointed the women again in
1884 when the resolutions committee refused to adopt a plank
in its platform giving any recognition to women. While none
of the other parties had done any better, Republicans certainly
had not lived up to their Civil War–won reputation as the
party of freedom.[7]

The frustration with the political parties led to the revital-
ization of the Equal Rights Party, begun in 1872 by Victoria
Woodhull. The party in 1884 nominated attorney Belva Lockwood for president. Lockwood never minced words, as evidenced by a speech at the 1878 NWSA convention, a summary
of which is included in this chapter.

Lockwood's feminist credentials were impressive. Her first
client was a battered woman whose alcoholic husband had left
her. Lockwood won a divorce and alimony for the woman. Determined that women lawyers should be able to represent their
clients without restrictions, Lockwood drafted a bill enabling
them to practice in all the higher courts, including the Supreme

Court, and lobbied the bill for six years, with the backing of the NWSA, until it finally passed Congress. Lockwood then moved admission of the first southern African American man to practice before the high court. She drafted a bill requiring the government to give its employees equal pay for equal work, which Congress passed in 1872. Concerned about the vulnerability of women prisoners placed in the hands of male jailers and guards, Lockwood and others worked for the placing of matrons at the District of Columbia jail and police stations until one was finally appointed in 1884. She successfully argued an important case establishing the legality of slave marriages. Mandatory, binding arbitration among all the nations of the world was a goal high on Lockwood's agenda. She wrote the Sherman Resolution, a bill to grant the president authority to mediate when war is imminent between two nations.[8]

Vice-presidential candidate Marietta Stow's credentials were likewise impressive. Stow had founded a Woman's Republic in San Francisco to create an independent center of thought and action for women in 1881. A vegetarian and dress reformer (she invented and wore a modified Bloomer costume, which she called the triple S costume: sensible, scientific, simple), Stow was one of many feminists advocating collective kitchens, collective businesses, and collective housing.[9]

The party's stirring call to action read:

> Rouse woman! Rouse Justice! Rouse Truth! The she eagle has left her nest to tear with beak and talons, the ravergers of her unfledged brood . . . Is this treason? No! It is a slave insurrection which while supporting a tyrannical government will maintain its own.[10]

The campaign inspired poems, like this one published in the November 1884 issue of Stow's newspaper, the *Woman's Herald of Industry*:

> Wake sluggard, wake! Behold the flame
> That bursts to life when woman's name
> Is etched in splendor on the wall

> That topples ere its final fall.
> The wall of Prejudice is rent,
> And bails of ridicule e're-spent.[11]

Although some of the planks, like the forced assimilation of Native Americans, we understand today as repressive, much of the 1884 platform of the all-woman Equal Rights Party stands as one of the most progressive of any party in history. An outline of its platform is included in this chapter.

The media were divided over Lockwood's candidacy, as was the NWSA. Gage ran as one of the two electors-at-large on the ticket,[12] while Stanton and Anthony came out with a circular titled "Stand By the Republican Party."[13]

Belva Lockwood clarified her vision of what the campaign could do in a letter to Clara Foltz published in the October 1884 *Woman's Herald of Industry*:

> If we can get one elector elected on our ticket so that, that person will form one of the Electoral College that meets here in December, this Campaign of our Equal Rights Party will pass into the history of 1884, and become the entering wedge—the first practical movement in the history of Woman Suffrage, and will be the beginning of the end. It will open a door to be shut no more forever, and four years from now will sweep the country. Already every newspaper in the land has caught up the refrain and all over the country earnest men and women are saying "Why not?"[14]

Daily mentions of Lockwood's campaign in the press brought audiences of thousands who paid to hear her speak. On election day she received 4,149 popular votes.[15]

More important, Lockwood received the entire electoral vote of Indiana, presumably cast as a joke. Whatever the motive for their action, the electorate had spoken and Lockwood had achieved her goal—that is until the government illegally refused to recognize the votes cast for her. Lockwood petitioned Congress, "asking that the ballots cast for her shall be counted, and that the electoral vote of Indiana be adjudged to her."[16] While the Senate didn't support her claim, Lockwood reflected:

> I have had a splendid campaign, well received and attentively listened to everywhere. My campaign fund was my lecture receipts and I more than covered expenses. I had more fun and less worry than any of the other candidates and have accomplished a great deal. . . .
> Reforms are slow, but they never go backwards. Their originators may die, but the reform will live to bless millions yet unborn.[17]

While Victoria Woodhull had announced her candidacy for president in 1872, she didn't carry on a campaign or receive votes. This historic event marked the first time a woman campaigned for the office of president of the United States, which Lockwood would do again four years later.

The American Woman Suffrage Association, in its plan of work for 1884, continued qualified support for the federal amendment, while maintaining its concentration on getting woman suffrage state by state and in the territories. School suffrage was enacted in twelve states; now it was time, the AWSA said, to go after the vote in local elections.[18]

The AWSA further supported federal suffrage the following year, resolving at their 1885 convention:

> *Resolved*, That the association send a deputation to Washington in behalf of its memorial to Congress to frame a statute prohibiting the disfranchisement of women in the Territories, and to cooperate with the National Woman Suffrage Association (at its January meeting) for a Sixteenth Amendment forbidding political distinctions on account of sex.[19]

As the NWSA, and especially Susan B. Anthony, also supported work in the states while concentrating on the federal constitutional amendment, the two organizations no longer were antagonistic in their suffrage work. However, the NWSA would continue to prioritize a federal amendment, while the AWSA concentrated on the states.[20]

There were victories to celebrate, and in each instance where women won the right to vote in an election, the arguments of the antis lost credibility. The *History of Woman Suffrage* editors tongue-in-cheek asserted that women voting didn't destroy the family, as conservatives predicted.

> In the territories of Wyoming and Utah, woman suffrage still continues after five years' experiment, and we have not learned that households have been broken up or that babies have ceased to be rocked.[21]

Anti-suffragists like Mrs. Admiral Dahlgren continued to counter that women didn't want to vote. Kingsbury county in Dakota Territory tested that assumption, as reported in an article in the *Bismarck Tribune* signed "Justice." "A more orderly election was never known" when women voted in a local election," the paper reported, and "no self-respect was lost and no woman was lowered in public esteem." If 222 women turned out to vote in a snowstorm with only a week's notice, Justice challenged, "is it to be supposed they do not appreciate the right?"[22]

The legislature of newly settled Dakota Territory followed Wyoming and Utah in passing a woman suffrage amendment. While today all governors in the five U.S. territories are directly elected, in the past many territorial governors were appointed by the president of the United States. Dakota governor Pierce, a presidential appointee in office only six months, vetoed the bill.

The Washington Territory Legislature had come within one vote of granting women's suffrage in 1854, and strong organizing by the Washington Woman Suffrage Association finally won the right in 1883. Victory was short-lived when four years later the Territorial Supreme Court overturned the woman suffrage law in 1887. Back on its feet, the organization pushed through the passage of the law again in 1888, but once again the Supreme Court overturned it. The liquor industry was the power behind the reversals, when women voted to shut down bars and brothels in several cities.[23]

Rights won were rights that could be taken away, the suffragists learned. As early as 1876 the NWSA resolved to support Utah women as Congress began considering legislation to disenfranchise them. Polygamy, or the practice of plural marriage, was the real issue behind the scenes.[24]

Congress was considering the Edmunds-Tucker Act, which became law in 1887. The bill made polygamy illegal, punishing it with a fine of from five hundred to eight hundred dollars and imprisonment for up to five years. The act also disincorporated the Church of Jesus Christ of Latter-day Saints (Mormon), authorized seizure of church real estate not directly used for religious purposes, and dissolved its Perpetual Emigrating Fund Company, on the grounds that they all fostered polygamy. Women had been voting in Utah Territory for seventeen years, and the Edmunds-Tucker Act took that right away from them, abolishing woman suffrage in Utah Territory. The NWSA protested the legislation with the following resolutions at its 1886 convention:

> Whereas, The Anti-Polygamy bill passed by both Houses of Congress provides for the disfranchisement of the non-polygamous women of Utah; and
>
> Whereas, The women thus sought to be disfranchised have been for years in the peaceable exercise of the ballot, and no charge is made against them of any crime by reason of which they should lose their vested rights; therefore,
>
> *Resolved*, That this association recognizes in these measures a disregard of individual rights which is dangerous to the liberties of all; since to establish the precedent that the ballot may be taken away is to threaten the permanency of our republican form of government.[25]

Another issue fought during the decade was jury duty. Among the rights denied women by the misogynist Blackstone code of law, adopted by the states after the Revolution, was the right to sit on a jury. How could a woman accused of a crime be tried by a jury of her peers if the entire jury was made up of men?

> [Blackstone] held that the common law requires jurors to be free and trustworthy "human beings," and that while the term "human beings" means man and woman, the female is, however, excluded on account of the defect of sex.[26]

Washington Territory overturned that manifestation of the Blackstone code when the legislature made jury duty legal for women the same year it granted women the vote in 1883. Clara Foltz sent an on-the-ground report to the feminist paper the *New Northwest*, describing this newly won right in action. The report is included in this chapter.

The gaining of this right to serve on juries was also short-lived. When the Washington Territorial Legislature, under pressure from the liquor industry, took away the right of suffrage four years later in 1887, it also passed legislation ending women serving on juries.

Suffrage, of course, wasn't the only NWSA issue. Stanton sent a letter to the 1886 convention along with a resolution holding the Christian teachings of woman's subordination to man, and the church's enforcement of these ideas, accountable for woman's oppression.

Unlike the positive response to similar resolutions in the previous decade, the NWSA membership now hesitated. A similar resolution had failed the year before, and now the NWSA was strongly divided on this issue, as demonstrated in the lively 1886 convention discussion reprinted in this chapter. The resolution was strongly opposed by conservative Helen Gougar of Indiana and supported by Virginia Minor. Clara Colby and two men, Lucretia Mott's son-in-law, Edward M. Davis, and an Episcopal clergyman, spoke in favor of Stanton's resolution, which eventually passed by a vote of thirty-two to twenty-four.

The organization had clearly become more orthodox. While some Christian denominations, challenged by those demanding their rights, had softened their position on man's authority over woman, even supporting woman suffrage, the dogma remained. The question continued of how, or even whether, to challenge the orthodox Christian biblical teaching requiring woman's oppression. As Gage and Stanton pointed out, each move to equality, from speaking in public to wearing pants to control of their bodies to voting, was met with conservative Christian opposition. If not challenged, would this orthodox voice fight each movement for greater rights?

Gage was now editing the *National Citizen and Ballot Box*, the official newspaper of the NWSA, and she confronted this Christian threat to women's rights in an 1881 article titled "Person and Things," included in this chapter.

Another sign of growing conservatism in some elements of the organization came with a shocking opposition to the main focus of the NWSA's suffrage work:

> The resolution calling upon Congress to take the necessary measures to secure the ballot for women through an amendment to the Federal Constitution, was vigorously opposed by the Southern delegates as contrary to States' Rights, but was finally adopted.[27]

Labor had organized with such strength in 1886 that when 350,000 workers in 11,562 establishments throughout the land struck for the eight-hour day on May 1, the results were instantaneous. By the next day half of the strikers had won their demand. Friedrich Engels was amazed at the succession of labor victories that followed, and wrote that in ten months, U.S. workers achieved a "revolution" that in another country "would have taken at least ten years."[28]

When ten thousand people showed up for a mass rally organized by the Knights of Labor and the Central Labor Union in New York City on July 5, 1886, Lillie Devereux Blake was a featured speaker as president of the New York Woman Suffrage Association. Clara Colby brought the need for solidarity with the labor movement to the later NWSA convention with a speech and resolution, which were endorsed by the organization. Both Blake's and Colby's speeches are included in this chapter.[29]

When the Statue of Liberty was unveiled in New York Harbor a few months later, in October 1886, the New York Woman Suffrage Association protested:

> That the proposition of our French friends to erect a statue of Liberty on Bedloe's Island, in New York Harbor, points afresh to the cruelty of woman's present position, since it is proposed to represent Freedom as a majestic female form in a State where not one woman is free.[30]

Lillie Devereux Blake, president of the organization, described their action in detail. While the Statue of Liberty represented the hypocrisy of the United States government, it also represented the hope of the future. Her full account is included in this chapter.

In the midst of all this agitation, the NWSA continued its pressure on Congress for a constitutional amendment with yearly congressional hearings held during their annual Washington convention.

While the Senate Select Committee on Woman Suffrage had reported favorably on the woman suffrage amendment in 1883, the full Senate had never taken up the question until New Hampshire senator Henry W. Blair introduced it on January 25, 1887. For the first time in U.S. history, the Senate voted on the submission of an amendment to the federal Constitution that would protect the voting rights of women.

The opponents of suffrage, however, presented only three documents, each from individual women, one of them choosing to remain anonymous. The suffragists dramatically outshone them:

> Senator Blair presented a petition for the suffrage from the Woman's Christian Temperance Union of 200,000 members, signed by Miss Frances E. Willard, president, and the entire

official board. This was accompanied by a strong personal appeal from a number of distinguished women, and hundreds of thousands of petitions had been previously sent. The Senator also received permission to have printed in the *Congressional Record* the arguments made by the representatives of the suffrage movement before the Senate committee in 1880 and 1884.[31]

The vote was 16 yeas, 34 nays, 26 absent. This would be the first and only discussion and vote in the United States Senate on the woman suffrage amendment in the nineteenth century. It would take another thirty-two years of struggle before the Senate would finally pass this amendment.

While the AWSA minimally supported the federal amendment, and the NWSA, and especially Susan B. Anthony, also supported work in the states while concentrating on the federal constitutional amendment, the two organizations no longer were antagonistic in their suffrage work. However, the NWSA would continue to prioritize a federal amendment, while the AWSA concentrated on the states. As Gage clarified when Nebraska faced the ballot issue, the NWSA's position was clear:

> While we of the National are glad to see an amendment to a State constitution proposed, securing suffrage to woman, we must not be led by it to forget or neglect our legitimate work, an amendment to the national constitution, which will secure suffrage at one and the same moment to the women of each State. While all action of any kind and everywhere is good because it is educational, the only real, legitimate work of the National Woman Suffrage Association, is upon Congress.[32]

History of Woman Suffrage, begun by the leadership triumvirate of the NWSA—Stanton, Gage, and Anthony—in 1876, was now complete. The third volume, which took the movement through the mid-1880s, was published in 1886. This massive decade-long project of three volumes, a thousand pages each, was accomplished all by hand, without the help of even the recently invented typewriter, which was not yet in common use.

In the contract that Stanton, Gage, and Anthony had entered into in 1876, they agreed to the following distribution of labor, as Anthony's writing block prohibited her from doing the writing: Stanton and Gage would "write, collect, select, and arrange the material," while Anthony would "secure the publication of said work by and through some competent publishing house." They would equally share any net profit from the sale of the books.[33]

When funding for the project seemed impossible, help arrived. Eliza Jackson Eddy was the daughter of Francis Jackson, who gave the woman's rights cause $5,000 in 1858. A personal experience of the terrible injustice of the law precipitated the gift. Eliza had lost her children when her husband seized their two young daughters and took them to Europe without her consent. His daughter's legal powerlessness in fighting the loss of her children prompted Jackson to support women's rights. When she died in 1882, Eliza left a bequest of $50,000 to be divided between Susan B. Anthony and Lucy Stone. An indirect heir unsuccessfully challenged the will, and in 1885 Anthony and Stone each received $24,125, or $634,000 in today's purchasing power. It was to be used according to their own individual judgment, "for the advancement of woman's cause."[34]

After Stanton and Gage died, in 1898 and 1902 respectively, Ida Husted Harper, Anthony's hand-picked biographer, picked up where they had left the movement's history in the mid-eighties. With the help of Anthony, she edited two more volumes (this time with a typewriter). Harper then concluded the history with a sixth volume, bringing the history to 1920, when the suffrage amendment was finally ratified. Anthony used much of the Eddy endowment to give away copies of *History of Woman Suffrage* to individuals, schools, and twelve hundred libraries in the United States and Europe.[35]

History, of course, is written through the lens of the author, and the final three volumes of the *History*, filtered through Harper and Anthony's focus on the suffrage amendment, prioritized that work. They also smoothed out some of the rough edges of the movement, and toned down the radical edge. For example, the story Harper and Anthony tell of the Statue of Liberty action does not present it as a protest:

> In the fall an interesting observance was arranged by the State Suffrage Association when the statue of Liberty Enlightening the World, given to the American nation by France, was unveiled on October 28. There was a great excursion down the bay to witness this ceremony and the association chartered a boat which was filled with friends of the cause. A place was secured in the line between two of the great warships, and, while the cannon thundered a salute to the majestic female figure which embodied Freedom, speeches were made on the suffrage boat by Mrs. Blake, Mrs. Margaret Parker of England, Mrs. Harriette R. Shattuck of Massachusetts, Mrs. Gage, Mrs. Howell and others.[36]

While Anthony believed that the vote was the sole issue of importance and all other things in the long list of woman's wrongs could be solved by it, Stanton and Gage saw the vote differently, as they concluded the Preface of their final volume of the *History*. The vote, they believed, was not an end in itself, but simply the lever to push off woman's oppression by the state, the church, the capitalist, and the home:

> The narrow self-interest of all classes is opposed to the sovereignty of woman. The rulers in the State are not willing to share their power with a class equal if not superior to themselves, over which they could never hope for absolute control, and whose methods of government might in many respects differ from their own. The annointed leaders in the Church are equally hostile to freedom for a sex supposed for wise purposes to have been subordinated by divine decree. The capitalist in the world of work holds the key to the trades and professions, and undermines the power of labor unions in their struggles for shorter hours and fairer wages, by substituting the cheap labor of a disfranchised class, that cannot organize its forces, thus making wife and sister rivals of husband and brother in the industries, to the detriment of both classes. Of the autocrat in the home, John Stuart Mill has well said: "No ordinary man is willing to find at his

own fireside an equal in the person he calls wife." Thus society is based on this fourfold bondage of woman, making liberty and equality for her antagonistic to every organized institution. Where, then, can we rest the lever with which to lift one-half of humanity from these depths of degradation but on "that columbiad of our political life—the ballot—which makes every citizen who holds it a full-armed monitor?"[37]

These radical sentiments from the leadership of the NWSA were clearly not ones the rival AWSA would enforce. They had come a bit closer in their work for the vote, but the two organizations were still worlds apart in their organizational structures, tactics, and focus. Besides, the AWSA would never point fingers at the church as the source of woman's oppression. It came as a surprise to some, then, when among the resolutions adopted at the AWSA's 1887 convention was the following.

Whereas, The woman suffragists of the United States were all united until 1868 in the American Equal Rights Association; and

Whereas, The causes of the subsequent separation into the National and the American Woman Suffrage Societies have since been largely removed by the adoption of common principles and methods, therefore,

Resolved, That Mrs. Lucy Stone be appointed a committee of one from the American W. S. A. to confer with Miss Susan B. Anthony, of the National W. S. A., and if on conference it seems desirable, that she be authorized and empowered to appoint a committee of this association to meet a similar committee appointed by the National W. S. A., to consider a satisfactory basis of union, and refer it back to the executive committees of both associations for final action.[38]

The idea that they shared common principles was a stretch. While the NWSA continued to pass resolutions denouncing Christian dogma as the source of woman's oppression, the AWSA leadership saw it differently. Lucy Stone, describing the AWSA 1888 convention in the *Woman's Journal* of December 1, wrote:

It is always a matter of regret that the excellent speeches made at these meetings can not be phonographically reported, but it must suffice to say that they covered all the ground, from the principles on which representative government rests, to the teaching of the Bible, which Miss Laura Clay, in an able speech, warmly claimed was on the side of equal rights for women. Mrs. Zerelda G. Wallace, that noble mother in Israel, agreed with her, though from a different point of view, while Frederick Douglass claimed that the "Eternal Right exists independent of all books."[39]

While there were some orthodox women in the NWSA, and Frederick Douglass, dividing his time between the two organizations, was the voice of free thought at the 1888 AWSA convention, this difference loomed large between the two organizations. They also employed different methods, contrary to the AWSA resolution. The AWSA primary work for the vote in 1887 was outreach to the press, according to Lucy Stone in her report as chair of the Executive Committee.[40]

While the AWSA concentrated on education, the NWSA continued to employ the tactic of direct confrontation, facing down the government with protest. In 1887, the same year that the AWSA met in Philadelphia to celebrate its work enlisting the press to publish suffrage literature, NWSA representatives came to Philadelphia to challenge the president of the United States directly with a last-minute protest against celebrating the centennial of the Constitution. While the AWSA got the press to print articles, the NWSA continued to do actions that the press covered. The AWSA's newspaper, the *Woman's Journal*, even covered some of the events, publishing correspondent Lillie Devereux Blake's description of the protest at the Constitution's centennial celebration. The account is printed in this chapter.

The protest, signed by Anthony, Gage, Blake, Rachel G. Foster, and May Wright Sewall on behalf of the National Woman Suffrage Association in 1887, reminded the governmental officials: "In the midst of the pomp and glories of this celebration women are only onlookers, voiceless and unrepresented, a denial in defiance of the provisions of the Constitution you profess to honor." Delineating the ways in which the Constitution was being violated, the protest demanded "in the future all the people of the nation shall have an equal voice in choosing the rulers whose high mission it shall be to guide a true Republic on its course of glory."[41]

Stories of the unjust treatment of women kept issues alive in the press. Lillie Devereux Blake recounted one in an 1887 lecture, cited in a San Jose, California, paper and included in this chapter.

Stories of resistance also made the suffrage papers, such as one about a young woman homesteading in Dakota, published in the August 1889 *Wisconsin Citizen*. Receiving official notice that she needed to work out her poll tax, she refused, "unless the privilege of voting was given her." The tax wasn't collected. "If all the women who are assessed for taxes in Dakota would take this stand," the paper encouraged, "there would be no trouble in making the constitution of the new state one of equal rights."[42]

There could be no bystanders to this women's revolution, Sara Underwood claimed in the same issue of the *Wisconsin Citizen*. She called out women who failed to work for their rights.

Oh, you indifferent women, who in sheltered homes, under kindly masculine protective rule, sit serenely in your chair of ease, sneering perhaps at this clamor for rights. If it were possible to reach you we might ask if you think it noble, if you think it grand, if you think it just that you should not help in this battle which is for you and your daughters? That through your apathy the battle should be fought over and over again to gain each successive step toward enfranchisement by a determined band of your braver, more clear-sighted sisters?

We would like to set ablaze within your frigid souls the divine fire of Liberty.

Some day you will blush with shame, or your sons and daughters will blush for you, that while the one great progressive battle of this era was being fought for your liberties, you were enrolled in the coward's list of the indifferent.[43]

In 1888 the NWSA embarked on the challenging project of holding an International Council of Women. A call went out to ten thousand activists in Western Europe and North America to come to Washington to share tactics not just for woman suffrage but for equality and justice, "in the Church and in the Home," as well:

The first public demand for equal educational, industrial, professional and political rights for women was made in a convention held at Seneca Falls, New York, in the year 1848.

To celebrate the Fortieth Anniversary of this event, an International Council of Women will be convened under the auspices of the National Woman Suffrage Association, in Albaugh's opera house, Washington, D. C., on March 25, 1888.

It is impossible to overestimate the far-reaching influence of such a Council. An interchange of opinions on the great questions now agitating the world will rouse women to new thought, will intensify their love of liberty and will give them a realizing sense of the power of combination.

However the governments, religions, laws and customs of nations may differ, all are agreed on one point, namely: man's sovereignty in the State, in the Church and in the Home. In an International Council women may hope to devise new and more effective methods for securing in these three institutions the equality and justice which they have so long and so earnestly sought. Such a Council will impress the important lesson that the position of women anywhere affects their position everywhere. Much is said of universal brotherhood, but for weal or woe, more subtle and more binding is universal sisterhood.[44]

Forty-nine delegates from fifty-three English, Irish, French, Norwegian, Danish, Finnish, Indian, and Canadian women's organizations attended the week-long Council. Beyond the vote, the eighty speakers discussed a wide range of women's issues: education, philanthropies, temperance, industries, professions, organizations, and social purity, along with legal, political and religious conditions.[45]

The religious tone set early was decidedly not the NWSA's. A "prayer meeting group" of orthodox Christian women succeeded in getting each session opened with a prayer, and Anthony reached out to Frances Willard, the president of the Woman's Christian Temperance Union, to take part in the council.

The Woman's Christian Temperance Union (WCTU) was an army of "organized mother-love," under the banner, "For God and Home and Native Land," going into battle, initially, against the liquor traffic. When praying and singing proved rather unsuccessful, Frances Willard received divine inspiration, she said, to work for suffrage so women could vote liquor out of existence. She joined the American Woman Suffrage Association, as did many WCTU members. The WCTU wanted the vote for another, far more important reason than banning alcohol, as Willard proclaimed in her presidential address to the 1887 WCTU convention:

> The Woman's Christian Temperance Union, local, state, national and world-wide, has one vital, organic thought, one all-absorbing purpose, one undying enthusiasm and it is that *Christ shall be this world's King*. Yea, verily. THIS WORLD'S king in its realm of cause and effect; king of its courts, its camps, and its commerce; king of its colleges and cloisters; king of its customs and its constitutions.[46]

The wall of separation between church and state was under siege from a conservative orthodox Christian movement sweeping the country. Congress was considering bills requiring Christian school prayers and closure of all public facilities on Sunday, the biblically imposed day of rest. The Prohibition Party was the force behind much of this, and the WCTU supported it. Charismatic and widely popular with conservative

Christian women, Willard was elected president of the National Council of Women, a new organization that grew out of the council.

Abigail Scott Duniway, NWSA mainstay and editor of the Oregon feminist paper the *New Northwest*, had become convinced that the WCTU women were destroying the possibility of success because of their insistence on getting the vote to end the use of alcohol. The *Wisconsin Citizen* railed against bringing prohibition and suffrage together. Christianity-coated temperance was much more palatable to the public than women's empowerment. As Lucy Stone put it, "[I]t is so much easier to see a drunkard than it is to see a principle."[47]

Anthony recognized that fact. Drawn by Willard's charisma, she was equally dazzled by the number of women she led—about ten times the number of the two suffrage organizations combined. The vote had always been Anthony's greatest concern, and her commitment to this single issue had become entrenched over the years. Impatient at the suffrage progress, she had begun to formulate a new strategy.

Anthony had also asked AWSA founder Lucy Stone to take part in the council. For twenty years the AWSA and the NWSA had worked for women's rights in their own separate and different ways. Now their leaders appeared together on the same platform, for the first time since the 1869 break into the two groups. Appearing together changed the context for the merger offer the AWSA had sent to the NWSA.

Gage, who had stepped down as chair of the Executive Committee years before, was persuaded to return to the position after the International Council by other NWSA members who also saw impending danger to the organization. Under Gage's leadership, the NWSA's Executive Committee, in the post–International Council meeting, elected an eight-woman Advisory Committee, Gage among them, to consult with the merger group. They proposed a joint convention of the NWSA and the AWSA be held to decide the terms of union. Since the NWSA membership far outnumbered that of the AWSA, the smaller organization predictably declined the offer and there the matter rested. There would be no merger.[48]

As chair of the Executive Committee, Gage knew she would be informed of any important items, but Anthony did not tell her that she had received a new offer from the AWSA that would be acted upon at the next convention, in 1889. Gage was ill and didn't attend. Working with Anthony, May Wright Sewall was elected the new chair of the Executive Committee. Anthony announced receipt of the new AWSA union offer and appointed members of a committee to consider it, made up primarily of those who openly favored it. Anthony's pro-merger union committee brought a new constitution to the floor of the convention for endorsement just as it was concluding on the final night. Unsure of what was happening, members approved it, not realizing it replaced the NWSA nationally focused constitution with one that mirrored the AWSA's states' rights document. This new constitution had previously been approved by the AWSA, so nothing stood in the way of merger now, the union committee argued. Union advocates were united and tightly organized to push through the merger, while those opposed to it were stunned, confused, and disbelieving. Clara Colby moved unsuccessfully that the question be submitted to a mail vote of all NWSA members. The question of union was placed before the midnight session of the Executive Committee. It passed by a vote of 30 to 11.[49]

In the months that followed, many members of the NWSA, shocked and angry, protested to Gage that they had no warning a merger was to be voted upon and they had no voice in the decision, which they thoroughly opposed.

Examining the new constitution, Gage realized that it had removed the very structure that had focused the NWSA on working toward a national suffrage amendment. Where NWSA members had joined as individuals, the new constitution required that they join a state organization. Women could come into the national organization only if they were chosen as a delegate from their state. The state delegate structure of the AWSA replaced personal representation. This changed the very nature of their work from a national to a state focus and disenfranchised all the NWSA members except those chosen as state delegates.

Working with letters from Stanton, members of the Executive Committee and opponents of the merger, along with accounts in the AWSA's *Woman's Journal,* the NWSA's *Woman Tribune*, and the official Union Reports, Gage wrote a formal protest, signed by five officers of the NWSA and sent to the entire membership.[50] It is included in this chapter.

The protest was too late. This 30–11 vote of a nonrepresentative body would change the course of history. The grassroots, multi-issue focus of the NWSA was gone; conservative Christian women would come to control the new hierarchical, single-focused organization working for the vote at the expense of other women's rights issues. The NWSA was destroyed, not in a merger, but in a capitulation to the weaker AWSA. The new organization, the National American Woman Suffrage Association, formally came together the following year at an 1890 convention.

Stanton was elected president and Lucy Stone chosen to head the Executive Committee, positions primarily honorary. Uninterested in organizational work, Stanton was spending most of her time in Europe, and Lucy Stone was ill. Anthony, elected vice president at large, would control the direction of the organization.

Many of the long-time NWSA members left the movement. One of them was Matilda Joslyn Gage, who formed the Woman's National Liberal Union, an organization made up of anarchists, labor and prison activists, and suffragists determined to fight the religious forces trying to impose their conservative agenda on the country through governmental policy.

An unlikely newspaper source covered the conflict between Gage and Anthony. L. Frank Baum, who ten years later would publish *The Wonderful Wizard of Oz*, was the son-in-law of Gage and a newspaper editor in Aberdeen, South Dakota. He reported:

The two great factions of the national Woman Suffrage Association are openly arrayed against each other in Washington this week. At their heads are the two leaders who together were mainly instrumental in forming the organization 21 years ago, who have worked shoulder to shoulder as collaborators in the cause, who penned together that remarkable history of Woman Suffrage which stands today the best exponent of their claims for a sixteenth amendment—Matilda Joslyn Gage and Susan B. Anthony

Mrs. Gage, at Willard's Hall, is forming with her followers an advanced degree called the "Woman's National Liberal Union," separating themselves from the old body of suffragists because the latter "are not progressive, nor working intelligently to advance the interests of universal suffrage."

Miss Anthony, with headquarters at the Riggs House, is defying her old partner, and endeavoring to destroy the popularity of the new movement.

It is difficult to state at present which faction seems best calculated to win the battle for supremacy.[51]

A decade later, with Gage and Stanton both dead, Anthony sat beside her hand-picked biographer, Ida Husted Harper, instructing her as Harper wrote her biography and then edited the fourth volume of *History of Woman Suffrage*. Their interpretation of the merger process, recognized as the official history, has been repeated by historians for nearly a century.

Harper described the merger this way in her *History of Woman Suffrage*:

The feature of this occasion which will distinguish it in history was the formal union of the National and the American Associations under the joint name. For the past twenty-one years two distinctive societies had been in existence, both national as to scope but differing as to methods. Negotiations had been in progress for several years toward a uniting of the forces and, the preliminaries having been satisfactorily arranged by committees from the two bodies, the officers and members of both participated in this national convention of 1890.[52]

In Anthony's biography they maintained the merger was accomplished "in the most thoroughly official manner, according to the most highly approved parliamentary methods, and the final result was satisfactory to a large majority of the members of both societies, who since that time have worked together in unbroken harmony."⁵³

I.
Report of the House of Representatives Special Committee on Woman Suffrage, March 1, 1883

Mr. White, by unanimous consent, from the Special Committee on Woman Suffrage, reported back the joint resolution (H. Res., 255) proposing an amendment to the constitution, which was referred to the House calendar, and, with the accompanying report, ordered to be printed.

Mr. Springer: As a member of that committee I have not seen the report, and do not know whether it meets with my concurrence.

Mr. White: I ask by unanimous consent that the minority may have leave to submit their views, to be printed with the majority report.

The Speaker: The Chair hears no objection.

Mr. White, from the Select Committee on Woman Suffrage, submitted the following:

The Select Committee on Woman Suffrage, to whom was referred House Resolution No. 255, proposing an amendment to the Constitution of the United States to secure the right of suffrage to citizens of the United States without regard to sex, having considered the same, respectfully report:

In attempting to comprehend the vast results that could and would be attained by the adoption of the proposed article to the constitution, a few considerations are presented that are claimed by the friends of woman suffrage to be worthy of the most serious attention, among which are the following:

I. There are vast interests in property vested in women, which property is affected by taxation and legislation, without the owners having voice or representation in regard to it. The adoption of the proposed amendment would remove a manifest injustice.

II. Consider the unjust discriminations made against women in industrial and educational pursuits, and against those who are compelled to earn a livelihood by work of hand or brain. By conferring upon such the right of suffrage, their condition, it is claimed, would be greatly improved by the enlargement of their influence.

III. The questions of social and family relations are of equal importance to and affect as many women as men. Giving to women a voice in the enactment of laws pertaining to divorce and the custody of children and division of property would be merely recognizing an undeniable right.

IV. Municipal regulations in regard to houses of prostitution, of gambling, of retail liquor traffic, and of all other abominations of modern society, might be shaped very differently and more perfectly were women allowed the ballot.

V. If women had a voice in legislation, the momentous question of peace and war, which may act with such fearful intensity upon women, might be settled with less bloodshed.

VI. Finally, there is no condition, status in life, of rich or poor; no question, moral or political; no interest, present or future; no ties, foreign or domestic; no issues, local or national; no phase of human life, in which the mother is not equally interested with the father, the daughter with the son, the sister with the brother. Therefore the one should have equal voice with the other in molding the destiny of this nation.

Believing these considerations to be so important as to challenge the attention of all patriotic citizens, and that the people have a right to be heard in the only authoritative manner recognized by the constitution, we report the accompanying resolution with a favorable recommendation in order that the people, through the legislatures of their respective States, may express their views:

Joint Resolution *proposing an amendment to the Constitution of the United States*:

Resolved by the Senate and House of Representatives of the United States of America in congress assembled, (two-thirds of each House concurring therein), That the following article be proposed to the legislatures of the several States as an amendment to the Constitution of the United States, which, when ratified by three-fourths of the said legislatures, shall be valid as part of said constitution, namely:

Section 1. The right of citizens of the United States to vote shall not be denied or abridged by the United States or by any State on account of sex.

Sec. 2. The congress shall have power, by appropriate legislation, to enforce the provisions of this article.[54]

2.
Summary of Belva Lockwood's speech at the January 1878 NWSA convention

[T]he only way for women to get their rights is to take them. If necessary let there be a domestic insurrection. Let young women refuse to marry, and married women refuse to sew on buttons, cook, and rock the cradle until their liege-lords acknowledge the rights they are entitled to. There were more ways than one to conquer a man; and women, like the strikers in the railroad riots, should carry their demands all along the line.[55]

3.
Platform of the National Equal Rights Party, 1884

1 We pledge ourselves, if elected to power, so far as in us lies, to do equal and exact justice to every class of our citizens, without distinction of color, sex, or nationality.

2 We shall recommend that the laws of the several States be so amended that women will be recognized as voters, and their property rights made equal with that of the male population, to the end that they may become self supporting, rather than a dependent class.

3 It will be our earnest endeavor to revive the now lagging industries of the country by encouraging and strengthening our commercial relations with other countries, especially with the Central and South American States, whose wealth of productions are now largely diverted to England and other European countries for lack of well established steam-ship lines, and railroad communications between these countries and our own, encourage exports by an effort to create a demand for our home productions; and to this end, we deem that a moderate tariff—sufficient to protect the laboring classes, but not so high as to keep our goods out of the market, as most likely to conserve the best interests of our whole people. That is to say, we shall avoid as much as possible a high protective tariff on the one hand and free trade on the other. We shall also endeavor by all laudable means to increase the wages of laboring men and women. Our protective system will be most earnestly exerted to protect the commonwealth of the country from venality and corruption in high places.

4 It will be our earnest effort to see that the solemn contract made with the soldiers of the country on enlistment into the United States service viz: that if disabled therein they should be pensioned, strictly carried out, and that, without unnecessary expense and delay to them; and a re-enactment of the "Arrears Act."

5 We shall discountenance by every legal means the liquor traffic, because its tendency is to demoralize the youth of the land; to lower the standard of morality among the people; and we do not believe that the revenue derived from it would feed and clothe the paupers that it makes, and the money expended on its account in courts, workhouses and prisons.

6 We believe that the only solution of the Indian question is, to break up all of their small principalities and chieftainships, that have ever presented the anomaly of small kingdoms scattered through a republic and ever liable to break out in some unexpected locality; and which have been hitherto maintained at such great expense to the Government; and treat the Indian like a rational human being, as we have the negro—make him a citizen, amenable to the laws, and let him manage his own private affairs.

7 That it is but just that every protection granted to citizens of the United States by birth should also be secured to the citizens of the United States by adoption.

8 We shall continue gradually to pay the public debt and to refund the balance, but not in such manner as to curtail the circulating medium of the country so as to embarrass trade, but pledge ourselves that every dollar shall be paid in good time.

9 We oppose monopoly, the tendency of which is to make the rich, richer, and the poor, poorer, as opposed to the genius and welfare of Republican institutions.

10 We shall endeavor to aid in every laudable way the work of educating the masses of the people, not only in book knowledge, but in physical, moral and social culture, in such a manner as will tend to elevate the standard of American manhood and womanhood—that the individual may receive the highest possible development.

11 We recommend a uniform system of laws for the several States as desirable, as far as practicable; and especially the laws relating to the descent of property, marriage and divorce, and the limitation of contracts.

12 We will endeavor to maintain the peaceable relations which now exist between the various sections of our vast country, and strive to enter into a compact of peace with the other American as well as European Nations, in order that the peace which we now enjoy may become perpetual. We believe that war is a relic of barbarism belonging to the past, and should only be resorted to in the direst extremity.

13 That the dangers of a solid South or a solid North shall be averted by a strict regard to the interests of every section of the Country, a fair distribution of public offices, and such a distribution of the public funds for the increase of the facilities of inter commercial relations as will restore the South to her former industrial prestige, develop the exhaustless resources of the West, foster the iron, coal, and woolen interests of the Middle States, and revive the manufactures of the East.

14 We shall foster civil service, believing that a true civil service reform, honestly and candidly administered will lift us out

of the imputation of having become a nation of office seekers, and have a tendency to develop in candidates for office an earnest desire to make themselves worthy and capable of performing the duties of the office that they desire to fill, and in order to make the reform a permanent one, recommend that it be ingrafted into the constitution of the United States.

15 It will be the policy of the Equal Rights Party to see that the residue of the public domain is parceled out to actual settlers only, that the honest yeomanry of the land, and especially those who have fought to preserve it, shall enjoy its benefits.[56]

4.
Clara Foltz, "Testimony of an Eye-Witness," 1885

Mrs. Clara S. Foltz, who returned last week from a trip to Western Washington, took some pains while there to inform herself relative to jury service as applied to the newly enfranchised voters of that Territory. Having had, as an attorney at the California bar for the past five years, ample opportunity to consider the stuff that juries are made of, Mrs. Foltz is well qualified to judge of the matter, and she says that it has seldom been her lot to see as careful, earnest note taken of evidence as that taken by the women whom she saw in the jury-box. As regards their disinclination for this service, she says that after careful inquiry she found that most women are not only willing, but many of them are anxious, to perform the service. The exception is found among women of fashion and frivolity, whose uselessness in all active channels is their only passport to "womanliness," as they have been trained to view it. Said she: "I thought I had been fully prepared to see women acting in the capacity of jurors, but when I entered the court-room and saw that awful bugbear of 'woman's rights'—women among men in the jury-box—I was so overcome with this grand evidence of progress that I felt for a moment quite hysterical, and in my desire to laugh and cry, and my determination to do neither, I had hard work to maintain my self-control.

One of the 'ladies of the jury,' whom counsel with polite, deferential and earnest manner was addressing, was a motherly-looking, intelligent woman who, with hands encased in cotton gloves and bonnet strings tied snugly under her chin, listened with conscientious intent to the argument, her face written all over with earnest determination to discharge her sworn duty in the premises, according to the light furnished by evidence."

This is the spectacle which opponents of equal rights have been distorting into unwomanly proportions for these three decades. This the reality, the fiction of which has been made the theme of ribald jest and unseemly denunciation for lo! these many years. How simple a tale the earnest common sense of practice substitutes for the distorted imagery of theory.

To the masses of the women of Washington Territory the idea of jury service may be distasteful; but the masses have had no experience in the matter, and under any condition it must be years before they will. Those who have had experience almost universally testify that they do not find it disagreeable or irksome, do not seek to evade it, and on the contrary enjoy the breadth of view and the pocket money that such service brings. The truth of the matter is that the hue and cry heard against the innovation is raised by narrow men who make great assumption of virtue in declaring, "I do not want *my* wife to serve on a jury"; by mercenary men who see in every woman in the jury-box three dollars per day diverted possibly from their own pockets; by lawless men who fear with reason the conscience that women bring to the discharge of jury duty; and by timid women who are yet afraid of the scarecrow that custom has set up.

If the Legislature now in session at Olympia shall pass a law relieving women from jury duty, it will be at the behest of these classes rather than by the desire of the women of Washington Territory who, having served on juries, know that such service is not incompatible with womanly dignity.[57]

5.

Discussion by NWSA members of
Elizabeth Cady Stanton's church accountability resolution in the 1886 NWSA convention

Mrs. Helen M. Gougar (Ind.) moved that the resolution be laid upon the table, saying: "A resolution something like this came into the last convention, and it has done more to cripple my work and that of other suffragists than anything which has happened in the whole history of the woman suffrage movement. When you look this country over you find the slums are opposed to us, while some of the best leaders and advocates of woman suffrage are among the Christian people. A bishop of the Roman Catholic Church stood through my meeting in Peoria not long since. We can not afford to antagonize the churches. Some of us are orthodox, and some of us are unorthodox, but this association is for suffrage and not for the discussion of religious dogmas. I can not stay within these borders if that resolution is adopted, from the fact that my hands would be tied. I hope it will not go into open convention for debate."[58]

Mrs. Perkins (O.): I think we ought to pay due consideration and respect to our beloved president. I have no objection to sending missionaries to the churches asking them to pay attention to woman suffrage; but I do not think the churches are our greatest enemies. They might have been so in Mrs. Stanton's early days, but to-day they are our best helpers. If it were not for their co-operation I could not get a hearing before the public. And now that they are coming to meet us half way, do not throw stones at them. I hope that resolution, as worded, will not go into the convention.

Mrs. Meriwether (Mo.): I think the resolution could be amended so as to offend no one. The ministers falsely construe the Scriptures. We can overwhelm them with arguments for woman suffrage—with Biblical arguments. We can hurl them like shot and shell. Herbert Spencer once wrote an article on the different biases which distort the human mind, and among the first he reckoned the theological bias. In Christ's time and in the early Christian days there was no liberty, every one was under the despotism of the Roman Cæsars, but women were on an equality with men, and the religion that Christ taught included women equally with men. He made none of the invidious distinctions which the churches make to-day.

Mrs. Shattuck (Mass.): We did not pass the resolution of last year, so it could not have harmed anybody. But I protest against this fling at masculine interpretation of the Scriptures.

Mrs. Minor (Mo.): I object to the whole thing—resolution and letter both. I believe in confining ourselves to woman suffrage.

Mrs. Colby (Neb.): I was on that committee of resolutions last year and wrote the modified one which was presented, and I am willing to stand by it. I have not found that it hurts the work, save with a few who do not know what the resolution was, or what was said about it. The discussion was reported word for word in the *Woman's Tribune* and I think no one who read it would say that it was irreligious or lacked respect for the teachings of Christ. I believe we must say something in the line of Mrs. Stanton's idea. She makes no fling at the church. She wants us to treat the Church as we have the State—viz., negotiate for more favorable action. We have this fact to deal with—that in no high orthodox body have women been accorded any privileges.

Edward M. Davis (Penn.): I think we have never had a resolution offered here so important as this. We have never had a measure brought forward which would produce better results. I agree entirely with Mrs. Stanton on this thing, that the church is the greatest barrier to woman's progress. We do not want to proclaim ourselves an irreligious or a religious people. This question of religion does not touch us either way. We are neutral.

Madame Neymann (N. Y.): Because the clergy has been one-sided, we do not want to be one-sided. I know of no one for whom I have a greater admiration than for Mrs. Stanton. Her resolution antagonizes no one.

. . . Mrs. Gougar: I think it is quite enough to undertake to change the National Constitution without undertaking to change the Bible. I heartily agree with Mrs. Stanton in her idea of sending delegates to church councils and convocations, but I do not sanction this resolution which starts out—"The greatest barrier to woman's emancipation is found in the superstitions of the church." That is enough in itself to turn the entire church, Catholic and Protestant, against us.

Mrs. Nelson (Minn.): The resolution is directed against the superstitions of the church and not against the church, but I think it would be taken as against the church.

Miss Anthony (N. Y.): As the resolution contains the essence of the letter, I move that the whole subject go to the Plan of Work Committee.

The meeting adjourned without action, and on Friday morning the same subject was resumed. A motion to table Mrs. Stanton's resolution was lost. Miss Anthony then moved that both letter and resolution be placed in her hands, as the representative of the president of the association, to be read in open convention without indorsement. "I do not want any one to say that we young folks strangle Mrs. Stanton's thought."

The Rev. Dr. McMurdy (D. C.): I do not intend to oppose or favor the motion, but as a clergyman and a High Church Episcopalian, I can not see any particular objections to Mrs. Stanton's letter. The Scriptures must be interpreted naturally. Whenever Paul's remarks are brought up I explain them in the light of this nineteenth century as contrasted with the first.

It was finally voted that the letter be read without the resolution.

The resolution was brought up later in open convention and the final vote resulted in 32 ayes and 24 noes. This was not at that time a delegate body, but usually only those voted who were especially connected with the work of the association. Before the present convention adjourned a basis of delegate representation was adopted, and provision made that hereafter only regularly accredited delegates should be entitled to vote.[59]

6.
"Persons and Things," Matilda Joslyn Gage article in her *National Citizen and Ballot Box*, 1881

A few Sundays ago, the Rev. Knox-Little, an English high church clergyman preached a "Sermon to Women," in the large church of St. Clements, Philadelphia, which was an exposition of clerical opinion of woman, and an insult to the civilization and intelligence of the age. In the course of the revered gentleman's remarks, he said: "God made himself to be born of a woman to sanctify the virtue of endurance; loving submission is an attribute of woman, men are logical, but women lacking this quality, have an intricacy of thought. There are those who think women can be taught logic; this is a mistake. They can never by any power of education arrive at the same mental status as that enjoyed by men, but they have a quickness of apprehension, which is usually called leaping at conclusions, that is astonishing. There then, we have distinctive traits of a woman, namely endurance, loving submission, and quickness of apprehension."

After having defined woman's place in creation, the Rev. Knox-Little defined her duty. First her duty as a daughter and a sister, then, a wife's duty. "Wifehood," said the preacher, "is the crowning glory of a woman. In it she is bound for all time. To her husband she owes the duty of unqualified obedience. There is no crime which a man can commit which justifies his wife in leaving him or applying for that monstrous thing, divorce. It is her duty to subject herself to him always, and no crime that he can commit can justify her lack of obedience. If he is a bad or wicked man she may gently remonstrate with him, but refuse him never."

After this manner, blasphemous to womanhood, did the Rev. Knox-Little continue his sermon. Woman, according to his doctrine, is shorn of all responsibility; she is deprived of conscience, intelligent thought, self-respect, everything, to become an appendage to man, a thing. The clergy in the middle ages, divided rights into those of persons and things, themselves being the persons, the laity, things.

Rev. Knox-Little and his ilk of to-day divide the world into persons and things,—men being the persons and women the things.

It is said that among the Romans no divorce took place for 500 years, but during that period the wife was the husband's slave. She could not divorce herself from him, as she had no control over herself; the husband would not divorce her, because she was his slave over whom he had power of life and death. If she tasted of wine, he could kill her, if she even took the key of the wine cellar, he could kill her, and many a husband coming home after an absence treacherously kissed his wife to ascertain if her breath smelled of the forbidden drink. The Roman husband at that period had power also over the lives of his children; holding his wife as a slave, he did not divorce her, as divorcing her would have practically freed her.

Rev. Knox-Little has similar views of divorce as the old Roman husband. He said; "Let divorce be anathema; curse this accursed thing, divorce; curse it, curse it!"

From divorce he changed to children, giving women his advice upon this point. He said: "Think of the blessedness of having children. I am the father of many children and there have been those who have ventured to pity me, 'keep your pity for yourself,' I have replied. 'They never cost me a single pang.' In this matter let women exercise that endurance and loving submission which with intricacy of thought are their only characteristics."

But have I not quoted enough of this sermon to make every woman's cheek tingle with shame and indignation?

Every portion of it is an insult and a degradation to woman, but the advice in regard to children is the cap-sheaf of ministerial impertinence. My blood always boils at advice from a man in regard to a family. That, at least, should be the province of woman alone. To say when and how often she chooses to go down into the valley of the shadow of death, to give the world another child, should be hers alone to say. Rev. Knox-Little's children never cost him a single pang, but their mother did not speak. Through months and years of suffering she had given birth to those children; through days and weary, weary nights of care she had reared them, but all her husband has of compassion for her, or sympathy with her, is comprised in, "let women exercise that endurance and loving submission which with intricacy of thought are their only characteristics."

Rev. Henry Ward Beecher once said, the matter of having a family should have been thus arranged: the father and the mother to bear them alternately. First the mother, then the father, then the mother the third, which he declared would be the limit of the family as the father would refuse to again pass through all the suffering incident upon the birth of a child.

It requires but little thought upon woman's part for her to realize how closely her disabilities are interwoven with religious belief and religious despotism, but if she needs aid to thought the Knox-Littles will help her.[60]

7.

Clara Bewick Colby, "The Relation of the Woman Suffrage Movement to the Labor Question," NWSA convention, 1886, as edited in *History of Woman Suffrage* (and Resolutions)

She began by saying, "All revolutions of thought must be allied to practical ends." After sketching those already attained by women, she continued:

The danger threatens that, having accomplished all these so thoroughly and successfully that they no longer need our help and already scarcely own their origin, we will be left without the connecting line between the abstract right on which we stand and the common heart and sympathy which must be enlisted for our cause ere it can succeed. Why is it that, having accomplished so much, the woman suffrage movement does not force itself as a vital issue into the thoughts of the masses? Is it not because the ends which it most prominently seeks do not enlist the self-interest of mankind, and those palpable wrongs which it had in early days to combat have now almost entirely disappeared? . . .

We need to vitalize our movement by allying it with great non-partisan questions, and many of these are involved in the interests of the wage-earning classes. . . . We need to labor to secure a change of the conditions under which workingwomen live. We need to help them to educative and protective measures, to better pay, to better knowledge how to make the most of their resources, to better training, to protection against frauds, to shelter when health and heart fail. We must help them to see the connection between the ballot and better hours, exclusion of children from factories, compulsory education, free kindergartens; between the ballot and laws relating to liability of employers, savings banks, adulteration of food and a thousand things which it may secure when in the hands of enlightened and virtuous people.

. . . *Resolved,* That we call the attention of the working women of the country to the fact that a disfranchised class is always an oppressed class and that only through the protection of the ballot can they secure equal pay for equal work.

Resolved, That we recognize as hopeful signs of the times the indorsement of woman suffrage by the Knights of Labor in national assembly, and by the National Woman's Christian Temperance Union, and that we congratulate these organizations upon their recognition of the fact that the ballot in the hands of woman is necessary for their success.[61]

8.
Lillie Devereux Blake, president of the New York City Suffrage Association, description of the 1886 protest at the unveiling of the Statue of Liberty, in the *Woman's Journal*

Anxiously were the skies watched at nightfall with hopes of a brightening up at sunset, but alas! a steady down-fall kept up all night, and the morning of the great day dawned with thick clouds veiling the sun. It did not actually rain, however, when the hour for starting on the excursion arrived, and, despite the dampness, about two hundred people assembled on our boat, the John Lennox. After the usual delays we got under way, and took our place in the naval parade. Our steamer was a large one, and despite some discomforts and much disappointment at the fog and rain, the run down the bay was a memorable one.

Through some error our party had been placed in the wrong boat, and got assigned to one of the leading positions in the line, so that we felt entitled to assume the place given us, and thus the John Lennox, floating the woman suffrage flag, was one of the first steamers to reach Bedlow's [sic] Island, where it assumed one of the best positions, directly in front of the great bronze statue.

The sight at this time was magnificent. On the right and left of us were two vessels of war. We were almost under the guns of the Minnesota, while all about us were grouped excursion steamers, tugs, police-boats, and yachts. Every vessel was dressed out with bunting, while on the Island a crowd of people swarmed under the gay decorations of the President's stand.

And over all this scene of animation, above the land, above the sea, towering far above the pigmy men at her feet, rose the majestic woman form, Liberty, represented in fair feminine proportions, calm, majestic, mighty, seeming to say with her silent lips of bronze, "I am the embodied hope of the future, and the enthroned prediction of liberty for women."

Presently the veil was withdrawn from her beautiful calm face, and the air was rent with salvos of artillery fired to hail the new goddess; the earth and the sea trembled with the mighty concussions, and steam-whistles mingled their shrill shrieks with the shouts of the multitude,-all this done by men in honor of a woman. Amid the confusion, I looked into the faces of the tired veterans of our cause who stood about me, and saw how their eyes also glowed with hope.

At the prow of our boat there floated a long white pennon bearing on it the letters "New York State Woman Suffrage Association." It was worth much of effort and of toil to see that banner flying on that day before the front of our woman Liberty.[62]

9.
"Our New York Letter," Lillie Devereux Blake's
description of the 1887 Constitution centennial protest

Ever since the Constitutional Centennial has been talked of, it
has seemed to me an occasion which ought not to be allowed to
pass without some sort of protest on the part of the women of
the nation. Various attempts which were made failed to arouse
any enthusiasm among the friends of the cause in Philadelphia,
and it was therefore a great gratification to find Mrs. Lucy
Stone in the *Woman's Journal* editorially calling attention to
the injustice inflicted on women. Almost at the last minute Miss
Susan B. Anthony, on the part of the National Woman Suffrage
Association, authorized the preparation of a protest, and as
Chairman of the Committee of Presentation, I prepared the
document which will be found in another column.

Thursday noon brought me to Philadelphia, into streets
thronged with people and gay with banners. After considerable
delay, I succeeded in joining Miss Rachel G. Foster, who was
with a party of friends in the window of a church on Broad
Street, witnessing the industrial procession.

The matter of finding a fitting occasion on which to present
the protest to the President was one which caused us considerable anxiety, and after a brief rest we made a long struggle
through the thronged streets to the headquarters of the Centennial Committee. We were there shown the roster of the ceremonies and various engagements of the President during the
three days. We decided that the most fitting occasion for the
presentation would be at the public reception on Saturday
morning. We had no right to intrude upon social affairs. No
women had been invited to participate in any of the public ob-
servances. But when the President stood in the City Hall to receive all who chose to come, we certainly had the right to be
there. Though "only women," and representing "only women,"
yet it could not be denied that we were inhabitants of the land,
and therefore, among the people who might claim an entrance.

I was the guest of Miss Foster and her sister, Miss Julia, at their summer residence at Germantown, over Thursday night, the evening being devoted to addressing copies of the protest to the papers throughout the country. On Friday night Miss Adelaide Thompson, the veteran advocate of our cause, hospitably entertained me in her comfortable home, whose door is ever open to those who are laboring for our reform.

It was certain that the throng would be very great at the public reception on Saturday morning, so no attempt was made to form a large Presentation Committee. Those who started on the mission were Miss Rachel Foster and Miss Adelaide Thompson, of Pennsylvania, Miss Lucy Anthony, of Kansas, and myself. When we reached the closed iron gate of the city building, admittance was refused to all but the Chairman of the Committee, and I was only allowed because I was accompanied by a representative of the press, who persuaded the guardian at the door to admit us both.

The room in which the President was to stand was not large; it was dressed with flags, and guarded by policemen in double rows. Precisely at nine o'clock the cheering outside announced the coming of the Chief Magistrate. A moment later he entered the room, and was presented to the city officials. Then there was a pause, and this was my opportunity. I at once advanced, holding a copy of the protest with the autograph signatures. As Mr. Cleveland saw me, he smiled pleasantly, shook hands, and greeted me cordially.

"I have the honor, Mr. President," I said, "to present to you this protest, on behalf of the National Woman Suffrage Association. Will you give it your attention when you are more at leisure?"

"I will, certainly, my most careful attention," he said, taking the document, and as the head of the line of people advanced, I bowed and passed on."[63]

10.

Excerpt from Lillie Devereux Blake lecture "Is It a Crime to Be a Woman?," published in the *San Jose Daily*, July 27, 1888

In this country, which is proud of its claims of freedom to all, one-half of its people are treated as if they were guilty of a crime, and it were better for them, if possible, not to have been born women. A few years ago a young woman was arrested on the streets of New York in men's habiliments. It transpired that she had been a waiter in a restaurant, and as a woman had received $4 a week. She left that restaurant, and at another, attired as a man, she was paid $9, $5 more than her previous salary. She was convicted, and sentenced to six months' confinement on Blackwell's Island for no other reason than that she was a woman.[64]

11.

Matilda Joslyn Gage, A Statement of Facts. Private. To members of the National Woman Suffrage Association Only, 1889

We, the undersigned, regard it as due to members of the National Association who were not present at its annual convention last winter, and who possess no method of becoming informed upon the subject, to make a frank statement of what was done "by a vote of thirty," at nearly twelve o'clock at night, after denial of the right of absent members to a voice in the question, thereby changing, without their consent, the *status* of the large body of volunteer workers comprising the National Woman Suffrage Association.

. . . By adoption of this Constitution and change in method of work, the National Woman Suffrage Association has been virtually destroyed. As founded, it looked alone to securing suffrage for woman through action of the Nation, leaving each State free to do its own special State work. The fact that the National Woman Suffrage Association has at different times held conventions in different States, does not detract from this fact. All special work done by it in different States has been simply educational; it has never attempted, *as a body*, to interfere with State work, or to define State legislation.

. . . Under the new Constitution, individual members are disfranchised, its conventions made strictly delegate under such a basis of representation as entirely takes away the rights of its members *not delegated* by some auxiliary society. The National Woman Suffrage Association is therefore no longer exclusively National in its character, but has taken upon itself that species of State work heretofore the object of the American Society, explained by Lucy Stone, as "school and municipal suffrage," and which, under the old Constitution of the National Woman Suffrage Association, had been left solely where it belongs—under control of the respective States.

. . . Under the basis of representation the whole power of the Association is given to those states with the greatest number of members of Auxiliaries even though such States should send but a single delegate to its conventions.

. . . Rich States or those near by can send many delegates, while poor or distant States may scarcely be able to send one.

. . . A new comer with but little knowledge or experience as to the needs of the work may control a large number of votes; while a woman of very much greater experience, perhaps having traveled more than twice as far for purpose of attending the convention, having come at great personal expense to represent her State, although without having been sent as a delegate from some auxiliary Society would have no vote. This disfranchises some of our most devoted pioneer suffragists. States not having become 'Auxiliary,' although possessing many local societies and a large number of individual suffragists can take no part— have no representation in the conventions.

The Constitution was adopted by the "Committee of Conference on Union," before it had been presented to the Convention for action, and before the members of the convention even knew that any amendment was contemplated, the whole proceedings being unparliamentary and irregular; the call for the convention even containing no mention that a change was proposed.

Previous to the final vote, at the last Executive Session, it was moved and long discussed that the question of 'union' should be submitted by a circular letter to all National members and let their vote decide it. Great opposition was manifested. The "unionists" as a body combatted this proposition, declaring the members ought not to be consulted.

. . . Let us note the different method adopted by the American Woman Suffrage Association in regard to its own members. The *Woman's Journal* of December 1, 1888, says: "By a resolution passed at the American Woman Suffrage Association held in Cincinnati, November 21–22, 1888, such a change of Constitution as might be recommended by a majority of the representatives of that Association on the foregoing committee, and *afterwards accepted by a majority vote of the members* of the American Association, was to be accepted; and the Secretary was authorized to take the vote of the members of the American Woman Suffrage Association upon the new Constitution *by mail*, in order to secure as wide an expression of opinion as possible and avoid the necessity of calling a special convention for this purpose."

This course was honorable and just. How different that of the National, which neither called a special convention for the purpose of canvassing in regard to union, nor took "the vote" of its members "by mail," as did the American.

It cannot be said that the National Woman Suffrage Association "consented," for surely no person "consents" whose wishes are not even consulted.

In addition to all else wrong, the work of "union" was accomplished in a packed committee, two members having been requested to resign on the ground, as explicitly stated, that a person whose mind was made up against union was not a proper member of the committee. Although persons *not* in favor were considered unfit, two others who had declared themselves *in favor* were added after the committee convened, (one, however, refusing to accept the appointment).

. . . Constantly recurring instances prove that there is no real union between the two societies—can be none. Their methods have ever been diverse, and that of the National the subject of continual criticism by the American. As showing this difference it is only necessary to recall the fact that on the same day the 'Committee on Union' met, the forenoon of the convention was chiefly devoted to an article by Mr. Minor of the St. Louis bar, on 'The Law of Federal Suffrage' (read by Mrs. Minor), conclusively proving the nation to have sole and absolute power over the suffrage, as has always been held by the National Woman Suffrage Association. A portion of the session was also given to a statement regarding Mrs. Robinson's petition to Congress for relief from her political disabilities,—a method that has been in use by the National Association since 1878, and recognized as in direct line with its work. The form in use since that year was also read for the instruction of members of the National Woman Suffrage Association, who were urged to make similar appeal.

At that instant the *Woman's Journal* (organ of the American Society) was criticising the National method of work in an article headed, "Congress has no Jurisdiction." It was brought forth by Mrs. Robinson's appeal which it severely censured, but was no less in opposition to Mr. Minor's argument, and to the whole policy of the National Woman Suffrage Association since its formation.

Thus at the very moment of "union" the American Association through its organ was denouncing the action that very day recommended as the special policy of the National Association.

    Rev. Olympia Brown, Vice-President
      for Wisconsin.
    Charlotte F. Daley, member of the Executive Committee
      for New York.
    Marietta M. Bones, Vice-President
      for South Dakota.
    Matilda Joslyn Gage, New York.

The undersigned protest against the disfranchisement of the members of the National Woman Suffrage Association at its executive meeting of January 24th, 1889, when, by a vote of thirty to eleven, a formal "union" was effected between the National Woman Suffrage Association and the American Woman Suffrage Association. Submitting the question of union to the members of the National Woman Suffrage Association was refused by a small vote in a small meeting, and at the same meeting it was asserted by two members of the conference committee (as an inducement to the meeting to refuse this submission to the members) that the "American" members were not to be consulted, whereas, according to the *Woman's Journal*, all the "American" members were consulted directly afterward.

Against a "union" formed by means of such unjust and undemocratic methods, and by means of such a false representation, we earnestly protest.

HARRIETTE R. SHATTUCK,
Vice-President for Massachusetts.

HARRIET B. ROBINSON,
member of the Executive Committee
for Massachusetts.[65]

VII.

THE 1890s:
Suffrage Victories and Moral Decay

Women suffrage victories accompanied the merger of the National and American Woman Suffrage societies. However, the new organization, the National American Woman Suffrage Association (NAWSA), increasingly defined itself as religiously conservative and racist as it moved through the decade. African American women organized separately, and concerns about working women and body rights found voice outside the NAWSA.

The new NAWSA scored victories on the national and state fronts during the decade. Women won the right to vote in the first four states to endorse woman suffrage. Wyoming, which had adopted woman suffrage as a territory in 1869 once again made history in 1890 when it entered the Union as the first state in which women had full voting rights. The middle and western states gained three more victories during the decade. Colorado endorsed women voting in 1893 and Idaho three years later in 1896. Utah Territory, where women gained the vote in 1870, then lost it in 1887, regained it again when Utah came into the Union as a state in 1896. While these victories came three years apart, there would be no more state victories for fourteen years.

There were also losses. Despite raising $5,000 (about $96,150 in today's purchasing power), most of which was used for canvassing and providing national speakers in South Dakota, the 1890 suffrage campaign there lost. The New York

State Constitutional Convention received six hundred thousand signatures in 1894 asking that voters be allowed to consider a woman suffrage amendment, but it, too, failed.[1]

The NAWSA scored two major victories at the national level with the momentum the NWSA had gained over the years. A House Judiciary Committee heard testimony for the first time in 1892 and the Senate Committee on Woman Suffrage issued a favorable report.[2] Continual pressure could now show real progress.

Forces in the organization, however, wanted to bring the NAWSA to the states' rights focus of the old AWSA. This signaled the shift in focus the NAWSA would take. While the congressional hearings would continue, the NAWSA would not provide adequate funds, petitions, and focus to keep the momentum going at the federal level. Also, the suffragists' testimony increasingly lost its edge, and by 1898 the yearly hearings had become exercises in respectability, according to the *Washington Star* report of the hearing before the House Judiciary Committee:

> The members paid a tribute to the devotion of the woman suffragists, and at the same time showed appreciation of it by nearly all being in attendance at the hearing this morning. It is seldom that more than a quorum of any committee can be induced to attend a hearing of any sort. To-day fifteen out of seventeen members were present and manifested a deep interest in the remarks submitted by the women. The character of the assemblage was one to inspire respect, and the force and intelligence of what was said warranted the attention and interest shown. The people who not many years ago thought that every woman suffragist was a masculine creature who "wanted to wear the pants" would have been greatly embarrassed in their theories had they been present at the hearing to-day. There was not a mannish-appearing woman among the number. It was such an assemblage as may be seen at a popular church on Sunday, or at a fashionable afternoon reception. In fact there was not anywhere such an affectation of masculinity as is common among

the society women of the period. Each year there have appeared more young women at these hearings, and the average of youth seemed greater to-day than ever before. Fashionably attired and in good taste, representative of the highest grade of American womanhood, the fifty or sixty women present inspired respect for their opinions without destroying the sentiment of gallantry which men generally feel that they must extend towards women.[3]

Money poured in as the movement became more respectable. Louisa Southworth of Cleveland gave $1,000 ($20,400 today) to Anthony to open headquarters in Philadelphia in 1895. Total receipts for the year were $9,835 ($233,000 today), with a balance of several hundred dollars in the treasury.[4]

The AWSA position that states had the authority to decide who could vote appealed to white southerners who deeply resented the federal government's taking that authority and granting black men the vote with the Fifteenth Amendment to the Constitution.

Henry Blackwell, who more than twenty years before had courted southern men with the promise that woman suffrage would maintain white supremacy, now dusted off his old argument and published it in 1890 under the auspices of the NAWSA. Since white women outnumbered black men and women combined, the "Solution of the Southern Question" Blackwell proposed was educated suffrage for women, which would result in a clear white voting majority.[5]

"The distrust of the illiterate negro vote which is felt in the Southern States," and the resulting necessity to modify the Fifteenth Amendment, Blackwell wrote, "constitute the most perplexing problem in American politics," arousing prejudice and generating hate. "How can the negro vote be freely cast and fairly counted without endangering social order and political stability?" he asked, answering, "In only one way." "The illiterate, irresponsible voters, who now too often constitute a legal majority, must be controlled by the honest ballots of the civilized, responsible members of the community." That is, "by adding the votes of educated women." In Massachusetts, he goes on, "no man can vote unless he can read and write." So Massachusetts women are "demanding the ballot only for women who can read and write." Why not ask for it the same in all states to counter the illiterate "people of foreign birth" and "people of African race" along with the illiterate whites, since there are "more educated women than all the illiterate voters, white and black, native and foreign," in all but one state. Educated woman suffrage would, by the way, also create a "white voting majority" of 3,751,773. Educated female suffrage would maintain white supremacy in the South.[6]

The 1893 NAWSA endorsed Blackwell's strategy, passing the following resolution unanimously:

> That without expressing any opinion on the proper qualifications for voting, we call attention to the significant facts that in every State there are more women who can read and write than the whole number of illiterate male voters; more white women who can read and write than all negro voters; more American women who can read and write than all foreign voters; so that the enfranchisement of such women would settle the vexed question of rule by illiteracy, whether of home-grown or foreign-born production.[7]

The 1894 NAWSA convention delegates debated whether to even work for the suffrage amendment. Some held with Sallie Clay Bennett (Kentucky) "that instead of asking for an amendment to confer suffrage, we should demand protection in the right already guaranteed by the U. S. Constitution." Blackwell made his position clear. "I do not believe in Federal Suffrage. I agree with the State's Rights party in their views," he stated. Anthony closed the debate agreeing that the "spirit of the Constitution guarantees full equality of rights" and their protection but "until we can get a broader Supreme Court—which will not be until after the women of every State in the Union are enfranchised—we never will get the needed liberal interpretation of that document." The majority concurred in this view.[8]

The NAWSA in 1892 had voted to carry its state suffrage campaign into the South, and in 1895 it moved its annual convention out of Washington, D.C., for the first time, holding it in the South. When the NAWSA made this decision to meet in Atlanta, Georgia, the members knew the southern states were taking the vote away from African American men, enforcing segregation through Jim Crow laws, and murdering African American men, often by publicly lynching them. Anthony, who had taken over as NAWSA president when Stanton stepped down in 1892, asked Frederick Douglass, who was an honored regular attendee at the D.C. conventions, not to attend.[9] Douglass would have been appalled to hear Henry Blackwell urge the South to adopt woman suffrage as a solution of the "negro problem," echoing his argument in a widely published *Woman Suffrage Leaflet*, "A Solution of the Southern Question": "Ability to read and write is absolutely necessary as a means of obtaining accurate political information," Blackwell contended. Without literacy, he continued, one is almost certain to become a tool of "political demagogues, much like a "trained monkey," who goes through the motion of dropping a paper into a box. We have "two great bodies of illiterate citizens," he continued: immigrants in the north and African Americans and a number of uneducated whites in the South. "Against foreigners and negroes, as such, we would not discriminate," Blackwell assured.[10]

This was a direct play to southern racism during a critical time historically. The most blatant legal means southern legislatures were using to keep African American men from voting was the Grandfather Clause. This required the very educational qualification Blackwell was condoning, with one exception. Literacy tests were required, not for all voters, but only for those whose ancestors had not been legally allowed to vote before 1866, which, of course, applied only to black men, allowing illiterate white men to vote. Enacted by Mississippi in 1890, Grandfather Clauses quickly spread throughout the South. These laws remained until the Supreme Court finally struck them down in 1915. Combining the Grandfather Clauses with educated female suffrage was clearly a winning strategy for maintaining white power in the South, and one the NAWSA, through its silence on the former and its endorsement of the latter, had adopted.

The suffragists were well aware of the clauses, as well as the violence against African American men. Frances Ellen Watkins Harper, an African American organizer, poet, and lecturer, spoke about it at the 1891 National Council of Women, where she said in part:

> Our first claim upon the nation and government is the claim for protection to human life. That claim should lie at the basis of our civilization, not simply in theory but in fact. Outside of America, I know of no other civilized country, Catholic, Protestant, or even Mahometan, where men are still lynched, murdered, and even burned for real or supposed crimes. . . . A government which has power to tax a man in peace, and draft him in war, should have power to defend his life in the hour of peril. A government which can protect and defend its citizens from wrong and outrage and does not is vicious. . . . The strongest nation on earth cannot afford to deal unjustly towards its weakest and feeblest members. . . . Whether it was wise or unwise, the government has exchanged the fetters on his wrist for the ballot in his right hand, and men cannot vitiate his vote by fraud, or intimidate the voter by violence, without being untrue to the genius and spirit of our government, and bringing demoralization into their own political life and ranks. . . .
>
> It is said the negro is ignorant. But why is he ignorant? It comes with ill grace from a man who has put out my eyes to make a parade of my blindness,—to reproach me for my poverty when he has wronged me of my money. If the negro is ignorant, he has lived under the shadow of an institution which, at least in part of the country, made it a crime to teach him to read the name of the ever-blessed Christ. If he is poor, what has become of the money he has been earning for the last two hundred and fifty years? . . .
>
> Instead of taking the ballot from his hands teach him how to use it, and to add his quota to the progress, strength, and durability of the nation.[11]

In 1895 the NAWSA decided to permit state organizations to exclude black women if they chose, practicing the "states' rights" segregation that was also the policy of the Woman's Christian Temperance Union.[12]

The NAWSA leadership played on the resentment some white women felt when men of color received rights before they did. The 1890 South Dakota suffrage referendum had voters deciding on both votes for women and votes for Native American men. The Reverend Anna Howard Shaw, who would later become president of the NAWSA from 1904 to 1908 and again from 1909 to 1915, titled her 1891 convention speech reviewing the South Dakota campaign, "Women vs. Indians," described in the fourth volume of *History of Woman Suffrage*:

> In an address brimming and bubbling over with wit, satire and pathos, she showed how much greater consideration the Indians received from the men of that State than did women. She told how 45 per cent of the votes cast the preceding year were for male Indian suffrage and only 37 per cent for woman suffrage; how Indians in blankets and moccasins were received in the State convention with the greatest courtesy, and Susan B. Anthony and other eminent women were barely tolerated; how, while these Indians were engaged in their ghost dances, the white women were going up and down the State pleading for the rights of citizens; how the law in that State gives not only the property but the children to the husband, in the face of all the hardships endured by those pioneer wives and mothers. She suggested that the solution of the Indian question should be left to a commission of women with Alice Fletcher at its head, and said in closing: "Let all of us who love liberty solve these problems in justice; and let us mete out to the Indian, to the negro, to the foreigner, and to the woman, the justice which we demand for ourselves, the liberty which we love for ourselves. Let us recognize in each of them that One above, the Father of us all, and that all are brothers, all are one."[13]

Carrie Chapman Catt, who would follow Anthony as NAWSA president, serving from 1900 to 1904 and from 1915 to 1920, again brought up the South Dakota campaign in an 1893 convention speech, decrying the injustice of Lakota (Sioux) men exempted from taxation and allowed to vote, while the "law-abiding, intelligent women" of South Dakota were compelled to pay taxes and not allowed to vote.[14]

Ironically, after granting voting rights to Lakota (Sioux) men in November 1890, a month later more than two hundred unarmed Lakota, most of them women and children, were murdered by the U.S. Army in the Wounded Knee massacre. Clara Colby's husband, Leonard, head of the nearby Nebraska National Guard, was brought in to lead the clean-up of the frozen Lakota bodies from the scene of the massacre. Finding a baby whose mother he believed had been killed, he brought the child home for his wife to raise. Colby took Zintkala Nuni with her when she traveled to suffrage events, until instructed not to by Anthony, who wrote:

> As to your proposition to take the Indian baby to meetings with you—I say "No" most emphatically—for you to do so would be an imposition upon every household in which you should be entertained—and upon every audience as well—and beside that nuisance—you would distract the [thought] from the <u>one point</u> of woman's enfranchisement—to turn to adoption of Indian babies— the amalgamation of the races and all sorts of side thoughts—
>
> No, no—if you go anywhere in Kansas or New York—for the purpose of helping our work along—go by yourself—without adopted boy or girls! And if they were your own—or if it were Mrs. Foster Avery and her own baby or babies—I would say the same.
>
> Your newspaper baby is the only one that the friends could possibly welcome as your companion—in the homes and in the meetings—
>
> But—my dear—it is a crazy thought—even—and would be a crime if carried out—you had vastly better not go into either state campaign than to exhibit that untutored Indian girl of yours—so don't think of it—.[15]

Lottie Wilson Jackson, a delegate from Michigan described by Anthony and Harper as "so light-complexioned as hardly to suggest a tincture of African blood," introduced a resolution in the 1899 NAWSA convention that "colored women ought not be compelled to ride in smoking cars, and that suitable accommodations should be provided for them." The motion to adopt the resolution was tabled after a lively discussion, "as being outside the province of the convention."[16]

James Jacks, the president of the Missouri Press Association, sent out an article describing African American women as thieves and prostitutes. It may have been the straw that broke the camel's back, leading to an organization dedicated to "[l]ifting as we climb," to demonstrate to "an ignorant and suspicious world that our aims and interests are identical with those of all good aspiring women." The National Association of Colored Women would work against lynching, Jim Crow laws, and segregated transportation. Education, child care, job training, and pay equity were on the to-do list. Excluded from some segregated NAWSA state organizations, they would also work for women's suffrage. The organization described its own history:

In 1895 an obscure man in an obscure Missouri town sent a letter broad-cast over this country and England, reflecting upon the character and morals of our Women. So utterly false were the vile statement, that the women were aroused as never before and when Mrs. Josephine St. Pierre Ruffin, President of the New Era Club of Boston, called a meeting of protest in July 1895, the indignant women from North, South, East and West flocked to the "Classic Hub", and in no uncertain terms vindicated the honor of the Race. The National Federation of Colored Women's Club was the result of that meeting, with Mrs. Booker T. Washington at its head. However, another National organization, the Women's Loyal Union, with Mrs. Cooke (née Helen Appo Cook) as President existed at Washington and the women soon realized that two organizations so identically similar could not work harmoniously as separate units. Therefore, the two organizations met in July 1896, and each appointed a committee to arrange for a consolidation, which was effected and the National Association of C.W.C. came into existence with Mrs.

Mary Church Terrell, of international fame, as President. This joint session was attended by some of the most notable women of our Race, among whom were Harriet Tubman, Francis E.W. Harper, poet and writer, Victoria E. Matthews, founder of the White Rose Mission of New York, Josephine S. Yates, teacher and writer, and others. Mrs. Ida B. Wells Barnett and Elizabeth Lindsay Davis were the delegates from Illinois."[17]

Sunday should be a day of rest, just as God rested on the seventh day after creating the earth, religious conservatives believed. Beyond practicing this themselves, these evangelical Christians wanted laws forbidding any business or activity on Sunday. By 1892 their drive focused on the upcoming World's Fair in Chicago. Besides the serious threat of religion intruding into government posed by this Sunday closure, many workers, who had only Sunday off, would be denied the opportunity to attend the fair. NAWSA president Stanton introduced a resolution supporting the World's Fair staying open on Sunday. While a majority favored the measure, many were religiously opposed to any Sunday activity, and others believed the organization shouldn't address the issue. In the midst of the controversy, Stanton withdrew the resolution, saying she'd proposed it "largely for the sake of discussion." Anna Howard Shaw promptly presented a resolution opposing the sale of liquor on the fair grounds, which she did "as a matter of conscience and in order that it might go on record."[18]

This was the last convention Stanton or Lucy Stone attended. Stone died in the following year, 1893. Stanton remained as honorary president of the NAWSA, while Anthony took over the presidency. The following year, the 1893 NAWSA convention adopted all the resolutions presented without dissent, except the last. They refused to endorse this one:

Whereas, The Constitution of the United States promises noninterference with the religious liberty of the people; and

Whereas, Congress is now threatening to abridge the liberties of all in response to ecclesiastical dictation from a portion of the people; therefore,

Resolved, That this association enters a protest against any national attempt to control the innocent inclinations of the people either on the Jewish Sabbath or the Christian Sunday, and this we do quite irrespective of our individual opinions as to the sanctity of Sunday.

Resolved, That we especially protest against this present attempt to force all the people to follow the religious dictates of a part of the people, as establishing a precedent for the entrance of a most dangerous complicity between Church and State, thereby subtly undermining the foundation of liberty, so carefully laid by the wisdom of our fathers.[19]

In the midst of this religious backsliding by the NAWSA, The National Council of Women hosted a monumental celebration of Stanton's eightieth birthday at the Metropolitan Opera House in New York City on November 12, 1895. Seated on the platform like Queen Victoria, surrounded by garlands of flowers, Stanton listened as tributes poured forth from speakers, songs, and letters from around the world. She rose to speak and began by lauding all the changes in women's lives won by the movement. Having warmed up the audience she then, in her typical style, pushed the envelope. "We who have made our demands on the State have nearly finished this battle," she asserted. "The principle" of woman suffrage "is practically conceded." And then she dropped the bombshell. Her full speech is included in this chapter.

During her eightieth birthday year, Stanton also published *The Woman's Bible*, a collection of thoughtful essays by Stanton and a Revising Committee of seven women examining the Bible's passages that either ignored or injured women.

Carrie Chapman Catt, Reverend Anna Howard Shaw, and the conservative women who increasingly came to control the NAWSA were furious at Stanton for alienating orthodox Christian women. While Stanton had issued *The Woman's Bible* in her private capacity and the NAWSA had not hosted her controversial birthday speech, she was still associated with the organization as its honorary president. Two months later, Rachel Foster Avery submitted her recording secretary's report to the NAWSA annual convention, stating that the "work of our Association" has been "much hindered" and "damaged" by "a volume with a pretentious title, covering a jumble of comment . . . without either scholarship or literary value, set forth in a spirit which is neither that of reverence or inquiry."[20] Avery called for a resolution denouncing Stanton's work.

A lengthy and volatile debate ensued, following the old AWSA–NWSA lines of division over religion, with Henry Blackwell and Alice Stone Blackwell, joined by Reverend Anna Howard Shaw and Carrie Chapman Catt among those supporting the resolution while Clara Colby, Lillie Devereux Blake, and others opposed it. After much internal wrangling, a watered-down committee resolution was brought to the convention floor declaring:

> This association is non-sectarian, being composed of persons of all shades of religious opinion, and has no official connection with the so-called "Woman's Bible" or any theological publication.[21]

Angered at this slap in the face of her old friend, Anthony stepped down temporarily as president chairing the convention to give an impassioned speech about keeping the organization open to all views on religion. The speech is included in this chapter.

Despite Anthony's appeal, the resolution censuring *The Woman's Bible* was adopted, with 53 yeas, 41 nays.[22]

An outraged and hurt Stanton asked Anthony to resign from the NAWSA; Anthony considered it, but ultimately refused. While this caused a further rift in their friendship, Stanton didn't back down.

Three years later, in 1898, she pushed forward with a second volume of *The Woman's Bible*. Her introduction documented Christianity's primary role in the oppression of women and is included in this chapter.

While the religious conservatives were rising in power in the NAWSA, religious forces in the country were strengthening their attack on women's reproductive choices. Stanton and Gage both signed a petition against the infamous Comstock laws, under which women and men were being arrested and imprisoned for issuing publications educating about sexuality and birth control. There were two freedoms under attack: freedom of the press and reproductive freedom. The petition read:

> We Append Our Names to This Paper for the Purpose of Protesting—
>
> Against any and all laws violating and invading the constitutional pledges which guarantee to American citizens the rights of Free Speech and Free Press.
>
> Against the enforcement of laws by the instrumentality of private amateur detective associations.
>
> Against the establishment of a censorship of the press and of the mails as is now attempted in the Post Office Department.
>
> And having seen that such laws, and prevailing methods of enforcing them, open great opportunities for fraudulent practices, for the accomplishment of private revenges, and for the suppression of unpopular sentiments by fanatical persecutions, we hereby pledge ourselves to do all that good citizens may properly do to overcome these mischiefs and to reverse the current of this class of legislative and official aggression.[23]

Gage published her major work in 1893, and immediately raised the attention of Comstock. *Woman, Church and State*, a thoroughly documented treatise on Christianity's essential role in causing and maintaining women's oppression, also condemned the absence of legal consequences for the age-old practice of sexual abuse by priests and for sex traffickers operating in the United States. When she gave a copy to her local school library, Anthony Comstock threatened to arrest the school board members if they placed the book on the shelves. "The incidents of victims of lust told in this book are such," Comstock threatened, "that if I found a person putting that book indiscriminately before the children I would institute a criminal proceeding against them for doing it."[24] Asked by a reporter for her opinion of Comstock, Gage answered:

I look upon him as a man who is mentally and morally unbalanced, not knowing right from wrong or the facts of history from 'tales of lust.' Being intellectually weak, Anthony Comstock misrepresents all works upon which he presumes to pass judgment, and is as dangerous to liberty of speech and of the press as were the old inquisitors, whom he somewhat resembles. A fool as a press censor is more to be feared than a knave, and Comstock seems to be a union of both fool and knave. Buddha declared the only sin to be ignorance. If this be true, Anthony Comstock is a great sinner.[25]

Lois Waisbrooker, a Freethought colleague of Stanton and Gage, served as guest editor of *Lucifer, the Light-Bearer*, a Freethought, body-right newspaper, while its sixty-two-year-old editor, Moses Harman, spent time in jail on obscenity charges under the Comstock laws. Waisbrooker published an excerpt about male horse genitals from a Department of Agriculture report, showing the contradiction of the Comstock law in outlawing description of human anatomy. Comstock banned the issue from the mails. And then, in 1894, he arrested the seventy-year-old woman for obscenity.[26] Gage came to her defense:

> Well, what has struck Mrs. Waisbrooker? Had not heard of it. Does the "church" or the "state" expect to gag the universe? I intend to live a good while yet to help put the vile tyrant down. Give us *free* thought, *free* speech, a *free* pen, a *free* people.[27]

While Alice Stone Blackwell, the daughter of Lucy Stone and Henry Blackwell, could not support the progressive ideas of the *Lucifer*, freedom of the press was an issue that even a conservative suffragist could support when it came close to her own newspaper, the *Woman's Journal*. Stone Blackwell editorialized on the subject in an article that is included in this chapter.

Mary L. Doe brought greetings from the American Federation of Labor to the 1899 NAWSA convention, encouraging the suffrage organization to work with the labor movement, since "[w]oman suffrage would find its most hopeful and fertile field among the labor organizations," and "the workingmen stood for weak and defenseless women even before they did for their own rights."[28]

The NAWSA took no further steps toward aligning the suffrage cause with organized labor, but simply passed the following resolution:

> We appreciate the friendly attitude of the American Federation of Labor, the National Grange and other public bodies of voters, as shown by their resolutions indorsing the legal, political and economic equality of women.[29]

As Stanton moved further away from the issue of suffrage and toward the underlying causes of woman's oppression, she also became committed to economic justice. On the fiftieth anniversary of the 1848 woman's rights convention, Stanton penned a challenge to suffragists. Look beyond the vote, or any other single issue, she encouraged, and envision the creation of an economy based on cooperation, not competition. Her motto toward the end of her life became, "The few have no right to the luxuries of life while the many are denied the necessities," taken from her letter to the 1898 NAWSA convention, "The Co-Operative Ideal will Remodel Codes and Constitutions," included in this chapter.

1.
"Woman's Imperative Duty," an address by
Elizabeth Cady Stanton upon her eightieth birthday,
November 12, 1895

It is a long time, near half a century, since a few persons met in 1848, in a little Methodist church in Seneca Falls, to discuss the status of women under the laws of New York.

That was the first woman's rights convention ever held in the world. . . . A declaration was read and signed by most of those present, and a series of radical resolutions adopted. But the majority of women ridiculed the idea of political rights for themselves, the press caricatured the convention, the pulpit denounced it, and some who took part withdrew their names, and appeared no more on our platform. But above this wave of petty clamor, that rolled from Maine to Louisiana, arose the clarion voice of Phillips: "This is the inauguration of the most momentous reform yet launched upon the world, the first organized protest against the injustice that has brooded for ages over the character and destiny of one-half the human race."

Within two years conventions were held in half a dozen different States, letters of sympathy came from women in this country, from Italy, France and Germany, all taking an active part in the revolutions of 1848. Just at that time, too, the earthquakes began in California, showing that old mother earth sympathized in the general upheaval, in the rebellion of her daughters against the creeds and codes and customs of effete civilizations. And the invisibles began at that time to knock and move tables, gradually awakening a deep interest in psychological manifestations. But I will not use any of my allotted time in dwelling on the past and noting the steps of progress, except to say that James Mott, a dignified Quaker, presided over the first convention, and his noble wife Lucretia, and her sister Martha Wright, and Frederick Douglass were the leading speakers.

Paulina Wright Davis called the first convention in old Massachusetts, and Lucy Stone kept the watchfires of liberty burning there until the day of her death. She was the first woman in the nation to protest against the marriage laws at the altar, and to manifest sufficient self-respect to keep her own name, to represent her individual existence through life.

Frances D. Gage responded to the call for Ohio, Mary F. Thomas for Indiana, Lucinda Stone for Michigan, Mary Grew for Pennsylvania, Elizabeth B. Chace for Rhode Island, Ernestine L. Rose, a beautiful Polish lady, and Antoinette Brown, made their appeals in most of the States and before several legislative assemblies. Matilda Joslyn Gage and Susan B. Anthony made their debut on our platform in 1852. Later came Mary A. Livermore, Isabella Beecher Hooker and Julia Ward Howe, Rev. Phebe Hannaford, Rev. Olympia Brown and others, who all did good service. Those who follow will pay fitting tributes to all these noble women.

I have just two thoughts I wish to emphasize:

1. Woman's sphere. That ground has been traveled over so often that there is not a single tree nor flower nor blade of grass to be found anywhere. Yet excursions of men are continually going to survey that old worn-out land. Ever since Eve left Paradise, the trend of thought has been in the direction of woman's sphere. Those who could write in prose or verse have written about it; those who could orate have talked about it. Statesmen have declared its limits in laws and constitutions; bishops in Scriptures and sermons; editors in journals, and scientists in osseous formations, muscles, nerves, and the size and quality of the feminine brain. They have all sung in chorus the same old song, and will continue, like Poe's raven, to sing it "evermore," unless some one shall arise to solve this tangled problem.

Fortunately, to remove this subject from human thought and give place to more profitable discussions, I arose on the 12th of November, in the year of our Lord 1815, and have spent a great part of my life in elucidating this question. I propose now to give you the result of my explorations.

Those who are capable of drawing logical conclusions from facts, will leave this house to-night with their minds forever at rest as to the limits of woman's sphere. While Franklin, Kane, Greeley and Peary have been sailing 'mid the Polar ices to find the North Pole, I have been traveling in the realm of the possibilities to find woman's sphere and the voting poll. Spyglass in hand, I crossed the imaginary lines of diameter and circumference bounding its limits; I took reckonings at every degree of latitude and longitude; in the temperate, frigid and torrid, Arctic and Antarctic zones. In halting one day, I found an old document, said to have been written at the dawn of creation, when the Gods were in consultation about the creation of man. They said:

"Let us make man in our own image, male and female, and give them dominion over the whole earth and every living thing therein."

They did so. Here we have the first title deed to this green earth, given alike to man and woman, and the first hint of "God's intentions." Those who will make some logical concessions must admit that wherever woman has been and maintained a foothold, and whatever she has done and done well, it must have been the "Creator's intentions" that she should occupy that position and do that special work. Unless you admit this, you impeach the wisdom of the Creator and exalt the woman as able to set at defiance the laws of her being. While everything in the universe moves according to immutable law, the sun, the moon, the stars and every planet revolving in its own elliptic, the fish of the sea, the birds of the air, all in their appointed places, moving in harmony together, how can woman get out of her sphere? The moment you declare she is, you make her all powerful, greater than her Maker. To do this she must defy the laws of attraction, cohesion and gravitation, the centripetal and centrifugal forces, the positive and negative electricity, to be scattered into space herself, and be seen no more forever.

Instead of this fatal escapade, lo! She is here; tied to the plane just as man is, and compelled to follow in his footsteps. He is happy and contented, and always stays in his sphere, and nobody writes nor talks about it. He has gone everywhere, and done everything his genius made possible. Diving to ocean depths, he gives us pictures of coral caves and the monsters of the sea; sailing with his balloon in the blue ether, he tells us of the wonders above the clouds. With his railroads he has linked together the Rocky and Alleghany mountains, the Atlantic and Pacific, and with his ocean cable he has anchored continents side by side and welded the nations of the earth in one. The seven wonders of the world are so many tributes to his genius; the magnificent cathedrals, the museums, the libraries, the art galleries—all proclaim his divine origin, his creative power.

He has labored by turns in every department of science and industry, and has gathered knowledge and riches from every quarter of the globe. He has filled all stations, high and low, governed nations, led armies, and by his marvelous inventions has shifted the heavy burdens of labor from human shoulders to tireless machines. Every day he has some new surprise in store for us, and new promises of the future, when we are to make the journey of life by electricity, when all our present modes of locomotion, even the bicycle, will be thrown into the shade. He will thus make life like a sweet dream, the realization of a fairy land.

Thus we see that women need no longer knit or weave, make butter or cheese. Cunning arms and fingers of steel now do it all. Women need no longer cook or wash or iron, or bake or brew; for men do it all in restaurants, laundries, bakeries and breweries. Women need no longer sew, for with cunning machines men now make underclothes for women and children, and even the man-milliner bonnets and the tailor-made dresses are superior to what women themselves can produce.

And man is not only making our earthly dwelling all that we could desire, but he is giving us new and delightful anticipations of the life to come. Learned revising committees have cast serious doubts on the Inferno and the Prince of Darkness. They have even, in the last version of the New Testament, eliminated the words "hell" and "everlasting punishment," a most praiseworthy concession to the emotional nature of women and children. They have even added some new touches of gladness and hospitality to our heavenly home. Instead of a fuming Judge, driving three-fourths of the human race like goats into outer darkness and despair, we have pictures of a loving Father who welcomes us to his presence; instead of a bigoted Peter at the gate questioning our entrance there, smiling angels open wide the portals, and all shades and colors of humanity walk in together—Jew and Gentile, bond and free, white and black, rich and poor, male and female, without regard to color, sex or previous condition of servitude.

This is the beautiful vision liberal Doctors of Divinity and Spiritualists give us of the future. Milton and Dante, they say, threw their doleful poems into the Jordan as they passed over; and Swedenborg, on the shore, got out an expurgated edition of his melancholy prose writings. Now, I suppose, carping women all over the house are saying to their neighbors, "Where do we come in? If man is such a wonderful being, and fills all space, where is our sphere?" Why, it is plain to every rational mind that if man is everywhere and woman of necessity must remain on the planet, then their sphere is the same. They are and ever must be indissolubly bound together, as mother, father, husband, wife, brother, sister, in childhood, in marriage, in all life's struggles, ever sharing each other's joys and sorrows. With tears of affection and immortal wreaths they perform the last sad offices of love and friendship for each other, and in the bosom of mother earth, side by side, they rest at last together.

Yes, the spheres of man and woman are the same, with different duties according to the capacity of the individual. Woman, like all created things, lives, moves and has her being obedient to law, exploring with man the mysteries of the universe and speculating on the glories of the hereafter. In the words of Tennyson, they must be together:

> "Everywhere
> Two heads in council, two besides the
>   hearth,
> Two in the tangled business of the world,
> Two in the liberal offices of life,
> Two plummets dropped for one to sound
>   the abyss
> Of science, and the secrets of the mind."[30]

The question is no longer the sphere of a whole sex, but of each individual. Women are now in the trades and professions, everywhere in the world of work. They have shown their capacity as students in the sciences, their skill as mariners before the mast, their courage as rescuers in life boats. They are close on the heels of man in the arts, sciences, and literature; in their knowledge and understanding of the vital questions of the hour, and in the every-day, practical duties of life. Like man, woman's sphere is in the whole universe of matter and mind, to do whatever she can, and thus prove "the intentions of the Creator."

2. The other thought I would emphasize is the next step in progress we should take in our march to complete emancipation. We who have made our demands on the State have nearly finished this battle. The principle is practically conceded.

We now have full suffrage in Colorado, Wyoming and Utah; municipal suffrage in the great State of Kansas, and school suffrage in half the States of the Union. They have had municipal suffrage in Great Britain and her colonies for over twenty years, and some form of suffrage, on a property qualification, either in person or by proxy, in several European countries. Most of those who fought this battle have passed to another sphere of action, and our younger coadjutors will ere long, like Miriam of old, with tumbrels and dances and songs of victory, lead the hosts of women into the promised land of freedom. As learned bishops and editors of religious newspapers are warning us against further demands for new liberties, and clergymen are still preaching sermons on the "rib origin," and refuse to receive women as delegates to their synods, it is evident that our demands for equal recognition should now be made of the Church for the same rights we have asked of the State for the last fifty years, for the same rights, privileges and immunities that men enjoy. We must demand that the canon law, the Mosaic code, the Scriptures, prayer books and liturgies be purged of all invidious distinctions of sex, of all false teaching as to woman's origin, character and destiny.

To make her the author of sin, cursed in her maternity, a subordinate in marriage, an afterthought in the creation, and all by the command of God, was so to overweight her in the scale of being that centuries of civilization have not as yet been able to lift the burden. Charles Kingsley said long ago, "This will never be a good world for women until the last remnant of the canon law is swept from the face of the earth," and Lord Brougham echoed back the same sentiment as to the civil law for women. "It is," said he, "a disgrace to the Christianity and civilization of the nineteenth century." Here is the opinion of two distinguished men as to woman's degraded position under the canon and civil law in Church and State. Can it be that what such men see and denounce women themselves do not feel and repudiate?

We must demand an equal place in the offices of the Church, as pastors, elders, deacons; an equal voice in the creeds, discipline, and all business matters, in synods, conferences and general assemblies.

Women of wealth are all the time giving large sums of money to build and maintain churches; they fill the pews each returning Sunday; they swell the numbers of the devotees; they supply the enthusiasm for revival seasons, and worship the priesthood. They are ever loyal to the sons of Aaron, the house of Levi, the very powers that through the centuries have done more to block their way to freedom than all other influences put together. It is the perversion of the religious element in woman that has held her for ages the patient victim under the care of Juggernaut, on the funeral pyre, in iron shoes, in the Turkish harem, in the Catholic nunnery, and in the Protestant world beggars ever for fairs, donation parties, church decorations, embroideries of altar cloths, surplices and slippers. In return for this devotion they are entertained with sermons from the texts: "I suffer not a woman to speak in the churches";[31] "As Christ is the head of the Church, so is man the head of the woman."[32]

Women must demand that all unworthy reflections on the dignity and sacred office of the mother of the race be expunged from religious literature, such as the allegory as to the creation of woman, and Paul's assumptions as to her social status. These ideas conflict with the Golden Rule and the fifth commandment: "Honor thy mother," and should no longer be rehearsed in the pulpit. Such sentiments cannot inspire the rising generation with respect for their mothers.

We must demand that the pulpit be no longer desecrated by men who read passages of Scripture or preach from texts that teach the subordination of one-half the human race to the other.

What sight could be more inexpressibly sad and comic than a young man fresh from Princeton, preaching his first sermon to a congregation of educated middle-aged women from the text: "Wives, obey your husbands";[33] "If you would know anything, ask your husbands at home."[34] In view of the character and higher education of the women of the present day, the time has fully come for the Church to take an advance step on this question.

Jewish women should demand an expurgated edition of their liturgy. It must be very humiliating to them to have every man stand up in the Synagogue each returning Sabbath day, and say: "I thank thee, O Lord, that I was not born a woman."[35]

Nothing that has ever emanated from the brain of man is too sacred to be revised and corrected. Our National Constitution has been amended fifteen times, our English system of jurisprudence has been essentially modified in the interest of woman, to keep pace with advancing civilization. And now the time has come to amend and modify the canon laws, prayerbooks, liturgies and Bibles. Gladstone said the American Constitution, considering the circumstances under which it was written, is the most wonderful document that ever emanated from the brain of man. Yet from time to time, with the growth of the people, amendments were demanded. So with our statute laws. Why should we hold the Mosaic code and church decretals more sacred than the Saxon civil code and the legal opinions of Blackstone, Story and Kent? The trouble in both cases is that the laws and customs in Church and State alike are behind the public sentiment of our day and generation.

Woman's imperative duty at this hour is to demand a thorough revision of creeds and codes, Scriptures and constitutions. Petitions for a sixteenth amendment to the National Constitution for the enfranchisement of women have been annually presented to Congress for the last quarter of a century. Similar petitions for equal recognition in the Church should now every year press into the synods, conferences and general assemblies.

Twenty-five years ago a church in Illinois was rent in twain because some women persisted in praying in the weekly meetings. Ten years ago the Presbyterian General Assembly discussed this question for three days, and finally adopted a resolution leaving the matter to the discretion of the pastor. Now women not only pray in church meetings, but on many public occasions, in missionary and charitable conventions. Fifteen years ago the General Conference of the Methodist Episcopal Church, by a large majority, voted down a resolution to ordain women as missionaries, and four years later they voted down a resolution to ordain women as lay delegates; while thus far this autumn every State conference held has given a majority vote in favor of women as lay delegates. Last May (1895), the Episcopal Church of California passed a resolution that women might vote in vestry meetings, and also be eligible as church officers.

When the Church obeys the command, "Honor thy mother," and the State heeds the declaration, "Equal rights to all"; when the two powers join hands to exalt the mother of the race, who has gone to the very gates of death to give every man life and immortality, then we shall see the dawn of a new day in woman's emancipation. When she awakes to the beauty of science, philosophy, true religion and pure government, then will the first note of harmony be touched; then will the great organ of humanity be played on all its keys, with every stop rightly adjusted, and with louder, loftier strains, the march of civilization will be immeasurably quickened.[36]

2.

Susan B. Anthony's speech during *The Woman's Bible* debate in the National American Woman Suffrage Association 1895 convention

The one distinct feature of our association has been the right of individual opinion for every member. We have been beset at each step with the cry that somebody was injuring the cause by the expression of sentiments which differed from those held by the majority. The religious persecution of the ages has been carried on under what was claimed to be the command of God. I distrust those people who know so well what God wants them to do, because I notice it always coincides with

their own desires. All the way along the history of our movement there has been this same contest on account of religious
theories. Forty years ago one of our noblest men said to me:
"You would better never hold another convention than allow
Ernestine L. Rose on your platform;" because that eloquent
woman, who ever stood for justice and freedom, did not believe in the plenary inspiration of the Bible. Did we banish
Mrs. Rose? No, indeed!

Every new generation of converts threshes over the same old
straw. The point is whether you will sit in judgment on one
who questions the divine inspiration of certain passages in the
Bible derogatory to women. If Mrs. Stanton had written ap-
provingly of these passages you would not have brought in this
resolution for fear the cause might be injured among the *liberals* in religion. In other words, if she had written *your* views,
you would not have considered a resolution necessary. To pass
this one is to set back the hands on the dial of reform.

What you should say to outsiders is that a Christian has neither more nor less rights in our association than an atheist.
When our platform becomes too narrow for people of all
creeds and of no creeds, I myself can not stand upon it. Many
things have been said and done by our *orthodox* friends which
I have felt to be extremely harmful to our cause; but I should
no more consent to a resolution denouncing them than I shall
consent to this. Who is to draw the line? Who can tell now
whether these commentaries may not prove a great help to
woman's emancipation from old superstitions which have
barred its way?

Lucretia Mott at first thought Mrs. Stanton had injured the
cause of all woman's other rights by insisting upon the demand
for suffrage, but she had sense enough not to bring in a resolution against it. In 1860 when Mrs. Stanton made a speech before the New York Legislature in favor of a bill making
drunkenness a ground for divorce, there was a general cry
among the friends that she had killed the woman's cause. I
shall be pained beyond expression if the delegates here are so
narrow and illiberal as to adopt this resolution. You would
better not begin resolving against individual action or you will

find no limit. This year it is Mrs. Stanton; next year it may be I or one of yourselves who will be the victim.

If we do not inspire in women a broad and catholic spirit, they will fail, when enfranchised, to constitute that power for better government which we have always claimed for them. Ten women educated into the practice of liberal principles would be a stronger force than 10,000 organized on a platform of intolerance and bigotry. I pray you vote for religious liberty, without censorship or inquisition. This resolution adopted will be a vote of censure upon a woman who is without a peer in intellectual and statesmanlike ability; one who has stood for half a century the acknowledged leader of progressive thought and demand in regard to all matters pertaining to the absolute freedom of women.[37]

3.
The Woman's Bible Introduction, by Elizabeth Cady Stanton and the Revising Committee, 1898

From the inauguration of the movement for woman's emancipation the Bible has been used to hold her in the "divinely ordained sphere," prescribed in the Old and New Testaments.

The canon and civil law; church and state; priests and legislators; all political parties and religious denominations have alike taught that woman was made after man, of man, and for man, an inferior being, subject to man. Creeds, codes, Scriptures and statutes, are all based on this idea. The fashions, forms, ceremonies and customs of society, church ordinances and discipline all grow out of this idea.

Of the old English common law, responsible for woman's civil and political status, Lord Brougham said, "it is a disgrace to the civilization and Christianity of the Nineteenth Century." Of the canon law, which is responsible for woman's status in the church, Charles Kingsley said, "this will never be a good world for women until the last remnant of the canon law is swept from the face of the earth."

The Bible teaches that woman brought sin and death into

the world, that she precipitated the fall of the race, that she was arraigned before the judgment seat of Heaven, tried, condemned and sentenced. Marriage for her was to be a condition of bondage, maternity a period of suffering and anguish, and in silence and subjection, she was to play the role of a dependent on man's bounty for all her material wants, and for all the information she might desire on the vital questions of the hour, she was commanded to ask her husband at home. Here is the Bible position of woman briefly summed up.

Those who have the divine insight to translate, transpose and transfigure this mournful object of pity into an exalted, dignified personage, worthy our worship as the mother of the race, are to be congratulated as having a share of the occult mystic power of the eastern Mahatmas.

The plain English to the ordinary mind admits of no such liberal interpretation. The unvarnished texts speak for themselves. The canon law, church ordinances and Scriptures, are homogeneous, and all reflect the same spirit and sentiments.

These familiar texts are quoted by clergymen in their pulpits, by statesmen in the halls of legislation, by lawyers in the courts, and are echoed by the press of all civilized nations, and accepted by woman herself as "The Word of God." So perverted is the religious element in her nature, that with faith and works she is the chief support of the church and clergy; the very powers that make her emancipation impossible. When, in the early part of the Nineteenth Century, women began to protest against their civil and political degradation, they were referred to the Bible for an answer. When they protested against their unequal position in the church, they were referred to the Bible for an answer.

This led to a general and critical study of the Scriptures. Some, having made a fetish of these books and believing them to be the veritable "Word of God," with liberal translations, interpretations, allegories and symbols, glossed over the most objectionable features of the various books and clung to them as divinely inspired. Others, seeing the family resemblance between the Mosaic code, the canon law, and the old English common law, came to the conclusion that all alike emanated from the same source; wholly human in their origin and inspired by the natural love of domination in the historians. Others, bewildered with their doubts and fears, came to no conclusion. While their clergymen told them on the one hand, that they owed all the blessings and freedom they enjoyed to the Bible, on the other, they said it clearly marked out their circumscribed sphere of action: that the demands for political and civil rights were irreligious, dangerous to the stability of the home, the state and the church. Clerical appeals were circulated from time to time conjuring members of their churches to take no part in the anti-slavery or woman suffrage movements, as they were infidel in their tendencies, undermining the very foundations of society. No wonder the majority of women stood still, and with bowed heads, accepted the situation.

Listening to the varied opinions of women, I have long thought it would be interesting and profitable to get them clearly stated in book form. To this end six years ago I proposed to a committee of women to issue a Woman's Bible, that we might have women's commentaries on women's position in the Old and New Testaments. It was agreed on by several leading women in England and America and the work was begun, but from various causes it has been delayed, until now the idea is received with renewed enthusiasm, and a large committee has been formed, and we hope to complete the work within a year.

Those who have undertaken the labor are desirous to have some Hebrew and Greek scholars, versed in Biblical criticism, to gild our pages with their learning. Several distinguished women have been urged to do so, but they are afraid that their high reputation and scholarly attainments might be compromised by taking part in an enterprise that for a time may prove very unpopular. Hence we may not be able to get help from that class.

Others fear that they might compromise their evangelical faith by affiliating with those of more liberal views, who do not regard the Bible as the "Word of God," but like any other book, to be judged by its merits. If the Bible teaches the equality of Woman, why does the church refuse to ordain women to preach the gospel, to fill the offices of deacons and elders, and to administer the Sacraments, or to admit them as delegates to the Synods, General Assemblies and Conferences of the different denominations? They have never yet invited a woman to join one of their Revising Committees, nor tried to mitigate the sentence pronounced on her by changing one count in the indictment served on her in Paradise.

The large number of letters received, highly appreciative of the undertaking, is very encouraging to those who have inaugurated the movement, and indicate a growing self-respect and self-assertion in the women of this generation. But we have the usual array of objectors to meet and answer. One correspondent conjures us to suspend the work, as it is "ridiculous" for "women to attempt the revision of the Scriptures." I wonder if any man wrote to the late revising committee of Divines to stop their work on the ground that it was ridiculous for men to revise the Bible. Why is it more ridiculous for women to protest against her present status in the Old and New Testament, in the ordinances and discipline of the church, than in the statutes and constitution of the state? Why is it more ridiculous to arraign ecclesiastics for their false teaching and acts of injustice to women, than members of Congress and the House of Commons? Why is it more audacious to review Moses than Blackstone, the Jewish code of laws, than the English system of jurisprudence? Women have compelled their legislators in every state in this Union to so modify their statutes for women that the old common law is now almost a dead letter. Why not compel Bishops and Revising Committees to modify their creeds and dogmas? Forty years ago it seemed as ridiculous to timid, time-serving and retrograde folk for women to demand an expurgated edition of the laws, as it now does to demand an expurgated edition of the Liturgies and the Scriptures. Come, come, my conservative friend, wipe the dew off your spectacles, and see that the world is moving. Whatever your views may be as to the importance of the proposed work, your political and social degradation are but an outgrowth of your status in the Bible. When you express your aversion, based on a blind feeling of reverence in which reason has no control, to the revision of the Scriptures, you do but echo Cowper, who, when asked to read Paine's "Rights of Man," exclaimed "No man shall convince me that I am improperly governed while I *feel* the contrary."

Others say it is not *politic* to rouse religious opposition. This much-lauded policy is but another word for cowardice. How can woman's position be changed from that of a subordinate to an equal, without opposition, without the broadest discussion of all the questions involved in her present degradation? For so far-reaching and momentous a reform as her complete independence, an entire revolution in all existing institutions is inevitable.

Let us remember that all reforms are interdependent, and that whatever is done to establish one principle on a solid basis, strengthens all. Reformers who are always compromising, have not yet grasped the idea that truth is the only safe ground to stand upon. The object of an individual life is not to carry one fragmentary measure in human progress, but to utter the highest truth clearly seen in all directions, and thus to round out and perfect a well balanced character. Was not the sum of influence exerted by John Stuart Mill on political, religious and social questions far greater than that of any statesman or reformer who has sedulously limited his sympathies and activities to carrying one specific measure? We have many women abundantly endowed with capabilities to understand and revise what men have thus far written. But they are all suffering from inherited ideas of their inferiority; they do not perceive it, yet such is the true explanation of their solicitude, lest they should seem to be too self-asserting.

Again there are some who write us that our work is a useless expenditure of force over a book that has lost its hold on the human mind. Most intelligent women, they say, regard it simply as the history of a rude people in a barbarous age, and have no more reverence for the Scriptures than any other work. So long as tens of thousands of Bibles are printed every year, and circulated over the whole habitable globe, and the masses in all English-speaking nations revere it as the word of God, it is vain to belittle its influence. The sentimental feelings we all have for those things we were educated to believe sacred, do not readily yield to pure reason. I distinctly remember the shudder that passed over me on seeing a mother take our family Bible to make a high seat for her child at table. It seemed such a desecration. I was tempted to protest against its use for such a purpose, and this, too, long after my reason had repudiated its divine authority.

To women still believing in the plenary inspiration of the Scriptures, we say give us by all means your exegesis in the light of the higher criticism learned men are now making, and illumine the Woman's Bible, with your inspiration.

Bible historians claim special inspiration for the Old and New Testaments containing most contradictory records of the same events, of miracles opposed to all known laws, of customs that degrade the female sex of all human and animal life, stated in most questionable language that could not be read in a promiscuous assembly, and call all this "The Word of God."

The only points in which I differ from all ecclesiastical teaching is that I do not believe that any man ever saw or talked with God, I do not believe that God inspired the Mosaic code, or told the historians what they say he did about woman, for all the religions on the face of the earth degrade her, and so long as woman accepts the position that they assign her, her emancipation is impossible. Whatever the Bible may be made to do in Hebrew or Greek, in plain English it does not exalt and dignify woman. My standpoint for criticism is the revised edition of 1888. I will so far honor the revising committee of wise men who have given us the best exegesis they can according to their ability, although Disraeli said the last one before he died, contained 150,000 blunders in the Hebrew, and 7,000 in the Greek.

But the verbal criticism in regard to woman's position amounts to little. The spirit is the same in all periods and languages, hostile to her as an equal.

There are some general principles in the holy books of all religions that teach love, charity, liberty, justice and equality for all the human family, there are many grand and beautiful passages, the golden rule has been echoed and re-echoed around the world. There are lofty examples of good and true men and women, all worthy our acceptance and imitation whose lustre cannot be dimmed by the false sentiments and vicious characters bound up in the same volume. The Bible cannot be accepted or rejected as a whole, its teachings are varied and its lessons differ widely from each other. In criticising the peccadilloes of Sarah, Rebecca and Rachel, we would not shadow the virtues of Deborah, Huldah and Vashti. In criticising the Mosaic code, we would not question the wisdom of the golden rule and the fifth Commandment. Again the church claims special consecration for its cathedrals and priesthood, parts of these aristocratic churches are too holy for women to enter, boys were early introduced into the choirs for this reason, woman singing in an obscure corner closely veiled. A few of the more democratic denominations accord women some privileges, but invidious discriminations of sex are found in all religious organizations, and the most bitter outspoken enemies of woman are found among clergymen and bishops of the Protestant religion.

The canon law, the Scriptures, the creeds and codes and church discipline of the leading religions bear the impress of fallible man, and not of our ideal great first cause, "the Spirit of all Good," that set the universe of matter and mind in motion, and by immutable law holds the land, the sea, the planets, revolving round the great centre of light and heat, each in its own elliptic, with millions of stars in harmony all singing together, the glory of creation forever and ever.[38]

4.

Letter of support for Moses Harman by Alice Stone Blackwell, associate editor of the *Woman's Journal*, 1894

I heartily congratulate Moses Harman upon his release from prison. His sentence to a year in the penitentiary was a gross miscarriage of justice.

My attention was forcibly drawn to the arbitrary way in which the postal officials were dealing with him when an issue of his paper was refused transmission through the mails because it had copied an editorial from the *Woman's Journal*. That editorial was afterwards submitted to Mrs. Julia Ward

Howe, Jane Addams and a number of clergymen, all of whom declared that they could not see the slightest impropriety in it. It did not discuss social questions at all, but was merely a criticism of the methods of the post office. It had been allowed to circulate freely through the mails in the *Woman's Journal*. But as soon as it was copied into *Lucifer* the Chicago postal officials pronounced it indecent and unmailable, and the higher postal authorities at Washington upheld their decision.

Mr. Harman is entitled to the respect of all who esteem unselfishness, sincerity and courage, whether they agree with his opinions or not. In my judgment, some of the doctrines preached in his papers are highly objectionable, but it is a thousand times more objectionable that the right of free discussion should be denied to any doctrines, however erroneous. Yours for a free press.–Alice Stone Blackwell, associate editor of the *Woman's Journal*.[39]

5.
"The Co-Operative Ideal Will Remodel Codes and Constitutions," a letter of Elizabeth Cady Stanton to a Woman Suffrage Convention, 1898

. . . You ask me to send a letter as to woman's position in regard to the war. Many women with whom I talk feel aggrieved that they have no voice in declaring war with Spain, or in protesting against it. The vast majority of men are in the same position. Why care for a voice in an event that may happen once in a lifetime more than in those of far greater importance continually before us? Why groan over the horrors of war when the tragedies of peace are forever before us?

Our boys in blue, well fed and clothed, in camp and hospital, are better off than our boys in rags, overworked in mines, in factories, in prison houses and in bare, dingy dwellings called homes, where the family meets at scanty meals, working ten hours, to talk over their hopeless situation in the despair of poverty.

A friend of mine visited the bleaching department in one of

our New England factories where naked boys, oiled from head to foot, are used to tramp pieces of shirting in a large vat. The chemicals necessary for bleaching are so strong as to eat the skin unless well-oiled. In time they affect the eyes and lungs. There these boys, in relays, tramp all day, but not to music, or inspired with the love of country. In England they have machinery for such work, but in the land of the Puritans boys are cheaper than machinery.

On a platform of ONE IDEA, mothers cannot discuss these wrongs. We may talk of the cruelties in Cuba now, on any platform, but not of the outrages of rich manufacturers of Massachusetts. Under the present competitive system existence is CONTINUAL war; the law is each for himself, starvation and death for the hindmost.

My message today to our coadjutors is that we have a higher duty than the demand for suffrage. We must now, at the end of fifty years of faithful service, broaden our platform and consider the next step in progress to which the signs of the times clearly point—namely, co-operation, a new principle in industrial economics. We see that the right of suffrage avails nothing for the masses in competition with the wealthy classes, and, worse still, with each other.

Women all over the country are working earnestly in many fragmentary reforms, each believing that her own, if achieved, would usher in a new day of peace and plenty. With woman suffrage, temperance, social purity, rigid Sunday laws and physical culture, could any, or all, be successful, we should see NO CHANGES in the condition of the masses. We need all these reforms, and many more, to make existence endurable.

What is life today to the prisoner in his cell, to the feeble hands that keep time with machinery in all our marts of trade, to those that have no abiding place, no title to one foot of land on this green earth? Such are the fruits of competition.

Our next experiment is to be made on the broad principle of co-operation. At the end of fifty years, whose achievements we celebrate here today, let us reason together as to the wisdom of laying some new plank in our platform.

The co-operative idea will remodel codes and constitutions,

creeds and catechisms, social customs and conventionalism, the curriculum of schools and colleges. It will give a new sense of justice, liberty and equality in all the relations of life. Those who have eyes to see recognize the fact that the period for all the fragmentary reforms is ended.

Agitation of the broader questions of philosophical Socialism is now in order. This next step in progress has been foreshadowed by our own seers and prophets, and is now being agitated by all the thinkers and writers of all civilized countries.

The few have no right to the luxuries of life while the many are denied its necessities. This motto is the natural outgrowth of the one so familiar on our platform and our official paper "Equal Rights for All." It is impossible to have "equal rights for all" under our present competitive system. "All men are born free, with an equal right to life, liberty and happiness." The natural outgrowth of this sentiment is the vital principle of the Christian religion, "Love thy neighbor as thyself."

In broad, liberal principles the suffrage association should be the leader of thought for women, and not narrow its platform, from year to year, to one idea, rejecting all relative ideas as side issues.

Progress is the victory of a new thought over old superstitions![40]

VIII.

THE 1900s:
Consolidating Power

Frederick Douglass's widow attended the NAWSA conference in 1900 and came away deeply troubled. Helen Pitts Douglass was a white woman, Frederick Douglass's second wife, and she wrote to a friend after the convention:

> The colored people do not like Miss Anthony, and she has lost the chance of a life time, the chance to endear herself and her cause to thousands to whom suffrage is as important as it is to herself,—the chance to put the association on record as standing squarely for humanity and loyalty—the chance to stay the advance of a spirit that is encroaching upon the safety of our Republic and to lead and strengthen the moral purpose of the women of the land.[1]
>
> Sat. evening Louisiana spoke, and three times the little thing declared for "white supremacy"—apparently to no one's discomfort.[2]

"Louisiana" was Kate Gordon, who spoke for the first time at this NAWSA convention in 1900. Impressed by her, Carrie Chapman Catt recruited her to be the organization's national corresponding secretary in 1901.

Anthony had decided it was finally time to step down as president of the organization and turn over the reins to younger women. The question of who would replace her hung in the air. Lillie Devereux Blake seemed the logical choice. Active in the movement for more than twenty years, she was a longtime president of the New York Woman Suffrage Association and officer in the NWSA and NAWSA. Her legislative track record included successful work to bring women into civil service positions and to get them appointed as census gatherers. She fought for and won pensions for war nurses. In New York, she led successful struggles for school suffrage, joint custody of children, seats for saleswomen, and a wife's right to create a will without her husband's consent. Endorsed by Stanton and widely popular, she had the inside track. There was a glitch, however. Despite Blake's success in winning rights for women through changes in the law, Anthony had abolished her Legislative Committee. Legislative success, after all, undercut Anthony's argument that change could only be accomplished through the vote. Unbeknown to Blake, Anthony had already hand-picked her successor. Blake's diary documents the sequence of events that followed in the next three months, including the contentious presidential campaign, her subsequent withdrawal of her candidacy "in the interest of harmony," and her formation of a National Legislative League, to do the work she was not allowed to do within the NAWSA. The diary entries are included in this chapter.

Blake had quickly realized that, despite the support she had, the leadership would decide the presidency in this top-down, hierarchical organization. The degree to which the organization had ceased to be democratic is reflected in the matter-of-fact way Harper and Anthony in *History of Woman Suffrage* described the process by which the president, and not the organization, chose the successor.

> It had been known for several years that Mrs. Chapman Catt was Miss Anthony's choice as her successor; she was considered the best-equipped woman in the association for the position, and the vote of the delegates showed how nearly unanimous was her election. The Rev. Anna Howard Shaw, who for a number of years had been vice-president-at-large, could have had Miss Anthony's sanction and the unanimous vote of the convention if she would have consented to accept the office.[3]

Mary Church Terrell, president of the National Association of Colored Women, also spoke at the 1900 NAWSA convention. It was her second talk to the organization. Two years before she had delivered an impassioned address on "The Progress of Colored Women." Sitting now through the call for white supremacy, she held steady to the important goal of suffrage, ensuring that African American women had a place at the table:

> . . . To assign reasons in this day and time why it is unjust to deprive one-half of the human race of rights and privileges freely accorded to the other, which is neither more deserving nor more capable of exercising them, seems like a reflection upon the intelligence of the audience. As a nation we professed long ago to have abandoned the principle that might makes right. Before the world we pose to-day as a government whose citizens have the right to life, liberty and the pursuit of happiness. And yet, in spite of these lofty professions and noble sentiments, the present policy of this government is to hold one-half of its citizens in legal subjection to the other, without being able to assign good and sufficient reasons for such a flagrant violation of the very principles upon which it was founded.
>
> When one observes how all the most honorable and lucrative positions in Church and State have been reserved for men, according to laws which they themselves have made so as to debar women; how, until recently, a married woman's property was under the exclusive control of her husband; how, in all transactions where husband and wife are considered one, the law makes the husband that one—man's boasted chivalry to the disfranchised sex is punctured beyond repair.
>
> These unjust discriminations will ever remain, until the source from which they spring—the political disfranchisement of woman—shall be removed. The injustice involved in denying woman the suffrage is not confined to the disfranchised sex alone, but extends to the nation as well, in that it is deprived of the excellent service which woman might render. . . .
>
> The argument that it is unnatural for woman to vote is as old

as the rock-ribbed and ancient hills. Whatever is unusual is called unnatural, the world over. Whenever humanity takes a step forward in progress, some old custom falls dead at our feet. Nothing could be more unnatural than that a good woman should shirk her duty to the State.

If you marvel that so few women work vigorously for political enfranchisement, let me remind you that woman's success in almost everything depends upon what men think of her. Why the majority of men oppose woman suffrage is clear even to the dullest understanding. In all great reforms it is only the few brave souls who have the courage of their convictions and who are willing to fight until victory is wrested from the very jaws of fate.[4]

By the 1890s serious cracks began to appear in the hierarchical edifice of the NAWSA. Many state workers felt the national leadership's control of the state campaigns was hampering the state in the Washington campaign, as Laura Peters wrote to Lillie Devereux Blake. The full letter is included in this chapter.

Catt had been chairing the Organizational Committee, proceeding on its own without direction from the officers, resulting in a rift. A battle of the titans ensued as Anthony maneuvered to bring her successor into line. An angered Catt considered resigning, but biding her time, allowed the Business Committee to be reaffirmed as the executive organ of the NAWSA. Anthony, however, had met her match. Catt was as committed to one-woman rule as was Anthony. Catt's taking control of the state suffrage campaigns demonstrated this.[5]

Ironically, the NAWSA, which had endorsed the right of states to determine suffrage, now denied the state suffrage organizations the right to determine how their campaigns would be run by withholding money. Catt explained her reason for the drastic measure at the 1901 convention. She believed that they would never win victories at either the federal or state level "until national and State officers and workers were better trained for the work required." As their opposition was increasingly unified and politically experienced, "the cause would never be won unless its campaigns were equipped, guided and conducted by women fully aware of the nature of opposition tactics and prepared to meet every maneuver of the enemy by an equally telling counteraction."[6]

The 1902 convention in Washington, D.C., hosted delegates from ten countries who had come to attend the First International Woman Suffrage Conference and then took part in the NAWSA convention. Clara Colby read a paper Stanton had sent on educated suffrage. This would be Stanton's final address to the organization she had led as president and then honorary president; she died later that year. In her final address to the NAWSA, Elizabeth Cady Stanton argued the vote should be given only to those who were educated.[7] The speech as published in *History of Woman Suffrage* is included in this chapter.

The NAWSA convention moved South for the 1903 convention for ten days in New Orleans. This was the longest suffrage convention held to that point, and the crowded sessions, "never to be forgotten by the visitors or the residents . . . undoubtedly gave a decided impetus to favorable sentiment for woman suffrage in that section of the South," according to the report.[8] The success was a measure of how much the leaders played to the racism and religious conservatism of the region.

The first evening session was opened with prayer by the Right Reverend Davis Sessums, Episcopal bishop of Louisiana, who said in the course of it: "Prosper, we beseech thee, the deliberations of this association . . . so that their work may . . . contribute to the growth of true religion and civilization, to the happiness of homes and to the advancement of Thy Kingdom."[9]

The NAWSA board, now under the control of conservative southerners and their sympathizers, was forced to publicly explain its attitude on the race question when challenged by a New Orleans newspaper. The *Times-Democrat* accused the suffragists of encouraging "social equality" between blacks and whites. The board of officers immediately prepared a statement disavowing the charge, signed by Anthony, Carrie Chapman Catt, Anna Howard Shaw, Kate Gordon, and Alice Stone Blackwell. The full statement is included in this chapter.

That was not enough for some of the locals, who continued

to raise the "color question . . . notwithstanding the utmost care and tact on the part of those who had the convention in charge."[10] Reverend Anna Howard Shaw explained how she handled the repeated query in her speech at this 1903 convention. The speech is included in this chapter.

During the New Orleans convention Hala Hammond Butt, president of the Mississippi Suffrage Association, made the argument for educated suffrage in a symposium on the question: "Would an educational qualification for all voters tend to the growth of civilization and facilitate good government?" Butt "denounced with much severity the 14th and 15th Amendments" and claimed they had been "practically set at naught" by the restrictive educational qualifications southern states had generally adopted, an action "born of the instinct of self-preservation," she said. While she "deplored the political crimes it made possible," she claimed there was "an undercurrent of thought" running through the South that educated suffrage was the only "honorable solution" to "those questions that are vexing not only the body political but the body social of this Southern country." Those questions, of course, were how to maintain white supremacy.[11]

Mary Wood Swift, a California delegate, opposed educated suffrage but came down on the same racist, xenophobic side as the Mississippi delegate: A "great mass of ignorance," from male "immigrants who almost go from the steerage to the polls"; to "the half-civilized Indian"; to "paupers, delinquents, and defectives," all go to the polls, she said. "An ignorant voter may be an honest one but unless he is intelligent enough to study public questions for himself he is an easy prey for the political sharper," she warned. Still, she said educational requirements were not necessary, because "there are more white women in the United States than colored men and women together," and "more American-born women than foreign-born men and women combined." She echoed the underlying argument of the NAWSA that woman suffrage would maintain white, native-born supremacy. Then Swift went one step further. Women are only one-eleventh of those in prison, they compose more than two-thirds of the church membership, and the percentage of illiteracy is "very much less among women than among men." In short, she argued, women make up a large proportion of "patriotism, temperance, morality, religion and intelligence" and should be allowed to vote.[12] Charlotte Perkins Gilman, an activist and author best known for her novels and for short stories such as "The Yellow Wall-Paper," was the only panelist who opposed educated suffrage. Then the audience voted, and only five opposed educated suffrage. However, Harper asserted in *History of Woman Suffrage*, "The policy of the association had always been and continued to be to ask and work only for the removal of the sex qualification."[13]

Sylvanie Williams, a school administrator, suffragist, and founding vice president of the National Association of Colored Women's Clubs, attempted to attend the NAWSA convention and was banned because she was black. Founder/president of the local Phyllis Wheatley Club, which, among other things, sponsored a nursing school, a hospital, and a free clinic in the African-American community, Williams then invited Dr. Elizabeth Blackwell, Elizabeth Smith Miller, and Anthony to attend a meeting of their club to speak with them about black women's role in the suffrage movement.[14]

Williams presented Anthony with a large bouquet tied with yellow satin ribbon and said:

> Flowers in their beauty and sweetness may represent the womanhood of the world. Some flowers are fragile and delicate, some strong and hardy, some are carefully guarded and cherished, others are roughly treated and trodden under foot. These last are the colored women. They have a crown of thorns continually pressed upon their brow, yet they are advancing and sometimes you find them further on than you would have expected. When women like you, Miss Anthony, come to see us and speak to us it helps us to believe in the Fatherhood of God and the Brotherhood of Man, and at least for the time being in the sympathy of woman.[15]

The NAWSA leadership was institutionalizing racism by not allowing African American women into convention while allowing southern affiliates to segregate and work for educated suffrage. Anthony understood right from wrong. While she opposed racism personally, Anthony explained to Ida B. Wells why she felt it necessary to practice racist "expediency." Wells, an editor, lecturer, anti-lynching activist, and founder of the Alpha, the first suffrage club for black women, described these two sides of Anthony in her autobiography, an excerpt from which is included here.

Catt stepped down as NAWSA president in 1904, and Shaw took the helm at the annual convention, which was held in Washington, D.C.

The organization now had various committees, reflecting an expansion of concerns beyond the vote. Colby reported for the Industrial Problems Affecting Women and Children Committee in 1902 that six- and seven-year-old children were working twelve-hour days in southern factories, while legislation for their protection had been defeated in Georgia, Alabama, and South Carolina.[16]

Women, however, had won protective child labor laws, primarily in the North, in the last ten years, Florence Kelly, executive secretary of the National Consumers' League, who chaired the NAWSA's Committee on Industrial Problems Affecting Women and Children, reported in 1905. These victories proved, she said, "that women can do very much" toward legal reform "even without the ballot."[17]

Speakers from other organizations made pitches for their work. Mrs. Nathan, president of the New York Consumers' League, asserted that "some of the evils" from which working women suffered would be alleviated if they could vote, and the ballot would also give women who bought manufactured products a voice in the way in which they were produced.[18]

The conventions now were hearing about a variety of issues that women could influence once they could vote on them. Lucia Ames Mead, president of the Massachusetts State Suffrage Association and a peace activist, made an "impassioned plea" for a world peace organization, a World Court, and "arbitration treaties with every nation on earth."[19]

Blackwell, chair of the Business Committee, presented a series of surprisingly wide-ranging resolutions, which were adopted at the convention:

Whereas, the children of today are the republic of the future; and whereas two million children today are bread-winners; and whereas the suffrage movement is deeply interested in the welfare of these children and suffragists are actively engaged in securing protection for them; and whereas working-men voters are also vitally interested in protection for the young bread-winners; therefore,

Resolved, That it is desirable that our bills for civil rights and political rights, together with the bills for effective compulsory education and the proposal for prohibiting night work and establishing the eight-hour day for minors under eighteen years of age, be submitted to the organizations of labor and their cooperation secured.

The frightful slaughter in the Far East shows the imperative need of enlisting in government the mother element now lacking; therefore we ask women to use their utmost efforts to secure the creation of courts of international arbitration which will make future warfare forever afterwards unnecessary.

We protest against all attempts to deal with the social evil by applying to women of bad life any such penalties, restrictions or compulsory medical measures as are not applied equally to men of bad life; and we protest especially against any municipal action giving vice legal sanction and a practical license. . . . We recommend one moral standard for men and women.[20]

The organization had moved beyond Anthony's vote fixation, but it had also become more religiously conservative. While the NWSA had challenged the religious orthodoxy that dictated women's God-decreed submission to men, the NAWSA now embraced the churches that preached this message. There was now a Committee on Church Work, and Antoinette Knowles, the chair, reported to the 1906 convention a list of "orthodox churches" that had been willing to hold meetings if temperance were combined with suffrage. She called for a church committee in every state.[21]

Where the NWSA had collaborated with working women, the NAWSA now spoke about them. "A speaker should have been chosen from their ranks," Gertrude Barnum, secretary of the Women's National Trade Union League, schooled the convention. "We have been preaching to them, teaching them, 'rescuing' them, doing almost everything for them except knowing them and working with them for the good of our common country."[22]

Moving back to Baltimore for another set of lackluster congressional hearings following the 1906 convention, a feature of the meetings was a speech by Jane Addams of Hull House, Chicago, on "The Modern City and the Municipal Franchise for Women," which became part of the standard suffrage literature. Addams argued for woman suffrage to correct the problems developing in congested cities, since women better understood how to solve them. Her full speech is included in this chapter.

While the immigrant women with whom Jane Addams worked did not appear on the NAWSA platform, women of other countries were welcome, as was "Señorita Carolina Holman Huidobro," speaking about "The Women of Chili and Argentina in the Peace Movement." Another peace activist also spoke:

Mrs. Mead spoke on The World's Crisis, and, with an unsurpassed knowledge of her subject, pointed out the vast responsibility of the United States in the cause of Peace and Arbitration, saying in part: "Protected by two oceans, with not a nation on the hemisphere that dares to attack her; with not a nation in the world that is her enemy, rich and with endless resources, this most fortunate nation is the one of all others to lead the world out of the increasing intolerable bondage of armaments. If the United States will take a strong position on gradual, proportional disarmament the first step may be made toward it at the second Hague conference soon to be held. . . . Of all women the suffragists should be alert and well informed upon these momentous questions. Our battle cry today must be 'Organize the world!' War will cease when concerted action has removed the causes of war and not before."[23]

The NAWSA had now become a well-organized machine, which required uniformly trained suffrage salespeople and a well-honed, consistent message. Hence the organization distributed 62,000 copies of its quarterly publication, *Progress*, 106,753 pieces of literature, and many thousands of suffrage stamps, picture postals, and souvenirs in 1906.[24]

Progress would now be the official NAWSA publication. The press committee was abolished, its job to be done now at the national headquarters in Warren, Ohio, which had just moved to a spacious room on the ground floor of the county court house that had previously housed the public library.

The consolidation of work and decision-making was increasingly top-down. The national leadership would concentrate the organization's resources on state suffrage campaigns, sending Ida Porter Boyer from Pennsylvania to supervise the press work of the Oregon campaign.[25] The Executive Committee sent the state auxiliaries a Plan of Work, directing them to work for a uniform federal suffrage resolution; state laws for women's suffrage, property, inheritance, and guardianship; and initiative and referendum laws. Every club was to organize one new one and each member recruit a new one.[26]

On the ground, NAWSA members spread out to national and state conventions as well as local events throughout the country. As delegates or speakers at county fairs, granges, farmers' institutes, summer assemblies, and educational and religious societies, they asked for an endorsement of women suffrage, with good results. National endorsements reported in 1906 came from:

The American Federation of Labor, National Association of Letter Carriers, National Grange, National Council of Jewish Women, Supreme Commandery Knights of Temperance, National Associations of Universalists and of Spiritualists.[27]

Anthony came from her home in Rochester to the 1906 convention with a cold, which got worse. She spent most of the time under a doctor's care at the home of a couple who had been her long-time friends, Mary E. Garrett and Dr. M. Carey Thomas, president of Bryn Mawr College, but finally roused herself to attend the proceedings.

> On account of her extreme weakness it was not expected that Miss Anthony would speak but at the close of the evening she seemed to feel that she must say one last word, and rising, with a tender, spiritual expression on her dear face, she stood beside Miss Shaw and explained in a few touching words how the great work of the National Association had been placed in her charge; turning to the other national officers on the stage she reached out her hand to them and expressed her appreciation of their loyal support, and then, realizing that her strength was almost gone, she said: 'There have been others also just as true and devoted to the cause—I wish I could name every one—but with such women consecrating their lives'—here she paused for an instant and seemed to be gazing into the future, then dropping her arms to her side she finished her sentence—'failure is impossible!' These were the last words Miss Anthony ever spoke in public and from that moment they became the watchword of those who accepted as their trust the work she laid down. One month later to the day she was laid to rest with her loved ones.[28]

Anthony's last act was, characteristically, fundraising. When asked by her hosts "what was the greatest service they could render to advance the movement?" Anthony answered, "to raise a large fund for the work." These partners had previously together raised $500,000 to open a co-educational Medical Department at Johns Hopkins University. The two women pledged $12,000 (about $337,000 today) a year for the next five years and promised to find other women of means to join them.[29]

While the 1907 NAWSA convention was happening in Chicago the next year, a flurry of state suffrage votes were being held, as the *Woman's Journal* reported:

One of the striking features of the recent national suffrage convention in Chicago was the large number of very close votes on
woman suffrage bills that were announced from different States,
all taking place at about the same time. While the convention
was in session, the Chicago charter convention defeated woman
suffrage by a tie vote. The Nebraska delegates got word that it
had been lost in their Lower House by a vote of 47 to 46, with a
tie in the Senate. In the Oklahoma constitutional convention,
where the gambling and liquor forces as usual lined up against
woman suffrage, it came so near passing that a change of seven
votes would have carried it. In the West Virginia Legislature, where the last time it was smothered in committee, the
House vote this time stood 38 yeas to 24 nays. In South Dakota
the measure passed the Senate and came so near passing the
House that a change of seven votes would have carried it. In
the Minnesota House the vote showed a small majority for suffrage but not the constitutional one required. All these close legislative votes followed hard upon the remarkable vote in
Vermont, where the suffrage bill passed the House 130 to 25 and
came so near passing the Senate that a change of three votes
would have carried it.[30]

So near and yet so far from victory. Fearing the promise
made by the conservative suffragists that they would outlaw
liquor and vice (read gambling and prostitution) when women
won the vote, the liquor and gambling industry poured money
into campaigns to stop women from gaining suffrage.

Despite the previous admonition that the NAWSA should
invite working women to speak for themselves at the convention, working women were once again only talked about, this
time by Anna E. Nicholes of Chicago, who named another
enemy of woman suffrage: Business owners who made more
profits off women workers because they paid them less feared
that women voters would enact pay equity legislation.

A unique feature of this convention was the presence of an
African American woman. Fannie Barrier Williams of Chicago, a suffragist lecturer and a founder of the National Association of Colored Women (NACW), was selected to eulogize

Susan B. Anthony at a tribute to the deceased leader during the convention. In a carefully worded speech she called forth the early, anti-slavery Anthony while choosing not to remember Anthony's opposition to the Fifteenth Amendment and the enfranchisement of black men if women did not also get the vote or her later capitulation to expedient racism. The full eulogy is included here.

Just as the NAWSA's outreach brought woman suffrage resolutions from such other organizations as the American Federation of Labor, World's Woman's Christian Temperance Union, National Free Baptist Woman's Missionary Society, International Brotherhood of Teamsters, and the United Mine Workers of America, the presence of speakers from peace, labor, and consumer organizations at the NAWSA conventions resulted in wide-ranging resolutions passed by the delegates at the 1907 convention, including one on human trafficking:

> In view of the fact that in only 14 of our States have married mothers any legal right to the custody, control and earnings of their minor children, we urge the women of the other States to work for laws giving to mothers equal rights with fathers.
>
> The traffic in women and girls which is carried on in the United States and in other countries is a heinous blot upon civilization and we demand of Congress and our State Legislatures that every possible step be taken to suppress the infamous traffic in this country.
>
> We urge upon Congress and State Legislatures the enactment of laws prohibiting the employment of children under 16 years of age in mines, stores or factories.
>
> We favor the adoption of State amendments establishing direct legislation by the voters through the initiative and referendum.
>
> Inasmuch as in the second Hague Peace Conference there will be offered the greatest opportunity in human history to lessen the burden of militarism, therefore we request the President of the United States to approve the recommendations for the action of that conference which were presented by the Inter-

Parliamentary Union, to-wit: (1) An advisory world congress; (2) a general arbitration treaty; (3) the limitation of armaments; (4) protection of private property at sea in time of war; (5) investigation by an impartial commission of difficulties between nations before declaration of hostilities.[31]

From a low-budget grassroots organization run by volunteers out of their homes through most of its early history to a well-tooled, smoothly running top-down organization, the woman's movement now reported funding impressive by today's standards. Receipts by year with relative current value in brackets were:

1901: $22,500 [$460,000].

1902: $13,581 [$277,150].[32]

1903: $18,310 [$373,650].[33]

1904: $21,117 [$414,000].[34]

1905: $14,662 [$282,000].[35]

1906: (no report) Establishment of the Garrett-Thomas fund of $12,000 [$226,500] annually.

1907: $15,420 [$200,000]. A major gift was received during the convention, with a note attached stating: "In memory of Susan B. Anthony will you accept the enclosed check for $10,000 to be used as the national officers deem best in the work, so dear to her and to all true lovers of justice, for the enfranchisement of women?" As she showed the enclosure Dr. Shaw said: "This is the largest check I ever held in my hand." The convention rose in appreciation of Mrs. Lewis's generous gift.[36]

1908: $14,480 [$273,000] The Garrett-Thomas fund of $12,000 [$226,500] annually was used to provide annual salaries of $3,500 [$66,000] for Dr. Shaw and $1,000 [almost $19,000] each for the secretary and treasurer, leaving $6,000 [$113,000]

for campaign work. Mrs. George Howard Lewis of Buffalo
gave Dr. Shaw a check in memory of Susan Anthony of
$10,000 [$188,700] for campaign work.[37]

1909: $21,466.[38] This year marked the establishment of national
headquarters in New York City where they rented the entire
twentieth floor of a new building on Fifth Avenue for two
years. Alva Smith Vanderbilt Belmont provided the rent
difference between the Warren, Ohio, headquarters and the
new locale. Belmont's gifts also included $146,000 for the
Sewell-Belmont house.[39]

The president's salary of $3,500 was hardly needed by Car-
rie Chapman Catt, an independently wealthy woman. It would,
however, have meant a great deal to Lillie Devereux Blake,
whose existence depended upon her salary, and the Legislative
League she had founded when she withdrew her candidacy as
president. Her organization was floundering, as was the fate of
all the organizations that sprang out of discontent with the
NAWSA's vision and policy.

For the last convention of the decade, the NAWSA moved to
Seattle in July 1909, where the Alaska-Yukon-Pacific Exposition brought reduced railroad rates.[40] Kate Gordon, the corresponding secretary, in reporting on the specialized literature
that had been sent out:

> . . . spoke of the letter of the Brewers' and Wholesale Liquor
> Dealers' Association, so widely circulated during the recent Or-
> egon Suffrage campaign, calling the attention of all retailers in
> the State to the necessity of defeating the amendment, and to the
> postal instructing them how to mark their ballot, with a return
> card signifying their willingness. . . . Miss Gordon urged that
> clergymen of all denominations should be circularized with it.
> She said: "I believe the association should not be dissuaded from
> this undertaking because of the amount of work and its costli-
> ness. The burden of responsibility rests upon us to prove with
> such evidence that the worst enemy of the church and the most

active enemy of woman suffrage is a mutual foe, the 'organized liquor and vice power.' If in the face of such direct evidence representatives of the church still allow prejudice, ignorance or indifference to woman suffrage to influence them, then they knowingly become the common allies of this power.[41]

Having allowed the suffrage movement to be aligned with temperance, the NAWSA now turned to the church as an ally against the liquor enemy it had created.

The Business Committee once again strengthened the national leadership's power over the state workers on the ground, stating:

Appropriations shall be made for educational, church and petition work; financial aid shall not be given to States having campaigns on hand unless there be perfect harmony within the ranks of the workers of those States; an organizer shall be sent to Arizona to prepare the Territory for constitutional or legislative work and a campaign organizer to South Dakota.[42]

The work to create permanent peace in the world looked increasingly hopeful. As Belva Lockwood had pointed out in her 1884 presidential campaign, if all nations would agree to mandatory, binding arbitration of disputes, war would be taken off the table. The Committee on Peace and Arbitration's report celebrated the various international agreements made by the representatives of forty-six nations who established the principles of war at the tenth anniversary of the 1899 Hague Conference in 1909. In pointing out the work that should be done in the United States for peace, however, the report challenged the primacy of woman suffrage:

Pre-eminently among women's organizations, the National American Woman Suffrage Association, which opposes the injustice of refusing the ballot to women, should stand against the grossest of all injustices which leaves innocent women widowed and children orphaned by war, and which in time of peace diverts nearly two-thirds of the federal revenue from constructive work to payment for past wars and preparation for future wars. Thus far this association has been so absorbed in its direct methods of advancing suffrage that it has not perhaps sufficiently realized the power of many agencies that are furthering its cause by indirect means. I firmly believe that substituting statesmanship for battleship will do more to remove the electoral injustices that still prevent our being a democracy than any direct means used to obtain woman suffrage, important and necessary as these are. Women, though hating war, quite as frequently as men are deluded by the plea that peace can be ensured only by huge armaments. It is a question whether woman suffrage would greatly lessen the vote for these supposed preventives of war, but there is no question that more reliance on reason and less on force would exalt respect for woman and would remove the objection that woman's physical inferiority has anything to do with suffrage.[43]

While the NAWSA focused on state suffrage, the national suffrage amendment didn't fare well during the decade of the 1900s, as a summary of the work during the ten years demonstrates.

The 1900 convention was held in Washington, D.C., with the usual Senate and House hearings on woman suffrage and the usual results:

No one can read the arguments for the enfranchisement of women as presented before these two committees without a profound conviction of the justice of their cause and the imperative duty of those before whom they pleaded it to report in favor of submitting the desired amendment. This report would simply have placed the matter before the respective Houses of Congress. But neither committee took any action whatever and as far as practical results were concerned these eloquent pleas fell upon deaf ears and hardened hearts.[44]

A dozen anti-suffragists showed up. They had no tickets for admission, and the chairmen of the two congressional committees said they would hold hearings for them at another time. Anthony then "persuaded the doorkeeper to admit them, introduced them herself to the chairman of the committee, and placed them in good seats near the front." She invited these anti-suffragists to testify, and they had the last word after the NAWSA speakers, who were not allowed to correct the false information of the antis.[45]

The 1901 convention was held in Minneapolis, but the NAWSA returned to Washington the following year, with no report made by the Senate or House committees.[46]

In 1903 the NAWSA again left Washington for its convention, this time meeting in New Orleans, then back to Washington in 1904 for the usual hearings before the Senate and House committees, when once again there were no reports that would bring the suffrage amendment before Congress. In a token gesture, the Senate Committee gave the NAWSA ten thousand copies of the hearings and the House Committee sent fifteen thousand copies.[47]

Portland was the site of the 1905 convention, then back to the Washington area for a Baltimore convention in 1906 and the congressional committee hearings, which resulted again in nothing but thousands of franked copies of the hearings sent to the national suffrage headquarters to be distributed throughout the states.[48]

Anthony, reporting for the Congressional Committee in 1900, had explained that there was no progress for a federal amendment because the organization had no one in Washington keeping constant tabs and pressure on Congress. The full report is included in this chapter.

Despite Anthony's warning, the NAWSA held more conventions outside Washington than in the nation's capital throughout the decade. The last three NAWSA conventions of the decade were held outside the nation's capital with no congressional hearings: 1907 in Chicago, 1908 in Buffalo, and 1909 in Seattle. Catt took personal charge of one final petition drive in 1909 but Congress didn't budge.[49]

State suffrage fared no better. The four victories in the previous decade had been matched by eleven defeats and, despite major funding and work, women did not gain the right to vote in a single state during the entire decade.

The greatest success of the decade was the change in laws for women and children, with eleven state societies in 1909 reporting a series of victories, including an improvement in the position of teachers and property rights of wives. Minnesota reported thirty acts improving conditions, while Maine reported nearly a dozen such new laws. All this was done without women having the vote.[50]

While the NAWSA, as it grew more conservative, shunned discussion of reproductive justice, Anthony Comstock continued his war on women's bodies. Stanton and Gage, who had signed a petition opposing Comstock's moral crusade the previous decade, were now both dead. In 1902 the movement for a woman's right to ensure that she would birth only children she could welcome, love, and support claimed a martyr to the cause. Ida Craddock killed herself rather than spend the rest of her life imprisoned under the Comstock laws. Her suicide note is excerpted in this chapter.

Anthony Comstock died in 1915. His legacy was 3,600 people imprisoned, 15 suicides, including Ida Craddock's, more than 120 tons of literature burned, and 100 years of loss of legal access to contraceptives and abortion until the last Comstock Act was finally overturned by the Supreme Court in *Griswold* v. *Connecticut* in 1965.

I.
Lillie Devereux Blake Diary entries selected from January 23 to March 28, 1900

January 23: At the S.P.S and then went to see Mrs. Stanton who signed a paper asking delegates to vote for me as President of N.A.W.S.A.

January 27: Have sent a protest to every member of the Business Committee of the N.A.W.S.A. against the unwarranted action last spring, when they agreed with Miss Anthony to abolish my Committee and my work. I am very busy preparing my constitution argument for Washington. I called on Dr. Mary Putnam Jacobi and she gave me her endorsement.

February 4: The canvass for the presidency waxes hot. I prepared documents and the other side for Mrs. Catt, is sending out interviewers. I have worked over my speech, and my articles till my head is tired.

February 5: There was a caucus of my friends here, and then Mrs. Whitney stayed to dinner.

February 7: Started for Washington with Mrs. Goss, and Dr. Mary Brinkman. Went to the Riggs House there. In the evening went to meeting of Executive Committee of the N.A.W.S.A. and was brought to trial without the least warning, in regard to the destruction of my legislative committee. The women sat there like cowards, only a few daring to express sympathy with me. I stated my case, and said I was deeply hurt at the action of the business committee, but as a last word, "I did not weep then, and I shall not weep now, there are other avenues of usefulness open to me."

February 8: Went to Convention in the Church of Our Father during the morning. Caucus in the afternoon, Mrs. Howell, Mrs. Hood, Miss Keyser and Mrs. Ricker have arrived for the caucus. In the evening, talked with Mrs. Ricker and other friends.

February 10: Sent out the circular advocating my candidacy, signed by Mrs. Stanton, Dr. Jacobi and Mrs. Russell Sage. It made a great sensation. Mrs. Catt asked me to sit on the platform and speak in the afternoon. She was presiding.

February 11: Sunday. Very tired, rested and wrote letters, saw friends. Everything is being done to secure my defeat.

February 12: Presented my amendment to the constitution. It was lost, of course. In the afternoon went with Mrs. Wilbur to the reception at the White House, and then to the Willard reception of Miss Lowe. Miss Helen Morris Lewis of North Carolina dined with me.

February 13: Went to the Capitol and made an address before the Judiciary Committee of the House of Representatives on the constitutional arguments. I made a fine address and delivered it well. Was given only 15 minutes and had to speak first. After a hasty lunch, went to convention just in time to withdraw my name as a candidate. I said that "while I thanked many friends throughout the nation and in the Convention for their support, that in the interest of harmony, and for the sake of the future of the Association, I wished to withdraw my name from any consideration it might have had." Then I walked directly out of the convention and I was warmly applauded all the way to the door. I went to the hotel, took a nap, had Mrs. Howell come to dinner, and I received many kindly expressions from many delegates.

March 11: Thinking much of forming a National Legislative League. Mrs. Victoria Conkling Whitney urges it, and I have many letters from friends and strangers to the same effect.

March 15: Mrs. Whitney came in the morning and stayed all day, working with me on our National Legislative League.

March 27: I am working very hard on the constitution and program of the National Legislative League.

March 28: At 3 o'clock went to the Park Avenue Hotel, 25 people came representing many different societies. Letters were read from all over the United States. Mrs. Whitney called the meeting to order. I acted as temporary chairman and was elected president of the N.L.L. with a good set of officers. The Constitution and the Platform were adopted.[51]

2.
Laura Peters letter to Lillie Devereux Blake, January 18, 1900

. . . Some months ago I wrote a letter to the *Wisconsin Citizen* in which I enclosed a complaint against the National for not assisting us in our time of need, with funds.

Mrs. Catt wrote a long letter to me, in which she said I labored under a mistake, that the National had offered to assist, that she had written to the officers of the Washington Association and <u>planned</u> for them a system of campaign, and asked if they would like to have the National carry out this preliminary work, and told them it was her belief that the National would not like to attempt anything less systematic and thorough. I replied that I did not labor under any mistake, that I knew of her letter planning a campaign, and knew that it was completely impracticable, that it was impossible for the Washington State executive Com' to comply with its demands.— She said, "that I insinuated that the National refused to help Washington and because of it defeat came." I replied I do not insinuate I state facts. I insist that if the National had bent its energies to financially assist the two states that had reached the crisis of an election, without attempting to foist upon them, burdens and obligations which it was impossible for them to meet, that the National would have done something practical—and that is what I am trying to have done for Oregon.

Mrs. Catt says, "You say that you asked officials for $100.00 to assist you as an organizer. I do not remember that you ever made that request of our Organization Com'. Certainly the request was not made by the Washington Association, and naturally we could not send money to individuals who might ask for it for their own use in the work." I realize that situation to be correct, but I did not write exactly as an individual, but as first VP and State Organizer. I wrote to Miss Anthony and told her the condition of finances in this state. The executive Com' could not write and ask for help since they had refused the 'plan' of Mrs. Catt. Mrs. Catt says the Amendment was defeated in Washington because of the smallness of the campaign, and I say the campaign was small because of lack of funds.

"But the National has long since declared its unwillingness to contribute to state campaigns unless it can control the manner in which the money was expended, and says Mrs. Catt, it may be for this reason that Washington refused aid." Exactly. And in my opinion the same reason prevails in Oregon. Mrs. Duniway cannot under the circumstances ask for financial help, but as you say so truly, that is no reason why you of the East cannot help her, and as I wrote to Mrs. Catt, ". . . Help the Officers there with all the funds you can, and do not, I beg of you, handicap them by or with any rules and regulations as to their method of spending the money. Remember that the National has failed a time or two, though they have been permitted to run things their own way, in states that were hoping to secure an amendment. Urge the friends of the cause through your official papers to <u>give</u> to the Oregon Campaign. Announce through those channels that all funds contributed for the purpose will be sent directly to the Officers of the Oregon State Association to be used as in their judgment may seem best, and thereby the National can throw the responsibility of its expenditure upon the state officers and relieve the National of any responsibility, for the 'wise' or otherwise expenditure of the money."[52]

3.
"Educated Suffrage," Elizabeth Cady Stanton's last speech, read by Clara Colby at the 1902 NAWSA convention, excerpted in *History of Woman Suffrage*, volume 5

The proposition to demand of immigrants a reading and writing qualification on landing strikes me as arbitrary and equally detrimental to our mutual interests. The danger is not in their landing and living in this country but in their speedy appearance at the ballot-box, there becoming an impoverished and ignorant balance of power in the hands of wily politicians. While we should not allow our country to be a dumping-ground for the refuse population of the old world, still we should welcome all hardy, common-sense laborers here, as we have plenty of room and work for them. . . . The one demand I would make for this class is that they should not become a part of our ruling power until they can read and write the English language intelligently and understand the principles of republican government. . . . To prevent the thousands of immigrants daily landing on our shores from marching from the steerage to the polls the national Government should prohibit the States from allowing them to vote in less than five years and not then unless the applicant can read and write the English language. . . . To this end, Congress should enact a law for "educated suffrage" for our native-born as well as foreign rulers, alike ignorant of our institutions. With free schools and compulsory education, no one has an excuse for not understanding the language of the country. As women are governed by a "male aristocracy" we are doubly interested in having our rulers able at least to read and write.

The popular objection to woman suffrage is that it would "double the ignorant vote." The patent answer to this is, abolish the ignorant vote. Our legislators have this power in their own hands. There have been various restrictions in the past for men. We are willing to abide by the same for women, provided the insurmountable qualification of sex be forever removed. . . . Surely, when we compel all classes to learn to read and write and thus open to themselves the door of knowledge not by force but by the promise of a privilege all intelligent citizens enjoy, we are benefactors, not tyrants. To stimulate them to climb the first rounds of the ladder that they may reach the divine heights where they shall be as gods, knowing good and evil, by withholding the citizen's right to vote for a few years will be a blessing to them as well as to the State. . . . [53]

4.
NAWSA board of officers' response to an accusation by the New Orleans *Times-Democrat* that the suffragists were encouraging racial equality, signed Susan B. Anthony, Carrie Chapman Catt, Anna Howard Shaw, Kate Gordon, and Alice Stone Blackwell, 1902

The association as such has no view on this subject. Like every other national association it is made up of persons of all shades of opinion on the race question and on all other questions except those relating to its particular object. The northern and western members hold the views on the race question that are customary in their sections; the southern members hold the views that are customary in the South. The doctrine of State's rights is recognized in the national body and each auxiliary State association arranges its own affairs in accordance with its own ideas and in harmony with the customs of its own section. Individual members in addresses made outside of the National Association are of course free to express their views on all sorts of extraneous questions but they speak for themselves as individuals and not for the association. . . .

The National American Woman Suffrage Association is seeking to do away with the requirement of a sex qualification for suffrage. What other qualifications shall be asked for it leaves to each State. The southern women most active in it have always in their own State emphasized the fact that granting suffrage to women who can read and write and who pay taxes would insure white supremacy without resorting to any methods of doubtful constitutionality. The Louisiana association asks for the ballot for educated and taxpaying women only and its officers believe that in this lies "the only permanent and honorable solution of the race question." . . .

The suffrage associations of the northern and western States ask for the ballot for all women, though Maine and several other States have lately asked for it with an educational or tax qualification. To advise southern women to beware of lending "sympathy or support" to the National Association because its auxiliary societies in the northern States hold the usual views of northerners on the color question is as irrelevant as to advise them to beware of the National Woman's Christian Temperance Union because in the northern and western States it draws no color line; or to beware of the General Federation of Women's Clubs because the State Federations of the North and West do not draw it; or to beware of Christianity because the churches in the North and West do not draw it. . . . [54]

5.

Reverend Anna Howard Shaw in her autobiography,
The Story of a Pioneer, recalled how she handled the
repeated query about the "color question"
at the 1903 NAWSA convention

. . . We were all conscious of the dangers attending a discussion of the negro question, and it was understood among the Northern women that we must take every precaution to avoid being led into such discussion. It had not been easy to persuade Miss Anthony of the wisdom of this course; her way was to face issues squarely and out in the open. But she agreed that we must respect the convictions of the Southern men and women who were entertaining us so hospitably.

On the opening night, as I took my place to answer questions, almost the first slip passed up bore these words:

What is your purpose in bringing your convention to the South? Is it the desire of suffragists to force upon us the social equality of black and white women? Political equality lays the foundation for social equality. If you give the ballot to women, won't you make the black and white woman equal politically and therefore lay the foundation for a future claim of social equality?

I laid the paper on one side and did not answer the question. The second night it came to me again, put in the same words, and again I ignored it. The third night it came with this addition:

Evidently you do not dare to answer this question. Therefore our conclusion is that this is your purpose.

When I had read this I went to the front of the platform.

"Here," I said, "is a question which has been asked me on three successive nights. I have not answered it because we Northern women had decided not to enter into any discussion of the race question. But now I am told by the writer of this note that we dare not answer it. I wish to say that we dare to answer it if you dare to have it answered—and I leave it to you to decide whether I shall answer it or not."

I read the question aloud. Then the audience called for the answer, and I gave it in these words, quoted as accurately as I can remember them:

"If political equality is the basis of social equality, and if by granting political equality you lay the foundation for a claim of social equality, I can only answer that you have already laid that claim. You did not wait for woman suffrage, but disfranchised both your black and your white women, thus making them politically equal. But you have done more than that. You have put the ballot into the hands of your black men, thus making them the political superiors of your white women. Never before in the history of the world have men made former slaves the political masters of their former mistresses!"

The point went home and it went deep. I drove it in a little further.

"The women of the South are not alone," I said, "in their humiliation. All the women of America share it with them. There is no other nation in the world in which women hold the position of political degradation our American women hold to-day. German women are governed by German men; French women are governed by French men. But in these United States American women are governed by every race of men under the light of the sun. There is not a color from white to black, from red to yellow, there is not a nation from pole to pole, that does not send its contingent to govern American women. If American men are willing to leave their women in a position as degrading as this they need not be surprised when American women resolve to lift themselves out of it."

For a full moment after I had finished there was absolute silence in the audience. We did not know what would happen. Then, suddenly, as the truth of the statement struck them, the men began to applaud—and the danger of that situation was over. . . .[55]

6.

Ida B. Wells, in this excerpt from her autobiography,
Crusade for Justice, recalls an 1894 visit with
Susan B. Anthony

. . . At the close of my address a young man in the audience,
whom we afterward learned was a southerner, sneeringly
asked, "If the colored people were so badly treated in the
South, why was it that more of them didn't come North?" Before I could answer, Miss Anthony sprang to her feet and said,
"I'll answer that question. It is because we, here in the North, do
not treat the Negroes any better than they do in the South,
comparatively speaking."

She then went on to tell that she had been visiting me the
week before and that a little girl of my colored hostess came in
and asked her mother for ten cents with which to attend the
school dance that afternoon. The mother gave her the dime
and had her put on her best dress, and she went away very hap-
pily. When the child went up to give her dime to the teacher so
that she, too, could go into the room where the school dance
was being held, the teacher said, "Why, Rosa, I didn't mean
you," and let the child know that because she was colored she
could not take part in that social recreation.

Of course Miss Anthony's statement created quite a sensation, and it was in all the daily papers of Rochester next morning. And when Miss Anthony's sister and I went out to do
some shopping Monday morning, the proprietor, recognizing
Miss Anthony, stepped up and asked me if I was the Miss
Wells who had spoken the night before. When I said yes, he
said that he and his wife had read the account that morning at
the breakfast table and they both agreed that Miss Anthony
had been very unjust to the North. Miss Anthony, all this time,
was over at the counter attending to her shopping, but she
came up in time to hear a very spirited defense of her famous
sister's position; for I, too, could tell of much segregation that
was going on in the North—in school, in church, in hotels, to
say nothing of social affairs.

Nor was this the only incident by which Miss Anthony

strove to inform her fellow townsmen on this subject. One morning she had engagements in the city which would prevent her from using the stenographer whom she had engaged. She remarked at the breakfast table that I could use the stenographer to help me with my correspondence, since she had to be away all the morning, and that she would tell her when she went upstairs to come in and let me dictate some letters to her.

When I went upstairs to my room, I waited for her to come in; when she did not do so, I concluded she didn't find it convenient, and went on writing my letters in longhand. When Miss Anthony returned she came to my room and found me busily engaged. "You didn't care to use my secretary, I suppose. I told her to come to your room when you came upstairs. Didn't she come?" I said no. She said no more, but turned and went into her office. Within ten minutes she was back again in my room. The door being open, she walked in and said, "Well, she's gone." And I said, "Who?" She said, "The stenographer." I said, "Gone where?" "Why," she said, "I went into the office and said to her, 'You didn't tell Miss Wells what I said about writing some letters for her?' The girl said, "No, I didn't." "Well, why not?" Then the girl said, "It is all right for you, Miss Anthony, to treat Negroes as equals, but I refuse to take dictation from a colored woman." "Indeed!" said Miss Anthony. "Then," she said, "You needn't take any more dictation from me. Miss Wells is my guest and any insult to her is an insult to me. So, if that is the way you feel about it, you needn't stay any longer." Miss Anthony said the girl sat there without moving, whereupon she said, "Come, get your bonnet and go," and the girl got up and went.

Miss Anthony tells about this incident in the history of her own life so that you can see it was not a star chamber proceeding. Those were precious days in which I sat at the feet of this pioneer and veteran in the work of women's suffrage. She had endeavored to make me see that for the sake of expediency one had often to stoop to conquer on this color question. This was when we discussed Miss Willard's attitude, and of course I could not see what she was trying to make clear to me. She added that she supposed she, too, belonged to Miss Willard's

class, for she had done that very same thing in the Women's
Equal Suffrage Association. She said when women called their
first convention back in 1848 inviting all those who thought
that women ought to have an equal share with men in the government, Frederick Douglass, the ex-slave, was the only man
who came to their convention and stood up with them. "He
said he could not do otherwise; that we were among the friends
who fought his battles when he first came among us appealing
for our interest in the antislavery cause. From that day until
the day of his death Frederick Douglass was an honorary member of the National Women's Suffrage Association. In all our
conventions, most of which had been held in Washington, he
was the honored guest who sat on our platform and spoke in
our gatherings. But when the Equal Suffrage Association went
to Atlanta, Georgia, knowing the feeling of the South with regard to Negro participation on equality with whites, I myself
asked Mr. Douglass not to come. I did not want to subject him
to humiliation, and I did not want anything to get in the way
of bringing the southern white women into our suffrage association, now that their interest had been awakened. Not only
that," said Miss Anthony, "but when a group of colored women
came and asked that I come to them and aid them in forming a
branch of the suffrage association among the colored women I
declined to do so, on the ground of that same expediency. And
you think I was wrong in so doing?" she asked. I answered un-
compromisingly yes, for I felt that although she may have made
gains for suffrage, she had also confirmed white women in their
attitude of segregation. . . .[56]

7.

"The Modern City and the Municipal Franchise for Women," Jane Addams's speech at the 1906 NAWSA convention

It has been well said that the modern city is a stronghold of in-
dustrialism quite as the feudal city was a stronghold of milita-
rism, but the modern cities fear no enemies and rivals from

without and their problems of government are solely internal. Affairs for the most part are going badly in these great new centres, in which the quickly-congregated population has not yet learned to arrange its affairs satisfactorily. Unsanitary housing, poisonous sewage, contaminated water, infant mortality, the spread of contagion, adulterated food, impure milk, smoke-laden air, ill-ventilated factories, dangerous occupations, juvenile crime, unwholesome crowding, prostitution and drunkenness are the enemies which the modern cities must face and overcome, would they survive. Logically their electorate should be made up of those who can bear a valiant part in this arduous contest, those who in the past have at least attempted to care for children, to clean houses, to prepare foods, to isolate the family from moral dangers; those who have traditionally taken care of that side of life which inevitably becomes the subject of municipal consideration and control as soon as the population is congested. To test the elector's fitness to deal with this situation by his ability to bear arms is absurd. These problems must be solved, if they are solved at all, not from the military point of view, not even from the industrial point of view, but from a third, which is rapidly developing in all the great cities of the world—the human-welfare point of view. . . .

City housekeeping has failed partly because women, the traditional housekeepers, have not been consulted as to its multiform activities. The men have been carelessly indifferent to much of this civic housekeeping, as they have always been indifferent to the details of the household. . . . The very multifariousness and complexity of a city government demand the help of minds accustomed to detail and variety of work, to a sense of obligation for the health and welfare of young children and to a responsibility for the cleanliness and comfort of other people. Because all these things have traditionally been in the hands of women, if they take no part in them now they are not only missing the education which the natural participation in civic life would bring to them but they are losing what they have always had.[57]

8.
Fannie Williams's eulogy to Susan B. Anthony at the 1907 NAWSA convention, excerpted in *History of Woman Suffrage*, volume 5

My presence on this platform shows that the gracious spirit of Miss Anthony still survives in her followers. . . . When Miss Anthony took up the cause of women she did not know them by their color, nationality, creed or birth, she stood only for the emancipation of women from the thraldom of sex. She became an invincible champion of anti-slavery. In the half century of her unremitting struggle for liberty, more liberty, and complete liberty for negro men and women in chains and for white women in their helpless subjection to man's laws, she never wavered, never doubted, never compromised. She held it to be mockery to ask man or woman to be happy or contented if not free. She saw no substitute for liberty. When slavery was overthrown and the work of reconstruction began she was still unwearied and watchful. She had an intimate acquaintance with the leading statesmen of the times. Her judgment and advice were respected and heard in much of the legislation that gave a status of citizenship to the millions of slaves set free.[58]

9.
Anthony's report for the Congressional Committee at the 1900 NAWSA convention explaining why Congress had not acted favorably on the woman suffrage amendment

One reason why so little has been done by Congress is because none of us has remained here to watch our employees up at the Capitol. Nobody ever gets anything done by Congress or by a State Legislature except by having some one on hand to look out for it. We need a Watching Committee. The women can not expect to get as much done as the railroads, the trusts, the corporations and all the great moneyed concerns. They keep hundreds of agents at the national Capital to further their interests. We have no one here, and yet we expect to get something done, although we labor under the additional disadvantage of having no ballots to use as a reward or punishment.[59]

10.
Ida Craddock's suicide note extracted, 1902

To the Public:

I am taking my life, because a judge, at the instigation of Anthony Comstock, has decreed me guilty of a crime which I did not commit—the circulation of obscene literature—and has announced his intention of consigning me to prison for a long term.

. . . This little book, "The Wedding Night," and its companion pamphlet, "Right Marital Living," have been circulated with approval among Social Purity women, members of the W.C.T.U., clergymen and reputable physicians; various physicians have ordered these books from me for their patients, or have sent their patients to me to procure them or to receive even fuller instruction orally; respectable married women have purchased them from me for their daughters, husbands for their wives, wives for husbands, young women for their betrothed lovers. On all sides, these little pamphlets have evoked from their readers commendation for their purity, their spiritual uplifting, their sound common sense in treating of healthful and happy relations between husbands and wives.

In contrast with this mass of testimony to their purity and usefulness, a paid informer, who is making his living out of entering complaints against immoral books and pictures, has lodged complaint against one of my books as "obscene, lewd, lascivious," and proposes to indict the other book later on, so as to inflict legal penalties on me a second time. This man, Anthony Comstock, who is unctuous with hypocrisy, pretends that I am placing these books in the hands of minors, even little girls and boys, with a view to the debauchment of their morals. He has not, however, produced any young person thus far who has been injured through their perusal; nor has any parent or guardian come forward who claims even the likelihood of any young persons being injured by either of these books; nor has he even vouchsafed the addresses of any of the people from whom he states he has received complaints.

. . . On Friday last, October 10, I underwent what was supposed to be a fair and impartial trial by jury; but which was really a most unfair trial, before a thoroughly partisan judge, at the close of which he abolished my right of trial by jury on the main question at issue, namely the alleged obscenity of "The Wedding Night" book. . . . My evidence was almost wholly choked off; neither my counsel nor myself was permitted to endeavor to justify the book by argument.

. . . He said he would not let the question go to the jury; he considered the book "obscene, lewd, lascivious, dirty." He added that he would submit to the jury only the question of fact. Did the defendant mail the book? (The charge was "mailing an obscene book.") He said, "Gentlemen of the Jury, the question for you to pass upon is, Did the defendant mail the book? You know that she admits having mailed the book. Please render your verdict. I do not suppose you will care to leave your seats." And the poor little cowed jury could do nothing but to meekly obey the behest of this unrighteous judge, and to pass in their ballots, "Guilty of mailing the book." Which, of course, was no crime at all.

I fully expected that the public press of New York city would duly chronicle this most remarkable invasion of the rights of the people by such an abolishing of the trial by jury; but so far as I could learn, the press remained totally silent.

It is evident that the political pull of the party which fathers Anthony Comstock is too powerful for any newspaper in New York to dare to raise a protest when, at the instigation of this *ex officio* informer, an innocent woman, engaged in a laudable work of sex reform, indorsed by reputable citizens, is arrested on false information and denied her right of trial by jury.

Since Friday last, people of influence and respectability have written to the judge on my behalf and have been to see him; but he announces his inflexible intention of sending me to prison, and, he is careful to malignantly add, "for a long, *long* term." I am a "very *dangerous* woman," he adds: Mr. Comstock has told him most shocking things about me—not in court, however, this paid informer being far too cute to dare to face his victim openly with any such lies.

At my age (I was forty-five this last August) confinement under the rigors of prison life would be equivalent to my death-warrant. The judge must surely know this; and since he is evidently determined to not only totally suppress my work, but to place me where only death can release me, I consider myself justified in choosing for myself, as did Socrates, the manner of my death. I prefer to die comfortably and peacefully, on my own little bed in my own room, instead of on a prison cot.

. . . I earnestly hope that the American public will awaken to a sense of the danger which threatens it from Comstockism, and that it will demand that Mr. Comstock shall no longer be permitted to suppress works on sexology. The American people have a right to seek and to obtain knowledge upon right living in the marriage relation, either orally or in print, without molestation by this paid informer, Anthony Comstock, or by anybody else.

Dear fellow-citizens of America, for nine long years I have faced social ostracism, poverty, and the dangers of persecution by Anthony Comstock for your sakes. I had a beautiful gospel of right living in the marriage relation, which I wanted you to share with me. For your sakes, I have struggled along in the face of great odds; for your sakes I have come at last to the place where I must lay down my life for you, either in prison or out of prison.

—Ida C. Craddock.[60]

IX.

1910:
Nearing the Finish Line for Suffrage

The National American Woman Suffrage Association had now secured its focus on the vote, and created a well-oiled, top-down suffrage machine. The decade saw resistance from the workers on the ground, the creation of a new, vibrant organization following the British militant model, and ultimately, victory.

The ground for suffrage became more favorable in several ways during the decade. Women were now voting in several states, a progressive movement was sweeping the country, and the Constitution had been amended twice. The Sixteenth Amendment, establishing a federal income tax, was ratified in 1913. Also in 1913 the Seventeenth Amendment, which took the election of U.S senators out of the hands of state legislatures and gave it directly to the people, was ratified. The women who had gained suffrage now were voting for the senators to represent them. *History of Woman Suffrage* described the result.

In 1910 an insurgent movement developed in Congress and extended into various States to throw off the party yoke and the domination of "special interests" and adopt progressive measures.[1]

The effect upon Congress of the addition of between three and four million women to the electorate was immediately apparent. A woman suffrage amendment to the Federal Constitution had suddenly become a live question. A circumstance greatly in its favor was the shattering of the traditional idea that the Federal Constitution must not be further amended, by the adoption of two new Articles—for an income tax and the election of U. S. Senators by the voters.[2]

The 1910 convention meeting in Washington celebrated the achievement that year of forty associations' passing resolutions for woman suffrage, from Federations of Labor to Federations of Women's Clubs.[3] The leadership called for a change in tactics from "general argument and abstract appeal" to "statistics, laws, definite citations, instances of industrial conditions, legal status of women and children, etc.," to be gathered by the state organizations.[4]

Woman suffrage debates at colleges and universities were now all the rage, with such institutions as Dartmouth, Yale, the University of Texas, and Tulane University participating on their campuses.[5]

For the first time a president was invited to address the convention, not for an endorsement (which he didn't give) but just to welcome the participants. President Taft proceeded to insult the women, especially the delegates who had won suffrage in their states, by saying:

> . . . it seems to me that the danger is, if the power is conferred, that it may be exercised by that part of the class least desirable as political constituents and be neglected by many of those who are intelligent and patriotic and would be most desirable as members of the electorate.[6]

Hissing was heard in the hall. Alice Stone Blackwell in the *Woman's Journal* reported, "[I]t was as if the speaker had struck those women in the face with a whip." Appalled, not by the president's insult but by the hissing, NAWSA president Anna Howard Shaw sent the president an apology, which he graciously accepted.[7]

The Committee on Church Work report at this 1910 convention claimed that women were beginning to realize that their efforts were wasted in trying to effect "moral and social reforms" and questioning whether to take a stand "which will show that we are in earnest and demand the weapon of the ballot which is necessary before we can do our part as Christian citizens in advancing the kingdom of God on earth?"[8]

With the death of her father, Henry Blackwell, Alice Stone Blackwell appealed to the organization for assistance with her newspaper by making the *Woman's Journal* the official voice of the association. The arrangement lasted only three years; the paper was returned to Stone Blackwell in 1912 when it proved a financial burden to the NAWSA.[9]

New speakers appeared on the platform, including Max Eastman, assistant professor at Columbia University, who represented the New York Men's League for Woman Suffrage, of which he was secretary. Eastman spoke at the 1910 NAWSA convention in Washington, stating the following:

> The other day I had a letter from a man who said he wouldn't join my society because he feared I was "striking a blow at the family, which is the cornerstone of society." Well, I am not much of an authority on matrimony but that sort of language sounds to me like a hysterical outcry from a person whose family is already tottering. It is at least certain that a great many of these cornerstones of society are tottering, and why? Because there dwell in them triviality and vacuity, which prepare the way of the devil. Who can think that intellectual divergence, disagreement upon great public questions, would disrupt a family worth holding together? On the contrary, nothing save a community of great interests—whether in agreement or disagreement—can revive a fading romance. A high and equal comradeship is the one thing that can save those families which are the tottering cornerstones of society.[10]

Two women who would prove pivotal to the future of the movement appeared for the first time, having been schooled by working with the militant British suffragettes. Harriot Stanton Blatch, the daughter of Elizabeth Cady Stanton, had returned from England several years before and organized what became the Women's Political Union to bring working-class women into the movement.

Believing that people were more drawn to music and marchers than logical argument, the Women's Political Union organized the first of what would be many suffrage parades. At the NAWSA convention Blatch presided at a symposium on open air meetings, another way that was then being much discussed "of bringing the movement out of the convention halls and into the streets."[11]

The other woman on the 1910 platform influenced by the British movement was Alice Paul. She spoke about her time in prison, where she had gone on a hunger strike and been forcibly fed. Newspapers such as the *New York Times* had been carrying her story. The full article, "Suffragette Tells of Forcible Feeding," is included in this chapter.

"Differences in regard to administration" had appeared in the NAWSA, leading to corresponding secretary Professor Potter's resignation. "The Official Board was divided in opinion and this led to several changes in its personnel," the official report vaguely stated.[12]

Adopting Harriot Stanton Blatch's strategy of public demonstration, the suffragists staged a motorcade, described in the report as "the most picturesque incident of the convention":

> . . . the long line of fifty decorated automobiles which bore the petitions and delegates of each State from the Hotel Arlington to the Capitol, where the petitions were personally delivered to the various Senators and Representatives who were to present them to Congress. The large piles of rolled petitions, the respect of the people who lined the streets, the courtesy of the Congressmen and the crowds which watched the presentation in Senate and House were all impressive.[13]

Impressive as the spectacle may have been, it resulted in no report from either the House or the Senate.[14]

Two more suffrage states were added, Washington in November 1910 and California in October 1911,[15] the culmination of years of organized effort.[16] Organizations representing 26 million members had now endorsed suffrage.[17] The National Association Opposed to Woman Suffrage (NAOWS) brought together wealthy, well-connected women with the liquor industry (which feared women would enact prohibition), southern politicians, corporations, and businessmen fearing equal pay, along with some Catholic clergy. While the antis organized nationally, men organized internationally into a Suffrage League.[18]

Carrie Chapman Catt, who had stepped down as NAWSA president several years before due to ill health, was now recovered and making a trip around the world as president of the International Woman Suffrage Alliance.[19] At least three thousand supporters marched in a second New York City suffrage parade in 1911—eight times the size of the 1910 parade, with ten thousand attending the rally that followed.[20]

A unique feature of the annual NAWSA convention, which was held in Louisville, Kentucky, in 1911, was a speech by Emmeline Pankhurst, the militant British suffragette and organizer of the Woman's Social and Political Union. Her association declared war on the property of the men of England, which the men of England cared more about than life, the suffragettes charged. Pankhurst's full speech is included in this chapter.

Conflict appeared as new women with new ideas came into the NAWSA and the previous unanimity in the election of officers disappeared. Delegates also questioned changes to the organization's constitution. However, the NAWSA report assured, "[T]he differences of opinion were peaceably adjusted by compromise."[21]

The Resolutions Committee, consisting now of one member from each state delegation, proposed a wide range of actions, including ratification of President Taft's Arbitration Treaties; support for the proposed federal amendment for the election of U.S. senators by popular vote with women voting; pure food and drugs; an end to the moral double standard, and the placing of a colossal statue representing Peace at the entrance to the Panama Canal.[22]

These resolutions were easily adopted by the convention. An African American and white delegate together, however, asked for one to be introduced that caused controversy:

> Resolved, that women who are trying to lift themselves out of the class of the disfranchised . . . recognize that it is as unjust and as undemocratic to disfranchise human beings on the ground of color as on the ground of sex.[23]

President Shaw blocked the introduction of this resolution. The organization continued its policy of allowing state societies to practice segregation and indirectly endorsing white supremacy by standing silent when these southern auxiliaries lobbied for suffrage for white women only and for educated suffrage. Desha Breckinridge spoke on the prospect for woman suffrage in the South at this 1911 convention, reiterating the recurrent NAWSA appeal to white supremacy and adding an appeal to southern male chivalry as an argument for woman suffrage:

> A conference of southern women suffragists at Memphis a few years ago, in asking for woman suffrage with an educational qualification, pointed out that there were over 600,000 more white women in the southern States than there were negroes, men and women combined. If the literate women of the South were enfranchised it would insure an immense preponderance of the Anglo-Saxon over the African, of the literate over the illiterate, and would make legitimate limitation of the male suffrage to the literate easily possible. . . .
>
> Conditions of life in the South have made and kept Southerners individualists. The southern man believes that he should personally protect his women folk and he does it. He is only now slowly realizing that, with the coming of the cotton mills and other manufactories and with the growth of the cities, there has

developed a great body of women, young girls and children who either have no men folk to protect them or whose men folk, because of ignorance and economic weakness, are not able to protect them against the greed and rapacity of employers or of vicious men. It is a shock to the pride of southern chivalry to find that women are less protected by the laws in their most sacred possessions in the southern States than in any other section of the Union; that the States which protect their women most effectively are those in which women have been longest a part of the electorate. . . . [24]

More suffrage victories piled up as Oregon, Arizona, and Kansas amended their constitutions and conferred equal suffrage on women by large majority votes. The Michigan result was still in doubt when the NAWSA met in Philadelphia for the 1912 convention.[25] Theodore Roosevelt's Bull Moose Party became the first major political party to support woman suffrage. Twenty thousand suffrage supporters joined the third New York City suffrage parade—twice the number at the rally the previous year.

Reenacting the 1876 protest, the convention began a great outdoor rally in Independence Square with a reading of the Declaration of Rights of Women, which Stanton and Gage had written and five NWSA officers had illegally presented at the great centennial celebration in that very square. This was, however, a protest in memory only. No one risked arrest as had the NWSA suffragists.[26]

Resolutions adopted by the convention included the usual call for woman suffrage; arbitration, not war; an end to child labor and also sex trafficking. They defined the last, however, in the way typical of the times. Sex trafficking was a violation of morality, not women's bodies, and one applying only to white women:

That we commend the efforts of our National Government to end the white slave traffic; that we urge the passage in our States of more stringent laws for the protection of women; that we demand the same standard of morals for men and women and the same penalties for transgressors; that we call upon women everywhere to awake to the dangers of the social evil and to hasten the day when women shall vote and when commercialized vice shall be exterminated.[27]

A unique feature of the 1912 convention was Men's Night, with James Lees Laidlaw, president of the 20,000-member National Men's League for Woman Suffrage chairing. One of the most popular of the all-male speakers was Reginald Wright Kauffman, who shared from his recently published book about sex trafficking, or the "white slave traffic," entitled *The House of Bondage*.[28]

"From the very beginning of the equal rights movement," Alice Stone Blackwell editorialized in the *Woman's Journal*, "courageous and justice-loving men have stood by the women and have been invaluable allies in the long fight." Now men were organized nationally to work for women's rights.[29]

A problem was emerging in the western states, where women were winning the most suffrage victories but were feeling unrepresented in the NAWSA, as were midwestern suffragists who had not achieved suffrage. From 1869 to 1895 the annual conventions were all held in Washington, D.C., and since then, nine of the seventeen had been held in eastern states. Because of the expense of travel, western women were far fewer in attendance at the conventions than women from the East. In addition, all the national presidents were from the East, along with most of the board. Feeling the need of "getting together, becoming acquainted, developing leadership and planning their work," these suffragists formed the Mississippi Valley Conference in 1912 and worked for the vote in their own states until 1917.[30]

Conflict at this 1912 convention also arose over who could vote. Large states with many delegates currently ran the organization, since delegates at a convention cast the entire number of votes to which the state was entitled by its paid membership. The convention amended the constitution to give the vote only to the delegates present, which might even out representation if more conventions were held west of the Mississippi.[31]

Further disagreement arose because a number of officers and delegates had taken part in political campaigns that year, in opposition to the organization's nonpartisan policy.[32]

When the delegates passed a resolution reaffirming "the position for which it always has stood, of being an absolutely non-partisan, non-sectarian body," the officers interpreted it to mean that "the association must not declare officially for any political party, implying that individual members and officers could support a party or candidate."[33]

The House committee hearing following the convention found the antis raising the frightening specter of woman suffrage resulting in women serving in the military and refusing to marry and have children. Further, "Is it not true that every free-lover, socialist, communist and anarchist the country over is openly in favor of female suffrage?" they charged.[34]

The NAWSA had a Congressional Committee to work for the federal amendment, but focused as they were on state suffrage, they only allotted ten dollars for the committee's national activity in 1912. They cared so little for the suffrage amendment that it was not surprising when they accepted Jane Addams's motion to put two young newcomers at the head of the Congressional Committee. NAWSA president Shaw had marched in the British suffrage parades, so she endorsed Alice Paul as chair of the Congressional Committee to organize a parade under the NAWSA umbrella, but with all the money to be raised by the committee alone. Paul and her team raised $27,378, mostly from small donations, the biggest a thousand dollars from John McLean, the owner of the *Washington Post*. This Washington suffrage parade turned out to be the big NAWSA event of 1913.[35]

While Harriot Stanton Blatch's organization had sponsored major parades in New York City for the last three years, this parade was the NAWSA's first. Pennsylvania Avenue was lined with 250,000 people from the Capital to the Treasury

Department on March 3, 2013, the day before Woodrow Wilson's presidential inauguration. A horse-drawn float led the parade, waving a banner that read, "We demand an amendment to the constitution of the United States enfranchising the women of the country." Somewhere between 5,000 and 10,000 (Paul reported the higher figure) women marched in groups: college men, a foreign contingent, and so on, behind three heralds with trumpets, four mounted brigades, nine bands, and more floats. Almost immediately men—many drunk—broke through the steel cables protecting the marchers and began attacking the women, cursing, shoving, and tripping, throwing lighted cigarettes, and injuring 100 while the police watched.

The southern women refused to march with the black suffragists, and the organizers initially ordered segregation: The black women would march at the end of the parade. Protests immediately flooded in, leading the organizers to bumble in confusion, as the National Association for the Advancement of Colored People (NAACP) newspaper reported:

> . . . the woman's suffrage party had a hard time settling the status of Negroes. At first Negro callers were received coolly at headquarters. Then they were told to register, but found that the registry clerks were usually out. Finally, an order went out to segregate them in the parade, but telegrams and protests poured in and eventually the colored women marched according to their State and occupation without let or hindrance.[36]

Interviewed years later, Alice Paul remembered it differently. There was in fact a Negro women's section from the National Association of Colored Women, led by Mary Church Terrell. When the southern delegations refused to march if the black women were in the parade, a Quaker leader suggested the men march between the southern women and the African American women's contingents, and the problem was solved, Paul said.[37]

Paul's Congressional Committee was active beyond organizing the parade. On April 7, when women from congressional districts went to Congress with petitions and resolutions, they scored a major victory. The Senate and House Joint Resolution

Number One for Federal Amendment was reported unanimously by the Senate Woman Suffrage Committee. For the second time in history there was a favorable report from the
Woman Suffrage Committee of the U. S. Senate.[38]

The activist Congressional Committee now ratcheted up its
activity. A dozen pilgrimages coming from all parts of the
country met in Washington on July 31, when an automobile
procession met the "pilgrims" at the end of their "hike" and
escorted them through the streets of Washington to the Senate,
where they presented petitions with about two hundred thousand signatures to the Senate.[39]

They held eight theater meetings in Washington with smaller
meetings both indoors and out almost daily, often as many as
five or ten a day. A suffrage play, two banquets, a reception
and a luncheon, and a fund-raising benefit and a luncheon
were among the Congressional Committee's numerous activities There was a problem, however. Paul and her group had
formed another organization in April, the Congressional
Union (CU), which worked with the Congressional Committee
on all these events. The CU rapidly grew to more than a thousand members. This threatened the NAWSA leadership's control of the suffrage work.

This dynamic new Congressional Committee took charge of
all the arrangements for the late November convention, raising
the funds for all its expenses, including those of the national
officers, and securing hospitality for the delegates. Alice Paul
was at its head, with the support of Harriot Stanton Blatch and
Jane Addams. Lucy Burns, Crystal Eastman Benedict, Dora
Lewis, and Mary Ritter Beard all joined the committee.[40]

The tone of this 1913 NAWSA convention was dramatically
changed by this emerging leadership. Two years before, the
deadly Triangle Shirtwaist Factory fire had killed 123 women
and 23 men who were locked on the top floors of the New
York City building. The horror of the event raised awareness
of the working conditions of women workers, leading to a call
for better conditions.

At this NAWSA convention two years later, the voices of
working women were finally heard, as labor organizers had

suggested for years. Margaret Hinchey, a laundry worker, Rose Winslow, a stocking weaver, and Mary Anderson, member of the executive board of the National Boot and Shoemakers' Union, all spoke. Hinchey's speech is included in this chapter.

With the impact of Paul's Congressional Committee, the NAWSA suddenly switched direction and now the board instructed the state organizations to work for a federal amendment, and to get congressional candidates to endorse it. Maintaining top-down power, the leadership instructed that their traveling Suffrage School would spring into action when six or more states requested it, and agreed to share the expense. The delegates, however, once again asserted their authority, instructing the national organization to appoint a committee to come up with a plan for "more definite connection" with the states where women had won suffrage.[41]

Now that the Senate suffrage committee had favorably reported the joint resolution for a suffrage amendment, the NAWSA asked the Senate to pass it, President Wilson to put his executive power behind it, and the House Rules Committee to support the creation of a Committee on Woman Suffrage. Further, it demanded legislation to stop U.S. women from losing their citizenship when they married male immigrants, thereby ending this vestige of the religious edict that "the two shall become one and the one is the man" in marriage. While working to protect the citizenship of (presumably white, native-born) women who married immigrants, the NAWSA was also working to deny citizenship to the immigrant men those women married, unless they were fluent in English.[42]

After the 1913 convention, Paul and the Congressional Committee organized an official delegation of 100 convention delegates along with 55 women representing all the associations auxiliary to the NAWSA in a march two by two to the White House executive offices to meet with President Wilson. This was the first time a president had ever officially received a woman suffrage delegation. While this march of 150 women from the Congressional Committee headquarters through the streets of Washington raised attention, the delegation did not get the suffrage endorsement they requested from President Wilson. Once again, he waffled.[43]

When my private opinion is asked by those who are cooperating with me, I am most glad to give it, but I am not at liberty until I speak for somebody besides myself to urge legislation upon the Congress.[44]

It was a tense time, with a great deal of reason for women to be frustrated and angry. President Shaw, in her satirical speech, which is included in this chapter, contrasted the emotional reserve of the suffragists with the emotional excess of male politicians.

The states' rights issue reared its ugly head again in response to the NAWSA Congressional Committee, whose purpose was to pursue a federal amendment exclusively. The southern suffragists organized into the Southern Woman Suffrage Conference, then called for a meeting with their governors to strategize how to protect states' rights by extending woman suffrage by state enactment rather than by the federal amendment.[45]

At the November convention, Paul presented her Congressional Committee report, which was signed by her as "chairman of the Congressional Committee and president of the Congressional Union," as it was impossible to separate the work of the two. Catt immediately sprang into action, questioning the relationship between the two and asking why, if the Congressional Committee "was a regular committee of the National American Association, no appropriation had been made for its work during the coming year and why there was no statement in the treasurer's report of its expenditures during the past year." When it was explained that the committee had raised and spent its own funds, and the Congressional Union was formed to assist the NAWSA committee, Catt successfully moved that the board continue the Congressional Committee and "cooperate with it in such a way as to remove further causes of embarrassment to the association." An amendment was added that the board "should appropriate what money could be spared for the work of this committee."[46]

At the NAWSA board meeting after the 1913 convention, the board discussed the magnitude and independent nature of the Congressional Union. Beyond simply assisting the NAWSA Congressional Committee, it was a national organization whose purpose was to work for the federal amendment; therefore, the board felt, it duplicated the "work which the National Association had been formed to do in 1869." The NAWSA letterhead had been used to solicit money for the Congressional Union, and people donated, believing they were supporting the NAWSA. Therefore, the board decided, "there must be complete separation of the work of the committee and the Union," and the same person couldn't head them both. Plus the Congressional Union had to regularly submit its plans to the NAWSA board in the future. Paul couldn't accept these conditions, and she was immediately removed as chair of the Congressional Committee. The other members then resigned. The Congressional Union was now a separate organization in competition with the NAWSA.[47]

The Congressional Committee, aided by the Congressional Union, had delivered a congressional victory when the Senate Woman Suffrage Committee voted on May 14 to report the woman suffrage resolution favorably and did so unanimously, with one senator abstaining. The previous anti-suffrage committee chair had been replaced by a pro-suffrage one, Senator Charles S. Thomas of Colorado.

For years the NAWSA had funded state campaigns at the expense of the national amendment and made only a half-hearted attempt at congressional hearings, often not even waiting in Washington for the committee reports. This new flurry of dramatic suffrage activity, which caught the eye of the public and the media, had brought the question of a federal amendment to the fore, and brought the first major victory at the federal level in years.[48]

The House, however, once again dug in its heels over establishing a Committee on Woman Suffrage like the one that had long existed in the Senate, despite Congressional Committee member Helen Hamilton Gardener's reminder that "over one-fifth of the Senate and one-seventh of the House were elected by the votes of women,"[49] By 1913 women voted in nine states: Wyoming, Colorado, Utah, Idaho, Washington, California, Arizona, Kansas, and Oregon. Illinois women gained presidential suffrage in 1913, and Alaska Territory gave women the limited suffrage men possessed. Gardener also used the race card to shame the representatives. Her full speech is included in this chapter.

When the antis brought into the hearings a "poor, misguided working girl," as History of Woman Suffrage described her, who said wage-earning women didn't want the vote, the suffragists asked Rose Winslow, the stocking weaver who had addressed the convention, to respond and read the resolution demanding the suffrage that was passed by the National Women's Trade Union League:

> I have not had any choice as to whether I should walk on the Bowery or on Fifth Avenue, because I walk nowhere in the sunshine. I am one of the millions of women who work in the shadow of these women of whom men speak as though they are the only ones in the country, in order that they may parade the avenue in all the beauty and glory of everything brought from all over the world for their decoration, but I do not come with merely my personal opinion and experience. I have the opinion of the organized working women of America in convention assembled. These women represent all the trades that women work at in the United States and they have passed this resolution demanding the ballot without a dissenting vote.[50]

The House decided by a vote of 123 to 55 that "suffrage was a State and not a Federal question," and failed to set up the special suffrage committee the women had once again requested.[51]

Suffrage activity had really heated up in the states by 1914. Nevada and Montana adopted woman suffrage. In another five western states, however, suffrage went down to defeat. In four of the seven states where suffrage was on the ballot—Nevada, Montana, and North and South Dakota—the amendment was submitted by legislative act. In three—Nebraska, Missouri, and Ohio— it was submitted by initiative petition.

Massachusetts and New Jersey voted overwhelmingly to submit the suffrage amendment to their legislatures, whose approval was required before the amendment could be submitted to the voters for their final approval. Suffragists also got an amendment introduced into eight other legislatures.[52]

Young people joined the suffrage phalanx with the organization of a National Junior Suffrage Corps.

World War I began in Europe in July 1914, and when the annual NAWSA convention met in November, Rosika Schwimmer, a Hungarian who had come to the United States with a petition to President Wilson, "made an eloquent and impassioned address." She represented the women of fifteen countries that were at war who implored Wilson to use his influence to bring about peace. She appealed to U.S. men to end war in the future by giving women the vote, since they "would always use it for peace."[53]

Believing that the war would never have happened if women, "with their deep instinct of motherhood and desire for the conservation of life," had voted, the NAWSA called for universal woman suffrage. Commending President Wilson's peace efforts, the convention expressed deep sympathy "with the plea of the women of fifteen nations," calling on Wilson and the representatives of all the other neutral nations "to use their best endeavors to bring about a lasting peace founded upon democracy and world-wide disarmament."[54]

The Congressional Union (CU) now was working independently from the NAWSA, and a major tactical difference emerged.

Paul had learned from the British Woman's Social and Political Union their practice of holding the entire political party in power responsible for the failure to enact woman suffrage; campaigning against individual candidates of the party even though they supported women voting. These were the very politicians whom the NAWSA courted and lionized. The Democrats were in power, and the NAWSA strategy was to support individual pro-suffrage politicians and work for the election of pro-suffrage candidates, whatever their party. The CU's tactic was to oppose Democratic candidates, whether they supported woman suffrage or not, because they were the party in power.

The CU circulated a petition among the Democrats asking them to caucus about establishing a Suffrage Standing Committee, thereby putting the party in power on record for or against suffrage. The Democratic Party in the South, of course, was committed to states' rights, so this action was an invitation to the party to oppose a federal amendment.

The NAWSA predictably opposed this plan, since its nonpartisan policy meant holding the individual and not the party responsible. Its Congressional Committee "tried desperately hard" to block the petition, but the well-organized CU had forty women lobbying against the NAWSA's three. The party caucus not only voted against a Standing Committee on Suffrage but went further, following the southern Democrats' lead and stating that woman suffrage was a question to be determined by the states and not by the national government.[55]

The NAWSA board endorsed their conservative-led Congressional Committee's plan to introduce in Congress a federal amendment for woman suffrage radically different from the one for which the association had been working since 1869. The Shafroth Amendment called for each state to hold a referendum on woman suffrage if more than 8 percent of the legal voters in the previous election signed a petition for it. This tactic had proven extremely costly with little success in the past.

The Shafroth Amendment, named after the Colorado senator who introduced it at the request of the NAWSA Congressional Committee, was favorably reported to the Senate in May. It became the Shafroth-Palmer Amendment, after the Pennsylvania representative who introduced it in the House.

Ruth Hanna McCormick, the new NAWSA Congressional Committee chair, explained that this shift from the senators and representatives to the people of their respective states

would satisfy the southern supporters of the states' rights doctrine. Their opposition, McCormick claimed, "is primarily the
greatest obstacle to federal legislation on any subject and is
recognized as a valid objection by the members of Congress
and particularly those from the North, who feel that they owe
to the members of the South the justice of refraining from interference in matters vital to the South."[56]

The NAWSA leadership played right into the states' rights
racism of the South with their introduction of this alternative
amendment that would recognize the states' authority to determine who could vote, thereby setting a dangerous precedent. If
the states could confer suffrage on women, could they not decide to let white women only vote, and take voting rights away
from black men to restore white supremacy?

While the amendment had been discussed for months in the
Woman's Journal, the 1914 convention, held in Nashville, was
the first one in which the NAWSA delegates had a chance to
vote on it. The debate lasted several sessions and "more bitterness was shown than ever before at one of these annual meetings," the *History* reported. The board stood by its endorsement
of the amendment, but for "most of those delegates who had
been in the movement for years it meant the abandonment of
the object for which the association had been formed and for
which all the founders, the pioneer workers and those down to
the present day, had devoted their best efforts."[57]

The final result was a compromise. The organization would
continue to work for the federal amendment, but the NAWSA
leadership could support the alternative amendment. And the
next day the southern suffragists were back with their new
form of states' rights, which the Southern Woman Suffrage
Conference had endorsed. Getting a bill allowing women in
each state to vote for their members of Congress placed the
focus for suffrage back on the states. The southern suffragists
explained their position:

The next day an informal conference was held at which Miss
Laura Clay and Mrs. Sallie Clay Bennett explained a bill for
Federal Suffrage, which they, with others, had long advocated,

to enable women to vote for U. S. Senators and Representatives. Congress had the power to enact such a law by a simple majority vote of both houses. The association for many years had had a standing committee on the subject, which was finally dropped because it was believed that the law could not possibly be obtained. It found much favor at this convention, which instructed the Congressional Committee to "investigate and promote the right of women to vote for U. S. Senators, Representatives and Presidential Electors through action of Congress."[58]

Clara Colby, who for the last twelve years had been working with the Federal Women's Equality Association, another dissident spinoff of the NAWSA, asked for time to speak in this convention. Although her organization had been created to obtain a bill enabling women to vote for senators and representatives, it now switched its efforts to support the federal amendment.[59]

The Congressional Committee's plan for "blacklisting" congressional candidates with a bad woman suffrage record came under attack, the delegates voting that this could only be done with the approval of a majority of the societies in the state affected. The delegates further took back control from the national organization by voting that the Congressional Committee "should send out information and suggestions for congressional work," but the state workers would decide how to use the material. If a majority of them in a state couldn't agree upon a plan, the Congressional Committee wouldn't work in that state.[60]

The election of officers at the 1914 NAWSA convention demonstrated how unhappy the members were with the leadership. The new board included only two members of the old one besides President Shaw. There was a silent protest against Shaw's leadership. Thirty-two delegates didn't vote and ninety-one left their ballots empty rather than cast a vote for Shaw.[61]

It was about this time that one of the movement's wealthiest donors, Alva Belmont, switched her allegiance—and money—from the NAWSA to the CU.

Resolutions in the 1914 convention reaffirmed the organization's support for the federal amendment, asking Congress to endorse it, and the convention also demanded equal pay for equal work. Reaffirming the association's past policy of non-partisanship, it came out strongly opposed to the CU's strategy, declaring:

> . . . the National American Woman Suffrage Association is absolutely opposed to holding any political party responsible for the opinions and acts of its individual members, or holding any individual public official or candidate responsible for the action of his party majority on the question of woman suffrage.[62]

While dissent raged in the NAWSA, the CU conducted another direct action, carried out by five suffragists sitting in the front row of the visitors' gallery at the president's December formal address to Congress. As Wilson spoke, the women unfurled a banner that read, "Mr. President, What Will You Do for Woman Suffrage?" This was at a time when the NAWSA sought his goodwill.

The CU also named the federal amendment the Susan B. Anthony Amendment, and the NAWSA picked up the new name, until Stanton's relatives and friends objected, since she "had been equally associated with it from the beginning, and all the pioneer workers had been its staunch supporters." The NAWSA then formally named it the Federal Suffrage Amendment.[63]

There was progress with the president in 1915 when finally Wilson, along with seven of the ten members of his cabinet, came out in public support of woman suffrage. Wilson cast his vote in favor of it in the New Jersey election, where the measure failed, as it did in three other of the most populous states—Massachusetts, New York, and Pennsylvania. Ironically, in the eastern states, where the women's rights movement began, woman suffrage was failing, while the West scored success.[64]

During the 1915 NAWSA convention, held December 14–19 in Washington, delegates visited the White House opening day, Shaw in the lead, now asked the president to take the next step and use his influence to get the federal amendment through Congress, and if that failed, to get a woman suffrage plank in the Democratic platform. As reported in *History of Woman Suffrage*, he answered, to their great joy, by saying that he had it under consideration. He looked at his hand a little ruefully and said: "You ladies have a strong grip." "Yes," Shaw responded, "we hold on."[65]

Harriot Stanton Blatch's Women's Political Union merged with the CU, and the New York City suffrage parade once again doubled in size, with forty thousand women marching, many dressed in white and carrying signs with the names of their states.

Shaw stepped down as president and a reluctant Carrie Chapman Catt once again agreed to lead the NAWSA. In addition to the usual resolutions for suffrage and peace, there was a new one in the 1915 convention, sheepishly offering assurance that women would do nothing with the ballot to change the status quo. Affirming a belief in the home as "the foundation of the State" and "the sacredness of the marriage relationship," they held that the vote would allow women to "strengthen the power of the home and sustain the sacredness and dignity of marriage." The NAWSA denounced "as gross slander" any statements by the antis to the contrary.[66] Perhaps only the enemies of woman suffrage remembered the early suffragists' call to end loveless marriages and give married women full rights to their bodies and their lives.

The NAWSA Congressional Committee would only work in a state when all its societies agreed to the plans of the committee, the delegates voted. Further, it also seemed to be the opinion of the convention that states considering a suffrage campaign should first demonstrate to the Survey Committee that they were ready for it. If the committee felt they weren't prepared and the state went ahead with the campaign, the NAWSA would not support it.[67]

The delegates, however, prevailed in the question of the Shafroth-Palmer Amendment by passing a strong resolution endorsing the federal suffrage amendment, "for which it has been working" for forty-five years, and forbidding support for any other suffrage amendment.[68]

The NAWSA was deeply concerned about the CU's

campaign and voted to meet with its members to see if they could cooperate, as explained in the *History*:

> Another problem came before this convention—the policy of the recently formed Congressional Union to adopt the method of the "militant" branch of the English suffragists and hold the party in power responsible for the failure to submit the Federal Suffrage Amendment. They had gone into the equal suffrage States during the congressional campaign of 1914 and fought the re-election of some of the staunchest friends of this amendment, Senator Thomas of Colorado, for instance, chairman of the Senate Committee which had reported it favorably and a lifelong suffragist. The press and public not knowing the difference between the two organizations were holding the National American Association responsible and protests were coming from all over the country . . . and there was a considerable feeling that some plan for united action should be found.[69]
>
> The meeting came to naught.
>
> The committee of five representing the National American Association recommends that no affiliation shall take place because it was made quite clear that the Congressional Union does not denounce nor pledge itself not to resume what we term its anti-party policy and what they designate as their election policy; also because it is their intention, as announced by them, to organize in all States in the Union for congressional work, thus duplicating organizations already existing.[70]

The CU sponsored Sara Bard Field in a transcontinental cross-country automobile tour from San Francisco to Washington, D.C., carrying petitions with a half-million suffrage signatures collected during the 1915 Panama-Pacific International Exposition, the World's Fair held in San Francisco. Field presented the petitions to Congress at the Senate suffrage committee hearings. An angry Senator Thomas refused to preside, since the CU had worked against his re-election. A committee member asked Shaw to explain the difference between the NAWSA and the CU, as members were confused. Shaw answered:[71]

It is, perhaps, like two different political parties, which believe in different procedure. The National Woman Suffrage Association has two fundamental ideas—to secure the suffrage through State and national constitutions—and we appeal both to Congress and to the States. The Congressional Union, as I understand it, appeals only to the Congress. Another essential difference is that the policy of the Union is to hold the party in power responsible for the acts of Congress, whether they are acts of that party by itself or of the whole Congress. They follow a partisan method of attacking the political party in power, whether the members of it are friendly to the woman-suffrage movement or not. For instance, Senator Thomas of Colorado, Senator Chamberlain of Oregon and other Senators and Representatives who have always been favorable to our movement and have aided us all the way along, have been attacked by this Union not because of their personal attitude toward our question but because of the attitude of their party.

The National Suffrage Association pursues a non-partisan method, attacking no political party. If we could defeat a member of any political party who persistently opposed our measure we would do it, whether in the Republican or the Democratic or any other, but would never hold any party responsible for the acts of its individual members.[72]

Three weeks before the House voted down woman suffrage it had approved an amendment to ban the use of alcohol in the United States, a measure the Senate would also approve in 1919. Many congressmen opposed suffrage on states' rights grounds, yet these same men supported a measure to take the control of alcohol away from the states, a contradiction the NAWSA's Congressional Committee duly noted and acted upon. Identifying the states' rights congressmen who voted for federal prohibition but probably wouldn't support a federal suffrage amendment, the Congressional Committee chair sent their names to the state chairs, suggesting they call the congressmen on their hypocrisy. While this shamed several of them into supporting suffrage, seventy-two ended up voting *for* the National Prohibition Amendment but *against* the Federal Woman Suffrage Amendment.[73]

While the segregated NAWSA continued its work, using the maintenance of white supremacy as one of its arguments for woman suffrage, the CU followed suit. One of its campaign handouts took on the question, "Will the federal suffrage amendment complicate the race problem?" and answered: "White women greatly outnumber Negro women in fifteen southern States, except Mississippi and South Carolina and in nine of these States, white women outnumber the total Negro population by 2,017,286. In Mississippi and South Carolina, where there are more blacks than whites, they have educational qualifications. South Carolina also has a property qualification for voting." Along with the NAWSA, the CU now appeased southern white men by assuring them that woman suffrage would maintain, and even strengthen, white supremacy.[74]

African American women and men continued to work for woman suffrage on their own. The National Association for the Advancement of Colored People (NAACP) held a symposium on "Woman Suffrage and the Fifteenth Amendment" in the pages of its official magazine, *The Crisis,* in August 1915. Mary Church Terrell, a founder and president of the National Association of Colored Women (NACW) contributed the essay "Women Suffrage and the Fifteenth Amendment," which is included in this chapter.

The CU sponsored a convention in June 1916 for women in the western states that had achieved voting rights, the women who had felt left out of the NAWSA and formed their own group. The convention resulted in the establishment of the National Woman's Party (NWP). The CU continued to exist in states where women did not have the vote, while the NWP replaced the CU in western states that had passed women's suffrage. A smart strategic move, this gave state-enfranchised women an organization from which to work for the federal suffrage amendment.

The NAWSA, NWP, and CU all concentrated on the national political conventions in the 1916 presidential election year, resulting in a full sweep of woman suffrage support from all of the conventions. While the Progressive, Socialist, and Prohibition platforms declared support for a federal amendment, the Republican and Democratic platforms favored suffrage for women without specifying how it should be achieved.[75]

While the CU and NWP opposed all Democratic Party candidates, the NAWSA invited Democratic presidential candidate Wilson to speak at its September 1916 convention in Atlantic City. It also invited the Republican candidate, Judge Charles Evans Hughes, who had declared in favor of the federal suffrage amendment. He wasn't able to attend. In his convention address, Wilson continued to waffle in his willingness to push forward the suffrage amendment and ended with an appeal to that most incendiary advice to feminists: patience.[76]

Dr. Anna Howard Shaw, now honorary president, would have none of it.

"We have waited long enough for the vote, we want it now," she exclaimed, and then turning to the President with her irresistible smile she finished, "and we want it to come in your administration!"[77]

The NAWSA convention debated what had become a paramount question: Should the organization drop work on the federal amendment and confine its activities to state legislation? With momentum gathering on the federal amendment, President Catt now shifted her position, arguing "that the Federal Amendment was the one and only way."[78] The convention, however, voted overwhelmingly in favor of continuing to work for both national and state constitutional amendments, the southern delegates refusing to give up the states' rights approach.[79]

Catt gave the example of her home state, Iowa, to show what they were up against. The liquor industry rounded up "every drunkard and outcast" to vote against the suffrage amendment, resulting in thirty-five thousand more votes on the suffrage proposition than on the governor. "This story differs in coloring and detail with each campaign but varies little as to general fact," she warned. The state suffrage campaigns, she concluded, "must be so good that these purchasable and controllable elements will be outvoted."[80]

The convention called for a thorough and comprehensive Corrupt Practices Act that would make public all funds used in political campaigns and provide punishments for offenders. This legislation would bring to light the real donors behind the anti-suffrage movement.[81]

The House once again proved recalcitrant in moving suffrage forward. While the Senate suffrage committee again reported favorably on the federal amendment, the House Judiciary Committee voted to postpone all constitutional amendments indefinitely.[82]

The year 1916 saw the first woman elected to the House of Representatives, Jeannette Rankin of Montana, where women had gained the vote in 1914. The year also marked the first martyr to the suffrage cause. Inez Milholland Boissevain, unwilling to halt her grueling suffrage tour for the CU despite illness, collapsed while speaking on stage in Los Angeles. She died shortly after, on November 25.

The NAWSA concentrated its work on getting Congress to approve the federal amendment in 1917 with a move away from its nonpartisan stand. The organization stood ready to work for candidates in both parties and both Houses of Congress who would vote for the federal amendment, with the Executive Board and the boards of the States in question to decide which candidates to oppose. The NAWSA resolution called for the formation of a compact of state associations, "willing and ready to conduct such campaigns."[83]

The Congressional Committee asked the senior senator from each nonsuffrage state to set up a meeting between his state's congressional delegation and the NAWSA state delegates during the suffrage convention. This new strategy was successful; thirty of these meetings were held, often with the entire state delegation attending.[84]

Catt testified at the hearing in a dramatic call to the legacy of liberty but pitting privileged women against veterans and immigrants. The full speech is included in this chapter.

While the NAWSA women were welcomed into senators' offices to discuss suffrage, the "silent sentinels" of the NWP (merged in March with the CU) were picketing in front of the White House. College students, working women, state delegates, and various professions and organizations took their assigned days to stand vigil with signs outside the gates.

With the NAWSA working on the inside and the NWP applying pressure from the outside, the combined forces finally got the House to create the Woman Suffrage Committee for which the NAWSA had so long strived. However, the Judiciary Committee, which for forty years had kept the question of woman suffrage from coming before the House, reported the federal amendment "without recommendation" and tried to prevent its being referred to the new committee.[85]

When the United States entered World War I on April 6, 1917, the NAWSA jumped into action, the annual convention reaffirming the organization's "unswerving loyalty to the Government in this crisis," with each state association establishing War Service and Liberty Loans committees, the latter to cooperate with the state divisions of the Woman's Committee of National Defense.[86]

The NWP, on the other hand, did not publicly support the war effort, and continued its pickets, now calling out the government's hypocrisy in supporting democracy abroad while denying its women citizens the right to vote at home. The picketers, who eventually numbered about two thousand, were seen by many as unpatriotic and even seditious, and mobs began to attack them. Instead of arresting those committing violence, on June 22, 1917, the police began arresting the suffrage picketers on charges of obstructing sidewalk traffic, with some sentenced up to six months in jail. Many of those imprisoned demanded to be treated as political prisoners and went on hunger strikes when they were not. Force-fed if they refused to eat, sometimes beaten, the 168 imprisoned suffragists held out, even Alice Paul, who was put in solitary confinement in the mental ward of the prison to break her spirit. The suffragists won. The public outcry against their treatment forced the government to unconditionally release the picketers in

November. A report on the arrest of the picketers is included in this chapter.

While the NAWSA denounced the pickets, the organization carried on the tradition of parades, generated by Harriot Stanton Blatch, whose organization had merged with the NWP.

Before New York held a referendum, suffragists showcased a petition bearing more than a million women's signatures in a New York City march in April 1917, and Carrie Chapman Catt led a suffrage parade in the city that fall.

During the summer of 1917 ten thousand black women, men, and children marched in silence in a New York City parade organized by the NAACP in the first major public protest of racial violence in U.S. history.

African American support for woman suffrage continued. A black monthly magazine, *The Messenger*, published an editorial, "Woman Suffrage and the Negro" by A. Philip Randolph, in November. The article is included in this chapter.

The NAWSA instructed its state affiliates to lobby state legislatures to give women voting rights for presidential electors. Illinois did so in 1913; women there voted for the electors at the 1916 presidential election and the Electoral College accepted Illinois' vote, establishing the precedent. National headquarters promptly sent state legislators across the country copies of the opinion of Chief Justice Walter Clark of North Carolina that the federal Constitution empowered state legislatures to determine who should vote for presidential electors. The presidents of the state suffrage associations picked up the ball and convinced the legislatures of North Dakota, Nebraska, Indiana, Michigan, Ohio, and Rhode Island to pass this legislation.[87]

Arkansas gave women full primary voting suffrage while Vermont extended the municipal franchise to women. In November 1917 came the great New York full suffrage victory, which added forty-five members of Congress elected partly by votes of women and presumably obligated to support a federal amendment. The critical mass, suffragists believed, had been achieved. Republican Theodore Roosevelt and Democrat William Jennings Bryan headed numerous members of both parties who jumped on board the suffrage bandwagon. While President Wilson continued to hesitate about pushing his party to endorse the amendment, both Republican and Democratic opponents now began to feel the best they could do was to hold off the inevitable victory of woman suffrage as long as they could.[88]

So certain were they that the suffrage amendment would now be passed that the National College Equal Suffrage League, formed in 1908 and an active force in the suffrage work, voted to dissolve the organization, as did the Mississippi Valley Conference, formed in 1912.[89]

Following the lead of the NWP, Catt outlined a plan for an auxiliary organization to the NAWSA that would bring together suffragists from the enfranchised states. Each state association would automatically become a member upon enfranchisement. By this plan enfranchised states would work for the federal amendment, and ultimately be part of a central body of all the states once national suffrage was achieved. The organization would be known as the National League of Women Voters.[90]

The cumulative effect of the years of persistent work, the state victories resulting in millions of women voters, the respect for the NAWSA's war efforts, and what the NWP picketers had endured in their imprisonment, coupled with the critical work of African American suffragists and other organizations, had brought the suffrage struggle to the tipping point.

The newly formed Woman Suffrage Committee in the House gave a five-day-long hearing to the NAWSA, the NWP, and the Anti-Suffrage Association from January 3 to 7, and the stenographic report filled 330 closely printed pages, which Harper lauded in *History of Woman Suffrage*:

> It was the last of the committee hearings on a Federal Suffrage Amendment which began in 1878 and had been held during every Congress since that date. If an investigator of this subject has time to read only one document it should be the report of this hearing.[91]

Although they felt confident of victory, the NAWSA leaders continued to court the southern legislators with promises of delivering white supremacy with the women's vote. Mrs. Guilford Dudley, president of the Tennessee Equal Suffrage Association, represented the women of the South in the House Woman Suffrage Committee hearing, assuring the representatives with the same argument the NAWSA had been using for years. There are more white women than blacks in fifteen southern states; South Carolina and Mississippi countered their black majority with property and education requirements; the four other states in the "black belt" also have an education test. Finally, she countered, blacks were moving north in large numbers, so "it appears that we must transfer part of our rather hysterical anxieties with regard to the southern negro vote to some other States."[92]

NAWSA President Catt followed up with a unique framing of a racist argument. The idea prevails with some members of Congress, she said, that "the colored women are more intelligent, ambitious and energetic than the men," but that white women, if they had the vote, would only "vote as their husbands do," implying the white women "are too weak-minded to have an opinion of their own." So basically you men are saying "that the colored woman is superior to the colored man but that the white woman is the inferior of the white man," she challenged. "Or is it possible that the climate of the South produces a stronger 'female of the species' than male, and that the men of the South are afraid of both the white and the black women?" she asked.[93]

The anti-suffragists chose as their spokesperson one of the South's most noted orators, former U.S. senator Joseph W. Bailey of Texas. "The two most important personal duties of citizenship are military service and sheriff's service, neither of which is a woman capable of performing," Bailey boldly asserted. Women were actually performing the duty of sheriff, constable, marshal, and police in many places, the chair countered. "They may be playing at them but they are not really performing them," Bailey insisted. The "women of this country will never go into our armies as soldiers," Bailey went on to predict, so "I hardly think they have the right to make the laws under which you and I must perform those services." The chair asked, "When the men go to the front with the cartridges and guns the women assisted in making are the latter not participating in the war the same as men?" "They are doing their part and it may be just as essential as the man's," Bailey agreed, "but it is not military service." Not content with having dug himself into two holes, Bailey went for a third, adding an additional duty of citizenship: jury service. There are "natural, moral and domestic" reasons, "which render them wholly unfit for it." No one had apparently told Mr. Bailey that women had been serving on juries for from twenty to forty years in the western states. He wasn't done. The effect of the woman's movement on civilization would be disastrous, as in the Roman republic when women attained their rights: "They married without going to church and were divorced without going to court." He wrapped-up his tour de force of misogyny by declaring, "A single standard of conduct for men and women is an iridescent dream. We cannot pay women a higher tribute than to insist that their behavior shall be more circumspect than ours."[94]

Catt responded by recounting an anti–woman suffrage speech by Prime Minister Herbert Asquith in the House of Commons in which he argued that the British Empire would always have to be defended militarily, and "what do women know about war?" Three years later he "humbly confessed" that he was wrong. During the recent war, men and women had made equal sacrifices, so he demanded woman suffrage and voted for it in the House of Commons. "Remembering Mr. Asquith" Catt concluded, "I think there is hope for Mr. Bailey."[95]

This last hearing that would ever be held on the federal suffrage amendment closed on January 7, 1918, and on January 8 the suffrage committee made a favorable report to the House of Representatives, debate on the amendment to be three days later. The day before the debate twelve Democratic members called on President Wilson, who finally advised the submission of the amendment.[96]

Representative Jeannette Rankin opened the debate on the suffrage amendment and a five-hour deliberation followed. In a historic move, the House, by a slim two-thirds majority, voted to submit the amendment to the state legislatures.

The suffrage amendment now would go to the Senate for ratification. Over the months following, anti-suffrage senators stalled the amendment while pro-suffrage leaders delayed it when it appeared they didn't have the necessary votes. Even when President Wilson made an appeal, Democratic senator Oscar Underwood from Alabama immediately followed with a prolonged states' rights argument against the amendment. A variety of amendments were proposed and defeated, including one by another Democrat, Mississippi senator John Sharp Williams to make the resolution read: "The right of *white* citizens to vote shall not be denied, etc.,"[97]

Both the NAWSA and the NWP now shifted into unprecedented action. The NWP established picket lines in front of the U.S. Capitol and the Senate Office Building for a continuing, visible reminder while the NAWSA carried out its 1917 convention resolution:

> If the 65th Congress fails to submit the Federal Amendment before the next Congressional election the association shall select and enter into such a number of campaigns as will effect a change in both houses of Congress sufficient to insure its passage.[98]

Both organizations redoubled their efforts in this midterm election to ensure Congress would have enough pro-suffrage members to pass the suffrage amendment. They won; the necessary two-thirds majority in the Sixty-sixth Congress had been secured. This left the victory for the new Republican-controlled Congress that would convene in 1919 to claim.[99]

The NAWSA spent $30,720—almost half a million dollars today—on three 1918 state campaigns in Michigan, South Dakota, and Oklahoma, and suffrage was won in all three.

Although President Wilson had publicly come out in favor of

the suffrage amendment and promised to support the measure, he failed to follow up his words with action, adopting a hands-off policy rather than stand up to the racist members of his party in the South. Three hundred indignant NWP members gathered in Lafayette Park on December 16, 1918, in front of a fiery cauldron into which they tossed President Wilson's speeches about democracy.

The NWP continued to keep its "watchfire" burning. Each time Wilson made a stirring pro-democracy speech, the NWP members would toll a large and loud bell they had acquired, and one of them would go outside their headquarters into La-fayette Park carrying a copy of the speech and, with great dignity, burn it in their cauldron. When Wilson had still not delivered on his promise to get his party on board with the suffrage amendment, one hundred women gathered in front of the White House on February 9, 1919, and burned the president's image in effigy. Thirty-nine of them were arrested and twenty-five were sent to jail. The organization then dramatically sent suffrage prisoners on a cross-country speaking tour aboard a train appropriately named "Democracy Limited" in February and March 1919.

State legislatures in twenty-five states called on every senator to vote for submission of the amendment while Vermont, Indiana, and Wisconsin enacted presidential suffrage in the winter of 1919.[100]

Wanting one more chance to take credit for passing the suffrage amendment before the Republicans took power, the pro-suffrage Democrats held a caucus. Twenty-two senators voted in favor of the suffrage amendment, with only ten voting in the negative, but the anti-suffrage Democratic floor leader sabotaged the victory. He allowed the ten negative senators to withdraw their votes so that he could declare that the vote stood 22–0, a quorum had not voted, and the resolution was lost.[101] The Democratic-controlled Senate then voted and the amendment was lost by one vote. The Democrats had lost their last opportunity to take credit for enacting woman suffrage.[102]

The NWSA had been founded fifty years before and, anticipating victory, the 1919 NAWSA convention had been planned
as a Jubilee celebration. Nevertheless, victory was imminent,
and the delegates divided their time between the convention
and organizing the League of Women Voters, which Catt had
proposed earlier.

In her presidential address, Catt now laid out an agenda for
the new organization to work toward: compulsory education,
English the national language, education of adults, higher qualifications for citizenship, direct citizenship for women and not
through marriage, compulsory lessons in citizenship through
foreign-language papers, an oath of allegiance as qualification
for citizenship, schools of citizenship in every city ward and
rural district, and an educational requirement for voting.[103]

Alice Stone Blackwell presented wide-ranging resolutions at
the NAWSA convention, which were adopted:

Whereas, women may now vote for President in twenty-six
States of the Union, and for all elective officers in England, Scot-
land, Ireland, Canada and throughout the largest part of Europe; our eastern and southern States are now the only
communities in the English-speaking world in which women are
still debarred from self-government; our nation has just emerged
from a war waged in the name of making the world safe for democracy and ought in consistency to establish real democracy at
home; and every political party in the United States has endorsed woman suffrage in its national platform; therefore be it

Resolved, that we call upon the 66th Congress to submit the
Constitutional Amendment for nation-wide woman suffrage to
the States at the earliest possible moment.

Whereas, one-fourth of the men examined for the army were
unable to read English or to write letters home to their families,
be it

Resolved, that we urge the establishment at Washington of a
national department of education with a Secretary of Education
in the Cabinet.

Resolved, that this association earnestly favors a League of

Nations to secure world-wide peace based upon the immutable principles of justice.

Resolved, that we protest against the unfair treatment of professional women by the United States authorities in declining the services of women physicians, surgeons and dentists in the recent war, thus compelling loyal, patriotic women to serve under the flag of a foreign government. We recommend that in future our Government recognize the fitness of accepting the services of professional women for work for which their training and experience have qualified them.

Resolved, That we urge our Government to bring about the prompt redress of all legitimate grievances, as the removal of the sense of injustice is the surest safeguard against revolution by violence.

Whereas, the Woman in Industry Service of the U. S. Department of Labor was established as a result of the war emergency,

Resolved, that we call upon Congress to establish this service as a permanent Women's Bureau in the U. S. Department of Labor with adequate funds for the continuance and extension of its work.

Resolved, that we ask the U. S. Government in its next census to classify definitely the unpaid women housekeepers as homemakers, thus recognizing their important service to the nation.

Resolved, that we call upon Congress to give military rank to army nurses.

Resolved, that we tender to our national president, Mrs. Carrie Chapman Catt, our deep appreciation of her sagacity, good judgment, fairness and indefatigable devotion to the cause of equal rights, and we pledge our best efforts to carry out her wise and far-reaching plans for ultimate victory.[104]

On January 29, 1919, the full Congress ratified the Eighteenth Amendment, which the House had ratified in 1915. The amendment banned the sale, transportation, and use of alcohol in the United States. The temperance women had achieved their goal before the suffragists. This kicked the legs out from under the liquor industry's argument that woman suffrage would result in prohibition. The adoption of the amendment also strengthened the federal government's authority over the states, and "the suffragists saw the bitterest opponents of their amendment on the ground of State's rights throw this doctrine to the winds in their determination to put through the one for prohibition," Harper reflected in *History of Woman Suffrage*. However, this weakening of the states' rights argument against the suffrage amendment strengthened the prospects for its passage, which quickly happened.

Four months later the U.S. House of Representatives again passed the federal suffrage amendment, with forty-two more votes than needed. The Senate, now with a Republican majority, passed the amendment June 4, with 56 ayes and 25 nays. It was on to the states for ratification.

I.
"Suffragette Tells of Forcible Feeding,"
the *New York Times*, February 18, 1910

To take part in the welcome planned by the Equality League of Self-Supporting Women to Miss Alice Paul, the American woman who was one of the hunger strikers in the late militant movement carried on by the Suffragettes in England, an audience that filled only about two-thirds of Cooper Union turned out last night.

Resolutions were passed condemning Senator Brackett's plan for a poll of women on the suffrage question and Assemblyman Dana's bill requiring a majority of all the electors voting to pass an amendment to the Constitution, but the interest of the gathering centred in what Miss Paul had to tell of forcible feeding. She seemed unwilling to dilate on it, but justified it as a form of passive resistance. In her speech she thus described it:

"They tied us down with bonds around our legs, chests, and

necks. Then the doctors and warders held us down and forced a tube five or six feet long, about the size of a finger, through the nostrils to the stomach. Many doctors wrote to Mr. Asquith protesting against this method as inhumane, barbarous, and dangerous, and protests were received from Massachusetts and many European countries, including even Spain."

Some one in the audience sent up a question asking why the prison officials did not use the throat as a means of access for the food. Miss Paul explained that the suffragettes could make a very effectual resistance against the placing of the tube in the mouth, and then touched on her own feelings.

"It always caused my nose to bleed and brought out a perspiration all over me. I had fits of trembling, and I never went through the experience without weeping and sometimes crying aloud."

Miss Paul, though she protested that no one disliked the militant methods more than the suffragettes themselves, spoke of their doings with a good deal of humor. She said they had reduced England to a state of civil war, and thus described the sending of a deputation of eight women to Mr. Asquith from a mass meeting in Trafalgar Square:

"He had only eight women to meet, but he called out 10,000 police. The deputation was headed by a band playing the "Marseillaise," It seemed a far cry to the time when that tune was played in Paris, but I doubt if feeling ran any higher. It was only the trick of the Government, by which the rumor was spread that the deputation had been received that prevented a riot in the streets of London.

Miss Paul said that the women who interrupted political meetings only asked questions very politely and expatiated on the necessity of having the halls searched to oust intruders before the meetings began and even having the roofs examined as great pieces of fun.

Her apology for the policy of throwing stones at public buildings was that in England the smashing of windows is a recognized form of political agitation, and that in Ireland they had lately smashed $5,000 worth of glass because they always do things on a big scale in that country.

"We never smashed windows," she asserted "except in Government offices and then with great care lest anyone be hurt. On many a prison wall in England is carved 'Resistance to tyranny is obedience to God' and in this spirit we smashed windows."

She alleged that certain Suffragettes were placed in punishment cells, into which light only came for one hour a day through thick bottle glass, and the only furniture was a rough seat and a plank bed, which had not always a mattress. Being pressed to tell of her exploit at the Guildhall, which resulted in her imprisonment and hunger strike, she said:

"With a hospital nurse I disguised myself as a charwoman, and we hid in the building all day. We heard the police searching it, and one man, seeing me lying behind a heap of lumber, thought I was a policeman taking a nap. We could not get into the banquet hall, but we established ourselves in the gallery of the Council Chamber and broke a pane of the window looking into the banquet hall.

"I began to make a speech to Mr. Asquith. The band started playing and the police hurried to the roof. They always look for suffragettes for some reason on the roof. The band stopped and we went on with our speech. Then they took us and we got a month each."

Miss Inez Milholland, the Vassar graduate, who has been prominent in the shirtwaist strike, was one of the other speakers answering questions on the suffrage movement sent up from the audience.[105]

2.

Report of Emmeline Pankhurst's speech at the 1911 NAWSA convention in *History of Woman Suffrage*, volume 5

Mrs. Emmeline Pankhurst of England, received an ovation when she rose to speak and soon disarmed prejudice by her dignified and womanly manner. She began by pointing out the fallacy that the women of the United States had so many rights and privileges that they did not need the suffrage and in proof she quoted existing laws and conditions that called loudly for a change. She then took up the situation in Great Britain and explained how many years the women had tried to get the franchise by constitutional methods only to be deceived and spurned by the Government. She told how at last a small handful of them started a revolution; how they had grown into an army; how they had suffered imprisonment and brutality; how the suffrage bill had again and again passed the second reading by immense majorities and the Government had refused to let it come to a final vote. "We asked Prime Minister Asquith to give us a time for this," she said. "For eight long hours in a heavy frost some of the finest women in England stood at the entrance to the House of Commons and waited humbly with petitions in their hands for their rulers and masters to condescend to receive them but the House adjourned while they stood there. The next day, while they waited again, there was an assault by the police, acting under instructions, that I do not like to dwell upon outside of my own country."[106]

3.
Speech of Margaret Hinchey, a laundry worker, at the 1913 NAWSA convention

It was a comparatively new thing to have women wage-earners on the woman suffrage platform and their speeches made a deep impression, as that of Miss Hinchey, for instance, who said in part:

> When we went to Albany to ask for votes one member of the Legislature told us that a woman's place was at home. Another said he had too much respect and admiration for women to see them at the polls. Another went back to Ancient Rome and told a story about Cornelia and her jewels—her children. Yet in the laundries women were working seventeen and eighteen hours a day, standing over heavy machines for $3 and $3.50 a week. Six dollars a week is the average wage of working women in the

United States. How can a woman live an honorable life on such a sum? Is it any wonder that so many of our little sisters are in the gutter? When we strike for more pay we are clubbed by the police and by thugs hired by our employers, and in the courts our word is not taken and we are sent to prison. This is the respect and admiration shown to working girls in practice. I want to tell you about Cornelia as we find her case today. The agent of the Child Labor Society made an investigation in the tenements and found mothers with their small children sitting and standing around them—standing when they were too small to see the top of the table otherwise. They were working by a kerosene lamp and breathing its odor and they were all making artificial forget-me-nots. It takes 1,620 pieces of material to make a gross of forget-me-nots and the profit is only a few cents.

Four years ago 30,000 shirtwaist girls went on strike and when we went to Mayor McClellan to ask permission for them to have a parade he said: "Thirty thousand women are of no account to me." If they had been 30,000 women with votes would he have said that? We have in New York 14,000 women over sixty-five years old who must work or starve. What is done with them when their bones give out and they cannot work any more? The police gather them up and you may then see in jail, scrubbing hard, rough concrete floors that make their knees bleed—women who have committed no crime but being old and poor. Don't take my word for it but send a committee to Blackwell's Island or the Tombs and see for yourselves. We have a few Old Ladies' Homes but with most of them it would take a piece of red tape as long as from here to New York to get in. Give us a square deal so that we may take care of ourselves.[107]

4.

Anna Howard Shaw's speech at the 1913 NAWSA convention

I know the objections to woman suffrage but I have never met any one who pretended to know any reasons against it. . . .

By some objectors women are supposed to be unfit to vote because they are hysterical and emotional and of course men would not like to have emotion enter into a political campaign. They want to cut out all emotion and so they would like to cut us out. I had heard so much about our emotionalism that I went to the last Democratic national convention, held at Baltimore, to observe the calm repose of the male politicians. I saw some men take a picture of one gentleman whom they wanted elected and it was so big they had to walk sidewise as they carried it forward; they were followed by hundreds of other men screaming and yelling, shouting and singing the "Houn' Dawg"; then, when there was a lull, another set of men would start forward under another man's picture, not to be outdone by the "Houn' Dawg" melody, whooping and howling still louder. I saw men jump up on the seats and throw their hats in the air and shout: "What's the matter with Champ Clark?" Then, when those hats came down, other men would kick them back into the air, shouting at the top of their voices: "He's all right!!" Then I heard others howling for "Underwood, Underwood, first, last and all the time!!" No hysteria about it—just patriotic loyalty, splendid manly devotion to principle. And so they went on and on until 5 o'clock in the morning—the whole night long. I saw men jump up on their seats and jump down again and run around in a ring. I saw two men run towards another man to hug him both at once and they split his coat up the middle of his back and sent him spinning around like a wheel. All this with the perfect poise of the legal male mind in politics!

I have been to many women's conventions in my day but I never saw a woman leap up on a chair and take off her bonnet and toss it up in the air and shout: "What's the matter with" somebody. I never saw a woman knock another woman's bonnet off her head as she screamed: "She's all right!" I never heard a body of women whooping and yelling for five minutes when somebody's name was mentioned in the convention. But we are willing to admit that we are emotional. I have actually seen women stand up and wave their handkerchiefs. I have even seen them take hold of hands and sing, "Blest be the tie that binds." Nobody denies that women are excitable. Still, when I hear how emotional and how excitable we are, I cannot help seeing in my mind's eye the fine repose and dignity of this Baltimore and other political conventions I have attended![108]

5.

Helen Hamilton Gardener's 1913 speech to the House of Representatives calling for the establishment of a Committee on Woman Suffrage

Mrs. Helen H. Gardener (D. C.), after showing that woman suffrage was a mere side issue with the Judiciary Committee and that it would be busier than ever the coming session, said: "Those of us who live here and have known Congress from our childhood know that an outside matter has less chance to get any real consideration by such a committee under such conditions than the proverbial rich man has of entering the kingdom of heaven." She pointed out that over one-fifth of the Senate and one-seventh of the House were elected by the votes of women and continued:

You will remember that there is a committee on Indian Affairs. Are the Indians more important than the women of America? They did not always have a special committee, they used to be a mere incident, as we now are. They used to be under the War Department and so long as this was the case nobody ever doubted for an instant that the "only good Indian was a dead Indian"—just as under the incidental administration of the Judiciary Committee it is not doubted by some that the only good woman is a voteless woman. When the Indians secured a committee of their own they began to get schools, lands in severalty and the general status of human beings. . . . It became the duty of that committee to investigate the real conditions, the needs, the grievances and the best methods of promoting the interests of the Indians. That was the beginning of the end of Indian wars; the first hope of a possibility—previously sneered at—of making real and useful citizens of this race of men who now have Representatives in Congress. It was precisely the same with our island possessions, only in this case we had profited by our experience with Indian and labor problems, and it did not take so long to realize that a committee whose duty it should be to utilize, develop and conserve the best interests of these new charges of our Government and to develop them toward citizenship as rapidly as possible was the safe and sane method of procedure. . . .

We want such a committee on woman suffrage in the House. We do not ask you to appoint a partisan committee but only one open-minded and honest, which will really investigate and understand the question, its workings where it is in effect—a committee which will not accept wild statements as facts, which will hear and weigh that which comes from the side of progress and change as well as that which is static or reactionary. . . . The recommendation that we have such a committee does not in any way commit you to the adoption of a belief in the principle of self-government for women. This is not much to ask and it is not much to give, nor will it be needed for very many more years.[109]

6.
Carrie Chapman Catt, *Address to the Congress on Women's Suffrage*, November 1917

Woman suffrage is inevitable. Suffragists knew it before November 4, 1917; opponents afterward. Three distinct causes made it inevitable.

First, the history of our country. Ours is a nation born of revolution, of rebellion against a system of government so securely entrenched in the customs and traditions of human society that in 1776 it seemed impregnable. From the beginning of things, nations had been ruled by kings and for kings, while the people served and paid the cost. The American Revolutionists boldly proclaimed the heresies: "Taxation without representation is tyranny." "Governments derive their just powers from the consent of the governed." The colonists won, and the nation which was established as a result of their victory has held unfailingly that these two fundamental principles of democratic government are not only the spiritual source of our national existence but have been our chief historic pride and at all times the sheet anchor of our liberties.

Eighty years after the Revolution, Abraham Lincoln welded those two maxims into a new one: "Ours is a government of the people, by the people, and for the people." Fifty years more passed and the president of the United States, Woodrow Wilson, in a mighty crisis of the nation, proclaimed to the world: "We are fighting for the things which we have always carried nearest to our hearts: for democracy, for the right of those who submit to authority to have a voice in their own government."

All the way between these immortal aphorisms political leaders have declared unabated faith in their truth. Not one American has arisen to question their logic in the 141 years of our national existence. However stupidly our country may have evaded the logical application at times, it has never swerved from its devotion to the theory of democracy as expressed by those two axioms. . . .

With such a history behind it, how can our nation escape the logic it has never failed to follow, when its last un-enfranchised class calls for the vote? Behold our Uncle Sam floating the banner with one hand, "Taxation without representation is tyranny," and with the other seizing the billions of dollars paid in taxes by women to whom he refuses "representation." Behold him again, welcoming the boys of twenty-one and the newly made immigrant citizen to "a voice in their own government" while he denies that fundamental right of democracy to thousands of women public school teachers from whom many of these men learn all they know of citizenship and patriotism, to women college presidents, to women who preach in our pulpits, interpret law in our courts, preside over our hospitals, write books and magazines, and serve in every uplifting moral and social enterprise. Is there a single man who can justify such inequality of treatment, such outrageous discrimination? Not one.

Second, the suffrage for women already established in the United States makes women suffrage for the nation inevitable. When Elihu Root, as president of the American Society of International Law, at the eleventh annual meeting in Washington, April 26, 1917, said, "The world cannot be half democratic and half autocratic. It must be all democratic or all Prussian. There can be no compromise," he voiced a general truth. Precisely the same intuition has already taught the blindest and most hostile foe of woman suffrage that our nation cannot long continue a condition under which government in half its territory rests upon the consent of half of the people and in the other half upon the consent of all the people; a condition which grants representation to the taxed in half of its territory and denies it in the other half; a condition which permits women in some states to share in the election of the president, senators, and representatives and denies them that privilege in others. It is too obvious to require demonstration that woman suffrage, now covering half our territory, will eventually be ordained in all the nation. No one will deny it. The only question left is when and how will it be completely established.

Third, the leadership of the United States in world democracy compels the enfranchisement of its own women. The maxims of the Declaration were once called "fundamental principles of government." They are now called "American principles" or even "Americanisms." They have become the slogans of every movement toward political liberty the world around, of every effort to widen the suffrage for men or women in any land. Not a people, race, or class striving for freedom is there anywhere in the world that has not made our axioms the chief weapon of the struggle. More, all men and women the world around, with far-sighted vision into the verities of things, know that the world tragedy of our day is not now being waged over the assassination of an archduke, nor commercial competition, nor national ambitions, nor the freedom of the seas. It is a death grapple between the forces which deny and those which uphold the truths of the Declaration of Independence.

Do you realize that in no other country in the world with democratic tendencies is suffrage so completely denied as in a considerable number of our own states? There are thirteen black states where no suffrage for women exists, and fourteen others where suffrage for women is more limited than in many foreign countries.

Do you realize that when you ask women to take their cause to state referendum you compel them to do this: that you drive women of education, refinement, achievement, to beg men who cannot read for their political freedom?

Do you realize that such anomalies as a college president asking her janitor to give her a vote are overstraining the patience and driving women to desperation?

Do you realize that women in increasing numbers indignantly resent the long delay in their enfranchisement?

Your party platforms have pledged women suffrage. Then why not be honest, frank friends of our cause, adopt it in reality as your own, make it a party program, and "fight with us"? As a party measure—a measure of all parties—why not put the amendment through Congress and the legislatures? We shall all be better friends, we shall have a happier nation, we women will be free to support loyally the party of our choice, and we shall be far prouder of our history.

"There is one thing mightier than kings and armies"—aye, than Congresses and political parties—"the power of an idea when its time has come to move." The time for woman suffrage has come. The woman's hour has struck. If parties prefer to postpone action longer and thus do battle with this idea, they challenge the inevitable. The idea will not perish; the party which opposes it may. Every delay, every trick, every political dishonesty from now on will antagonize the women of the land more and more, and when the party or parties which have so delayed woman suffrage finally let it come, their sincerity will be doubted and their appeal to the new voters will be met with suspicion. This is the psychology of the situation. Can you afford the risk? Think it over.

We know you will meet opposition. There are a few "women haters" left, a few "old males of the tribe," as Vance Thompson calls them, whose duty they believe it to be to keep women in the places they have carefully picked out for them. Treitschke, made world famous by war literature, said some years ago, "Germany, which knows all about Germany and France, knows far better what is good for Alsace-Lorraine than that miserable people can possibly know." A few American Treitschkes we have who know better than women what is good for them. There are women, too, with "slave souls" and "clinging vines" for backbones. There are female dolls and male dandies. But the world does not wait for such as these, nor does liberty pause to heed the plaint of men and women with a grouch. She does not wait for those who have a special interest to serve, nor a selfish reason for depriving other people of freedom. Holding her torch aloft, liberty is pointing the way onward and upward and saying to America, "Come."

To you and the supporters of our cause in Senate and House, and the number is large, the suffragists of the nation express their grateful thanks. This address is not meant for you. We are more truly appreciative of all you have done than any words can express. We ask you to make a last, hard fight for the amendment during the present session. Since last we asked a vote on this amendment, your position has been fortified by the addition to suffrage territory of Great Britain, Canada, and New York.

Some of you have been too indifferent to give more than casual attention to this question. It is worthy of your immediate consideration. A question big enough to engage the attention of our allies in wartime is too big a question for you to neglect.

Some of you have grown old in party service. Are you willing that those who take your places by and by shall blame you for having failed to keep pace with the world and thus having lost for them a party advantage? Is there any real gain for you, for your party, for your nation by delay? Do you want to drive the progressive men and women out of your party?

Some of you hold to the doctrine of states' rights as applying to woman suffrage. Adherence to that theory will keep the

United States far behind all other democratic nations upon this question. A theory which prevents a nation from keeping up with the trend of world progress cannot be justified.

Gentlemen, we hereby petition you, our only designated representatives, to redress our grievances by the immediate passage of the Federal Suffrage Amendment and to use your influence to secure its ratification in your own state, in order that the women of our nation may be endowed with political freedom before the next presidential election, and that our nation may resume its world leadership in democracy.

Woman suffrage is coming—you know it. Will you, Honorable Senators and Members of the House of Representatives, help or hinder it?[110]

7.
"Woman Suffrage and the Fifteenth Amendment," by Mary Church Terrell, published in *The Crisis*, August 1915

Even if I believed that women should be denied the right of suffrage, wild horses could not drag such an admission from my pen or my lips, for this reason: precisely the same arguments used to prove that the ballot be withheld from women are advanced to prove that colored men should not be allowed to vote. The reasons for repealing the Fifteenth Amendment differ but little from the arguments advanced by those who oppose the enfranchisement of women. Consequently, nothing could be more inconsistent than that colored people should use their influence against granting the ballot to women, if they believe that colored men should enjoy this right which citizenship confers.

What could be more absurd and ridiculous than that one group of individuals who are trying to throw off the yoke of oppression themselves, so as to get relief from conditions which handicap and injure them, should favor laws and customs which impede the progress of another unfortunate group and hinder them in every conceivable way. For the sake of consistency, therefore, if my sense of justice were not developed at all, and I could not reason intelligently, as a colored woman I should not tell my dearest friend that I opposed woman suffrage.

But how can any one who is able to use reason, and who believes in dealing out justice to all God's creatures, think it is right to withhold from one-half the human race rights and privileges freely accorded to the other half, which is neither more deserving nor more capable of exercising them?

For two thousand years mankind has been breaking down the various barriers which interposed themselves between human beings and their perfect freedom to exercise all the faculties with which they were divinely endowed. Even in monarchies old fetters which formerly restricted freedom, dwarfed the intellect and doomed certain individuals to narrow circumscribed spheres, because of the mere accident of birth are being loosed and broken one by one. In view of such wisdom and experience the political subjection of women in the United States can be likened only to a relic of barbarism, or to a spot upon the sun, or to an octopus holding this republic in its hideous grasp, so that further progress to the best form of government is impossible and that precious ideal its founders promised it would be seems nothing more tangible than a mirage.[111]

8.
"Arrest 41 Pickets for Suffrage at the White House,"
the *New York Times*, November 11, 1917

Forty-one woman suffragists from fifteen States were arrested this afternoon for picketing outside the White House. Their adventure was one of the quietest and at the same time most sedately spectacular of all the picketing affairs yet staged.

Of the group of forty-one pickets, twelve were from New York City. The prisoners included Mrs. Harvey W. Wiley, wife of the pure food expert; Mrs. William Kent, wife of former Representative Kent of California, now a member of the Tariff

Commission, and Miss Lucy Burns, Vice Chairman of the Woman's Party.

All of the forty-one pickets, after having a ride in the Black Maria to the police station, were registered and then promptly released under $25 bail each. Miss Mary Ingham of Philadelphia, who did not have herself arrested, furnished the bail, aggregating $1,025, and the prisoners were allowed to go pending hearing on Monday in the Police Court.

Crowd Watches Arrests.

The picketing had been heralded by the National Woman's party for 4 o'clock, and at that hour Pennsylvania Avenue, all along the roadway before the White House, was jammed with men and women to take in the sight. The police under Captain Flather had to push back the crowd to let the trolley cars pass.

Soon after 4 o'clock the cavalcade of forty-one picketers, formed into five divisions, left Cameron House, off Lafayette Square, and began their descent toward the east gate of the White House. On former raids by the picketers the crowds jeered, but today there was none of it. A murmur arose as the vanguard of suffragists, with Mrs. Brannan at their head, marched across Pennsylvania Avenue.

The suffragists carried their usual display of banners, one at the head of the line reading: "Mr. President, in your message to Congress urge the amendment enfranchising women." Various other banners conveyed the idea to the throng that the demonstration was intended to impress the President with the urgency of his advocacy of the suffrage amendment.

The marching pickets lengthened their line appreciably as the vanguard approached the east gate, so that the New York women advanced on it alone. Immediately the New York women reached the gate they were stopped by Captain Flather.

The police officer quietly informed them that they must "move on." Mrs. Brannan replied that they intended doing no such thing. The Captain gave them a moment to wait; then, motioning to half a dozen policemen standing at his elbow, he ordered the women escorted to the Black Maria. They went without protest, completely filling the conveyance.

While the Black Maria was driving off to the police station the second group of suffragists had worked its way to the west gate of the White House. In this group were women from Massachusetts, headed by Mrs. Agnes H. Morey of Brookline, followed by Pennsylvania and New Jersey women. Mrs. Lawrence Lewis, who marched in this group, was one of the sixteen pickets arrested last July and pardoned by President Wilson after being sentenced to Occoquan.

Picket Takes Her Child Along.

It took the police just three minutes to head off the group at the west gate, and they were soon in another Black Maria. While they were being disposed of the third group, led by Mrs. William S. Kent, wife of a member of the Tariff Commission, appeared at the east gate. In Mrs. Kent's division were suffragists from Oregon, Utah, and Colorado. With Mrs. Kent was her 10-year-old son, Sherman, who held her arm and stood with her until she and the others of her group were escorted to the wagon.

The watching throng by this time had got accustomed to the quick shift from one gate to the other, so that it was not surprised when the fourth group, led by Mrs. Charles W. Barnes and comprising picketers from Oklahoma, Minnesota, and Iowa, surged toward the west gate. Immediately the police broke up the attack and the Black Maria started off again.

The last assault was upon the east gate, Mrs. Harvey W. Wiley heading this force. In her ranks were women from the District of Columbia, Louisiana, Maryland and Florida, the latter State having as its picketer Mrs. Mary A. Nolan, who is 73 years old. The Southern group was bundled off to a police station and that ended the picketing. In the District of Columbia group was Miss Lucy Burns, who was released last Saturday after a sixty-day sentence at Occoquan.

Every detachment that went to jail carried its banners along with it, the crowd having made no attempt to seize the pennants and the police not bothering about it.

While the last group was being taken away in the Black Maria, President Wilson, who had been out motoring with Mrs. Wilson, entered the White House grounds through the gate leading to the executive offices. The President could not help seeing the huge throng clustered before the White House.

Bore Five-Foot Banners.

Miss Lucy Burns telephoned from Washington to the New York headquarters of the Woman's Party yesterday that each of the forty-one pickets arrested carried a five-foot banner in stripes of purple, green, and white with an inscription addressed to the President.

Of the women arrested, Mrs. John Winters Brannan, who has previously been imprisoned in Occoquan, is the wife of a New York physician who is President of the Board of Trustees of Bellevue and Allied Hospitals and lives at 125 East Fifty-seventh Street. Mrs. Brannan was an officer of the Women's Political Union, most of whose members went over to the National Woman's Party. Mrs. Henry Butterworth was another officer of the union. Mrs. Ella Guilford was for a long time a worker with the organizations of the conservative suffragists.

Miss Elsie Hill of Washington, daughter of the late Congressman Hill of Connecticut, said yesterday:

"Once more the Administration finds itself in an embarrassing position of arresting on technical charges the women relatives of strong Administration supporters. Mrs. William Kent of California is the wife of the National Chairman of the Wilson Independent League, ex-Representative Kent, who has recently been appointed member of the Tariff Board. Miss Mary Bartlett Dixon is *own cousin* of Mitchell Palmer of Pennsylvania, Democratic floor leader in Mr. Wilson's first Administration, and recently appointed receiver of enemy property.

"Others arrested were Mrs. Harvey Wiley, daughter of the late General Kelton, U. S. A., and wife of the pure food expert. Dr. Wiley stumped the country for the election of Mr. Wilson in his first Presidential campaign. One of the most interested prisoners the jail authorities will have under their control is Miss Paula Jacobi of this city, who was for four months matron of a prison in Massachusetts and has studied prison reforms ever since."

Mrs. Oliver H. P. Belmont, member of the National Executive Committee of the National Woman's Party, said:

"What have we come to in America when splendid women, loving liberty, are arrested for asking this simple question: 'Mr. President, in your message to Congress, urge the passage of the Federal suffrage amendment enfranchising women'?"[112]

9.
"Woman Suffrage and the Negro," by A. Philip Randolph, the *Messenger,* November 1917

Woman suffrage is coming!

Some women want it, and some women don't want it.

Women are taxpayers, producers and consumers just the same as men are, and they are justly entitled to vote.

The sentimental and puritanical objections advanced by the squeamish moralists won't stand. Sex is no bar to woman's participating in the industrial world and it should be none to her participating in the political world.

Negro men should realize their responsibility and duty in the coming election on the question of woman suffrage. Remember that if the right to vote benefits the Negro man, the right to vote will also benefit the Negro woman.

If white women ought to have the right to vote, then colored women ought to have the right to vote. If it will be beneficial to one, it will be beneficial to the other. Colored Women are taxpayers, producers and consumers and they have a right to express their sentiment as regards the school systems, sanitation, the high cost of living, war and everything else which affects the general public. Of course, there are some colored women who will speak against woman suffrage, just as there are some white women who will speak for it. There were some Negro slaves who were opposed to freedom. Such kinks in the mind of the common people are not unusual.

Of course, when they are seen among the aristocracy, the reason is not difficult to see. Throughout history the few have attempted to keep the many in economic and political slavery.

But the great sweep of democracy moves on. The artificial standards of sex or race should not stand against it.

All peoples, regardless of race, creed or sex will be drawn into the vortex of world democracy.

Just as there could not be any union while some men were slaves and some men were free, there can be no democracy while white men vote and white women, colored women and colored men in the South don't vote.

Mr. Negro Voter, do your "bit."[113]

X.

1920: The Final Victory

The National American Woman Suffrage Association's final convention was the largest it ever assembled, but for the second year in a row its members were disappointed in their plan to celebrate a suffrage victory. Still, with victory so near, the majority of the seven days were given to working out the organizational details of the League of Women Voters as a new and independent society bringing together the NAWSA state auxiliaries for a smooth transition after the suffrage amendment was ratified.[1]

The NAWSA held the convention from February 12 to 18 to commemorate both Susan B. Anthony's hundredth birthday and Valentine's Day; the latter celebrated by suffragists with a living "ratification valentine," where presidents of ratified states one by one appeared in the opening to recite satirical rhymes about the unratified states.[2]

Within a month after the convention thirty-five states had ratified the amendment, leaving only one more state to meet the required three-fourths of the states needed to place the amendment in the Constitution. Of the twelve unratified states, including Connecticut and Vermont, the suffragists decided to go South to get Tennessee as the thirty-sixth.

Suffragists from all over the country flooded the state, both the NAWSA and the NWP joining the state women who had worked for years, all wearing yellow roses to identify one another. The anti-suffragists sported red roses. The NAACP worked behind the scenes for the amendment. NAWSA members Kate Gordon and Laura Clay opposed it. The last holdouts of the Southern States Woman Suffrage Conference, they stayed firm for states' rights to the bitter end. Lobbyists buttonholed legislators to go with the antis, their salaries paid by corporate interests fearing woman suffrage might mean equal pay and lost profits.

The opposition was religious, sexist, and racist. In a flyer titled "That Deadly Parallel," antis warned:

MEN OF THE SOUTH: Heed not the song of the suffrage siren! Seal your ears against her vocal wiles! For, no matter how sweetly she may proclaim the advantages of female franchise,

REMEMBER that *woman suffrage* means a reopening of the entire *Negro suffrage* question, loss of State rights, and another period of reconstruction horrors, which will introduce a set of female carpetbaggers as bad as their male prototypes of the sixties.

DO NOT JEOPARDIZE the present prosperity of your sovereign State, which was so dearly bought by the blood of your fathers and the tears of your mothers by again raising an issue which has already been adjusted at so great a cost.

NOTHING can be gained by woman suffrage, and much may be lost.[3]

Harriet Taylor Upton described "The Story of the 36th State" in the Ohio Woman Suffrage Association's *News Bulletin*. The full report is included in this chapter.

On August 26, 1920, the Nineteenth Amendment, guaranteeing women the right to vote in the United States of America, was officially added to the Constitution. Alice Paul unfurled the banner bearing the final thirty-sixth star over the balcony of the National Woman's Party headquarters. Catt and the NAWSA workers rushed back from Tennessee for victory celebrations in Washington and New York City.

The enemies of woman suffrage would not go down to defeat quietly, however. Throughout the country they pressured state attorneys general to declare the ratification unconstitutional or to require further legislation by the states. The NAWSA retained former U.S. Supreme Court justice Charles Evans Hughes as counsel in May 1920. Two anti-suffrage lawsuits were brought; one in Washington, D.C., the other in Maryland. Both lost and were appealed to the Supreme Court.

Meanwhile, millions of women voted in the general election on November 2, 1920, and in the state and local elections that followed through 1921, and the cases were almost forgotten. Finally, the Supreme Court heard the anti-suffrage arguments, and on February 27, 1922, it handed down its decision on the two cases. It upheld the authority of Congress under the Constitution of the United States to submit the amendment; declared that "the validity of the 15th Amendment had been recognized for half a century"; that "the Federal Constitution transcends any limitations sought to be imposed by the State"; that "the Secretary of State having issued the proclamation the amendment had become a part of the National Constitution."[4]

The victory must have been bittersweet. How much time, energy, and money had been consumed in finally achieving a simple right that should have been women's from the founding of the government? What might women have achieved toward gaining full personhood and rights that they still don't have today in the United States if they had not been tied up in pursuing this fundamental right? Catt reminisced a few years later:

> It is doubtful if any man, even among suffrage men, ever realized what the suffrage struggle came to mean to women before the end was allowed in America. How much of time and patience, how much work, energy and aspiration, how much faith, how much hope, how much despair went into it. It leaves its mark on one, such a struggle. It fills the days and it rides the nights. Working, eating, drinking, sleeping, it is there.[5]

The NAWSA folded into the League of Women Voters, and the organization continues its voter education work to this day.

The NWP closed its headquarters after ratification and temporarily stopped operations, concentrating on paying its bills. Then on February 15, 1921, the members held a convention to decide whether to disband or continue the work. The vote, they decided, was just a piece of the broader issues of women's rights, and the guarantee of equal rights for women needed to be embedded in the Constitution. At a follow-up meeting held in Seneca Falls in 1923 on the seventy-fifth anniversary of that first 1848 local women's rights convention, the National Woman's Party wrote a simple amendment, which was introduced in Congress in 1924.

While modified several times, the language of the Equal Rights Amendment (ERA) remains simple:

Section 1. Equality of rights under the law shall not be denied or abridged by the United States or by any State on account of sex.

Section 2. The Congress shall have the power to enforce, by appropriate legislation, the provisions of this article.

Section 3. This amendment shall take effect two years after the date of ratification.

It took women seventy-two years of work from the 1848 Seneca Falls convention until the suffrage amendment was finally ratified in 1920. Women have fought for the Equal Rights Amendment for ninety-five years, and of this writing, in 2019, women still do not have equal rights guaranteed in the Constitution of the United States. The struggle for the full personhood and equality our foremothers envisioned remains today for us to complete.

I.
"The Story of the 36th State," Harriet Taylor Upton in the *Headquarters News Bulletin*, September 1, 1920

Nearly every day of the Tennessee ratification campaign there was a scenario for a motion picture if any one had had time to write it.

Some 7 weeks ago Mrs. Catt went to Tennessee to help plan the campaign. She expected to stay a few days. In Tennessee there were the suffragists of the original organization and the League of Women Voters. By the time the legislature opened it was deemed advisable to form a new Ratification Committee with Miss Chart Williams, vice chairman of the National Democratic Committee as chairman. From that time on Mrs. Catt acted in an advisory capacity only and the Tennessee women were the active workers.

The Sunday preceding the opening of the session the National Republican Committee sent me to Tennessee to assist the Republicans in their work for ratification. No one person, no group, no party brought about the result in Tennessee but it was the combination of all of these. Mrs. Catt, whose experience has been a long one, said she never saw so vicious a lobby as that opposed to us and as for myself, sometimes I was terrified by the terrible hostility. No group of women ever worked harder than did the Tennessee women; they were largely young women and they started in full of vigor and I saw them grow pale and weak and fairly prostrated before they were through. They feared nothing, they left no stone unturned, they were resourceful beyond anything I have ever known. They were fearless, relentlessly calling down their adversaries as occasion required. Their men worked with them and for them with the same sort of valor that they would have fought a physical battle.

The legislature opened on the morning of August 9. It was the intention to introduce the ratification resolution in the lower house but as the speaker of that house, who had been a friend of the Governor and who had put through the presidential suffrage bill of the year before, suddenly became opposed to the ratification, the tactics were changed and the resolution was put into the Senate. The Senate had 23 members, 25 Democrats, 8 Republicans. Of the 8 Republicans, 7 voted for ratification. Of the 25 Democrats 18 voted for, 3 against and 4 did not vote at all. It was thus clearly demonstrated that the Republicans were going to hold the balance of power in this fight. Too much cannot be said for these splendid Republican

mountaineers who from the beginning to the end of that wonderful battle, stood their ground and never flinched. Going up
in the elevator one day a man was overheard to say, "We have
got to get some men of our own, we can't budge those Republicans."

The bill passed the Senate on Friday, the 13th. Everybody
said it was going to be our unlucky day but in order to have
the superstition proven it was the unlucky day for the antis. The
legislature adjourned over Sunday and upon their return the
House took up the matter. There were 99 members originally in
the House, one had resigned, a constitutional quorum was 50.
In the House were 28 Republicans and 71 Democrats. Two of
the 28 Republicans were absent on account of sickness, 26 were
present. On the ratification 15 voted for, 11 against. Of the
Democrats present there were 70, 36 voted against and 34 for,
a majority of the Democrats of the House therefore were
against. On the total there were 49 favorable votes and these
men were called the immortal 49 and there were 47 against.

As one looks back on the days spent in Tennessee and re-
members how we sat at the window and looked out on the
Capitol waiting for the verdict, how we encouraged and assisted the men who were with us, how we sympathized with
and helped as we could the Tennessee women, how we each in
turn grew brave when the others were despondent, how elated
and happy we were sometimes, how perfectly despairing we
were at others, the thing that stands out above all these things
was the vicious lobby which centered in Tennessee. There were
women wearing red roses from Massachusetts and from Louisiana, women who probably were sincere in their beliefs that
the enfranchisement of women meant ruination to the country.
There were Miss Kate Gordon and Miss Laura Clay working
against the ratification because they believe in State's Rights.

. . . The anti women were of course trying to us and I never
had seen them so strenuous. One jostled me in the elevator as
if she felt I ought not to be there but Oh! The subtilty and the
wickedness and the viciousness of the men lobbyists who were
there. The whiskey lobby was there in all its strength. The railroad lobby was there and one member on the floor said that

that lobby had dominated the state for fifty years and it had taken the question of woman suffrage to free the legislature from it. The manufacturers' lobby was there and on one day a certain manufacturer dismissed the girls in his factory and put red roses on them and had them go to the Capitol to swell the numbers of the antis. There were mysterious men nobody knew where they came from, whom they represented. For the first time in my life I would open my door suddenly and find a man standing there as if he expected to find that I had been doing something unlawful in regard to ratification. A telegram of mine was stolen between my room and the operating desk and so bold was the thief that he gave it to a newspaper and it was published facsimile. One of the ratification men was carried off and hidden and a most thorough search had to [be] instituted before he could be found and brought back. Harry Burns who voted as his mother asked him to and, as he announced from the floor, because his party had promised to, was the object of a most scandalous attack. The governor was visited by a very influential citizen who was financially and other ways very powerful and told that if he did not retrace his steps and come out against ratification he would be ruined. A young man who was for ratification was called out of bed every half hour throughout a whole night and almost as often during the second night and was asked to come down town, that he was needed. He constantly refused but this calling to the telephone kept him awake all night and the purpose of the whole thing was to get him so tired and sleepy that his morale would be broken. He was a youth too and it did not seem as if such tactics could be resorted to. Alcohol was as free as air and men who had any weakness in that direction were soon silenced in sleep. The wife of a prominent official in a southern state, immediately after Harry Burns had voted for ratification, took a train and went to his home in Niota, called upon his mother and tried to make her say that she had not written the letter to her son, tried to make her say she was not a suffragist, tried to make her write her son to change his mind but this woman of the Tennessee mountains, who never had seen a living suffragist, who never had been identified with them, knew so well the justice of the cause that nothing moved her. In speaking of it afterwards, she said gently she had almost to show the lady the door in order to get rid of her.

Yes, as I write I can see plainly the State House in Nashville. It stands out so strong against the sky. I can feel again the palpitation of my heart and can hear the cheers and not know what happened inside. I can see the people as they rush out of that capitol, as they come to tell us the news. It is all so plain to me, that building surrounded by its hills and its beautiful valleys and it seemed almost suitable that our fight should have been ended in that very state, the state of Andrew Jackson and his beloved Rachel for whom he fought.

Speaker Walker left the chair and took charge of the forces on the floor. In the Senate Senator Candler the only Republican who voted against it made a most vicious old time anti suffrage appeal on sex lines. It was disgusting. There was talk of asking him either to openly apologize or expel him from the Senate. In the House a number of speeches were made for and against and Speaker Walker closed the debate. On all subsidiary motions the vote had stood 48 to 48. One cannot imagine the tension that was on as these votes were being taken. As Speaker Walker closed his speech, the capitol surging full of people, he marched down the aisle and said, "The battle has been fought and we have won, I call for the previous question" and then the roll call was taken. A Republican mountaineer named Anderson was the first on the roll call. He was told to shout his "aye" and this he did. In a moment or two there was a sensation. Harry Burns a mountain lad of 24 years who had been voting "no" on all the subsidiary motions raised his voice and voted loudly "yes." The leaders knew they were lost unless they could bring over some ratificationist to the anti ratification side and Seth Walker walked down the aisle and put his arm around Mr. Turner's shoulders and held him fast. Mr. Turner had in the beginning been rather inclined not to ratify but on the subsidiary roll call he had voted for the ratificationists. It was now up to Mr. Walker to persuade him in the few seconds that were before him to go back to his original place. It was terrible for the ratificationists to stand and see the arm of the most powerful man in the legislature resting on the shoulders of a man who had voted both ways and yet the ratificationists knew that Mr. Turner had been converted to the ratification side and was conscientiously for it. There was a breathless silence when his name was called but he voted right and everybody knew as soon as his voice had died away and the clerk had reiterated his vote after him that the ratificationists had won. Mr. Walker, pale and trembling, walked down the aisle of the House of Representatives and asked to have his vote changed from "no" to "yes" and by that change of 50 to 46 the ratificationists were given a constitutional quorum which they otherwise would not have had and which made impossible some litigation which they had feared. The House immediately adjourned amid great excitement. There was hardly a person in that capital that did not wear either a yellow flower or a red rose.

Under the law of the Tennessee legislature, a man voting for reconsideration controls the question of that reconsideration for two days. No one else can bring it up, he is at liberty to bring it up at any time. So for two days the legislature had to wait for Mr. Seth Walker to bring up his re-consideration. He did not do it the first day and that night, Thursday, the anti suffragists held a great meeting. Miss Beatrice Shillito of Cincinnati, paid for the great auditorium and for the band. Speeches were made by prominent citizens, the suffragists were accused of being every kind of awful thing, Mr. Seth Walker said they would go to vote the next morning, that they had made three converts and that was sufficient to carry. People hardly slept that night, canvassing their men, looking over the situation, thinking what they could possibly do. The next morning when the House was called to order Mr. Walker did not dare bring up the re-consideration, as three men had disappeared and he did not have the votes. Up to this time each side was afraid of the other it was so desperately close, no wonder. Then the antis moved to adjourn until Monday. This would give them three days in which to work for converts but the ratificationists were too strong for them, and voted it down and passed a resolution to convene the following morning at

10 o'clock. It would be no use to bring up the question of re-consideration that day because the time had not expired.

As dramatic as was the ratification vote the vote to re-consider was more so. A man whose wife had been danger-ously ill and who had been home on a special train and come back to vote so that the Republicans had gained one vote. On the afternoon of this second Friday there were rumors abroad that the anti ratificationists were going to try to break the quo-rum. Everybody was on the qui vive. Every member of the leg-islature was watching and being watched. If a man went through the hall with a bag he was questioned as to where he was going. It was not alone the lobbyists who suffered during that session, no legislator had a happy time. As the night wore on the railroad stations were watched so that it might be known whether men were buying tickets to leave town and after the last train had gone, along towards three a.m. watch-ers all went to bed with the idea in a few hours more our ques-tion would be settled. We had counted without reason, 34 legislators had taken taxis for the station below town, bought tickets for Decatur, Ala., and as a reward a Baptist minister had made arrangements for them to attend his services on Sun-day morning. At 10 o'clock on Monday 50 ratificationists were in their seats and 9 anti ratificationists. Among the latter was Seth Walker. His only hope was to get a roll call on the fact that there was not a quorum present. That would make the ac-tion illegal. However the ratificationists were too hopeful to be careless and a number of subsidiary motions were lost and when the motion to reconsider was brought up it was defeated by 50, a constitutional majority and the question of no quorum did not appear on the record. It is easy to read that the vote stood 50 for and none against it but it was not such an easy thing to get that one vote.

Mr. Dodson, a young mountaineer who had been sticking closely to his job, received word a day or two before the vote was taken that his baby was sick. On Friday night late he got word that the baby was dying and he must come home imme-diately. Trains in Tennessee do not run often. There are few small towns which demand local trains and it was impossible at the time he got word to get a train until 11 o'clock the next morning. He telephoned to his wife that he would take the first train and he would be home the next night. Distances are great in Tennessee. The ratificationists therefore, in order to have the constitutional quorum, intended to have action taken before Mr. Dodson should leave. However they were delayed and at a quarter of 11 some suffragists took him to the train in a high power motor and bade him goodbye. Hardly was he gone when the ratificationists realized that if the motion to reconsider was voted down by less than a constitutional quorum, question might be raised, so taking another motor they hurried to the train and were obliged to sign two different papers in order to be let through, got to the Pullman car, brushed away the porter, grabbed Mr. Dodson, told him he must come back or all would be lost. He stood for a minute wavering between his sick baby and his political duty and then he was told that they would get a special train to take him home if possible and grabbing his bag the three men jumped off the train after it was in motion. He went back to the Capitol, voted "no" on reconsideration and saved the day. A special train was secured to reach Chattanooga in time to make the connection he would have made if he had taken an earlier train.

The ratification resolution having been signed by the Clerk of the House was sent back to the Senate where it originated and then to the Governor for signature. In the meantime the Governor had been enjoined from signing the certificate and he called in a number of legal authorities and every question in regard to it was settled. We of the outside heard that if the Governor disobeyed the injunction and was sent to prison he would be all right because he could pardon himself. Just what all the legal part of it was few of us knew but the Governor signed the certificate and sent it to the Secretary of State in Washington.

Yes, it was the most terrible fight that was ever made anywhere for suffrage and it was everybody's victory. It was woman's victory, it was man's victory, a Democratic Governor made the session of the legislature possible, a Republican minority held the balance of power and furnished the votes which

put it over and last of all the women of the north, in many
states, have really received their right to vote from the men of
the south. It was a terrible battle but it was worth while. Mrs.
Catt said in summing up the situation that it was brought
about by the political parties and a New York paper denied
this and said it was brought about by the women themselves.
Both statements were true, the women themselves fought the
battle and when they were strong enough and brave enough
the political parties saw the victory and espoused the cause. If
it had not been for the stand of the Democratic Party Governor
Roberts never would have called the legislature. If it had not
been for the stand of the Republican Party, the Republican
mountaineers would never have put over ratification.

Mrs. Catt, Miss Williams of the National Democratic committee and myself immediately boarded the train in order to
get into Washington when the certificate arrived. It preceded
us by a few hours because it was sent by special delivery and
we were not. When we arrived in Washington we went directly
to the Secretary of State's office and the Secretary of State read
his proclamation which was founded on the fact that he had
received the certificate of ratification from Governor Roberts.
We then proceeded to the Attorney General's office to see if
there was any possible action which our enemies could bring.
We talked the situation over from every angle and came away
satisfied that Tennessee was the 36th state to ratify the 19th
amendment and that the women of the United States would
vote in the election in November.

On the evening of Friday the 27th of August, the Poli theater
in Washington, was entirely filled. There was no more standing room even and at this meeting, Secretary of State Colby
brought a message from the President of the United States,
Miss Marjorie Shuler who had done the publicity in the Tennessee campaign spoke on the Immortal 49. Miss Charl Williams spoke on Women and Politics and I spoke on the 34 that
ran away. Mrs. Catt closed the evening meeting by reviewing
the whole Tennessee campaign. It was well that nationally
the work for the woman suffrage amendment was finished in the
capital where Susan B. Anthony, the woman who wrote the

19th amendment and had it presented in 1878 did most of her work.

The following day we all went to New York where the suffragists had planned a home-coming for Mrs. Catt. They had previously invited the rest of us. Philadelphia suffragists came down to the train and presented Mrs. Catt with flowers and paid her homage. In New York the Governor met Mrs. Catt, Democratic officials and Republican officials met Miss Williams, Mrs. Upton and Mrs. Catt and the moving picture machine got in its work and the procession moved to the Waldorf headed by a mounted policeman, a band and the carriage containing the speakers, Mrs. Catt being laden with flowers. At the Waldorf another meeting was held at which the same speakers spoke as had been at the Washington meeting and it was all over.[6]

Afterword:
Now That Our Journey Is at an End

This has been a journey of courage and cowardice; of principle and capitulation; of allies and racists. Examining our heroes and heras up close can be a painful process. Some may drop by the wayside to be replaced by others in our estimation as models of working for the greater good for all.

In her 1862 flag presentation speech sending the local boys off to the Civil War, Matilda Joslyn Gage predicted, "Unless liberty is attained—the broadest, the deepest, the highest liberty for *all*,—not for one set alone, one clique alone, but for man and woman, black and white, Irish, Germans, Americans, and negroes, there can be no permanent peace." Perhaps this is our new litmus test for historical respect: How well did this person work for liberty for "the broadest, deepest, and highest" liberty for all?

"We the people," the very first words of the Constitution, never meant all the people. The Founding Fathers meant themselves, white men with property. Our country's road to democracy has been a tug-of-war; progressives pulling for groups to be recognized as people with citizenship then entrenched power pushing them back by limiting that group. The Constitution recognized African American men as people in 1870; immediately the South imposed voting restrictions. Women legally became people in the United States in 1920, but money (poll taxes) and education requirements already in place in many states for men excluded many of those women from voting. Native Americans—like it or not—were told they were part of the people through the Indian Citizenship Act of 1924. Some chose to remain citizens in their own native nations, but many of those who wanted to vote as U.S. citizens were denied by states as late as 1957.

The exclusive club of U.S. citizenship kept being forced to expand its membership by those democracy-loving citizens who believed that "people" should mean everyone. Chinese American women and men weren't allowed into the club as United States citizens until 1943, after the repeal of the Chinese Exclusion Act. In 1946 Filipinos were allowed in; Japanese and other Asian Americans in 1952. In 1965, the Voting Rights Act made a valiant attempt to abolish the Jim Crow laws that kept African Americans from voting. The money requirement for voting was removed in 1966, when poll taxes were declared illegal. People with physical challenges gained access to the polls in 1990, with passage of the Americans with Disabilities Act.

This expanded definition of who are "we the people" is not secure or complete, nor will it be until there is a consensus in this country that it includes everyone. Citizens in our six territories: Washington, D.C.; Puerto Rico; American Samoa; Guam; the Northern Mariana Islands; and the U.S. Virgin Islands are considered only partial "people." Unable to vote for president, they have nonvoting representation in Congress. And those still determined to maintain white, native-born supremacy continue to try more and more devious means to push people out of the voting booth.

The Nineteenth Amendment, establishing the constitutional right of women to vote, doesn't constitute an end, a final victory. It's another benchmark in our progressive history of pushing open the door of citizenship to let more people in to take part in the decision-making process. The trajectory the Founding Fathers set was not toward equality. They practiced exclusion, but their words in the first sentence of the Constitution gave us a challenge to "establish Justice . . . promote the general Welfare, and secure the Blessings of Liberty to ourselves and our Posterity." It is up to us to continue to make manifest that challenge.

None of this history was inevitable. Each step along the way to equality, from the founding of the United States to the partial victory of the Nineteenth Amendment, history was made by the decisions people made, individually and as a group. Therein lies the "what if" of history, and the historical accountability.

While the Founding Fathers were schooled in democracy, watching it in action in the Haudenosaunee councils, what if they had also chosen to learn from the chiefs how essential women's voices were to the process? Further, if John Adams had listened to Abigail's counsel and warning to her husband, could the 144-year women's rebellion she predicted have been avoided?

When these men, many of them slave-owners, debated and then decided not to end the institution but to enable it in their founding document, they chose to abandon their own vision and create a partial democracy, an inherently unstable system built on liberty and justice for the minority of white men of means.

Later, the North may have won the Civil War, but it buckled under in the follow-up. If the Republican-controlled Congress had worried more about the future of democracy after the Civil War rather than maintaining the Republican majority, they could have created the Second American Revolution, guaranteeing political rights to all. Their self-serving behavior changed the course of history decisively. They pitted black men against women, with black women caught in the middle in a rupture we have yet to heal. Had women won political voice in that 1870 door-open moment, they could have concentrated, now with political power, on all the issues, such as body right, divorce reform, and equal pay, that they had raised before the Civil War. Instead, the white male representatives of the people, all elected by white men, set the woman's movement on a fifty-year uphill battle for full voting rights.

Our lives today would be different if individuals had made different choices. If another eleven women on the NWSA committee charged with deciding on the spot whether to merge with the AWSA in 1889 had joined the eleven who resisted the merger, they could have changed the course of women's history. Had they required a democratic vote of the whole membership, the merger offer of the AWSA probably would have once again been declined. The congressional momentum of the NWSA wouldn't have been lost, as it was, to the NAWSA's focus on state suffrage. Instead, the dynamic tension between the two original organizations would have been maintained. The AWSA state victories would have continued to produce congressional representatives elected partly by women voters to strengthen the unrelenting pressure the NWSA was putting on Congress to pass the federal woman's suffrage amendment. The NWSA's focus on the federal amendment would have kept everyone's eyes on the suffrage prize, a guarantee of the vote in the Constitution.

Movements are strengthened by a radical element pushing the envelope, which leaves the more conservative portion looking reasonable by comparison. The NWSA's direct action and civil disobedience opened people's ears to hear the tamer AWSA arguments. The loss of the NWSA, and the choices NAWSA leadership made, took the women's rights movement veering to the right.

When the merger favored the AWSA organizational structure, the grassroots process of the NWSA was lost. As the NAWSA leadership entrenched power at the top, disgruntled suffragists dropped out of the organization, often forming their own. State workers on the ground fought the national leadership's dictating their course of action and withholding money if the states didn't fall into line. Campaigns were disrupted and lost as a result. A grassroots movement had been turned into a top-down, authoritarian organization worthy of any corporation. Women made decisions that led to this outcome.

The result was a decade's standstill in the 1900s. Not a single suffrage victory, state or national, was achieved. Without the focused pressure of the NWSA, Congress, in fact, backslid, with not a single favorable report out of the committee hearings, unlike the previous decades. The hearings became a ceremony of respectability, as demonstrated by an Anthony anecdote after the 1900 hearings when the anti-suffragists were allowed to speak:

> Miss Anthony's love of the beautiful leads her always to clothe herself in good style and fine materials, and she has an eye for the fitness of things as well as for the funny side. "Girls," she said yesterday, after returning from the Capitol, "those statesmen eyed us very closely, but I will wager that it was impossible after we got mixed together to tell an anti from a suffragist by her clothes. There might have been a difference, though, in the expression of the faces and the shape of the heads," she added drily.[1]

Indeed. There might be a difference of opinion, but they were all fine, upstanding, white women. And respectable. "Beware, Susan," Stanton warned her friend, "as you become more respectable you become more conservative." The movement had lost its edge. Welcomed into congressional hearings and presidential receptions, the women were listened to respectfully by men who had no intention of acting on their requests. There was nothing to fear from these well-behaved women.

The Congressional Union and the National Woman's Party brought back the fighting edge of the movement. Although their confrontational tactics were denounced by the NAWSA, they put the fear of political loss into Congress and President Wilson, and got things moving again on the suffrage amendment. Their practice brought back the spirit of the NWSA, but, unlike the earlier organization, they focused only on the vote. And more important, they sometimes used racism to gain woman suffrage.

And then there was temperance, the legacy of the WCTU connection the NAWSA made, which had roused a sleeping giant. The liquor industry was not going to lose its lucrative trade without a fight, and the promise that women would make the use of alcohol illegal once they got the vote yielded the predictable results. The liquor lobby had plenty of money, and men wouldn't give up their beer, no matter what they thought about the justice of women voting. The anti-liquor women were a driving force behind the prohibition amendment, which was enacted before women could vote nationally.

The path of conservative, orthodox respectability chosen by the NAWSA leadership meant choosing allies. They chose a Christian orthodoxy that required women to be submissive to men rather than a "true religion," as Mary Grew said, "that sets people free." They chose racists over African Americans, figuring the latter would fall into line to give black women a voice no matter how racist the NAWSA policies were. They chose to capitalize on anti-immigrant prejudice rather than making a coalition with immigrants. They chose sides in the larger culture wars and they chose the wrong side; not the side of freedom but the side of repression. That is the legacy they left us.

Some made different choices.

When women abolitionists stepped out on their own in unsegregated societies to organize anti-slavery organizations separate from men, they gained the courage, organizational experience, and strong, eloquent voices that set the woman's rights movement on its way.

When the many men, like Frederick Douglass, Reverend Samuel J. May, and the international organization of prosuffrage men stepped out of the mainstream of prejudice and used their male privilege to further the cause of women's rights, they moved freedom forward and created a model for other men to follow.

But, one might say, the others were just products of their time, we may excuse them. No. They could be let off the hook if they didn't know better, but they did. When he created the southern strategy, promising that woman suffrage would maintain white supremacy, Henry Blackwell had a long history as a committed abolitionist. Ida B. Wells argued with Susan B. Anthony that she should carry her personal practice of opposing racism into her presidency of the NAWSA, rather than allowing racist expediency as policy. Other NAWSA presidents—Anna Howard Shaw and Carrie Chapman Catt—refused to let racial justice issues be discussed at their conventions, and all three leaders allowed the practice of segregation. These people knew the options, faced opposition, discussed and debated, and then chose self-interest and expediency.

History invites us to examine our tradition of political expediency, that process by which we bypass our principles and betray partners, all in the name of getting business done. We have come to collectively believe that within existing conditions it is the necessary thing to do, but what if instead we focus on creating different conditions? Different choices generate different conditions, which in turn produce different results. It may take longer, but the results are sustainable.

What if, for instance, instead of practicing expediency and caving in to southern white supremacy, the suffrage leadership had made alliance with African American male voters, North and South, working together to protect their voting rights? What if they had also courted the southern whites who favored equality? If the money spent on literature reinforcing racism had been spent on agitating, educating, and appealing against it, the conditions could have changed over time and the outcome then could have fostered African American rights.

People once believed that slavery could never be ended in the United States. Abolitionists changed the conditions and ended slavery. A coalition with southern white supremacists was not inevitable. It was a choice. The NAWSA and NWP leaders could have guided their organizations to build a different alliance, one with those working for freedom. Who knows where that would have led? Had they chosen a different path, our lives today might be quite different.

Had they also joined forces as an organization with the Freethought and reproductive justice movements, as Stanton and Gage did, we might not have had to wait until the 1960s for the use of contraceptives to finally be declared legal by the Supreme Court, or for women's right to abortion follow the following decade. We might not be living in a nation where, while finally legal, abortion and contraceptives come with an abortion education requirement and poll tax, available often only to those who can afford contraceptives or can sit through the required anti-abortion propaganda and have the money and time to travel to the constantly dwindling number of centers that provide abortions.

If the call for equal pay for equal work begun more than 150 years ago had not been dropped, might we have reached pay equity by now, rather than the 80 percent of men's wages women earn on average? What if the NAWSA had supported the *Woman's Bible* and continued to hold the conservative Christians accountable for using their religion to deny women their freedom? Would those religious forces be as strong today as they continue their fight against women's rights?

How strong would a coalition of women, people of color, and immigrants' rights activists have been, combined with the growing Freethought and reproductive rights movements?

How many black men's lives would have been saved if the NAWSA had supported African Americans in calling for an end to lynching, as the Female Anti-Slavery Societies bravely called out the institutionalized rape of enslaved women?

What if the NAWSA leadership had continued to fight the fourfold oppression of women by church, family, capitalism, and state that Gage and Stanton had identified? Where would we be today if the NAWSA had kept the vote in perspective, as simply a tool to gain our rights, not an end in itself? As the early cutting-edge issues got left by the wayside, one after another, our right to our bodies, to be free of violence, to have full legal rights and employment equity faded into the background.

As a result, when we got the vote, we forgot what to use it for. The fourfold oppressors of women identified by Gage and Stanton had been courted as allies: The vote would help maintain the orthodox Christian family, educated suffrage would ensure white, native-born, and class supremacy, and the oppressive laws of the state would have to await women voting.

Yes, we can continue to thank Anthony, Shaw, Catt, Paul, their followers, and their organizations for working so hard to get us the vote. But we must also hold them accountable for the legacy of racism, anti-immigrant sentiment, and class entitlement they left, as well as the issues they dropped. They had choices, all along the way. As we celebrate the movement that

brought women the vote, we may also consider a truth and rec-
onciliation process to take responsibility for the damage done
on the way to victory. There are still-festering wounds to be
healed.

None of this is inevitable. History is shaped by those who
swim with the tide as well as those who swim against it, stem-
ming the tide of injustice. To choose not to act is the worst possible action. There are no innocent bystanders to history.
Inaction ensures that injustice will continue in your name.

The overarching story, of course, is the deeply entrenched
sex/gender, race, class, and anti-immigrant systems in the history of our country. This institutional power that hooks those
of us in the dominant culture on our privilege also creates a
lesser life for every person who is oppressed by any of the systems, affecting everything in all our lives, as we all have multiple identities. It is not just a matter of having prejudice; it is
having the power to enforce that prejudice through laws, practices, and positions.

If every person who didn't act had fought as hard as he or
she could to turn things around, these embedded systems of
institutionalized power probably would have remained, but
they would have been significantly weakened. While power institutionalized feels intractable, that belief leads to inertia. The
institutional systems that leave rich, white, gender normative
males calling the shots and making the rules are not carved in
stone; they're not part of human nature; they didn't fall from
the heavens. *People* made them. And people, through individual actions and, most important, through collective action,
can unmake them.

History isn't then and now. It's as recent as the last breath
you took. If we don't have a system for holding our feet to the
fire in every "then" moment, where is our moral compass for
"now"? If we let our foreparents off the hook, do we thereby
let ourselves off also? What if we anticipate a future in which
our sisters in the future will judge our actions?

Our future can be one in which students reading their history won't just shake their heads, disbelieving that any woman
could have fought against women's right to vote, but will also

point the finger back to us and ask, "Why did you make that choice?" "What are the conditions, such as false religion and fake history, that cause people to act against their own self-interest and what can I do to change those conditions?"

We, the people, determine history by our choices. One person's boldness can fire others; two means someone has that person's back. A dozen can start a movement, a hundred can swing an election, a thousand can change the course of history. Individually, by our actions or our lack of action, we are a part of determining the world our children's children will inhabit. Can we do better than our foremothers and forefathers? The opportunity to do so is the gift we are given—and the responsibility.

Acknowledgments

Social media can transform the solitary experience of writing a book into a joyous crowd-sourced event. I posted my excitement at doing this anthology on Facebook, asking friends what they'd like to see in the book. The generous outpouring of ideas helped shape the content of the volume you hold in your hands. A book became a movement.

Thanks to all my co-conspirators in this venture.

Elizabeth Vogt, the gifted editor who shaped the final product, honing the excess and enhancing the rest, moving me forward with a skillful combination of encouragement and patience. Publicists Rebecca Marsh and Sara Leonard, and marketers Lydia Hirt and Molly Fessenden. I am deeply honored for this work to be part of the Penguin Classics collection, under the courageous vision of publisher Elda Rotor.

Early on the brilliant, passionate young women in the Matilda Joslyn Gage Girl Ambassador for Human Rights program explained to me how to be relevant. If I didn't get the lesson, it's not their fault.

Thanks to the Honors and Women/Gender Studies students—smart cookies to a person—in my "History of the Women's Suffrage Movement" class at Syracuse University, who have shaped my ideas and insights over the last nineteen years, and especially to the last group, who read the manuscript critically as a textbook, making invaluable edits.

To Rachel Hendricks, who began working with me through a field study with the St. John Fisher Executive Leadership program and quickly proved herself so invaluable that I hired her at the end of the study. "You probably won't be able to find this but . . ." I'd email her, and a short time later the obscure primary source would be in my in-box. Like every true artist, she thinks it's easy. Thank you, Rachel. This book, seriously, would not be in your hands without Rachel.

To my wonderful daughter Beth, who, as my personal assistant, took care of all the practical details of my life, clearing the path so I could write, and keeping me angry about the dreadful state of our country with daily updates that fueled my writing. To my irreverently funny son Dave, whose sharp wit kept things in perspective.

Thanks to Blythe Bennett, who continues the guiding gifts of clarity and love. My old friends and neighbors in the collective across the street, Karen Mihalyi, Cindy Squillace, Jack Manno, and Dik Cool, for feeding me with nourishing food and the wisdom from your years of dedicated, focused work creating a blessed community.

I am privileged that my closest colleagues are also my closest friends. Jeanne Shenandoah, Freida Jacques, Louise Herne, who, along with the many other Haudenosaunee women who continue to model the path to an egalitarian society and the continuation of life on Mother Earth, just as they showed the way to our feminist foremothers. Olivia Cousins, enthusiastically offering a platform for testing my analysis of the movement's racism, and Betty Jacobs, who twice brought me to United Nations–related events to share the story of the Haudenosaunee influence on women's rights. Michele Jones Galvin, who inspired with the spirit of her ancestor, Harriet Tubman. Theresa Corrigan, Bobbie Frances, Kath and James Fathers, Mary Ellen Kavanaugh, William Sunderlin, Phil Arnold, and Sandy Big Tree, who listened, discussed, and encouraged along the way. The synapse-popping sessions with Robin Kimmerer, Valerie Luzadis, Bill Wallauer, and Kristin Mosher, fueling our thoughts with great food.

Thanks to all my mentors who worked to school me in what to look for and how to think about what I saw. They are to be thanked for that which is good and true in these pages; I singly take responsibility for the warts.

Librarians, so many over the years, whose gift is bringing the world of words to our fingertips. One example, a placeholder for the rest, is Lisa Caprino, Reference Services Assistant at The Huntington Library, who transcribed and sent a letter when a copy could not be made without curatorial permission.

Michael Patrick Hearn, who generously shares his research finds—some of which are in this book—as a colleague and friend.

Friends and family and colleagues galore, a selection singled out. I ask the rest of you to forgive me for remembering your smart thoughts but neglecting to write down the instigator.

And to the Parkland students, who have inspired me, with your fearless and articulate calling out BS, to write from the very edge of what I know—and feel.

Notes

FOREWORD

1. Frederick Douglass, *The Life and Times of Frederick Douglass* (New York: Collier, 1962), 469.
2. Gunnar Myrdal, *An American Dilemma* (New York: Harper and Brothers, 1944), 1073
3. Ibid., 1077.

WOMEN VOTED BEFORE THE UNITED STATES WAS FORMED

1. "Capt. Oren Tyler," papers 1906, Seneca Falls Historical Society, Seneca Falls, New York.
2. Elizabeth Cady Stanton, *Eighty Years and More: Reminiscences 1815–1897* (London: T. Fisher Unwin, 1898), 430–31.
3. Theodore Stanton and Harriot Stanton Blatch, eds., *Elizabeth Cady Stanton as Revealed in Her Letters, Diary and Reminiscences* (New York: Harper, 1922), 271–72.
4. Alma Lutz, *Created Equal: A Biography of Elizabeth Cady Stanton* (New York: John Day, 1940), 287.
5. Frederick H. Martens, *Dictionary of American Biography III, Part 2,* "Fletcher, Alice Cunningham" (New York: Charles Scribner's Sons, 1959), 463–64; John Fiske and James Grant Wilson, *Appleton's Cyclopædia of American Biography,* "Fletcher, Alice Cunningham" (New York: D. Appleton and Company, 1900). Alice Fletcher's papers are housed at the National Anthropological Archives, Smithsonian Institution, Washington, DC.
6. Dr. Clemence S. Lozier founded the New York Women's Homeopathic Medical College.

7. Clemence Lozier, review of *Cases of the Legislature's Power Over Suffrage,* by Hamilton Wilcox, *The New Era,* October 1885, 308–9.

8. Elizabeth Cady Stanton, Susan B. Anthony, and Matilda Joslyn Gage, *History of Woman Suffrage, Vol. I* (Rochester, NY: Charles Mann, 1881), 208. From now on indicated as HWS I.

9. Quoted in Linda Grant DePauw, *Four Traditions: Women of New York During the American Revolution* (Albany: New York State American Revolution Bicentennial Commission, 1974), 13.

10. John Adams to James Sullivan, May 26, 1976, *Founders Online,* National Archives, last modified April 12, 2018, http://founders.archives.gov/documents/Adams/06–04–02–0091. Original source: *The Adams Papers,* Papers of John Adams, Vol. 4, *February–August 1776,* ed. Robert J. Taylor (Cambridge, MA: Harvard University Press, 1979), 208–13.

11. Letter of March 31, 1776, quoted, among other sources, in Elizabeth Cady Stanton, Susan B. Anthony, and Matilda Joslyn Gage, *History of Woman Suffrage, Vol. III* (Rochester, NY: Self Published, 1886), 19–20. From now on indicated as HWS III.

12. Leon F. Litwack, *North of Slavery* (Chicago: University of Chicago Press, 1961), 9.

13. Charles B. Waite, "Who Were Voters in the Early History of this Country?," *Chicago Law Times* 2 (1888), 397–412.

14. Edward Raymond Turner, "Women's Suffrage in New Jersey 1790–1807," *Smith College Studies in History* 1 (July 1916), 170.

15. Waite, "Who Were Voters in the Early History of this Country?," 397–412.

16. William Yates, *Rights of Colored Men to Suffrage Citizenship and Trial by Jury* (Philadelphia: Merrihew and Gunn, 1838), iii, 11.

17. Turner, "Women's Suffrage in New Jersey 1790–1807," 171.

18. HWS I: Preface.

19. Philip S. Foner and George E. Walker, *Proceedings of the Black State Conventions, 1840–1965, Volume I: New York, Pennsylvania, Indiana, Michigan, Ohio* (Philadelphia: Temple University Press, 1979), 8, 21, 23.

20. Ibid.

21. William Ray, "Petition to the Convention in Behalf of the Ladies. By their friend and counsellor." (Auburn, NY: E. F. Doubleday, 1821), 174–76.

22. Lori D. Ginsberg, *Untidy Origins: A Story of Woman's Rights in Antebellum New York* (Chapel Hill, NC: University of North Carolina Press, 2005).

23. Matilda Joslyn Gage, "The Remnant of the Five Nations," *(New York) Evening Post*, September 24, 1875.

24. Ibid.

25. "The first state of primitive man must have been the mere aggregation. The right of the mother was therefore most natural; upon the relationship of mother and child the remotest conception of the family was based.—*Wilkin*, p. 869." Footnote in Matilda Joslyn Gage, *Woman, Church and State: A Historical Account of the Status of Woman Through the Christian Ages: With Reminiscences of the Matriarchate* (New York: The Truth Seeker Company, 1895), 13.

26. "Where a god and goddess are worshipped together they are not husband and wife but mother and son. Neither does the god take pre-eminence, but the mother or goddess. This condition dates from the earliest days of society, when marriage in our sense of the word was unknown, and when kinship and inheritance were in the female line. The Babylonian Ishtur of the Iz-dubar legend is a deity of this type.—*W. Robertson Smith: Kinship in Ancient Arabia*." Footnote in Gage, *Woman, Church and State*, 13.

27. "Dr. Th. Achelis.—*Article on Ethnology, (The Open Court.)*" Footnote in Gage, *Woman, Church and State*, 13.

28. "In a country where she is the head of the family, where she decides the descent and inheritance of her children, both in regard to property and place in society, in such a community, she certainly cannot be the servant of her husband, but at least must be his equal if not in many respects his superior.—*Wilkin*." Footnote in Gage, *Woman, Church and State*, 14.

29. "*Motherright*." Footnote in Gage, *Woman, Church and State*, 14.

30. "Lubbuck.—*Pre-Historic Times and Origin of Civilization. Wilkin*." Footnote in Gage, *Woman, Church and State*, 14.

31. "Among many people the father at birth of a child, especially a son, loses his name and takes the one his child gets.—Tylor, *Primitive Culture*. Also see *Wilkin*." Footnote in Gage, *Woman, Church and State*, 15.

32. "Thus we see that woman's liberty did not begin at the upper, but at the lower end of civilization. Woman in those remote times, was endowed with and enjoyed rights that are denied to her but too completely in the higher phase of civilization. This subject

has a very important aspect, *i.e.* the position of woman to man, the place she holds in society, her condition in regard to her private and public (political) rights." Footnote in Gage, *Woman, Church and State*, 15.

33. Matilda Joslyn Gage, *Woman, Church and State: A Historical Account of the Status of Woman Through the Christian Ages: With Reminiscences of the Matriarchate* (New York: The Truth Seeker Company, 1895), 11–20.

34. Ibid., 454–55.

35. Matilda Joslyn Gage, "Indian Citizenship," *National Citizen and Ballot Box*, May 1878, 2.

36. "Deutsche *Mythology*." Footnote in Elizabeth Cady Stanton, "The Matriarchate, or Mother-Age," Rachel Foster Avery, ed., *Transactions of the National Council of Women of the United States, Assembled in Washington, D.C., February 22 to 25, 1891* (Philadelphia, PA: National Council of Women of the United States, 1891), 225.

37. "See Lecky's *History of Rationalism*, chapter 1." Footnote in Stanton. "The Matriarchate, or Mother-Age," 226.

38. For the details of woman's persecutions during centuries down to our own times see *History of Woman Suffrage, Vol. I*, chapter 15, by Matilda Joslyn Gage.

39. Printed in the Council proceedings, Stanton's speech appeared in Clara Colby's *Woman's Tribune* and headlined the *National Bulletin's* February 1891 issue. Elizabeth Cady Stanton, "The Matriarchate, or Mother-Age," Rachel Foster Avery, ed., *Transactions of the National Council of Women of the United States, Assembled in Washington, D.C., February 22 to 25, 1891* (Philadelphia, PA: National Council of Women of the United States,1891), 218–27; *Woman's Tribune*, February 28,1891; *The* (Washington, D.C.) *National Bulletin*, February 1891, 1, 5.

40. Alice C. Fletcher, "The Legal Condition of Indian Women," *Report of the International Council of Women Assembled by the National Suffrage Association, Washington D.C., March 25 to April 1, 1888* (Washington, DC: Rufus H. Darby, 1888), 237–41.

WOMEN ORGANIZED BEFORE SENECA FALLS

1. HWS I: 52.

2. "Constitution of the Female Anti-Slavery Society of Salem, Formed February 22, 1832," *Liberator*, November 17, 1832, 183.

3. Samuel Sillen, *Women Against Slavery* (New York: Masses & Mainstream Inc., 1955), 15, 42.

4. HWS I: 324.

5. HWS I: 15–18.

6. HWS I: 23.

7. HWS I: 163.

8. Wendell Phillips Garrison and Francis Jackson Garrison, *William Lloyd Garrison, 1805–1879: The Story of His Life Told by His Children in Four Volumes: Volume II 1835–1840* (Boston: Houghton, Mifflin & Company, 1894), 16.

9. HWS I: 406, f. 65.

10. Monroe Alphus Majors, *Noted Negro Women* (Chicago: Donohue & Henneberry, 1893), 194.

11. Ibid.

12. Ibid.

13. *Proceedings of the Anti-Slavery Convention of American Women, Held in Philadelphia, May 15th, 16th, 17th and 18th, 1838* (Philadelphia: Merrihew and Gunn, 1838), 7.

14. Laura H. Lovell, *Report of a Delegate to the Antislavery Convention of American Women, Held in Philadelphia, May 1838* (Boston: J. Knapp, 1838), 6–7.

15. Ibid., 14.

16. Ibid.

17. *Proceedings of the Anti-Slavery Convention of American Women, 1838*, 7–8.

18. *Circular of the Anti-Slavery Convention of American Women*, (Boston: Boston Public Library, 1837), 27–28.

19. George Bourne, *Slavery Illustrated in Its Effects Upon Woman and Domestic Society* (Boston: Isaac Knapp, 1837), 47–48.

20. Sillen, *Women Against Slavery*, 33. See also William Lee Miller, *Arguing About Slavery: John Quincy Adams and the Great Battle in the United States Congress* (New York: Vintage Books, 1995).

21. HWS I: 39, 404.

22. HWS I: 326.

23. HWS I: 39, 392–406; Sillen, *Women Against Slavery*, 30–31.

24. HWS I: 400.

25. *Circular of the Anti-Slavery Convention of American Women*, 27–28.

26. Sillen, *Women Against Slavery*, 33.

27. HWS I: 342. The author states that the resolution was passed "forty-three years ago," which apparently means 1838.

28. *Proceedings of the Third Anti-Slavery Convention of American Women, Held in Philadelphia, May 1st, 2d and 3d, 1839* (Philadelphia: Merrihew and Thompson, 1839).

29. HWS I: 51–52.

30. Sir William Blackstone, "Chapter XV: Of Husband and Wife," *Commentaries on the Laws of England, Volume I* (Oxford: The Clarendon Press, 1765), 430.

31. Sara Jane Brooks Sundberg, "Women and the Law of Property Under Louisiana Civil Law, 1782–1835" (Ph.D. thesis, Louisiana State University, 2001), 50–52.

32. "Current Topics March 5, 1892," *A Weekly Record of the Law and the Lawyers, Albany Law Journal*, Vol XLV, ed. Irving Browne (Albany, NY: Weed, Parsons, and Company, 1892), 199.

33. "Betsy Love and the Mississippi Married Women's Property Act of 1839," LeAnne Howe, accessed on April 12, 2018, http://www.mshistorynow.mdah.ms.gov/articles/6/betsy-love-and-the-mississippi-married-womens-property-act-of-1839.

34. Angela Boswell, "Married Women's Property Rights and the Challenge to the Patriarchal Order: Colorado County, Texas," in Janet L. Coryell, ed., *Negotiating Boundaries of Southern Womanhood: Dealing With the Powers That Be* (Columbia, MO: University of Missouri Press, 2000), 93–94, 100.

35. Linda E. Speth, "The Married Women's Property Acts, 1839–1865: Reform, Reaction, or Revolution?" in J. Ralph Lindgren et al., *The Law of Sex Discrimination*, 4th edition (Boston: Wadsworth, 2011), 13.

36. HWS I: 38–39.

37. HWS I: 99.

38. HWS I: 38–39.

39. Lewis Perry, *Radical Abolitionism: Anarchy and the Government of God in Antislavery Thought* (Ithaca, NY: Cornell University Press, 1973), 161.

40. Lucretia Mott, "Discourse on Woman" (speech, December, 17, 1849), in Anna David Hallowell, *James and Lucretia Mott: Life and Letters* (Boston: Houghton, Mifflin & Company, 1884), 500.

41. Sally Gregory McMillen, *Seneca Falls and the Origins of the Women's Rights Movement* (Oxford: Oxford University Press, 2008), 93–94.

42. "The women appeared uniformly in their old dress." Quoted in *Further Proceedings of the Joint Committee Appointed by the Society of Friends, Constituting the Yearly meetings of Genesee, New York, Philadelphia and Baltimore, for Promoting the*

Civilization and Improving the Condition, of the Seneca Nation of Indians, from the year 1847 to the year 1850 (Baltimore: Wm Woody & Son, 1850), 41.

43. "Council of the Seneca Nation," *New York Times*, August 11, 1845. Article begins: "We find in the Buffalo Commercial Advertiser a report of the proceedings of a Council of the Seneca Nation, held at Cattaraugus Creek Reservation on the 15th and 16th of July."

44. Margaret Hope Bacon, *Valiant Friend; The Life of Lucretia Mott* (New York: Walker and Company, 1980), 124.

45. Diane Rothenbert, "Erosion of Power an Economic Basis for the Selective Conservativism of Seneca Women in the Nineteenth Century," *Western Canadian Journal of Anthropology* 4, no. 3 (1976): 116–17.

46. Anna Johnson, *The Iroquois; or, The Bright Side of Indian Character* (New York: D. Appleton and Company, 1855), 306.

47. Ibid., 162.

48. HWS I: 32–34.

49. HWS I: 326–27.

50. Laura H. Lovell, *Report of a Delegate*, 17.

51. Ibid.

52. *An Appeal to American Women, on Prejudice Against Color* (Boston: Boston Public Library), 1839.

53. Sarah Grimke and Angelina Grimke, *On Slavery and Abolitionism: Essays and Letters*, Mark Perry, Introducer (New York: Penguin Classics, 2015).

54. *Remarks Comprising in Substance Judge Hertell's Argument in the House of Assembly of the State of New York, in the session of 1837, in Support of the Bill to Restore to Married Women "The Right of Property," as Guaranteed by the Constitution of This State* (New York: Henry Durell, 1839).

55. A harsh-tempered or overbearing woman.

56. 1 Corinthians 14:34—Let your women keep silence in the churches: for it is not permitted unto them to speak; but *they are commanded* to be under obedience, as also saith the law.

1 Corinthians 14:35—And if they will learn any thing, let them ask their husbands at home: for it is a shame for women to speak in the church.

Also these verses are related, although not in Corinthians.

1 Timothy 2:11—Let the woman learn in silence with all subjection.

1 Timothy 2:12—But I suffer not a woman to teach, nor to usurp authority over the man, but to be in silence.

1 Peter 3:1—Likewise, ye wives, *be* in subjection to your own husbands; that, if any obey not the word, they also may without the word be won by the conversation of the wives.

57. A stick or spindle onto which wool or flax is wound for spinning.

58. Clergymen.

59. John Milton, *Paradise Lost*.

60. HWS I: 82–83.

61. The Seneca Falls convention was followed by another woman's rights convention held in Rochester, NY.

62. "Letter from Lucretia Mott," *Liberator*, October 6, 1848.

63. Ibid.

THE 1850s: THE MOVEMENT TAKES OFF

1. HWS I: 224.

2. HWS I: 216.

3. HWS I: 220.

4. HWS 1: 215–26; 820–25.

5. HWS I: 821–22.

6. HWS I: 219.

7. "The Woman's Convention," *The* (Washington, D.C.) *National Intelligencer*, November 6, 1850.

8. Richard B. Morris, ed., *Encyclopedia of American History* (New York: Harper & Bros., 1961), 253.

9. "Thirty-sixth and Final Report of the Philadelphia Female Anti-Slavery Society" (Philadelphia: Merrihew & Son, 1870), 16. Quoted in HWS 1: 328 (the HWS editors attribute the writing to Mary Grew, corresponding secretary of the society).

10. HWS I: 882.

11. HWS I: 33.

12. HWS I: 109.

13. HWS I: 473.

14. HWS I: 455, f. 79.

15. *Syracuse Standard*, February 4, 1858.

16. *Woman's Tribune*, December 4, 1897, 193.

17. HWS I: 238.

18. HWS I: 247–48; *The Una*, April 1853.

19. Caroline H. Dahl, petition in the *Liberator*, June 11, 1858, quoted in HWS I: 262.

20. HWS I: 535.

21. *New York Tribune*, June 16, 1854.

22. *The Una*, April 1853, 44.

23. "Streetsville Review," *Syracuse Standard*, April 11, 1853.

24. *Louisville Focus*, c. 1828, as quoted in William Randall Waterman, *Frances Wright. Studies in History, Economics and Public Law, Volume 115* (New York: Columbia University, 1924), 162.

25. HWS I: 286.

26. *New York Tribune*, July 18, 1851.

27. Sherry Ceniza, *Walt Whitman and 19th-Century Women Reformers* (Tuscaloosa, AL: The University of Alabama Press, 1998), 21–23, 53, f. 14.

28. Lutz, *Created Equal*, 112.

29. HWS I: 105.

30. *Syracuse Standard*, May 7, 1855.

31. Alice Stone Blackwell, *Lucy Stone: Pioneer of Woman's Rights* (Charlottesville, VA, and London: University of Virginia Press, 1930), 171.

32. HWS I: 261–62.

33. *New York Tribune*, July 7, 1859.

34. Elizabeth Cady Stanton to Elizabeth Smith Miller, quoted in Lois Banner, *Elizabeth Cady Stanton: A Radical for Women's Rights* (Boston and Toronto: Little Brown and Co., 1980), 114.

35. *Syracuse Standard*, September 18, 1857.

36. HWS I: 223–24.

37. HWS I: 237–43.

38. HWS I: 612–13.

39. HWS I: 616–17.

40. HWS I: 527.

41. *New York Tribune*, November 16, 1853.

42. HWS I: 469–71.

43. HWS I: 836–39.

44. HWS I: 839–42.

45. "The Movement for Dress Reform," *New York Tribune*, January 20, 1857.

46. A portion of *Lalla Rookh: The Fire-Worshippers*, by Thomas Moore (1779–1852).

47. Children born with congenital syphilis to mothers who have been infected with the disease often die, and if they survive, may have deformities, or delays in development. They may develop rash, anemia, jaundice, and seizures. There was no cure for syphilis during this time.

48. A birth control advocate, Henry C. Wright authored *Marriage and Parentage: or, The Reproductive Element in Man, As a Means to His Elevation and Happiness* (Boston: Bela Marsh, 1855).

49. *Syracuse Standard*, July 1, 1858.

THE 1860s: IN FULL STRIDE, THE WAR'S SETBACK, AND REGROUPING AFTER

1. HWS II: 37.

2. HWS II: 14–15.

3. Sylvia Bradley, "Anna Ella Carroll, 1815–1894; Military Strategist—Political Propagandist," in *Notable Maryland Women* (Cambridge, MD: Tidewater Publishers, 1977), 62–70.

4. Matilda Joslyn Gage, *Who Planned the Tennessee Campaign of 1862? A Few Generally Unknown Facts in Regard to Our Civil War. Or Anna Ella Carroll vs. Ulysses S. Grant* (Washington, DC: 1880), 1–4.

5. Ibid., 8.

6. Ibid., 15–16.

7. Bradley, "Anna Ella Carroll, 1815–1894," 62–70.

8. *New York Times*, quoted in (Oneida Community) *Circular*, June 18, 1866.

9. HWS II: 54.

10. HWS II: 66–67.

11. HWS II: 815.

12. HWS II: 85.

13. A gifted orator, Anna Dickinson was instrumental in electing Republican Party candidates in the 1863 election. She was the first woman to deliver a political address before Congress.

14. HWS II: 90–91.

15. HWS II: 103.

16. "Negro Suffrage South and North," *New York Times*, July 8, 1865.

17. HWS II: 929–31.

18. HWS II: 228.

19. *Proceedings of the First Anniversary of the American Equal Rights Association* (New York: Robert J. Johnston, 1867), 60.

20. HWS II: 286–87.

21. HWS II: 230–31.

22. HWS II: 243.

23. Ibid.
24. HWS II: 264.
25. HWS II: 264–65.
26. George Frances Train, *Train's Great Speeches in England on Slavery and Emancipation, Delivered in London, on March 12 and 13, 1862*, (Philadelphia: T. B. Peterson & Brothers, 1862), 19–22.
27. HWS II: 264.
28. HWS II: 321–22.
29. HWS II: 309–10.
30. U.S. Constitution, Amendment XIV, § 1.
31. HWS II: 315.
32. "Appendix C: Women Who Voted, 1868 to 1873," *The Selected Papers of Elizabeth Cady Stanton and Susan B. Anthony, Volume 2: Against an Aristocracy of Sex 1866–1873*, Ann D. Gordon, ed. (New Brunswick, NJ: Rutgers University Press, 2000), 645–54. The Stanton-Anthony Project has done a fantastic service by compiling this information on women who voted during these early years, finally providing context for Anthony's much-referenced vote four years later.
33. HWS II: 325.
34. HWS II: 345.
35. HWS II: 333.
36. Paula Giddings, *When and Where I Enter: The Impact of Black Women on Race and Sex in America* (New York: W. Morrow, 1984), 66.
37. HWS II: 381–97.
38. Correspondence from Lucy Stone to Mr. Sanborn, August 18, 1869, A-1-10 Lutz Collection, Folder 12. Schlesinger Library, Cambridge, MA.
39. HWS II: 756–57.
40. HWS II: 757.
41. HWS II: 406.
42. HWS I: 743–44.
43. HWS I: 739–41.
44. HWS I: 742.
45. HWS II: 54–55.
46. HWS II: 79–80.
47. HWS II: 896–97.
48. HWS II: 171–72.
49. HWS II: 255–56.

50. Elizabeth Cady Stanton, *The Revolution*, October 21, 1869, and June 3, 1869. Reprinted in HWS II: 333–35.

51. HWS II: 345–58.

52. HWS II: 378–98.

53. Lutz, *Created Equal*, 173–74.

54. Ibid., 174.

THE 1870s: A DECADE OF PROGRESS, LOSS, AND REFINING TACTICS

1. Henry Blackwell, "American Woman Suffrage Association," *Woman's Journal,* January 8, 1870.

2. HWS II: 809.

3. Lutz, *Created Equal*, 162–63.

4. HWS II: 830.

5. HWS II: 872, f. 193.

6. U.S. Constitution, Amendment XIV, § 1.

7. HWS II: 408.

8. "Landmark Legislation: The Enforcement Acts of 1870 and 1871," United States Senate, April 12, 2018, accessed on April 14, 2018 https://www.senate.gov/artandhistory/history/common/generic/EnforcementActs.htm.

9. HWS II: 411.

10. HWS II: 586–755; (Portland) *New Northwest*, March 8, 1872, 3; Lutz, *Created Equal*, 198; Mayo.

11. HWS III: 828.

12. HWS III: 406.

13. This merger attempt was widely covered in the *Revolution* and the *Independent* and is summarized concisely by Lisa Tetrault, *The Myth of Seneca Falls: Memory and the Women's Suffrage Movement, 1848–1898* (Chapel Hill, NC: University of North Carolina Press, 2014), 35–37.

14. HWS II: 443.

15. Lois Beachy Underhill, *The Woman Who Ran for President: The Many Lives of Victoria Woodhull* (Bridgehampton, NY: Penguin Books, 1996), 94–107. See also, Tetrault, *The Myth of Seneca Falls*, 56–66.

16. Victoria C. Woodhull, "The Coming Woman," *New York Herald*, April 3, 1870. In Underhill, *The Woman Who Ran for President*, 77.

17. "German Communism—Manifesto of the German Communist Party," *Woodhull & Claflin's Weekly*, December 30. 1871.

18. Ida Husted Harper, *Life and Work of Susan B. Anthony*, Vol. 1 (Indianapolis and Kansas City: The Bowen-Merrill Company, 1899), 414–15.

19. HWS II: 811, f. 190.

20. HWS II: 813.

21. *Woodhull & Claflin's Weekly*, October 28, 1872.

22. Ibid.

23. Knowlton's book was reprinted years later by Charles Bradlaugh and Mrs. Annie Besant, *Fruits of Philosophy. An Essay on the Population Question* (London: Publishing Company, 1878), 48.

24. Robert Dale Owen, *Moral Physiology; Or, A Brief and Plain Treatise on the Population Question* (London: Holyoake and Co., 1859), 39.

25. Edward Bond Foote, *The Radical Remedy in Social Science; Or, Borning Better Babies Through Regulating Reproduction by Controlling Conception. An Earnest Essay on Pressing Problems* (New York: Murray Hill Publishing Co., 1886), 137–38.

26. E. H. Heywood, *Sexual Indulgence and Denial: Uncivil Liberty. An Essay to Show the Injustice and Impolicy of Ruling Woman Without Her Consent* (Princeton, MA: Co-operative Publishing Co., 1877), 11.

27. Matilda Joslyn Gage, *Syracuse Journal*, May 7, 1871.

28. "Women Tax Payers," Fayetteville *Weekly Recorder*, 1873; "Tea and Taxes," *Chicago Tribune*, 1873, and "Call for Dec. 16, 1873 Mass Meeting," Matilda Joslyn Gage Scrapbook, Library of Congress.

29. HWS III: 420.

30. *Minor v. Happersett*, 88 U.S. (21 Wall.) 162 (1874).

31. HWS II: 840.

32. HWS II: 837, f.196.

33. HWS II: 585, f.152.

34. Lillie Devereux Blake, *New Northwest*, February 26, 1875.

35. *New Northwest*, March 14, 1873.

36. HWS III: 4.

37. HWS III: 19–20.

38. HWS III: 57–58.

39. HWS III: 60.

40. HWS III: 104.
41. Ibid.
42. Madeline Vinton Dahlgren, *Thoughts on Female Suffrage, and in Vindication of Woman's True Rights* (Washington DC: Blanchard and Mohun, 1871).
43. HWS II: 488–89.
44. "The Woman Suffrage Question," *Syracuse Journal*, January 1872.
45. HWS III: 102–3.
46. HWS III: 60–61.
47. HWS III: 72–73; 149, f.21.
48. HWS III: 443, f. 206.
49. HWS III: 129.
50. Matilda Joslyn Gage editorial, *National Citizen and Ballot Box*, May 1879.
51. Dr. Clemence S. Lozier, *Child-Birth Made Easy* (New York: Robert J. Johnston, 1870), 3–4.
52. HWS II: 408.
53. "Woman's Rights Catechism," *Fayetteville Weekly Recorder*, July 27, 1871.
54. "Woman Suffrage. The Argument of Carrie S. Burnham before Chief Justice Reed, and Associate Justices Agnew, Sharswood and Mercur, of the Supreme Court of Pennsylvania, in Banc, on the Third and Fourth of April, 1873" (Philadelphia: Citizen's Suffrage Association, 1873), 5–6. For years, Burnham applied to practice and was denied by this court because she was a woman. Finally, her persistence paid off, and she was admitted to the bar in 1884. (HWS III: 475, f. 256.)
55. Victoria C. Woodhull, "And the Truth Shall Make You Free." Speech, Steinway Hall, November 20, 1871, Library of Congress, accessed on April 14, 2018, http://www.loc.gov/resource /rbnawsa.n8216.
56. "Women Tax Payers," *Fayetteville Weekly Recorder*, 1873; "Tea and Taxes," *Chicago Tribune*, 1873; and "Call for Dec. 16, 1873 Mass Meeting," Matilda Joslyn Gage Scrapbook, Library of Congress.
57. HWS II: 742, 744.
58. HWS III: 29–30.
59. HWS III: 31–34.
60. HWS III: 131–38.
61. HWS III: 124.

THE 1880s: A DECADE OF PROGRESS
AND DANGER

1. HWS III: 197, f. 53.
2. HWS III: 151–53.
3. HWS III: 198.
4. HWS III: 264.
5. HWS III: 177.
6. HWS III: 177–79; "The NWSA,—and the "National Republican Nominating Convention," *National Citizen and Ballot Box*, June 1880.
7. Elizabeth Cady Stanton and Ida Husted Harper, *History of Woman Suffrage*, Vol. IV (Rochester, NY: Self Published, 1902), 434–36. From now on indicated as HWS IV.
8. Belva Lockwood, "My Efforts to Become a Lawyer," *Lippincott's Monthly Magazine*, February 1888; Madeline B. Stern, *We the Women: Career Firsts of Nineteenth-Century America* (New York: Schulte Publishing Company, 1963), 212–13; HWS III: 109, 571; Sylvia Dannett, "Belva Ann Lockwood, Feminist Lawyer," *The Courier* 3, no 4, July 1971, 43–44; *The Alpha*, January 1, 1879, 6; *New Northwest*, May 26, 1876, 1.
9. *Herald of Industry*, November to December, 1884. This paper, edited by Marietta Stow, is the major source of information on the 1884 campaign of the Equal Rights Party. In December 1884, the paper became the *Woman's Herald of Industry*.
10. *Herald of Industry*, November 1884, 1.
11. Ibid.
12. *Woman's Herald of Industry*, December 1884.
13. *Woman's Herald of Industry*, November 1884.
14. Belva Lockwood, Washington, to Clara S. Foltz et al., San Francisco, September 25, 1884, in *Woman's Herald of Industry*, October 1884.
15. Belva Lockwood, "How I Ran for the Presidency," *National Magazine*, March 1903, 728–33.
16. Ibid.
17. (Oakland, CA) *National Equal Rights*, December 1884.
18. HWS IV: 410.
19. HWS IV: 417.
20. HWS III: 250–51.
21. HWS III: 6.
22. HWS III: 168.

23. "Woman Suffrage Crusade, 1848–1920," Mildred Andrews, accessed April 13, 2018, http://www.historylink.org/File/5662.
24. HWS III: 5.
25. HWS IV: 122.
26. Burnita Shelton Matthews, "The Woman Juror," *Women Lawyers' Journal 15*, no. 2 (January 1927).
27. HWS IV: 78.
28. Philip S. Foner, *We, The Other People* (Urbana: University of Illinois Press, 1976), 129.
29. HWS IV: 71.
30. New York Woman Suffrage Convention Resolution, May 1876.
31. HWS IV: 107–8; 100–111.
32. HWS III: 250–51.
33. *History of Woman Suffrage Agreement*, Ida Husted Harper Collection, The Huntington Library, San Marino, CA.
34. HWS IV: vii.
35. HWS IV: viii.
36. HWS IV: 840.
37. HWS III: vi.
38. HWS IV: 426.
39. HWS IV: 430.
40. HWS IV: 425.
41. Susan B. Anthony, Matilda Joslyn Gage, Rachel G. Foster, Mary Wright Sewall, and Lillie Devereux Blake, "Protest Against the Unjust Interpretation of the Constitution Presented on Behalf of the Women of the United States by Officers of the National Woman Suffrage Association, 17 September 1887," Blake collection, Missouri Historical Society, St. Louis, MO. *New York Times*, September 17, 1887, 2, and *New York Tribune*, September 18, 1887, 1, also carried the story of the protest.
42. *Wisconsin Citizen*, August 1889.
43. Sara Underwood, "To Women 'Indifferent' to Suffrage," *Wisconsin Citizen*, August 1889.
44. HWS IV: 125–26.
45. HWS IV: 125–27.
46. Frances E. Willard, "President's Annual Address," *Minutes of the National Woman's Christian Temperance Union, at the Fourteenth Annual Meeting, in Nashville, Tenn., 16 to 21 November, 1887* (Chicago: Woman's Temperance Publication Association, 1888), 71.
47. Paul E. Fuller, *Laura Clay and the Woman's Rights Movement* (Lexington, KY: University Press of Kentucky, 1992), 33.

48. Rachel Avery Foster, ed., *Negotiations between the American and National Woman Suffrage Associations: In Regard to Union* (Washington, DC, 1888); Scrapbook of clippings on union negotiations in Robinson Papers, Schlesinger Library, Cambridge, MA.

49. Ibid.

50. Correspondence from Matilda Joslyn Gage to Harriet Robinson, January 18, 1890, Papers of Harriet Jane Robinson and Harriette Lucy Robinson Shattuck, Schlesinger Library, Cambridge, MA.

51. L. Frank Baum, editorial, *Aberdeen Saturday Pioneer*, March 1, 1890.

52. HWS IV: 164.

53. Ida Husted Harper, *The Life and Work of Susan B. Anthony*, Vol. 2 (Indianapolis and Kansas City: The Bowen-Merrill Company, 1898), 632.

54. HWS III: 262–64.

55. HWS III: 73.

56. "Platform of the National Equal Rights Party," *National Equal Rights* 3, no. 11, November 1884.

57. "Testimony of an Eye-Witness," *New Northwest*, December 12, 1885.

58. HWS IV: 75–76.

59. HWS IV: 76–78.

60. Matilda Joslyn Gage, "Persons and Things," *National Citizen and Ballot Box*, January 1881, 2.

61. HWS IV: 122–23.

62. *Woman's Journal*, November 1886.

63. "Our New York Letter," *Woman's Journal*, September 24, 1887.

64. *San Jose Daily*, July 27, 1888, quoted in Katherine Devereux Blake and Margaret Louise Wallace, *Champion of Women: The Life of Lillie Devereux Blake* (London: Flemming H. Revell Company, 1943), 168.

65. Matilda Joslyn Gage, "A Statement of Facts," pamphlet distributed to National Women Suffrage Association by the author, 1889, Dr. Sally Roesch Wagner private collection, Syracuse, New York.

THE 1890s: SUFFRAGE VICTORIES AND MORAL DECAY

1. HWS IV: 174.

2. HWS IV: 189.

3. HWS IV: 318.
4. HWS IV: 257.
5. Henry Blackwell, "A Solution of the Southern Question," *Woman's Journal*, September 27, 1890.
6. Henry Blackwell, "A Solution of the Southern Question," *Woman Suffrage Leaflet 3*, no. 11, October 15, 1890.
7. HWS IV: 220, f.94.
8. HWS IV: 234.
9. Marjorie Julian Spruill, "Race, Reform and Reaction," in *Votes for Women: The Struggle for Suffrage Revisited,* Jean H. Baker, ed. (New York: Oxford University Press, 2002), 106; *Ida B. Wells, Crusade for Justice: The Autobiography of Ida B. Wells,* Alfreda M. Duster, ed. (Chicago: University of Chicago Press, 1970), 229–30.
10. HWS IV: 246.
11. Rachel F. Avery, ed., *Transactions of the National Council of Women of the United States, assembled in Washington, D.C. on Feb. 22–25, 1891* (Philadelphia: J.B. Lippincott, 1891), 86–91.
12. Amy Hackett, *Cloaking an Apology for Lawlessness: Ida B. Wells, Frances Willard and the Lynching Controversy, 1890–1894* University of Massachusetts, 2004).
13. HWS IV: 182–83.
14. HWS IV: 213.
15. Correspondence from Susan B. Anthony to Clara Colby, May 26, 1894, Box 2, Clara Dorothy Bewick Colby Papers, 1882–1914, The Huntington Library, San Marino, CA.
16. HWS IV; 344.
17. Elizabeth Lindsay Davis, *Lifting As They Climb* (Washington, DC: National Association of Colored Women, 1933).
18. HWS IV: 185–86.
19. HWS IV: 216–17.
20. *Woman's Journal*, February 1, 1896, 34.
21. HWS IV: 263.
22. Ibid.
23. "A Protest and a Pledge," *Lucifer the Lightbearer*, September 4, 1891. Also published in the September 18, 1891, and October 16, 1891, issues.
24. "Unfit to Read. Anthony Comstock Condemns a Noted Suffragist Book, Woman, Church and State," *Syracuse Standard*, August 12, 1894.
25. "Mrs. Gage's Book. A Statement of Her Side of the Case," *Weekly Recorder*, August 23, 1894.

26. Pam McAllister, "Introduction," *A Sex Revolution*, Lois Wais-brooker (Philadelphia: New Society Publishers, 1985), 38–42.

27. Matilda Josyln Gage, "Letter to the Editor," *Lucifer, The Light Bearer*, August 24, 1894, in Pam McAllister, "Introduction," 43–44.

28. HWS IV: 334.

29. HWS IV: 348.

30. From poet Alfred Lord Tennyson's "The Princess" (pt. 2, lines 155–60).

31. 1 Corinthians 14:34—Let your women keep silence in the churches: for it is not permitted unto them to speak; but they are commanded to be under obedience as also saith the law (King James version).

32. Ephesians 5:23—For the husband is the head of the wife, even as Christ is the head of the church: and he is the saviour of the body (King James version).

33. Ephesians 5:22. Wives, submit yourselves unto your own husbands, as unto the Lord (King James version).

34. 1 Corinthians 14:35—And if they will learn any thing, let them ask their husbands at home: for it is a shame for women to speak in the church (King James version).

35. The text, "Blessed are you, Lord, our God, ruler of the universe who has not created me a woman," is part of a sequence of blessings found in the Talmud. It is recited by traditional Jewish men at the beginning of daily morning prayers. Stanton refers to this blessing in her analysis of *Numbers XX* in *The Woman's Bible* (116–17): "To hold woman in such an attitude is to rob her words and actions of all moral character."

36. *Woman's Tribune*, December 28, 1895.

37. HWS IV: 264.

38. Elizabeth Cady Stanton, *The Woman's Bible* (New York: European Publishing Company, 1898), 7–12.

39. *The Persecution and the Appreciation: Brief Account of the Trials and Imprisonment of Moses Harman Because of His Advocacy of the Freedom of Women from Sexual Enslavement and of the Right of Children to Be Born Well* (Chicago: 1907), 20–21.

40. Elizabeth Cady Stanton, *The Co-operative Ideal Will Remodel Codes and Constitutions* (Chicago: The Progressive Woman, 1898).

THE 1900s: CONSOLIDATING POWER

1. Helen Pitts Douglass to My dear friend, 12 February 1900, Emily Howland Correspondence, Box 5, Friends Historical Library of Swarthmore College. Cited in Ann D. Gordon, "To Celebrate Worthily": When Birthdays Are No Longer Your Own. Posted on February 16, 2015, https://historicaldetails.wordpress.com/2015/02/16/to-celebrate-worthily-when-birthdays-are-no-longer-your-own/.
2. Ibid.
3. HWS IV: 389.
4. HWS IV: 358–59.
5. Correspondence from Susan B. Anthony to Laura Clay, April 15, 1900. University of Kentucky Library, Lexington, KY, quoted in Lutz, *Created Equal*, 292.
6. Ida Husted Harper, *History of Woman Suffrage*, Vol. V (Rochester, NY: National American Woman Suffrage Association, 1922), 8. From now on indicated as HWS V.
7. HWS V: 24.
8. HWS V: 85.
9. HWS V: 56.
10. HWS V: 75.
11. HWS V: 75–76.
12. HWS V: 76–77.
13. HWS V: 78.
14. Lee Sartain, *Invisible Activists: Women of the Louisiana NAACP and the Struggle for Civil Rights, 1915–1945* (Baton Rouge: LSU Press, 2007), 48; Adele Logan Alexander, "Adella Hunt Logan, the Tuskegee Women's Club, and African Americans in the Suffrage Movement," in *Votes for Women! The Woman Suffrage Movement in Tennessee, the South, and the Nation*, Marjorie Spruill Wheeler, ed. (Knoxville, TN: University of Tennessee Press, 1995), 89, 102; Darlene Clark Hine and Christie Ann Farnham, "Black Women and the Right to Vote," in *Civil Rights Since 1787: A Reader on the Black Struggle*, Jonathan Birnbaum and Clarence Taylor, eds. (New York: NYU Press, 2000), 256.
15. HWS V: 85, f 24.
16. HWS V: 19–20.
17. HWS V: 95, 141–42.
18. HWS V: 97.
19. HWS V: 97–98.

20. HWS V: 145–46.
21. HWS V: 162.
22. HWS V: 165–66.
23. HWS V: 187.
24. HWS V: 162.
25. HWS V: 162–63.
26. HWS V: 163.
27. HWS V: 161–62.
28. HWS V: 191–92.
29. HWS V: 183.
30. HWS V: 212.
31. HWS V: 212.
32. HWS V: 12–13.
33. HWS V: 94.
34. HWS V: 94, 99.
35. HWS V: 130.
36. HWS V: 236.
37. HWS V: 253.
38. HWS V: 276.
39. HWS V: 253.
40. HWS V: 253.
41. HWS V: 247–48.
42. HWS V: 253.
43. HWS V: 253–54.
44. HWS IV: 381.
45. HWS IV: 381–82.
46. HWS V: 54.
47. HWS V: 116.
48. HWS V: 191.
49. HWS V: 258.
50. HWS V: 259.
51. Journal of Lillie Devereux Blake. January 23, 1900, to March 28, 1900, Missouri Historical Society Archives, St. Louis, MO (Series II: Journals and Diaries, Subseries A: Originals. Folder 10).
52. Correspondence from Laura E. Peters to Lillie Devereux Blake, January 18, 1900, Missouri Historical Society Archives, St. Louis, MO.
53. HWS V: 32.
54. HWS V: 59–60.
55. Anna Howard Shaw, *Anna Howard Shaw, The Story of a Pioneer* (New York: Harper and Brothers, 1915), 311–13.

56. Alfreda M. Duster, ed., *Crusade for Justice: The Autobiography of Ida B. Wells* (Chicago: The University of Chicago Press: 1970), 227–30.

57. HWS V: 179.

58. HWS V: 203.

59. HWS IV: 365–66.

60. "Ida Craddock's Letter to the Public on the Day of Her Suicide," Ida Craddock, accessed on April 13, 2018, http://www .idacraddock.com/public.html.

1910: NEARING THE FINISH LINE FOR SUFFRAGE

1. HWS V: 624.

2. HWS V: 624–25.

3. HWS V: 281.

4. HWS V: 268.

5. HWS V: 268–69.

6. HWS V: 270.

7. HWS V: 273–74.

8. HWS V: 267.

9. HWS V: 289, 337.

10. HWS V: 285–86.

11. HWS V: 286.

12. HWS V: 282–83.

13. HWS V: 275.

14. HWS V: 309.

15. HWS V: 311.

16. HWS V: 317.

17. HWS V: 320.

18. HWS V: 311.

19. HWS V: 323.

20. *New York Times,* May 6, 1911.

21. HWS V: 324.

22. HWS V: 328.

23. W. E. B. DuBois, "Suffering Suffragettes," *The Crisis,* June 1912, 77.

24. HWS V: 329–30.

25. HWS V: 332.

26. HWS V: 333.

27. HWS V: 339–40.

28. HWS V: 340.
29. HWS V: 340.
30. HWS V: 668.
31. HWS V: 342.
32. HWS V: 341.
33. HWS V: 341–42.
34. HWS V: 354.
35. HWS V: 377–78.
36. "Politics," *The Crisis* 5, no. 6, April 1913, 1.
37. Robert S. Gallagher, "I Was Arrested, Of Course . . . ," *American Heritage*, February 1974.
38. HWS V: 380.
39. HWS V: 366–67.
40. HWS V: 366.
41. HWS V: 369.
42. HWS V: 373.
43. HWS V: 373–74.
44. HWS V: 376.
45. HWS V: 671.
46. HWS V: 377–81.
47. HWS V: 397, f. 80.
48. HWS V: 379–80.
49. HWS V: 384.
50. HWS V: 394.
51. HWS V: 397.
52. HWS V: 403.
53. HWS V: 410.
54. HWS V: 427.
55. Report of Ruth Hanna McCormick, chair of the NAWSA 1914 congressional committee, *Woman's Journal*. Reprinted in HWS V: 397.
56. HWS V: 412–18.
57. HWS V: 422–23.
58. HWS V: 424.
59. HWS V: 427–28.
60. HWS V: 424.
61. HWS V: 419–25.
62. HWS V: 426.
63. HWS V: 438.
64. HWS V: 439.
65. HWS V: 440.
66. HWS V: 460–61.

67. HWS V: 452.
68. HWS V: 452–53.
69. HWS V: 453.
70. HWS V: 454.
71. HWS V: 466–67.
72. HWS V: 470–71.
73. HWS V: 449.
74. *Will the federal suffrage amendment complicate the race problem?* Broadside 1916 (Caroline Katzenstein papers, Historical Society of Pennsylvania, Philadelphia, PA).
75. HWS V: 480.
76. HWS V: 498.
77. HWS V: 498–99.
78. HWS V: 498–99.
79. HWS V: 487.
80. HWS V: 486.
81. HWS V: 502.
82. HWS V: 630–31.
83. HWS V: 542.
84. HWS V: 516.
85. HWS V: 537–38.
86. HWS V: 543.
87. HWS V: 632.
88. HWS V: 634.
89. HWS V: 663, 668.
90. HWS V: 541.
91. HWS V: 577.
92. HWS V: 580–81.
93. HWS V: 582–83.
94. HWS V: 586–88.
95. HWS V: 591.
96. HWS V: 562.
97. HWS V: 640.
98. HWS V: 542.
99. HWS V: 564.
100. HWS V: 564–65.
101. HWS V: 565.
102. HWS V: 565–66.
103. HWS V: 553–54.
104. HWS V: 575–76.
105. "Suffragette Tells of Forcible Feeding," *New York Times*, February 18, 1910.

106. HWS V: 330–31.
107. HWS V: 364–65.
108. HWS V: 371.
109. HWS V: 384–85.
110. "Carrie Chapman Catt Address to the Congress on Women's Suffrage delivered November 1917, Washington, D.C.," accessed on April 13, 2018, http://www.americanrhetoric.com /speeches/carriechapmancattsuffragespeech.htm.
111. "Woman Suffrage and the Fifteenth Amendment," *The Crisis*, August 1915.
112. "Arrest 41 Pickets for Suffrage at the White House," *New York Times*, November 11, 1917.
113. A. Phillip Randolph, "Woman Suffrage and the Negro," the *Messenger*, November 1917.

1920. THE FINAL VICTORY

1. HWS V: 595, 608.
2. HWS V: 610–11.
3. "That Deadly Parallel," Broadside 1920 (Josephine A. Pearson papers, 1860–1942, Tennessee State Library & Archives, Nashville, TN, box 1, folder 4).
4. Harriet Taylor Upton, "The Story of the 36th State," *Headquarters News Bulletin* 5, no. 17, September 1, 1920.
5. Carrie Chapman Catt and Nettie Rogers Shuler, *Woman Suffrage and Politics: The Inner Story of the Suffrage Movement* (Buffalo, NY: C Scribner's Sons, 1926), 462.
6. Taylor Upton, "The Story of the 36th State."

AFTERWORD:
NOW THAT OUR JOURNEY IS AT AN END

1. HWS IV: 384.

Ready to find
your next great classic?

Let us help.

Visit prh.com/penguinclassics

PENGUIN
CLASSICS